REPORTAGE PRESS

ABOUT THE AUTHOR

NICK THORPE began reporting from Budapest in February 1986 and was the first western journalist to be based there. He covered the dying years of eastern Europe's regimes, and the revolutions which toppled them, for the BBC, the Independent and the Observer. He witnessed the collapse of Yugoslavia, popular uprisings in Bulgaria and Serbia and the transformation of non-violent to violent resistance in Kosovo. As the BBC's Central Europe correspondent he continues to report the successes, and the failures, of a revolution which never quite reaches its goal. Nick Thorpe is married with five children and lives in Budapest.

'89: The Unfinished Revolution

Power and Powerlessness in Eastern Europe

NICK THORPE

REPORTAGE PRESS

REPORTAGE PRESS

Published by Reportage Press
26 Richmond Way, London W12 8LY United Kingdom
Tel: 0044 (0)7971 461 935
e-mail: info@reportagepress.com
www.reportagepress.com

A catalogue record for this book is available from the British Library.

ISBN-13: 978–1–906702–17–5

Cover design by Henrietta Molinaro.

Typesetting by Florence Production Ltd.

Printed and bound in Great Britain by Cromwell Press Group.

For my sons
Samuel, Matthew, Daniel, Caspar and Jack

and

for my father
Peter
in loving memory

Will I be able
On this unrest-field
To make for you
A tent of my hands

Vasko Popa

Introduction

Wir haben nicht die Revolution, sondern die Revolution hat uns
gemacht . . .

We didn't make the revolution—the revolution made us.

Danton

NOW WHEN I GET BACK HERE
I EXPECT TO FIND
ALL OF YOU
MARCHING THROUGH THE STREETS
WITH GREAT BUNCHES OF WILD FLOWERS
IN YOUR ARMS

Kenneth Patchen

I first arrived in eastern Europe not to report, but to participate, in an
act of youthful solidarity with my fellow protesters.

It was the summer of 1983, a time of new tensions in an old, cold
war. The United States had just announced plans to introduce nuclear-
armed cruise missiles in western Europe. This was supposedly in response
to the deployment by the Soviet Union of vehicle-based ballistic missiles,
the SS20s, which had allegedly undermined the US superiority in
'intermediate range' nuclear missiles—those capable of hitting targets
500km to 5,000km away. The whole arms race seemed a mad, sad and
dangerous venture to me. In the spring of 1983, we organised a peaceful
blockade of the US airbase at Upper Heyford in Oxfordshire. At about
the same time, I read in a Campaign for Nuclear Disarmament (CND)
pamphlet that there was a small peace group in Hungary, which, like
us, opposed all nuclear weapons, East and West. I decided to go to
Budapest to try to find them.

They were planting flags in Vérmező Park in Buda. Ten or twelve
young men and women with handfuls of tiny paper flags with peace signs

on them, attached to pins. One on every tree and lamp post. There were posters too, explaining to the people of Budapest what the little flags meant. These young men and women were activists from the Diálógus independent peace group, and they had just declared the park, a shady expanse of beech and oak and acacia trees behind Castle Hill, a nuclear-free zone. This was a common tactic of the peace movement in those days. We might not have had much direct effect on the decisions of those in power. We might be dragged aside, time and again, when we lay in front of military vehicles—but we could declare small corners of our lives and our towns to be free of the violence we opposed. This far, we wanted to say, and no further.

While we in Britain risked only arrest, a few hours in a police cell and perhaps a small fine if they bothered to take us to court, in eastern Europe to stand up against nuclear weapons meant to risk your studies, your own job and possibly that of your partner or child.

The London office of CND advised against the trip. The last British peace activists to visit Hungary—women from the peace camp at Greenham Common airbase in southern England—had just been expelled, and their Hungarian hosts were in deep trouble. Best to stay away, they said on the phone, and not cause them more problems. Undeterred, I set out for Budapest, despite the fact I had no names or contact details for any members of the group.

Even late in the evening, the heat struck me like a wave as I got off the train at the East Station. A huge neon sign of an open-mouthed giant, advertising Orion television sets—Hungary's own—gazed down at us in the great hallway of the station. Without a word of Hungarian, map or guidebook, we somehow found our way to a campsite. My first impression, on that steamy July night, was that everyone was carrying flowers.

The ground in the campsite in the Óbuda suburb, once the old Roman town of Aquincum, was hard as stone. On our second day in the city, dazed by the summer heat and shortage of sleep, we sat in a bar near Moszkva Square, sipping cheap white wine and watching the world go by. A young man walked in, holding the hand of a small child. They looked nervously around, scanning the faces in the bar, then went out. But in those few seconds, I had had time to notice the badge pinned to his shirt—a flower, growing out of a peace sign. He was a member of the Diálógus group—the very people I had come to Budapest to find. We jumped up and ran after him. He was looking for his friends, he explained, who had taken part with him in the action in the park. As it turned out, they had mostly been arrested, but he had been overlooked. We sat down to have a drink. His name was Dániel Erdély, and he was with his seven-year-old son, Matyi.

Vérmező means 'The Field of Blood'. It was there, in 1795, that seven Hungarian conspirators against the Austrian emperor were executed.

'Field of blood, field of blood! How thirsty you were,' wrote the poet Sándor Petőfi in 1848, '... able to drink so much blood in a single draught.'

In 1849, the Prime Minister, Lajos Batthyány, and his colleagues were executed by Hungary's Habsburg rulers, for leading the next insurrection. The war of liberation in Hungary was one of many revolutionary events across Europe in 1848. It was reported at the time that the members of the Austrian firing squad clinked their beer mugs together before executing the Hungarian ministers. In honour of their martyrs the Hungarians made a vow not to clink their beer glasses together for one hundred and fifty years. In 1999, as the curse was lifted, I shut my eyes and waited for the tinkling of a million beer glasses. But nothing happened. People had forgotten how to do it.

*   *   *

In March 1985, I was in Petrozavodsk in Soviet Karelia, on the frozen shore of Lake Onega. This was my first trip as a journalist, following the footprints and the ski-tracks of the Finnish doctor and collector of folk stories, Elias Lönnröt. It was the one hundred and fiftieth anniversary of the first publication of the *Kalevala*, the Finnish epic poem which Lönnröt compiled from the material he collected, modelled on Homer's *Odyssey* and *Iliad*. A BBC World Service programme, *Outlook*, had commissioned an eight-minute radio feature about it. I borrowed a large, cumbersome reel-to-reel tape-recorder from Newcastle Polytechnic where my friends studied, and set out.

After days spent traipsing through the deep snow to talk to elderly writers in wooden cabins, it was my last evening in Petrozavodsk. I had tickets for the theatre, before my night train ride to Leningrad.

Suddenly, melancholy music sounded from loudspeakers in the streets. Konstantin Chernenko, the aged Soviet leader, was dead, after only a year in the job. The theatre performance was cancelled. The whole vast Union sank into compulsory, less-than-heartfelt mourning. After some time, I was allowed to board the train. But the mournful music continued in the sleeping car, which I found I was sharing with an Aeroflot ground engineer and his fiancée, who worked in a bookshop in Petrozavodsk. Both spoke excellent English—and, as we couldn't sleep, we talked. They spoke enthusiastically about the young man—by Soviet standards—who everyone already knew would be the next Soviet leader—Mikhail Gorbachev. After three dinosaurs in three years—Leonid Brezhnev, Yuri Andropov and Konstantin Chernenko—everything was now going to change, they hoped.

I bade farewell to them on the steps of the Finland Station in Leningrad, beside old women selling the last of the autumn apples in low winter sunlight. I decided to go and live in eastern Europe.

*   *   *

I moved to Budapest in February 1986, travelling by train from Greece through Yugoslavia. It was after midnight, and there was snow on the ground as I crossed Dániel Erdély's garden, in Virágárok, Ditch of Flowers Street. There were drunken conscripts singing in the road. I tapped on the window and a dog began barking inside.

Arriving from the south, rather than the north or west, and under a soft covering of snow, allowed me to slip into the country almost unnoticed. So did the fact that I had produced very little journalism. To the authorities, I was a completely unknown quantity. As I was to myself. I had to learn the trade, as well as the language and the history of the country, simultaneously. I had a rucksack of clothes, a small overdraft at a British bank and a half-finished notebook. It seemed the right moment to start a new life. I would stay for six months, I thought, and see how I got on.

I also knew it would not be easy to work behind the Iron Curtain. Apart from the large news bureaux in Moscow, there were no western journalists based in Hungary, and few in eastern Europe, though they did make regular forays from Vienna, or West Berlin. One British journalist from whom I had sought advice warned that I would be expelled almost immediately.

In my train carriage from Belgrade I befriended José, a film student from the Dominican Republic, who was studying in Kiev, capital of Ukraine and, at that time, still in the Soviet Union. He had just made a film about tigers at Kiev zoo. Intercut with film of Ukrainians shopping.

Tame, restless, potentially dangerous shoppers; tame, restless, potentially dangerous tigers. The censor was not amused, and ordered him to take out the shoppers. The Hungarian border police identified José as a troublemaker, and took him off the train to question him for so long that it set out without him, leaving his suitcase on the rack above my head. So I took it home with me, and got up early the next morning to meet the next train and give it back to him. I drank small glasses of very strong, very sweet coffee at the West Station, savouring my new life in this strange city. In due course, he arrived and was much relieved to retrieve his belongings.

At the Hungarian embassy in London, the head of the consular section had listened patiently to my plan to set up as a freelance journalist in Budapest. I was welcome, he said, provided I was named as a correspondent by a major British media organisation. A mere formality, I replied, and toured the editorial offices of several British dailies and weeklies. I told each that I was moving to Budapest anyway, and asked nothing more at this stage than that they read any reports or articles that I offered. No-one said no. No-one asked to see previous work. Only Martin Woollacott, foreign editor of the Guardian, tried to dissuade me.

'Let's say we like what you write, and we publish an article every two weeks,' he explained, through the thick cigarette smoke in his office in Farringdon Road. 'For which we will pay you the princely sum of £30. In two years time you will have a Hungarian girlfriend, perhaps a Hungarian wife and a baby on the way.' Better to go to journalism school in Britain, he suggested. Then get a job on a local paper and gradually work my way up. And perhaps one day become a foreign correspondent. I listened politely, and ignored his advice. Better to start at the top of the profession, I thought, than at the bottom.

*　　*　　*

What attracted me about eastern Europe from the start was exactly what repelled many western visitors. It was the disorder, the untidiness, the injustice. The sense of recent or impending disaster. The feeling that everything was both serious and funny at the same time. A buxom woman selling pink potatoes in an open market placed a pink rose among them, for effect; a man carrying a great sack of linen into a launderette bellowed 'CSÓK!' at the top of his voice to the assembled women, literally 'KISS!'—the much abbreviated form of the old greeting 'I kiss your hand'; at number 62, in the unpronounceable Bajcsy-Zsilinszky Street, the baker on the ground floor filled the whole building with the smell of fresh baked bread and cakes, while dissidents sold illegal publications, samizdat, on the first floor, and the country's first English language school functioned on the third. There were rumours that a large sum of money which had gone missing had turned up on the keys of its piano.

There were wooden barrels of sour cabbage in the markets, sold by women with sour cabbage-coloured hair whose ancestors were Swabians, Germans who had been invited to repopulate Hungary by the Habsburg Empress Maria Teresa, in the eighteenth century. The sour cabbage was eaten as it was, or stuffed in peppers with meat and stewed.

Everyone smoked or drank or cried. People wept and laughed more easily in public than in Britain. Strangers looked each other in the eye. Couples seemed to kiss with wilder abandon on the platforms of the underground. The Number 2 tram which ran along the eastern shore of the Danube, and the Number 19 which ran along the western shore, seemed always about to topple into the river. The river whose surface seemed to shift and change, in colour and texture, all the time.

Next to Parliament, a statue of the poet, Attila József, sat, chin in hand, blindly gazing out across the water.

> I sat there on the quayside by the landing,
> a melon rind was drifting on the flow.
> I delved into my fate, just understanding:
> the surface chatters, while it's calm below
> As if my heart had been its very source,
> troubled, wise was the Danube, mighty force.
> Like muscles when you work and lift the axe,
> or harvest, hammer, excavate a grave,
> so did the water tighten, surge, relax
> with every current, every breezy wave.
> Like Mother, dandled, told a tale, caressed,
> laundered the dirt of all of Budapest.

The poet died under a train at Szárszó on the southern shore of Lake Balaton, in December 1937, at the age of thirty-two. His death has always been described as suicide, but the former spokesman of the Budapest police, László Garamvölgyi, has written books and articles which attempt to prove it was an accident. That for some reason he was crawling over the tracks, when an engine started. Either way, suicide or tragic accident, his death seemed somehow typical of the Hungarian people. Always keen to sacrifice themselves for others, but rarely able to save themselves. It was as if everyone was terminally ill, but determined to make the most of each dying moment.

It also struck me that the deeper division of Europe was between not east and west, but south and north, and that Hungary belonged firmly to the south. But the east attracted me too, as I sought refuge from the west. The texture of time seemed different there, both slower and faster than the time I knew in northern Europe.

Politically speaking, time appeared to speed up, dramatically, just after I arrived.

The Solidarity movement in Poland, founded in 1980, had survived the imposition of martial law in 1981. Inspired and blessed by a Polish pope, the movement had continued its life underground, and was biding its time. The communist authorities had tried and failed to crush it.

Mikhail Gorbachev had been in power in the Soviet Union for less than a year, but there were already signs of change. My friends on the night train to Leningrad had been right. He had launched a policy of perestroika, a restructuring of the tattered Soviet economy which in turn needed a new glasnost, or openness. There was to be a freer discussion of carefully selected problems the country faced, which he hoped would raise public expectations with which he could break the resistance of the Party bureaucrats to limited reform. Unwittingly, he set in motion an avalanche of aspirations, not just in his own country, but right across eastern Europe.

Many observers in the West, their fingers burnt by previous Soviet leaders like Nikita Khrushchev, who had appeared to offer much, but had ended up delivering little, were unconvinced. But in eastern Europe, where every raised eyebrow and every hand-shake of a deputy prime minister had a meaning, the wind had definitely changed direction, and I was in the right place to feel it on my face.

In the Soviet Union, Gorbachev used journalists to carry his message to the public. In Hungary, journalists at regular dailies and weeklies began to strain at the leash, while the Party apparatus continued to act as if nothing had changed. But even its chief ideologist wrote of a 'lull' in Marxism, as though Marxism was a righteous storm which would soon resume, and that the waves of the proletariat would rise and rage once more.

Some commentators suggested that what was happening would be better summed up by the Russian word 'perelom', meaning a sudden break or turnaround.

The news leaked out slowly—first in hints, then in proper interviews from Gorbachev's inner circle, that the Brezhnev doctrine was dead. This was the principle that each communist country—in practice, the Soviet Union—was entitled to intervene in the affairs of others if socialism appeared to be endangered. If the Soviet army was no longer going to come marching in to topple the new skittles and prop the old skittles up next time they fell, the game was about to change completely.

As a young foreign journalist in Budapest in the mid-1980s, with no censors looking over my shoulder, the situation was perfect. My first reports were sent on an East German telex machine dated 1959, from the post office in Sándor Petőfi Street. Each time you hit a key it went down about three inches, bruising the knuckles on all the other fingers. They must have been designed for short, crisp telegrams, written by long-fingered typists with reinforced gloves. Not the long, analytical reports I began churning out. I finished each one with hands as sore as though I had boxed an opponent bare-fisted. My yellow machine produced a long snake of white tickertape, which I then fed back in, after I'd got through on the number. In London, my first customers, the language services of the BBC World Service, translated my reports into Hungarian, Czech, Russian, Polish and Romanian.

My sources were many—everyone wanted to talk, but few were able to publish. So what my Hungarian colleagues couldn't print, they passed on to me, in the hope that news of their small country might penetrate the wider world though the BBC airwaves. It was a constructive role, I thought and, true to my own past, a subversive one, as my reports were broadcast back into Hungary.

The strangest experience for a stranger to communism was the reverence with which the single Party was treated by its officials. The communist leader himself, János Kádár, after emerging from three years in prison in 1954, was interested mainly in finding out his own mistakes, and slavishly pledging to serve the Party better.

In *The Power of the Powerless*, an essay first published in 1982, the Czech dissident Václav Havel explained the 'hypnotic charm' of the communist ideology. 'To wandering humankind, it offers an immediately available home: all one has to do is accept it, and all mysteries ... and loneliness vanish.'

To that extent, the revolutions which overthrew it could be seen, on one level, as a restoration of mystery in a religious sense, and privacy in a middle-class sense.

'All we ever wanted was to be left alone, to be bourgeois!' the Hungarian writer, György Konrád, told me.

The memory, or the myth, of past revolutions had a great role in revitalising people who appeared to have bowed completely to the status quo. Schooled in the Great October Revolution of 1917 in Russia, they knew from the cinema that you have to seize key buildings—the headquarters of the secret police, for example. The French Revolution taught equality—and there was nothing that infuriated East German or Romanian workers more than reports of the luxury lifestyle enjoyed by comrades who ruled in the name of the working-class.

'Historical myths. . . .' wrote the Romanian historian of religions, Mircea Eliade, 'have a profound significance for the act of remembrance. A myth contains the story that is preserved in popular memory and that helps to bring to life some deep stratum buried in the depths of the human spirit.'

Eliade also wrote about the people of south-east Europe, in particular the peasantry, feeling 'left out of the tide of history', which only harmed them when they did get swept up in it. For me, the revolutions of 1989 and since appear like stepping stones in that tide, when the people find themselves, often to their own surprise, making progress across a river in flood.

Perhaps such moments were those Russian philosopher Nicholas Berdyaev wrote of, when he described history 'not as an external imposition, but as an interior event of spiritual significance', experienced actually on one's own skin.

*   *   *

On a rainy night in Moscow in October 2006, I tracked down Vitaliy Fomin. As an interpreter for the Soviet army command in Hungary in 1956, he was one of the few people still alive who had witnessed the crushing of the Hungarian revolution from the Soviet side. I missed a stop, and the bus carried me far beyond his dreary suburban block of flats. I retraced my tracks, on foot, and arrived at his front door drenched, more than an hour late, clutching a bottle of red wine. I had tried and failed to find a bottle with a red star on the label, and settled instead for a Bordeaux, with a simple but rather dramatic image of the sun.

He put the wine carefully to one side, and we sat in his kitchen on hard wooden stools, and drank cold, strong coffee. We spoke in our only common language, Hungarian.

'No revolution in human history has ever succeeded,' he said, paraphrasing Nicholas Berdyaev. The Hungarian word for revolution, forradalom, sat strangely in Vitaliy Fomin's mouth. Forradalom means literally 'a boiling up', from forrálni, the verb to boil. There is a powerful sense of ferment, but none of the movement, progress even, implicit in the word 'revolution' common to most European languages since the events of 1789 in Paris.

Vitaliy Fomin described arriving in Budapest on the night of 23 October 1956 in a Soviet jeep, without even so much as a pistol to defend himself. He slept under his own greatcoat, on the floor of an office of the Hungarian Ministry of Defence, his sleep interrupted by gun battles between young revolutionaries and secret policemen, who were fighting for control of the Zrínyi printing works next door.

Fifty years later, he said he was sorry about the loss of life, the thousands killed in street battles, as young Hungarians fought with Molotov cocktails and Second World War rifles against the might of the Soviet Southern Army. He regretted the retribution afterwards: the arrests, jail sentences and executions. But he still felt the Soviet intervention was justified, in the terms of reference of the time. An empire had the right to defend itself from inner subversion, he argued. Hadn't the British Empire, and all other empires, done the same?

On 23 October 1956, József Molnár was with hundreds of thousands of his fellow Hungarians on the streets of Budapest, to express his solidarity with the people of Poland. At least fifty-seven Poles, most of them protesters, had been killed by security forces at Poznań four months earlier, an act that paved the way for reforms by the Polish Communist Party. But the main scene of the ferment now spread to Budapest.

There is a traditional friendship between the Polish and Hungarian peoples, and it seemed a logical idea for Hungarian writers who, like the Poles, were trying to take advantage of a thaw in Moscow, to organise the march in solidarity with the reforms in Poland. But the events went further in Hungary, and ended even more bloodily.

In 1956, Hungarian students marched from the Technical University along the Buda bank of the Danube, while students from the Arts and

Humanities University marched along the Pest side of the river. The agreed meeting place was the statue of József Bem, a Polish general who had come to the aid of the Hungarians in their war of liberation against Austrian tyranny in 1848. Although the war culminated in humiliation and the execution of its leaders, Polish help was still fondly remembered more than one hundred years later.

As they marched, the crowd swelled, and the slogans they chanted became more radical—just as would happen again in 1989. Laughing children cycled alongside the marchers, sensing some kind of astonishing and marvellous carnival. Since the communist takeover in 1948, only official May Day demonstrations had been organised by the all-powerful Party. But this was something different. Photographs and films show a good-humoured crowd, all turned out in their best clothes, radiating serious joy. Despite the secret police, despite the years of Stalinist rule, they had overcome their fear.

At one point, near the Margit Bridge over the Danube, the crowd looked up. The famous composer Zoltán Kodály, already an old man, had come out onto his balcony, and was standing there with his arms upraised—a greeting, and a blessing.

At Bem Square, the noise was tremendous. In the excitement and the roar of the crowd, few could hear the speakers, who were shouting their words from Bem's plinth through nothing more than a small loud-hailer.

But József Molnár heard another sound. Something tinkling. He was standing on the west side of the square, near a five storey, nineteenth century block which housed an army barracks. Seeing the demonstrators coming, the commanding officers had locked the doors, to prevent any fraternisation by the soldiers.

So the soldiers had crowded round the windows to watch. And they began tearing the little red metal stars off their caps, and throwing them down, onto the pavement below. By the time József Molnár heard the sound, they were all doing it. It was raining red stars in Bem Square. 'At that moment,' József told me, fifty years later, 'I knew this was something more than a demonstration. I knew it was a revolution.'

*   *   *

This is a book about revolution, and regime change. It is about the brittleness of the regimes, and the comparative ease with which the people of eastern Europe in the last quarter of a century have toppled their rulers.

11

In 1989, in Hungary, Czechoslovakia, East Germany, Poland, and Bulgaria, miraculously without violence, but with the loss of more than a thousand lives in Romania. And then again in Bulgaria in 1997, in Kosovo in 1999 and in Serbia in 2000.

East of the Elbe, east and south of Vienna, government ministers quake in their boots when they hear the singing and chanting below. The jangling of keys on the streets of Prague, and Bratislava in November 1989. 'Time is up,' the crowd told the communist elite. 'It is time to leave the building. Lock the door when you go. Or better still, leave the key in the lock!'

* * *

It is also a book from street level, looking up at the windows and balconies of the powerful. It is about power, and powerlessness, as I have experienced them in eastern and central Europe, over the past twenty-five years. It is written from a position of sympathy with the street, but with an attempt at empathy with the balcony, and with the rooms and corridors of power behind. Seeing the problems of many countries, and the heavy burden of the past under which they toil, it is hard not to feel sympathy with those tasked with steering these countries, like old tramp steamers, towards harbour. Listing to port, or to starboard.

Few people, in war or peace-time, are granted the privilege of crossing the frontlines. But that for me is the joy of this job. To accost strangers in the street, and travellers on the train. To challenge elected, and unelected, leaders. To ask the council member why he gave permission to the developers to chop down that two hundred year old horse-chestnut tree in the courtyard of the Kisbuda restaurant to make way for an underground car-park. To ask the doctor why he feels compelled to intervene in every birth. To ask the prostitute why she feels driven to sell her body in an underpass—and through her to understand the degrees of prostitution that we all experience, as we try to earn a living. To experience the terror of those on whom tank shells are falling one day, and the justifications of the tank commanders the next. And to understand through them the degrees of fear and terror human beings inflict upon one another in everyday life.

* * *

What follows cannot hope to be exhaustive—and would be dull if I had tried to make it so. A great deal happened in central and eastern Europe during the past quarter century. I have largely restricted my narrative to places and events I witnessed myself, in the former Soviet satellite states of east and central Europe. My primary sources have been some three hundred and twenty, hand-written notebooks which I kept over this period, and several hundred hours of audio and video recordings.

There are, inevitably, exceptions. Adrian Bridge helped with his recollections of the fall of the Berlin Wall, and Konstanty Gebert with his memories of some of the key moments of the Solidarity experience in Poland.

I have tried throughout to see events through the prism of the ordinary people, in so far as this has been possible for me as a foreigner and a stranger.

An enormous number of people have helped me along the way—their names alone could fill a separate chapter. They translated for me when I had no money to pay them, drove through the night when I was too exhausted to go on, fed me and put me up in their homes, and, above all, patiently helped me understand the joy and pain of their lives, and of their nations.

I have been privileged to work for an organization, the British Broadcasting Corporation, which still remains true to its motto:

Nation shall speak Peace unto Nation.

Among the many colleagues, I will mention only a few names, without whose friendship and encouragement I could not have continued. István Siklós, the former head of the BBC Hungarian Section, and Mark Frankland, former eastern Europe correspondent of the Observer. Mike Popham and Tony Grant of the BBC's best programme, *From Our Own Correspondent*, and up on the bridge of the vast BBC ship, Mark James and Malcolm Downing.

My special thanks also to Nicola Balfour, Adam LeBor, Alison Mutler, Tim Judah, Victoria Clark, Danijela Mitić, Mihai Radu, Djordje Vlahić, Slobodan Stupar, Arber Vllahiu, Avni Ahmetaj, Vladislav Velev, Milorad Batinić, Peter Pallai and all at the former Hungarian, Romanian, and Bulgarian sections of the BBC.

This book is dedicated to my sons—in the full revolutionary pride of their youth, and to my father, who died suddenly when this narrative was still an infant in arms. It contains the seeds of conversations I still hope to have, or for which it is now too late. Some of the wood my father and I chopped together, four tons of elm and oak, on two October days, is still neatly stacked beside the garden shed. I can see it as I write.

My wife Andrea, my mother and father, my sister and brother, who gave me strength and love and encouragement at every turn. This book is also for them—an attempt at an explanation of where I have been, for so long.

I would also like to thank Rosie Whitehouse, Laura Keeling, and Jennifer Sandford at Reportage Press for inviting me to write this account in the first place, and for all their work and thought on the text, and Henrietta Molinaro for designing the cover. And finally Xandra Bingley, for her huge encouragement and advice.

At the end of the day, this is my account, and I alone take full responsibility for the selection of events, and the views expressed.

Dörgicse, September 2009

1. A Romanian Prelude

I sit in the crowded compartment of the train from Braşov to
Budapest and close my eyes, praying for the train to move. At
any moment, I expect the touch of a hand on my shoulder, and the
order to be given—'Come with us.' Will this train never leave? It seems
rooted in the station. I keep my eyes shut, and take deep breaths.
Then I feel something cold, dripping on my head. Steady, frozen
drops, through my hair, settling on my skull. I open my eyes, work
my arm loose from my nearest neighbour, and put my hand up
onto my head to investigate. I dip a cautious finger into the little
pool and lower the finger to eye level. My finger tip is scarlet, covered
in blood.

Pat Koza and I were lucky. We had applied for visas to visit communist
Romania in early November 1987. They had just been neatly stamped
into our passports when rumours began to circulate of an anti-regime
riot in the city of Braşov, high in the Transylvanian mountains. Eyewitnesses had crossed into Yugoslavia, and the Yugoslav news agency,
Tanjug—at that time one of the free-est in eastern Europe—had broken
the news of thousands of workers marching against the Romanian
dictator, Nicolae Ceauşescu. There were reports of posters of him being
burnt on giant bonfires, and of a savage retribution by the authorities.
The reports had been reprinted by the western press, but shadowed
by doubt and suspicions of exaggeration. There had been so little
dissent in communist Romania. Hadn't Radio Free Europe, broadcasting
from Munich, already reported that one in three Romanians were
informers for the Securitate, the dreaded secret police? Didn't everyone know that the Romanians even compared themselves to their
national dish, mamaliga? Polenta cooked in water and milk, and served
with cream and cheese—if anyone could find them. A kind of stodgy
pudding, capable of popping and sighing on a strong heat, but incapable
of exploding.

We flew into Otopeni airport in Bucharest on 25 November, ten days after the alleged protest in Braşov. On the day we set out, The Times of London questioned whether there had been any riot at all.

Pat was an experienced American journalist, bureau chief for United Press International in Warsaw. I was an inexperienced British one, but I had been to Romania several times from my home in neighbouring Hungary. I had travelled as a passenger in a bubble car, a little orange Polski Fiat, to visit remote Hungarian villages in Transylvania where peasants risked the wrath of the state to show their traditional hospitality to strangers. Such was the oppression in Romania under Nicolae Ceauşescu, that anyone who spoke to a foreigner was obliged to write a report of their encounter for the secret police. Transylvania then was like Narnia in *The Lion, the Witch and the Wardrobe* by C.S. Lewis— and Nicolae Ceauşescu was the white witch, keeping everything frozen in permanent winter.

* * *

In the spring of 1987, on my previous visit to Bucharest, I had taken a tram outside the Bessarabia Station, to visit an old man in his mid-eighties, whose name I so carefully concealed in my notebooks that I can no longer find it now. Having somehow negotiated the potholes in the street in the pouring rain, and lit match after match to find my way up the dark staircase, I knocked bravely on his door.

'You want to know the situation in this country?' he asked. 'It is a human catastrophe. This is not just the worst time for the past forty years, it is the worst in the last ten centuries!'

Every four or five days, he left his flat to visit the open market. To buy the rationed three hundred grammes of bread allowed each day, supplemented with milk if he could find it, jars of peas and, occasionally, a little meat or frozen fish.

'We survive by telling each other stories,' he smiled, 'like in Berlin, before the war.'

'It was my niece's birthday,' he went on, 'and I wanted to buy her flowers. When I couldn't find any, I went into a wine shop. The man in front of me in the queue asked for champagne. The sales assistant seized his arm, 'has he died then?" she asked.'

Popular legend had it that every household kept a bottle in their cupboard for the day Ceauşescu kicked the bucket.

'All that is needed is goodwill. The old leaders are dying. Everywhere young people are waking up and demanding freedom and democracy. There will be a united Europe, it is only a question of time, though I will not live to see it. I have lived too long already. One day you will remember what I said.' He said this to me standing, tall and thin as a rake despite his eighty-three years, his head almost brushing the bare light bulb, at least sixty watts strong, which blazed in defiance of the forty watt regulation.

The nearest I got to official criticism of the situation was this remark, off-record, from a senior government official.

'Our human rights record could be better. Bucharest is a mess, but will be beautiful again. You are lucky that there was no international press around to judge your country at the start of your industrial revolution.'

A young Hungarian woman, a factory worker in the same town and married to a Romanian, expanded the theme.

'We are no worse off economically than the Romanians. But when they have no food, they have at least the consolation of reading their own books and newspapers, of having their children taught at school in their own language.'

Driving through the Transylvanian countryside, there was a sense of official tension, but also of verbal solidarity between the Romanian majority and Hungarian minority. Ceauşescu had decided that all 13,000 villages in the country should be destroyed, and the population moved into agro-industrial complexes in the towns.

It was a policy opposed by all but the most fanatical supporters of Ceauşescu, but who was in a position to stop it?

'This is a policy of divide and rule,' I was told by a Romanian teacher who had been appointed to a school in the city of Tirgu Mureş, in an attempt to ensure that no teaching in Hungarian could take place. 'The regime is setting Romanian against Hungarian, Moldavian against Transylvanian, Orthodox against Catholic.'

In Iaşi, a Catholic priest was too scared to speak of the years of persecution, the shortage of Bibles and religious literature, or of contact with the outside world—his church, the second biggest in Romania, was not officially recognised. He would speak only about the fact that the churches were full every Sunday—'by the grace of God, a miracle!'

In the candlelit Orthodox cathedral nearby, the silver sarcophagus of

Saint Parascheva was surrounded by the faithful, kneeling, clutching the rim of the tomb as though it was the rim of their country, and praying for better times.

* * *

On arrival in Bucharest in November 1987, Pat and I decided to pay lip service to our original plan, on the basis of which our visas had been granted. We would talk to a few dull Communist Party officials, and state bankers and bureaucrats in the capital, before setting out for the hills, to find out what we could about the anti-communist protest.

We knew we would be closely followed by the Securitate, but trusted, naively, in our own skills to shake them off for a few hours and to find out what had really happened.

Pat stayed at the Intercontinental Hotel, while I stayed nearby in its more eccentric sister, the Hotel Continental, a wedding cake of a building in the city centre. The rooms were white and pink and gold, full of reflecting mirrors and uncomfortable chairs. A cake left over from a pre-communist wedding, perhaps, the icing hard enough to break your teeth on.

* * *

Unlike other communist rulers, who borrowed without restraint to keep the population warm with full stomachs, Ceaușescu decided, to the delight of the International Monetary Fund, to pay off the national debt. Anything and everything was exported. On the streets, the hunger of the people was most vividly illustrated by the fact that whenever you saw someone carrying a loaf of bread, they were chewing on it. A kilo of coffee cost more than $100 on the black market. A year's supply of birth-control pills $500. Ceaușescu had banned contraception and abortion, in an ultimately successful attempt to increase the population. In fact, the infant mortality rate was so high that births were not recorded until the child had been alive for a month.

In the countryside, an official permit was necessary even to kill a chicken, and most produce had to be sold, at low prices, to the state, where it immediately went for export. Each person in one small town in the mountains was required to give six days work, and $20, to the municipality each month.

'89: The Unfinished Revolution

There had been flickerings of discontent before the Braşov events, but these were few and far between. When white-collar female workers were summoned to a three-monthly pregnancy check, to prevent illegal abortions, no-one came despite the threat that their pay would be withheld. Wages were, eventually, paid in full. Spontaneous strikes by the glass-blowers of Turda, the IMGB heavy machinery works in Bucharest, the Cug metal works in Cluj and the Nicolina railway works in Iaşi had all taken place when wages were not paid, or food ran out in the shops. In Iaşi students had also marched on Party headquarters, demanding lighting, food and heat. In each case, conciliatory speeches were made, and the demands largely met. Occasionally, nonetheless, protest organisers mysteriously disappeared days, or weeks, afterwards.

The main television news dedicated two hours each day to the latest exploits of Nicolae Ceauşescu. Restaurants and bars closed at nine each evening, to conserve energy. Inspired by a trip to North Korea, Ceauşescu had decided to redevelop the historic city centre, destroying 40,000 buildings and dozens of ancient churches in the process.

*   *   *

On our first evening in Bucharest, as rare western visitors, we were invited for a drink at the British embassy club. I sipped a half of Guinness with Alp Mehmet, the first secretary. He regaled us with tales of the pleasures and discomforts of life in this most oppressive of societies, but seemed rather restrained in his criticism of the man in power.

At one point in the evening, he slipped his calling card across the table to me. Then he caught my eye, and with the subtlest gesture of his hand, mimed that I turn it over. A name, a street address and a telephone number were written on the back. Professor Silviu Brucan. It was a shock to realise that, even in his own club, a British diplomat did not dare speak openly.

The next day I shunned the hotel phone, and rang Brucan quickly from a public phone in an underpass near University Square. A deep, soft voice answered. He was keen to find out exactly which media we represented. I told him I was correspondent for both the BBC and the Independent newspaper in London, and Pat for a major US news agency. He sounded satisfied, and invited us to his home at eleven the next morning.

Pat and I hired a car, a small Soviet built Lada which looked pretty much the same from the front as the back. I found myself squinting inside to find the steering wheel, in order to work out which side to get in. Though we could have taken taxis around Bucharest, having our own transport would make it easier to escape from the capital as soon as we could, and establish a modicum of independence from the men who followed us everywhere, at a discreet distance. But first to the mysterious professor.

We realised he was important as we negotiated the tree-lined streets of elegant villas near Herastrau Park. At one point we got lost, and drove the wrong way down a one-way street. A uniformed policeman leapt out into the road in front of us, and furiously jabbed two fingers towards his eyes. Were we blind? he wanted to know. Had we not seen the sign? We played the stupid foreigner card and he let us go, with a curse.

A man in his mid-seventies opened the door. Silviu Brucan studied us with grey, intelligent eyes. Then ushered us quickly inside. In the hallway, we paused to look at black and white photographs of the professor with Edward Kennedy, Richard Nixon and Gerald Ford. Somewhat dazed, we sat down in his living room.

'First of all,' he asked firmly in impeccable, slightly accented English, 'do you know who I am?' We had to confess we had no idea.

The professor seemed unperturbed.

'I have prepared two papers for you,' he continued. 'Read this one first.'

And he handed each of us a single sheet—his curriculum vitae. Clearly typed himself on a typewriter, in just two copies, using a sheet of blue carbon paper between the white pages.

Pat and I read in silence. He had been editor-in-chief of Scînteia, the Communist Party daily, from 1944 to 1956, during both the communist takeover, and the most Stalinist period. During the late 1950s, he was Romanian ambassador, first to the United Nations in New York, then to the United States in Washington. In the 1960s, he was director of Romanian state television. Nowadays a member of the Central Committee of the Communist Party, and a Professor of Politics at the University of Bucharest, this was clearly no idle camp-follower. Least of all a dissident. But an insider, a heavy-weight Party ideologist.

'Now read this sheet,' he said, carefully, thrusting the next one at us.

I reproduce the text here exactly as he wrote it. He watched us intently as we read.

> The workers' demonstration in Brașov is a watershed in Romania's political history as a socialist state. A period of crisis has opened up

in the relationship between the Communist Party and the working class which until recently has ensured the political stability of the regime.

Here I must take issue with a misconception prevailing in the West that this regime owes its survival to the repressive organs of the state.

Surely this could not explain more than two decades of political stability. In fact, the main instrument of power has been the Communist Party with security forces playing only a marginal role and dealing with individual deviant cases.

The Party could successfully control the mass of workers because it became popular in the sixties when a turn for the better occurred in the Romanian economy and in the standard of living of almost three million peasants who joined the urban industrial workforce. There was plenty of food and there was no comparison with the 'idiocy of rural life' they had left behind.

In the eighties, however, their situation went from bad to worse and the Braşov eruption signals that the cup of privations is now full and the working class no longer accepts to be treated like an obedient servant. The recent decree on energy is actually asking the workers to commit suicide by freezing in their bedroom.

The leadership is now facing a hard choice: mass repression, because we are dealing with thousands of workers, or a sincere effort to come to terms with their legitimate grievances.

Certainly, the prevailing trend in the East today speaks loudly in favour of the second option. Repression might have incalculable repercussions both domestic and international. World public opinion is now a formidable force in the defence of human rights. Repression may only result in total isolation, this time not only from the West, but also from the East.

Moreover, repression will generate a rupture between the Party and the working class. As a veteran Party member I am worried that such a course of action might prevail. We have seen in Poland what such a rupture means and how difficult it is for the Party to regain the confidence of the workers, even when the best of intentions to improve their lot is apparent.

This was dynamite. A Marxist critique of Ceauşescu's personality cult, and its consequences. The 'rupture' he referred to in Poland was the rise of the Solidarity movement in 1980, and the suppression of it in 1981— only six years earlier. Silviu Brucan was, in Marxist terms, overtaking his own party 'on the left'. And laying down a direct challenge to a leader who tolerated no dissent, Nicolae Ceauşescu.

I expected the secret police to burst through the door at any moment, and arrest us all. I began to wonder whether Pat and I would get out of Romania alive.

The secret police had a way of arranging 'traffic accidents' for people they didn't like.

'Everything on the two pieces of paper I have given you is on the record,' Brucan continued. 'I can tell you anything else I know about Braşov, but that will be off-record—agreed?' We murmured our assent.

For the next two hours we listened as he described what had happened in Braşov on 15 November as he had heard the story from internal, Communist Party sources. How the workers from two factories, one producing tractors, the other heavy trucks, had been marched into town to vote for the single Communist Party candidate in local elections. It was a Sunday. These were the elite of the working class, he pointed out—skilled workers, well-educated and relatively well-paid—the chosen ones who had, in the words of his own statement to us, been brought in from the cold 'idiocy of rural life' to build socialism. This was perhaps the only phrase in his text with which his master might have agreed. Ceauşescu himself was the son of poor cobblers. His own hatred of village life informed his policies—especially when he decided to bulldoze three thousand villages.

On that famous Sunday, the Braşov workers reached a fork in the road, and instead of turning right to the polling stations, as they were supposed to, they had turned left instead, for the city centre. They were angry. They had just been told that their wages would be cut by a third, and that many would lose their jobs. During the night shift, there had been spontaneous meetings of workers in different sections of the giant factory to decide what to do. The Party, and the city, were about to find out.

When they reached Party headquarters in the main square, they easily overcame the unprepared guards and broke into the building. Their fury increased when they found large quantities of luxury foods inside—in preparation for the local Party officials to celebrate their 'victory' in the elections later that day—foods which could not be bought in ordinary shops. One worker scaled the building and tore down the Party flag. They smashed furniture and piled the broken wood—along with mountains of election posters of Ceauşescu and his wife Elena—onto a great bonfire in the square in front of the building. Then set fire to it.

Brucan related, too, how the authorities had stood back and watched, and waited. But they were not idle. They stopped traffic entering or leaving the city, cut the phone lines and tried to seal Braşov off from the outside world. For hours, the bonfire raged, the windows of the building were smashed and records, telephones, computers, and other Party objects destroyed.

Then as evening fell, and the crowds began to make their way home, the secret police struck. As many as ten thousand people had taken part in the protest. Thousands were questioned, and hundreds rounded up, piled into police vans and taken away. Brucan could not confirm whether or not they were still alive.

Uncertain what might now happen to the professor, or to ourselves, we bade him a solemn farewell, and drove on to our next meeting. In the car, we spoke in terse half-sentences. Our next appointment was at Agerpress, the state-controlled news agency in the Soviet-style press centre, modelled on a Stalinist building of the same ilk in Moscow. Lenin watched us, impassively, from his giant plinth outside. Inside a hot, stuffy room on an upper floor, two or three Party monkeys addressed us as 'dear colleagues', and asked how we were enjoying socialist Romania. Enormously, we told them, at least half-truthfully. They regaled us with statistics. How Romania was the only country in the communist bloc which had paid off its debts. How agricultural cooperatives produced record yields, year after year. How under the wise leadership of the Conducător, the Great Leader, and his scientist wife, Elena, the country was enjoying a golden age.

And how were we planning to spend the rest of our trip? they asked, politely. 'We thought we would just drive up to Brașov,' Pat disclosed, gently.

The man's smile froze. The room froze. Time stopped.

'Nothing happened in Brașov,' he croaked. 'Of course not,' we reassured him, 'but we thought we would just drive up there to have a look round, just in case.' To fulfil our duty as journalists, we explained. He had, after all, referred to us as 'colleagues'.

'Of course, you must go then—this is a free country, after all . . .' he hissed, with all the warmth and charm of a steel cat, '. . . but it will be a wasted journey. You will find nothing.' His anger was fuelled by the fact that he knew we knew he was lying.

We said our cold goodbyes and then made our way back down the musty staircase. The building smelt of old socks and stale cigarettes. There were portraits of Ceaușescu everywhere, stylised, with pudgy lips. With his wife. On his own. Or receiving flowers from doting children. As we came out of the main entrance, a rat shot past.

We got into the Lada and set off for Brașov. In a sense, we felt better. We had told the authorities where we were going. Our cards were open on the table in front of us. Just one concern gnawed at us—did they know

23

about Brucan's letter? Would they try to take it from us? Worst of all, we were afraid we would be involved in an 'accident'.

At some point, still in the suburbs of Bucharest, we noticed that one of our headlights wasn't working and got out to try to fix it. As we stood there looking foolishly at the headlamp in the softly falling snow, it suddenly came on again, without us even touching it. We burst out laughing. It was such a relief. We were so paranoid beforehand, we had hardly spoken a word in the car.

* * *

In Braşov, we booked into the only hotel in town, the Hotel Carpaţi, and set out on foot through the old town. After the drabness of communist Bucharest, this seemed a fairytale place of narrow, cobbled, medieval streets, dwarfed by mountains which appeared to have come into town themselves, to take a closer look.

Our presence had not gone unnoticed. Wherever we went a man in a puffy blue anorak followed our every step. This was a different class of minder to the ones who had chaperoned us in Bucharest. In the capital there were only fleeting glimpses: a car parked across the street with two men waiting; doors opening and shutting frequently in the next room in the hotel; men sitting silently at the next table in a restaurant, studiously ignoring us. You could never be one hundred per cent sure if they were really the police, or the product of our own, overworked imaginations. But here in Braşov, the gentlemen had a different role— not to find out who we were talking to, but to put us off even striking up a conversation.

So we developed a new tactic: to talk to as many people as possible. We played the dumb tourists.

'Excuse me, madam, can you tell us the way to the Black Church?' we would ask, in English or German. Braşov was traditionally a German town, known as Kronstadt, and both of us spoke fluent German. The church was the most famous monument in the city, a beautiful Gothic building left over from simpler, but perhaps no less brutal times. We would then tag on another question, 'We are journalists from England and America. Can you tell us what happened here last week?'

Some people fled from us as soon as we planted the second question. But several pondered briefly and then answered, gesticulating carefully.

'You turn left, then right, then left again. Thousands marched.

Party headquarters was completely trashed! You could see the bonfire two kilometres away!'

We thanked them hurriedly, and were away by the time blue anorak huffed up.

At the corner of Communist Party headquarters, the focal point of the disturbances, armed police with Alsatian dogs were on patrol. The windows were clearly new, the walls had been repainted and there was a large, freshly laid flower-bed in the square in front of the building. Many hints at attempts to conceal the events we now knew for sure had taken place, but no actual proof. As there was no point in pretending we were really tourists here, we rang the door bell. Eventually, a man in a long leather coat answered it. We gave our names, and the organisations we represented, and asked if it might be possible to speak to an official. Certainly not, he replied, but in a friendly manner. Perhaps he could tell us what had happened to this building just the previous week. 'Nothing, nothing at all.' He smiled. A better liar, or perhaps just further up the liars' chain, than the men from Agerpress.

Wandering back to our hotel, with blue anorak hot on our trail, twisting left and right down alleyways, getting deliberately lost, we resumed our game of questioning locals. A small man with a beard came up trumps. 'Meet me at the bus stop in front of your hotel at nine this evening,' he said in excellent English. 'Pretend you do not recognise me. Get on the bus then follow me home.'

It seemed too perfect; he was almost too well-rehearsed. Was he really going to risk his life, or was he working for them? Was it a trap, or a hidden trap-door?

Either way, we felt we had no choice but to meet him.

*   *   *

Both Pat and I kept our copies of Brucan's statement on us at all times, afraid to leave it in our hotel rooms. At the appointed time, we wandered down to the bus stop, and pretended to be discussing where to go and have supper. We spotted our man and leapt on through the back doors, just before they slammed shut, as he got onto the bus at the front.

We scrutinised our fellow passengers. No-one appeared to take any interest in us. In the dark, we couldn't tell whether the headlights on the road behind were innocent cars, or guilty ones.

The bearded man got off, near a housing estate in the suburbs. We followed. Glances over our shoulders suggested no-one was following us. We plunged into a dark stairwell, stumbling upwards—there were never lights in the stairways at that time in Romania. Electricity for households was rationed. It was all part of Ceauşescu's plan to pay off all Romania's foreign debts. All forms of domestic consumption, except for the Party elite, was drastically limited—the 'recent decree on energy' in Brucan's statement. If too many light bulbs burned in your windows, you were in danger of being reported by the neighbours.

We followed the man, at last, into his apartment. He shook our hands warmly for the first time, and introduced himself as Mihai Barsan, a thirty-two-year-old engineer at Steagul Roşu, the Red Flag truck factory. By now it was nine-thirty in the evening. There was no one else in the flat.

Before he began his story, he had a tale to tell us. 'I often listen to what we call Bucharest 3,' he said, laughing. With his beard, he really looked like the faun in Narnia. Bucharest 1, he explained, was Radio Free Europe. Bucharest 2 was the Voice of America. And Bucharest 3 was the BBC. I felt momentarily miffed that the BBC were demoted to third place, but it was not the right moment for professional vanity. All three radio stations broadcast in Romanian for several hours a day, and each provided airtime for Romanian, anti-communist émigrés, living in the West, as well as broadcasting uncensored news about the rest of the world in the Romanian language. But Mihai had another point to make.

'During the war in the Falklands—Malvinas,' he said, carefully using both the English and the Argentinean names for the islands in the South Atlantic, 'I heard an interview on the BBC with General Galtieri—the Argentinean leader. And I thought, this is the kind of radio we must have one day in Romania—one that could broadcast the words of the enemy leader, even during wartime!' And that was why, he said, he had decided to risk his life by talking to us tonight. My professional vanity was more than restored.

He went on to describe how, twelve days earlier at nine in the morning, several thousand workers from his factory, including himself, had been told to march together to vote in local elections. The city was already decorated with flags, celebrating the Communist Party's inevitable victory in the elections. There was, after all, only one candidate for each position. But there was already rebellion in the air. During the night shift, workers had openly expressed their anger about a twenty-eight to forty-one percent cut in wages, which had just been announced.

About three hundred men began marching from the factory, ostensibly to vote in the elections. But as they walked, a hum rose from the crowd, and no-one was quite sure where it began. It was a tune from the 1848 revolution, outlawed by the communist regime, called 'Romanian, awake!' People began singing the words:

> Awake, Romanian, from the deadly sleep
> Into which barbarian tyrants have lulled you,
> Now, as never before, forge for yourself a new fate,
> And make your cruel enemies bow before you . . .

Then they took their historic left turn, for the centre of the city—and Communist Party headquarters. People came to their balconies, looks of fear on their faces. Others wept. By now there were other chants: 'Down with Ceauşescu!' and 'We want bread!' As they passed through the Sunday morning streets, more and more people summoned the courage to join them.

Much of the detail of this he had found out later, from colleagues at work. Mihai had been playing bridge—illegal in Ceauşescu's Romania—in a friend's flat that morning, and had only joined the protest in the early afternoon. The demonstration was sparked, he said, both by the latest restrictions on basic goods in Romania, and by threatened job losses at his factory, and another, Tractorul. The austerity measures, ordered by Ceauşescu, and a fall in foreign orders, were taking their toll. As wages were tied to production, and there were no orders, unprecedented cuts of 5,000 jobs had also been announced at the factories. Unemployment in Romania, as in all communist countries, was illegal, so the workers were assured new jobs. Those they were allocated would be neither as prestigious nor as well paid, either on building sites or in the coal mines. They were being downgraded, and they knew it.

Braşov was Romania's second city, in terms of industrial production. The two factories alone, Tractorul and Red Flag, employed nearly 50,000 workers. As the workers from Red Flag turned left, the workers from Tractorul joined them. Ceauşescu's nightmare, and that of regimes across eastern Europe who claimed legitimacy from the working class, was about to come true. The workers were about to turn on their own party.

The rest of his account confirmed what Silviu Brucan had already told us.

There were also new details—the worker who scaled the front of the building and tore down the communist flag. Every picture of Ceaușescu they could find—and there were thousands—was taken out and piled high in front of the building. Other Party documents and papers were added. The bonfire was lit. Inside, young workers went from room to room, smashing computers. One policeman was reported to have been killed when the protesters attacked his patrol car.

Mihai also gave us details of the reprisals. Tanks and armoured vehicles began to cordon off the city centre. Local Party officials arrived by bus and started taking notes from the edge of the crowd, writing down the names of everyone they recognised. Those workers who could slipped quickly away, and the flames of the fire died down. The first arrests took place that evening.

The next morning, meetings were held in each section of the two big factories, Red Flag and Tractorul. Any worker who had participated was invited to confess.

Local managers already brandished lists. Workers who had not taken part in the action were invited to criticise it. A letter was sent to Ceaușescu by the 'loyal workers' of the factories, asking for the death penalty for those who had besmirched their city, and their country's good name.

Several hundred people had already been arrested, he said, and taken away. He didn't know where, but the roundups were continuing. One secret police tactic was to question children about the activities of their older brothers and fathers who worked at the plants.

By the time he had finished his tale it was two o'clock in the morning. We shook hands warmly, and left. We walked through the cold city, all the way back to our hotel.

Years later, after the revolution, I found out that Mihai was arrested within hours, before he set out for work. The Securitate had a full transcript of his conversation with us. He was roughed up by his interrogators, put in the back of a van with a dozen others arrested for alleged participation in the protest and driven towards Bucharest. At one point, the men were ordered to get out of the van and told to stand with their backs towards the guards, who loaded their rifles. Mihai waited for the end of his life.

But then they were ordered to get back into the van. Then driven on, to prison in Bucharest.

Pat and I still believed that our visit to his flat had gone undetected. Back in the hotel, we noticed that someone had gone through our luggage. We began to fear the worst when Mihai did not turn up to a meeting we had arranged—or rather, a walk past one another, outside a restaurant in the middle of the day.

Pat drove back to Bucharest, alone, to catch her flight for Warsaw. I decided to spend another day in Braşov, and take the evening train to Budapest. There were two men following me now, so close I could almost feel their breath on my neck. I had not been able to sleep for two nights because of the tension. For a while, I had sat in the bathroom of my room in the hotel, learning Brucan's statement off by heart. In case it was taken off me at the border, I reasoned. If I got that far.

I felt exhausted, exhilarated, and miserably lonely at the same time. As darkness fell, I started walking the streets of the town. Disco music came up from a basement.

I swerved suddenly, and dived down some stairs. Students were dancing in the dim light and, having nothing better to do, I started dancing with them. Then the music stopped. Two men came through the crowd for me. Everyone stared as I was taken out of the building, into the courtyard. The luckless organiser of the party was found, and brought out with me. He swore blind that he had never seen me before—which was completely true. Then I was questioned, civilly, in French, by a man who appeared to be the chief. Apparently satisfied that I had not had a chance to speak to anyone, they let me go, with an apology. 'A misunderstanding!' said the man from the secret police.

*   *   *

During the day, I had walked down to the station to buy my one-way ticket to Budapest. I sat in a public library for a while, trying to read. I imagined them questioning Brucan. If they knew the content of his statement, surely they would try to prevent it leaving the country? I had no way of finding out if Pat had made it safely to her flight.

Towards ten in the evening, I walked through the chilly streets to the railway station. My train to Budapest was supposed to leave at ten-thirty and the train was already standing at platform 1. I found my reserved seat in an already crowded, first-class compartment. I shut my eyes.

I felt something cold, dripping on my head and reached up to the growing puddle in my hair. I stared at my red finger and felt a scream rising in my lungs. And with the last of my strength, suppressed it. I stood up, unsteadily. There was a large, rectangular parcel, wrapped in news-paper and string, in the luggage rack immediately above my head. In the state of mind I was in, my first thought was that this was some trick of the state. Simply to freak me out even more. Or, perhaps, even to frame me, for murder. I asked around the carriage. Whose was the parcel? Everyone shrugged. It seemed to belong to no-one. I wanted to weep—should I put it back, and continue to be splashed with blood? It was not a fate I could wish on anyone else, either. So I wrestled the parcel down, took it out into the corridor of the train, and slid back the door of the next compartment. I then thrust it under the feet of a startled old lady. And returned, trembling, to my own seat.

A little later, the train finally moved off. I shut my eyes again, and sank into the deepest sleep.

The next thing I heard was shouting and banging, from far away. I opened my eyes to find myself lying on my side in a totally empty compartment. My own case was the only one in the luggage rack and I could hear someone going from compartment to compartment, sliding back the doors. Men were barking orders. The border! Before setting out, I had made half a plan of what to do with Brucan's statement, which still lay folded in my trouser pocket. I should conceal it somewhere, in case I was strip-searched. I leapt to my feet, and started running down the corridor, catching sight of a man in uniform as I fled towards the toilet at the end of the carriage. I went inside and locked the door. It was disgusting, shit-smeared and opening onto the track below, like most train toilets in eastern Europe at that time. But above the wash-basin there was a mirror. I took the precaution of lowering my trousers and underwear, then began to slowly slide Brucan's statement behind the glass. It was about half hidden when a fist began hammering on the door, and a voice shouted to me to open up. I froze. The next moment the soldier kicked open the door. My hands flew away from the mirror, and the incriminating document. A young conscript stood there, clutching an old, wooden-handled rifle. We stared at each other, almost equally horrified.

Noticing my state of undress, he mumbled an apology, and retreated. But had he seen the paper at the mirror? What would he report to his officer? With a heavy heart, I extracted the statement from its hiding place, and went back to my compartment, screwing it up into a ball in my hand as I did. Then I fitted it neatly under the apple cores and cigarette ash in the metal bin under the window. The lid was barely closed, when the plain clothes men arrived. They looked at my passport, then asked to take away my case. I assented. They disappeared with it. Soldiers marched up and down the train, checking for stowaways. There was little love lost between socialist Romania and socialist Hungary. Hungary had lost its beloved province of Transylvania to Romania less than seventy years earlier, and the loss of the Hungarians, and the joy of the Romanians, was barely dampened by the fact that they both, in theory, now belonged to the same communist camp.

The wait here, too, was interminable. I knew they would find little in my bag—my short-hand is unreadable, even on occasion, to myself. And I had been careful not to note anything incriminating, from Mihai or other people we had met in Braşov. Or from Brucan.

So what could they actually do with me? My main fear was that they would find some excuse to take me off the train. Once in their hands, I might disappear.

At last, the men arrived back with my case. My passport was stamped. The soldiers and their ladders clambered back onto the platform and the train groaned painfully back into motion. When the Hungarian border-guards got on the train at the next stop, I could have hugged them. I was free.

*　*　*

When I got to my flat in Budapest, I rang Pat in Warsaw. She was bleary, but safe as well. We agreed to release the Brucan statement simultaneously, that afternoon. But first, I needed more sleep.

Silviu Brucan's words, and our reports on Braşov, made headlines around the world.

'Romanian figure warns of repression', 'Party veteran denounces hardship under Ceauşescu.' Brucan himself was immediately placed under house arrest.

Foreign diplomats tried in vain to visit him, and reported his situation to the western media. Ceauşescu, clearly rattled, failed to attend a Warsaw Pact summit in early December, and sent his Foreign Minister instead. On 3 December, a meeting was held at the Red Flag factory, and our friends at Agerpress finally admitted that something had happened in Braşov.

'The arbitrary and abusive wage cuts were criticised, the manager was fired, and both the political leaders of the city and the organisers of the riots will be put on trial.'

After two weeks cut off from the outside world, Brucan was hauled in front of Ion Constantin, the man in charge of the discipline department of the Central Committee of the Romanian Communist Party.

'Comrade Brucan, we were surprised that an old Party member . . . could make a statement hostile to our Party and to our nation. Didn't you realise that such a statement gives aid and comfort to our class enemies? Didn't you see that you were addressing the worst imperialist agencies?'

Brucan was kept under house arrest until the following March. In June 1988, he was given a passport, and allowed to travel to the United States, in the hope that he would never come back.

In Braşov, workers like Mihai who had been arrested were kept in prison in Bucharest, interrogated and beaten regularly. Eugen Tudose, a trade union leader whom I met after the revolution, explained what happened next.

'On 2 December, two weeks after I was arrested, they brought us back to Braşov. There were sixty-one of us in my group, of over three hundred who were arrested. We were allowed to sleep one night at home, under a sort of house arrest. We were amazed to hear that all the shops were full of food, and our fellow workers had begun to receive one hundred percent of their salaries. People were happy about that, but very angry about all the arrests . . .'

'On 3 December we were put on trial for disturbing public order and hooliganism. We had no right to defend ourselves. We were simply ordered to say: "Yes, I recognise my crime, and I accept my punishment." I got eighteen months hard-labour, at Pogoanele, in Buzau county. I was twenty-seven years old.'

Ten years after the Braşov uprising, I asked another trade union leader, Gavril Filichi, why he thought that the death-sentences, demanded by the 'loyal' workers in their letter to Ceauşescu, had not been carried out.

'Because of public opinion, international public opinion first of all. Radio Free Europe, Voice of America, the BBC. And because of the students. While some in the town were demanding our execution, the students came to our rescue, chanting "The workers must not be killed!"'

Of those who were arrested, beaten or imprisoned by the authorities, three died in prison or in exile in other parts of Romania.

The lucky ones returned to Braşov during the revolution, two years later.

2. Twilight of the Grey King

We have had in our own history many and often bitter differences with the Hungarians, but we as a nation respect them. They are a strong and proud people. And Stalin, come to think of it, also had a healthy respect for them. He said to me on one occasion that nations which had been ruled by powerful aristocracies, like the Hungarians and the Poles, were strong nations. Stalin was a great admirer of powerful states and powerful institutions even when he was opposed to them; and his fear of the Hungarians and the Poles was a revealing backhanded recognition of Polish and Hungarian stamina.

Milovan Djilas, Yugoslav writer

The fifteenth of March 1986 was a Saturday. The sun was shining in Budapest though a chill wind blew off the river. The young crowd around the statue to the poet Sándor Petőfi on the Danube embankment just grew bigger and bigger. Some laid flowers at his feet, others planted little Hungarian flags in the grass. Most just hung around, half-pretending that they were not there to demonstrate at all, as though they just happened to be passing by and were magnetically drawn to the spot.

Petőfi himself, a high spirited youth with a slightly comical quiff in his hair, gazed over their heads, right hand in the air, his left clutching a rolled up scroll—the Twelve Demands of the Young Hungary movement, which he had formed, to the Habsburg regime. These included freedom of the press, the establishment of a Hungarian ministry based in Buda and Pest (which were still separate cities), a national guard, a national bank, the withdrawal of Austrian troops, the freeing of political prisoners, trial by jury and civil and religious equality.

The fifteenth of March is student's day in Hungary, in his honour. In 1848, a national uprising gathered momentum against Austrian rule. Less than twelve months later, Petőfi died a hero's death on the battlefield, probably from a Russian bullet. His body was never found.

The communists never knew quite what to do with Petőfi's legacy when they seized power in Hungary in 1948. They respected his revolutionary credentials, but were extremely nervous about his national ones. The Hungarians have a tendency to lump all foreign occupiers together in a kind of unpleasant ball. The Turks from 1541 to 1686, the Austrians from 1686 to 1867, and the Russians from 1945. It's given them a well-stocked storehouse of poems, songs and legends to deliver against each successive tyrant. Between the First and Second World Wars, 15 March was a national holiday. After the communist takeover it was demoted to a simple day off for schools and universities.

From the late 1970s, a few hundred students each year began staging symbolic, spontaneous gatherings at the Petőfi statue on that day. But in 1986 this looked like a serious escalation. It was hard to count the heads, because quite a few people were hanging about on the edge of the square, either out of fear or curiosity. Up on the old wooden scaffolding of the building overlooking the square, secret policemen patrolled with strangely disinterested expressions, photographing and filming. I took photos too. People gazed into my lens with a mixture of defiance and suspicion, which seemed to say—'even if you are a secret policeman too, we don't care any more.'

Soon after midday, three boys dressed in black unfurled a long national flag, the crowd fell into place behind them and they began to march through the narrow streets towards Parliament. They sang the Hungarian national anthem. Then the Székely hymn, from the old Hungarian lands in farthest Transylvania—but above all they chanted a poem by Petőfi:

We swear, by the God of the Hungarians,
We swear, we shall be slaves no more.

The words echoed back off the walls, doubling then redoubling the numbers present, just as in October 1956. This was starting to look like the biggest 'spontaneous' demonstration for years, and the people rushed to the street corners and balconies to watch. Some waved or clapped in support, but most looked worried. The students were rocking the boat, they thought. And boats which got rocked in Hungary had a tendency to capsize.

At first, there was no sign of the police at all. I walked beside the marchers, determined to separate my own past as a protester from my new, objective role as a reporter. It was tiring. To deliberately cut myself off from the solidarity, the sense of euphoria, of mutual love, the good chemistry of a march. My notebook was my shield, I realised, as was my speed. By taking side-streets, I could overtake and loop round to interview the lads at the front. Then calculate how many people were passing me a minute. Then multiply by the number of minutes it took the main body of people to pass. I counted 3,000—ten times the figure of previous years.

The marchers reached the domed octopus-like Parliament, which was guarded by just two sleepy stone lions. There was still no sign of the police. There were brief speeches from the steps of a statue to another hero of the 1848 revolution, Lajos Kossuth. Then they headed up the road to the Batthyány Flame, where a reddish light always flickers in memory of Lajos Batthyány, the Hungarian Prime Minister executed near this spot by the Austrians.

Here the authorities made their first, surreal intervention. Hastily erected loudspeakers began blaring tinny martial music from the sides of the square, drowning out the already faint speeches. Few could hear the words of Gáspar Miklós Tamás or János Kis, both philosophers and central figures in Hungary's small dissident community. At the end of the street, motorbike police began revving their engines. The atmosphere was becoming heavier.

'To Bem!' someone shouted. So the marchers wound their way across Margit Bridge, over the Danube. More police and speeches here, drowned out by more martial music. Burly plain clothes police protected the loudspeakers from the efforts of some students to 'accidentally' trip over them. The cameras clicked and whirred again. The crowd, four hours after it began to gather, was thinning a little by now, and someone suggested one more act of homage to an 1848 hero, the national poet and author of the Hungarian national anthem, Lajos Kölcsey.

Several times during the march I had noticed a thin girl rattling a bucket in which she was collecting contributions for Jenő Nagy, a dissident who had been fined for printing samizdat. I had carefully refused to give her a coin when she asked. 'I'm a journalist. ...' I explained. She seemed unimpressed.

Word spread now that she had been arrested. A group of students sat down in the road, blocked the traffic, and announced that they would stay there until the girl was released. The police suddenly swarmed like hornets, trying to drag the protesters out of the road. Tussles broke out. Some students were taken away. I started taking pictures.

Soon I noticed that whenever I raised my camera, a man in civilian clothes immediately stepped in front of me, blocking the shot. I backed away, and to my unease, he stayed close beside me. I tried to walk away but now there were three of them, blocking my escape. They barked questions at me in Hungarian. I had only been in the country a month, and understood very little of the language. I produced my British passport, which confused them. After a brief discussion, they shrugged and let me go, hopefully assuming that I was just a foreign tourist. I fled quickly, by metro, under the Danube to Kossuth Square, to hide my film at a friend's house. Before the police changed their mind.

That evening a smaller march of about 500 students set out from the Petőfi statue again, and were shepherded by the police on to the Chain Bridge over the Danube. Designed by Scottish architect Adam Clark to link the separate cities of Buda and Pest in the nineteenth century, the bridge rises in the middle, preventing the marchers from realising that police had already sealed off the Buda end. It was a trap. The police advanced from both ends, closing in on them in the middle. The authorities wanted to know the identity of the 'hard core'—those who still had the energy to march in the evening, after a whole day of protest.

As they started to confiscate identity cards, people panicked and tried to escape. The truncheons came out and many, including bystanders and car-drivers who had stopped to find out why the bridge was blocked, were beaten by the police.

In the following weeks, those whose identity papers the police had seized were ordered to report to their employers, or schools and universities, and were threatened with sanctions. Students quickly baptised the episode, 'The Battle of the Bridge.'

My reports to the BBC of the day's events were exclusives. There were no other western journalists in town, and Hungarian media were not allowed to touch the subject. What mattered was that they weren't just broadcast in the UK, but back into Hungary in both English and Hungarian, and into all the other eastern bloc countries in the native languages. The BBC, alongside Radio Free Europe and Voice of America, provided useful information which people could not get from their own media.

*　　*　　*

'89: The Unfinished Revolution

In 1986, Hungary was known as 'the merriest barracks in the Soviet camp', but it was a barracks, nonetheless. János Kádár had been in power for thirty years, since he was installed by the might of the Soviet Southern Army in November 1956. By 1986 there were still 65,000 Soviet soldiers in Hungary, dotted around the country in unlikely places—on the edge of otherwise innocuous towns, living behind outer perimeter walls made of long, reinforced concrete blocks. In Esztergom, north of Budapest, the seat of the Catholic archbishop of Hungary, the Soviet soldiers occupied a former monastery. They were let out in groups of three, an officer and two privates. In a bar opposite the barracks in Esztergom, there were Russian girls names scrawled in Cyrillic script on the walls of the urinal.

In Budapest, one could often see little clusters of Russians, especially in the main pedestrian thoroughfare, Váci Street, or at the zoo. The officer was distinguishable by his wide brimmed emerald-green cap, like a mini billiard table. On the whole, the Hungarians didn't hate the Russians and didn't even regard them as an occupying army. They just treated them with mild, sometimes ironic contempt, like slightly uncouth barbarians.

There were also 110,000 soldiers in the Hungarian army, mostly conscripts, serving their compulsory eighteen months or two years. It was a miserable time for most boys, their first prolonged period away from home, exposed to the brutality of corporals and sometimes of their fellow conscripts, and engaged in mindless tasks. Many were deployed along the Yugoslav border, to protect the country from the possibility of attack from a country where many of them went on holiday when they finished their term of duty. The idea of a Yugoslav threat to the Warsaw Pact countries was a hangover from the 1948–1952 period, when Tito's Yugoslavia refused to join other communist countries in the Warsaw Pact, and established the Non-Aligned Movement. If Hungarian conscripts thought of their supposed 'enemy' at all, it was more likely to be with longing for the azure waters and long-legged girls of the Adriatic coast than with fear of wild-eyed men with tin-hats and camouflaged faces, wriggling through the undergrowth towards them.

So Hungary was a country at peace, but not at peace with itself.

After the crushing of the 1956 revolution, tens of thousands of people were questioned, thousands imprisoned and nearly four hundred executed. The Hungarian Workers Party got an extra adjective and became the Hungarian Socialist Workers Party. Under János Kádár, who first appeared to join, but then betrayed, the revolution, changes began after the uprising had been safely crushed, and its main leaders and others caught up in it executed.

Men like József Molnár, who went into prison as national heroes in 1956 or 1957, came out as lepers. The Kádár regime initiated a series of economic reforms to improve the welfare of the people, and even some writers who had taken part in the Petőfi Circle, and initiated the revolution, were tempted to rejoin the establishment. Former friends, relatives even, crossed to the other side of the street to avoid bumping into former jail-birds. The betrayal of the revolution was complete.

Kádár's measures were carefully thought out to win over a recalcitrant population.

People were allowed to own land again—albeit only a small plot or allotment. There they could grow and, in many cases, even sell the surplus produce. This was a far cry from the dictatorship in Romania, but similar to the situation in Poland, where dogged rural resistance had prevented the communists from implementing their plans to nationalise the countryside. That there was not one single cast iron rule of how a communist country could and should be run was highly significant. It was to open the door for reform of first the economy and then the political process by the Communist Party itself.

In Hungarian cities, joint ventures were established with companies from other countries. Private banks were established, and in the mid-1980s the country joined the International Monetary Fund and the World Bank.

Economic freedoms included the possibility to change Hungarian forints into foreign currencies, to go abroad to western Europe every three years—provided of course one had been a good pupil, or a loyal citizen in the previous period. Hungarians set out for Austria and Italy, their car-boots filled with tins of food brought from home to save money.

At home, people earned enough to go out to a restaurant every week. Cinemas were always full—tickets were cheap. Eighty percent of the population owned, or at least had access to, a second home—often little more than a wooden hut on a hillside or lakeside, but a place to unwind from the stresses of office or factory. In the late 1950s, Budapest even got a new underground railway system, the Metro, with fast, efficient Soviet trains. A consolation, people muttered, for what they did to us during the revolution. Public transport cost a single one forint aluminium coin to ride the metro, and there were yellow two forint tickets for the excellent yellow trams or blue buses and red trolley-buses which plied the streets of the capital. There was no income tax, but people paid a quarter of their salaries in national insurance contributions.

In the 1960s in Hungary the carrots were many, and the sticks few.

'Those who are not against us are with us,' the Party leader, János Kádár, said in a famous speech in 1962. The country should be run 'for the people, but without them,' he said another time, like a pharmacist prescribing a cure, by a whole army of loyal Party bureaucrats. And what followed was a baby boom. The people drowned their defeat in the 1956 revolution in one another's arms.

To accommodate the surge in population, new housing estates shot up around Budapest and provincial towns, like battlements beyond the castle moat.

In the capital, the Roman ruins of the city of Aquincum, in the south-western districts of Óbuda and Békásmegye, disappeared among ten-storey blocks. The city expanded on the other shore of the Danube in Újpest. Gypsies from eastern cities like Miskolc and Debrecen, and the marshy villages along the River Tisza, were among the beneficiaries of the building boom. Their traditional lifestyle of travelling the roads of eastern Europe, plying their trades of tinkers and basket-weavers, blacksmiths and violinists at upper-class weddings, was banned in most countries in the early 1950s. In exchange, they were given cheap housing and guaranteed work. A bed to sleep in, a canteen in workers hostels in Budapest during the week and a train ticket home on Friday nights, on the so-called 'black trains', named after the colour of the skin of those who rode them.

One afternoon a friend took me to meet a Gypsy writer, Menyhért Lakatos. He met me at the door of his block of flats, a white cat perched on his shoulder. I took a photograph. When I got home, the film was blank. We spoke of his people, the old ways and the new.

'There were times in this country when we were mutilated, or killed on sight,' he said. One of his novels starts with a troop of Gypsies crossing a field. As the reader gets closer, he discovers that their ears have been cut off. It was little wonder, he concluded from this, that the non-Roma majority were still regarded as 'fair game' to steal from. What the Roma needed now was a new morality, appropriate to the times. But he couldn't say where or how it would be forged. In the meantime, the police were on their backs. Roma with police records received a little 'c' for cigány (Gypsy) next to their names on official statistics. Though they only made up five percent of the population, more than fifty percent of the inmates in Hungarian jails were Roma.

I stayed with Antal Kuklay, a Catholic priest in Köröm, a village near the River Tisza in eastern Hungary, who spent six years in prison for taking part in the 1956 revolution. He took me to meet his Roma congregation. They didn't mix easily with the old ladies who made up the hard core of worshippers, he said, but preferred to come at other times. They were drawn to religion, recognising an affinity between their own rich culture of blessings and curses, symbols and mysteries, and those of the church. To test the Gypsy stories of discrimination, I went with three or four teenagers to the village bar. A silence fell when we entered. We ordered soft drinks, and then the manager arrived and told us to drink up quickly, because he was closing. It was seven-thirty on a Saturday evening, and the place was full. We left our drinks on the table, and went out into the night. We walked to the next village down a road as straight as an arrow, under a vast canopy of stars. The girls turned cartwheels in the road and the boys leapt and beat on their knees and ankles, and hummed and clicked their tongues, forming a little moving orchestra across the Great Hungarian Plain. This was far better than the surly, smoky bar from which we had been excluded, anyway.

Apart from the flurries of rebellious youth each year on 15 March, and 23 October, the anniversary of the 1956 revolution, there was little visible dissent in Hungary.

The dissidents published a steady stream of books and samizdat articles, and a surprisingly wide circle of people read them. Visiting British and American diplomats took the dissidents out to lunch, but that was more or less it. The West did little to stir up dissent in eastern Europe and even, occasionally, stifled it. When Roger Golland, the first secretary at the British Embassy upset the authorities by regularly publishing samizdat articles in the embassy's daily English language summary of the Hungarian press, he was recalled to London. There was a sense that the division of Europe suited those in power in the West, as well as the East.

*　　*　　*

In Poland, the writer, Adam Michnik, had developed a theory of dissent known as 'new evolutionism'. After the crushing of the uprisings in East

Berlin, Poznań, Budapest and Prague, and especially after the Solidarity movement was suppressed in 1981, confrontation with the communist regimes seemed inadvisable, Michnik wrote. Instead, the strategy was to build a parallel world in which dissidents met and discussed and published their thoughts on democracy, human rights and the crimes of communist regimes. I had a feeling, sometimes, that they were like the early Christians, witnesses to a democratic truth which they thought was self-evident, undergoing greater or lesser repression, depending on which Roman emperor was in power, and patiently waiting for the day when everyone would believe in their creed of human rights. In Hungary, I enjoyed their company and only disagreed on one main point. They tended to dismiss Gorbachev—if he was really serious, the others would depose him, or worse, soon enough, they argued. While I was naively optimistic that his actions would—deliberately or inadvertently, I had no way of knowing—herald a revolution, the consequences of which we could not foresee.

Middle-class Hungarians openly kept copies of samizdat publications on their bookshelves, perhaps partly concealed by another magazine, but not exactly hidden behind the panelling. The print came off on your fingers, but the articles were well-researched, if a little dense. More importantly, there was an interesting overlap between the thirty or so 'open' dissidents, and a far wider stratum of sociologists, economists, psychologists and other 'intellectuals'. These were the people who passed on their more controversial research materials to the dissidents, as the only place where they would be able to publish them—albeit anonymously.

In Hungary, they translated and published books banned by the censors. Novels by George Orwell like *1984* and *Animal Farm*. And little vignettes of life in freer countries further West. One of my favourites was an article entitled *Protecting butterflies on the M4*. I found it strangely moving that people far from my own, fair island would risk arrest or fines to publish details of efforts to protect something so fragile. As though to contrast their own clumsy, unaccountable regime.

One of the most valuable activities of dissidents in Hungary, especially a subgroup of the people around the samizdat journal Beszélő, were their studies on poverty, discrimination, alcohol and drug abuse— all subjects which the communist authorities liked to think no longer existed. Ottilia Solt, from her ground floor flat next to the Komjádi swimming baths where samizdat literature was distributed, was a central figure in SZETA, which tried to ease the plight of the homeless and very poor.

The degree of repression varied from country to country, from period to period.

To their chagrin, I suspected, the Hungarian dissidents had a relatively easy time, compared to their Czech or Romanian or East German counterparts.

On the 'sensitive' dates in the calendar, however, the secret police flexed their muscles. Some dissidents were taken in for questioning—a euphemism for getting them off the streets, and thereby preventing them from making stirring speeches at the base of statues. But they would then usually be released without charge. The last openly political trial in Hungary had been of Miklós Haraszti in 1979, for his book *A Worker in a Workers' State*—a scathing diary of his six months in a factory where he had been sent for an earlier infringement. He was found guilty of subversion and given an eight month suspended prison sentence.

I was a regular visitor at his penthouse flat near Freedom Bridge in Pest. Like many of the Democratic Opposition, his father had been a devout communist in the 1950s, and Miklós had been a Maoist in the late 1960s. Nowadays he kept a small bust of Stalin on top of his television, 'to remind himself of the enemy,' he joked. His most recent book was *The Velvet Prison,* a scathing tract on the way in which artists were co-opted by the totalitarian state.

I found references to Stalin in Miklós Vásárhelyi's flat, too. The former press secretary to Imre Nagy, the Prime Minister in 1956, he had been imprisoned for several years after the revolution, and was seen by many as the 'father' of the dissidents. He told me once how he and his wife Edit, as communist journalists at the Szabad Nép newspaper after the Second World War, had been great admirers of Stalin, both as a communist, and because of the Soviet role in the defeat of Hitler. And how their love of the great leader had lasted until the so-called 'Doctor's plot' in 1952, when Stalin accused a group of doctors, who also happened to be Jewish, of planning to kill him. 'The scales suddenly fell from our eyes,' Miklós said. 'Edit and I looked at each other, and without a word, took the portraits of Stalin down from the walls, and carried them down to the dustbins outside.'

While the dissidents bore witness to a freer society, more compromised journalists in the mainstream media worked hard for it. I set out to tap into that stratum of the population—the 'establishment opposition' as the most likely engine for change, if change there was to be.

The most successful, legal weekly in Hungary was Heti Világgazdaság, a word of such complexity, even to Hungarians, that it was known to the public simply as HVG, standing for 'weekly world economy'. It had been built up from nothing to a circulation of 120,000 copies a week by its editor, Mátyás Vince.

'The trick is never to offend everyone at the same time,' he told me. You could only get away with criticising a certain minister, or government policy, if you cultivated powerful friends. It was in the ruling elite's interest to know what was really happening in the country, he explained. When his own journalists went too far, or he couldn't find an ally to please in the next edition, they would sometimes get their contributions back with the word 'Nyet' or 'No' scrawled in Russian across it.

But the relationship with Russia was changing and my new friends in the 'establishment opposition' took Gorbachev's words more seriously, and invested the most hope in the new Soviet leader. They identified him, in a sense, as a fellow traveller, longing for a gentler, more rational, more decentralised sort of rule.

On the surface, János Kádár and the old guard had little to fear from Mikhail Gorbachev. The Soviet leader's speeches on the need to restructure the economy sounded rather like what Hungary had been doing, in fits and starts, since 1967. A member of the Soviet Academy of Sciences, Oleg Bogomolov, even commented in an interview in HVG that the Soviets 'had much to learn from Hungarian economic experiments.' The 27th Congress of the Soviet Communist Party had taken place in the month I arrived, in February 1986—the first since Gorbachev had come to power.

'Maybe the atmosphere of the debates is the most interesting for Hungarian readers,' one journalist wrote at the time, in a mainstream newspaper, and went on to quote the demands of Soviet journalists that those responsible for censorship be named.

'Debates have always been impassioned in the Soviet Union,' he concluded, 'when there were debates at all . . .'

The big difference between the new Soviet reforms, under Gorbachev, and what had happened in Hungary, was the speed and extent of Gorbachev's moves. Small steps were the hallmark of Kádár's chess game, gifts directed from above towards a grateful population, too weary after the crushing of their revolution to demand anything more far-reaching. But Gorbachev was going hammer and tongs, appealing over the heads of the unwieldy apparatus directly to the people.

In the economy there were similarities, even direct borrowings from Hungary, like the granting of foreign trade rights to individual companies rather than to ministries, as had been the usual practice. Likewise, the setting up of joint companies with foreign partners. But Gorbachev was trying to prize open the tin of political reforms as well, in a way Kádár had never dared. And the writers and journalists were his tool.

The ruling elite was perhaps ten million in the Soviet Union, and half a million in Hungary. They became the target of the criticism of increasingly brave journalists, who exposed their inefficiency and their corruption. And in the process, they whetted their readers, viewers and listeners' appetites for a more open society.

But it was the Soviet leadership's ditching of the 'Brezhnev doctrine' which caused the biggest waves across the region.

The news that they were to be given more sovereignty was not much welcomed by the rulers of satellite countries who owed their power to the lack of national sovereignty granted their countries by Mr Gorbachev's predecessors.

*　　*　　*

'Communism is Soviet power plus the electrification of the whole country,' Lenin had said, and his successors had grasped his electric cable, as well as his power cable, with both hands. One of the biggest unfinished projects in the mid-1980s in the satellite countries of eastern Europe was a scheme to tap the slow-moving River Danube, where it flowed between Hungary and Czechoslovakia, for hydro-electric power. Exactly at the spot where the great river meandered most slowly, as it passed through one of the last wetland forests on its long, 2,800km length, between the Szigetköz region of Hungary and Žitný Ostrov, or Rye Island in Slovakia.

From the early 1950s onwards, Soviet, Hungarian and Czechoslovak engineers decided that the only way to get their hands on the prize of hydro-energy under such unfavourable conditions was to speed the river up—with the help of three dams.

The first, at Dunakiliti, would block the old river, and allow a storage lake to build up upstream. Water from there would be concentrated into a new artificial canal, 27km long, in the middle of which stood another set of turbines, at Gabčikovo. Meanwhile, a third dam and more turbines would be built at Nagymaros, 100km downstream where the Danube turns abruptly south, after flowing from west to east for so long. Electricity would be generated there by allowing great surges of water down from the earlier dams at times of high demand in winter, when the volume of water in the Danube was traditionally lower.

There were major environmental problems with the scheme. The draining of the wetlands would devastate animal and birdlife in a wide region. The surges down the Danube would erode the banks, requiring them to be shored up on both sides for long distances with concrete, further harming the ecological balance of the river. As would the deepening of the shipping channel by dredging. Some opponents argued that the whole scheme had more to do with shipping than harnessing electric power—that it was a way of turning the Danube into a 'motorway' for ever bigger container ships on their way from the Baltic to the Black Sea. Most seriously, the scheme threatened the biggest underground reservoir of fresh water in central Europe, replenished for tens of thousands of years by water filtering down through gravel beds beneath the river. And in the twenty-first century, as we all know, water would become more precious than oil.

In Hungary, the Danube Circle environmental group was established in 1984, led by a biologist, János Vargha. They held walks by the river, carrying banners. They printed badges of a curling blue river interrupted by a thick white line. They published detailed critiques of the plan, and laid their hands on official studies, which highlighted the same problems and which had consequently been hushed up. And I arrived, conveniently, just in time to report their regular protests.

János Bethlen, a young journalist at Hungarian Radio, also tried to offer a more critical take on the project in his late night reports. It was a general rule in the media at that time that the more readers, or listeners or viewers a report had, the more obedient it had to be to the Party line. So 'alternative' interpretations were tolerated on the periphery—very late at night on the radio, or in publications with the smallest circulation.

János set out to interview the engineer in charge of the Gabčikovo-Nagymaros project with twelve rather well-prepared and challenging questions, which he duly recorded. The next day, before the interview could be broadcast, he was called into his chief editor's office, and told to go back and do the interview again. This time with tamer questions to which the man in question would provide the appropriate, pro-dam answers, and everyone would be happy. 'If you already know the answers you need,' János retorted, 'I suggest you send a technician, not a journalist.' He was suspended for nine months.

My secret police file, obtained many years later, contains the following entry on one such walk beside the river. 'The so-called journalist makes no secret of his enthusiasm for the ideas of the organisers.' They, like other groups, were riddled with agents. But their message was increasingly popular. Hungary is a largely flat country, with few sites of outstanding natural beauty since the loss of the great horseshoe of the Carpathian Mountains in 1920.

The Danube Bend at Nagymaros, where the third dam was planned, was perhaps the most beautiful spot in the country, where the river speeds up to pass between the Pilis Hills on one shore, and the Börzsöny Hills on the other, overlooked by the medieval castle at Visegrád.

Do the communists really intend to destroy the most beautiful place in the country, people asked each other? And are we going to let them? At Nagymaros, the jazz composer and pianist, György Szabados, had his grand piano carried down to the shore, in protest against the scheme. There he played his elegy to the Danube, to the seagulls and to anyone brave enough to applaud him. His protest, like that of the Danube Circle, seemed hopeless. Nevertheless, some people found the courage, and the energy to raise their voices.

* * *

Easter, and the workers' holiday of 1 May, combined conveniently in 1986 to give almost a week's holiday. I set out on a hiking trip with friends through the wetlands of the Szigetköz. As I was packing my bag, I heard the first reports on the BBC of a possible accident at a nuclear power station in Ukraine. Two days later, it rained in western Hungary. We half-sheltered from the downpour under weeping willows on the Danube shore, drinking cheap red wine from a bottle, blissfully unaware that the radioactive cloud from neighbouring Ukraine was now directly overhead.

When workers at Hungary's lone nuclear power station, further down the Danube at Paks, went into work two days later, they set off the alarms. The entrance and the exit at Paks are the same, and carefully monitored by radiation detection equipment. The workers had spent the weekend in the open air, and many had been caught out in the same shower as I had. Equipment designed to measure radiation they might have picked up at work recorded instead the much higher levels they had picked up while at play.

Very little of all this was reported in the Hungarian media. The first mention came on page four of the Party daily on 29 April, three days after the accident. The rise in radioactivity in Hungary, the article suggested 'is not significant.' At about the same time, radiation measured on the roof of the British embassy in Budapest showed a dramatic increase.

That week I saw a rare, spontaneous protest on a Budapest street. Two punks, a boy and a girl, hair in spikes and their torn clothes dripping safety pins, staggered down the smart, pedestrian Váci Street, feigning fatal illness and groaning, 'sugárzás'—radiation!

In the West, polite middle-class shoppers might have been appalled. In Hungary, most people laughed, or applauded. The punks were expressing an emotion that they felt too, but had not been brave enough to articulate.

More news of the seriousness of the disaster leaked out, bit by bit. People were first advised to wash lettuces thoroughly, then not to eat them at all. They fell in price in the open markets of the city, until they were almost free. Pensioners snapped them up as a bargain. The British embassy was also informed that a whole day's milk had been poured away across the country—not an item which made it into any Hungarian media.

Chernobyl was a body blow to the Soviet Union and the whole Soviet system. Soviet power, even more than power in the capitalist world, was built on man's supremacy over nature. Tales of the brave helicopter pilots flying sortie after sortie to dump concrete into the smouldering core of the stricken reactor only served to restore a little faith in Soviet man. Soviet power had tripped a fuse. Lenin's electric balloon had burst.

Politics in the Soviet bloc was to take a dramatic turn. Chernobyl forced Gorbachev to admit in public the enormity of his country's problems and the corruption, bungling and cynicism that had produced the disaster and then, in turn, led the authorities to try to conceal what had happened. Moreover, he had also to admit that the Soviet system had become riddled with such corrupt and cynical behaviour to the point that it had become a threat to the system itself.

Gorbachev moved into top gear. Censorship was relaxed and Andrei Sakarov, the world's most famous dissident, was released. Then, in a

televised speech to the Party Central Committee in January 1987, he
made the case for a more inclusive democracy over the heads of the Party
elite, directly to the people. The vast majority of houses in the Soviet
Union had a television set. Gorbachev had opened a public debate on
reform and invited the public to offer their opinion. Although the Soviet
Union remained a one-party dictatorship, a slightly stunned public began
to organise themselves in informal organisations and find their voice.
Developments in the mother ship did not go unnoticed in her satellites.

* * *

Back in Hungary, the summer of 1986 was about to deliver a series
of blows to the Party in quick succession. In June, seventeen-year-old
Csilla Molnár, from a village near Lake Balaton in western Hungary,
committed suicide. A few weeks earlier she had been acclaimed 'Miss
Hungary' in a beauty competition, and was due to represent the country
in the Miss World tournament. Her tragedy was even taken up by the
usually obedient churches. 'What kind of country is this?' thundered the
bishops, in a message to their congregations, 'in which our prettiest
daughter takes her life?' A documentary film called *Szép Lányok*—
'Beautiful Girls', in which she starred, was already half complete. The
producers continued filming—her funeral, and the soul-searching which
followed. And the film played to packed houses in Budapest and in the
provinces.

Because it was all-powerful, the Communist Party was also all-
culpable. It was easy to blame everything which happened on those in
power.

In July 1986, the first ever Formula One race was held in Hungary at
Mogyoród, 20km east of the city, on a newly built track. Coach load
after coach load of spectators also arrived from abroad. And among them
many from neighbouring Romania. Such was the distrust between the
brotherly communist regimes in the two countries that Romanian
citizens, including ethnic Hungarians from Transylvania, were rarely
allowed a visa to visit Hungary. But a major sporting event like a motor
race seemed a safe bet. It wasn't. Many coaches went back to Romania
empty. It was the start of an exodus which Hungary had little choice
but to accept.

Three summers later, when East Germans poured into Hungary in the
hope of escaping across the western border into Austria, the authorities

had already cut their teeth on their 'own' refugees. Those fleeing Ceauşescu's repressive regime in Romania were cared for, first of all by the public and the churches, but eventually also by the regime, as fellow humans, and were shown solidarity. There was little solidarity left for socialist allies like Romania. The secret services, however, were very interested in any work I did on the subject. My police files are full of entries about meetings with priests who helped the refugees, and interviews with people who fled.

Also in July, the authorities finally lost their patience with my presence in Hungary, and my excuse that only 'bureaucratic delays' in my own country were delaying my accreditation as Budapest correspondent for one British media or another. I was suddenly told I had twenty-four hours to be named correspondent, or leave the country. I rang István Siklos of the BBC Hungarian section, and explained the situation. By then I was filing regular stories, not just for the Hungarian Service, but for the main radio newsroom. István promised to do what he could. Eighteen hours later, I received a telex. 'Congratulations. You are now the BBC correspondent in Budapest.'

As it turned out, the communist pressure had done my career the world of good. It was a close call. An entry in my secret police file from April 1986 reads: 'Despite repeated requests from the Foreign Ministry Press Department, he has failed to produce the documents necessary for accreditation, and therefore cannot be regarded as a journalist . . .' The information came from the Counter-Intelligence Service, who informed the political police, the regular police and the intelligence services. Blissfully unaware of such interest in me, I drank beer with a Russian colleague one day, in a basement bar opposite the Foreign Ministry. Why hadn't the British embassy provided me with a car? he asked, in all seriousness. In fact, my contacts with the embassy were rather modest; a pigeon hole where I picked up their summaries of the Hungarian press every few days, and lunches with the press officer. I had to write reports on the situation in the country nearly every day, which were broadcast immediately. He had to write his once a week, and they would not be published for thirty years.

The only blow that summer was a phone-call from my friend Richard at HVG. He had been called in by the Party, and told that he was behaving like a British spy, partly due to his contacts with me. Worried for his family in particular, he suggested it would be wise for us not to meet again for a while.

There was one other peculiar development. A visiting American journalist bought me a drink in the bar of the Hilton Hotel one July lunchtime, while the Soccer World Cup distracted me on a screen behind his head.

'There must be times,' he said, 'when you come across information which you cannot use in your reports, but which might be interesting to someone, somewhere . . .'

'It probably happens every day!' I replied, more interested in the next Brazilian free kick.

'What I would like to do is give you a name and phone number at our embassy in Bonn . . .' the journalist continued.

I suddenly woke up to what he was actually saying.

'No thanks,' I replied carefully. 'That would be too much like spying, and the basis of all my work here is openness. If the authorities want to know who I have been talking to, they just have to turn on their radios.' He didn't mention the subject again.

October 1986 was the thirtieth anniversary of the 1956 uprising, and like all patriotic anniversaries, a trial of strength between the dissidents and the regime. In 1969, the head of Agitation and Propaganda in the Party, János Berecz, carved the Party interpretation of 1956 in stone in his book, *1956—A Counter-Revolution in Words and Deeds*. This was vintage Marxism-Leninism—the uprising had been an attempt at a 'bourgeois restoration', a failed attempt to roll back the historical progress achieved in Russia in 1917, and in Hungary, for example, in 1948. Special emphasis was laid in Berecz's book on the excesses of the revolution—the lynching of nine communist officials outside the Budapest Party headquarters in Republic Square on 28 October 1956.

But by the mid-1980s, János Kádár himself seemed less certain. As he approached the end of his life, the crushing of the revolution, which he oversaw, appeared to weigh more and more heavily on his conscience. He preferred to use the phrase 'national tragedy' if he spoke about it at all. It was widely believed that the ghosts of those who had been executed for leading it, including his former Party comrade, Imre Nagy, still haunted him, even though it was popularly assumed that he had been ordered by Moscow to have them killed.

Party leaders knew the western media, including myself, would make a big deal of the thirtieth anniversary. So they tried to get in first with their own documentary film, presenting their own shades of meaning. The workers' outrage against the 'excesses' of the Stalinist period was understandable, the programme suggested. But wild reactionary elements had hijacked events. The lynching outside the Party headquarters on 28 October always figured high in the propaganda. The execution of Péter Mansfeld ten days after his eighteenth birthday was one of the many cards played by the dissidents. Mansfeld was a fifteen-year-old, like many of the kids on the barricades. Arrested in the aftermath of the revolution, he was too young to be killed. So the authorities patiently postponed the gallows until he reached the right age. I interviewed his brother, László, a hairdresser, through the steam and the suds of his barber's shop near the South Station.

At six in the evening on 23 October, a sixteen-year-old girl laid a small Hungarian flag at the foot of the statue of József Bem. The ever vigilant secret police pounced, wrote down her identity details, and let her go. Then the western journalists surrounded her. She seemed beautifully unperturbed by either. She had put the flag there partly for her father, who had taken part in the revolution, she said. But mainly for herself.

In a tumbledown two-storey wooden house in the suburb of Békásmegye in the north-west of Budapest about eighty people squeezed into a room to mark the anniversary. Candles were placed in the windows as a symbol of mourning for the dead. Sándor Rácz, a young workers' leader from 1956, in black suit and tie, reminded those present that the freedom which the people had fought for in 1956 had still not been achieved. Solemn hymns were sung. Then a joint statement was read out, linking the 1953 protest in East Berlin's Stalinallee with 1956 in Hungary, 1968 in Czechoslovakia and 1980 in Poland.

We took notes, and broadcast it around the world.

The next day I went with a BBC colleague to the city cemetery, in the distant suburb of Rákoskeresztúr, near the airport. We parked the car on the edge of a nearby industrial estate, and climbed a half-broken concrete fence into a remote corner of the cemetery, narrowly missing a dead Alsatian.

This was Plot 301, where those executed after the revolution were buried beside circus and zoo animals. It said something for the strangeness of Hungarian history—the remains of the martyrs resting uneasily among exotic beasts, lions and bears and elephants.

It was dusk when we got there, never the best time of day in a cemetery. But we were not alone. Parked some distance away was a green Lada with the AJ registration plates of state security. And near it, a tall thin man and a short fat one were loitering, like in a Cold War film.

They watched us sideways on, like birds, and appeared to be pretending not to have seen us. So we ignored them too, and set about exploring the undergrowth. There were row after row of unmarked graves, overgrown with hemp plants. A few had been cleared, and planted with makeshift crosses and flowers. When the revolutionaries were executed, between 1957 and 1962, several mothers of the victims managed to follow the vehicle at a distance, or bribe the guards into telling them where their children were buried.

The best kept of the graves had a large green bush planted on it, which had been scattered with white carnations. We took notes and photographs. Then sidled over to our watchers. 'Any idea who is buried here?' I asked the tall man in the leather jacket. He smiled, horribly, displaying long yellow teeth to match his long yellow face and yellow fingers. 'Among others, Imre Nagy,' he replied. To the best of my knowledge, it was the first time a state employee in communist Hungary had ever confirmed the whereabouts of the mortal remains of the leader of the revolution. We thanked them and left hurriedly, through our hole in the fence.

Three days later, the Party daily Népszabadság came out with its riposte to the statement of the dissidents. 'It was surprising,' the author commented 'how little ammunition these people managed to collect. If there is something to remember on this anniversary, it is that our policy of the last thirty years was correct.'

The signatories of the declaration had 'set themselves aside. . . . from a road which is making the country democratic, independent, and with increasing self-management of enterprises . . .'

The dissident philosopher Gáspar Miklós Tamás told me, 'The authorities are clever to recall it (1956), because this shows the people the limits of what can be done under this system. It is a lesson to be told again and again . . . the Kádár regime is kept in place by the feeling of impotence of the population.'

On 5 November, the Party ideologist János Berecz told a press conference, 'This anniversary is not a festival, not a holiday for us, but the closing of a chapter of tragic events.' Imre Nagy was 'justly sentenced', he said.

That particular chapter of Hungary's history, however, proved remarkably hard to close.

Cracks were also starting to emerge in the Party between hardliners like Berecz and Ernő Lakatos, known as the Party policeman, and 'pragmatists' like the leader of the Budapest Party, Károly Grósz. Grósz called for the closing down of loss-making factories, which would mean thousands of redundancies—anathema for the ideologists in a society where unemployment was supposed to be illegal.

At the end of November 1986, the Writers' Union held its first congress for five years. In 1981, their congress had ended in scandal, when they issued a statement in support of the Solidarity movement in Poland which had just been banned.

This time the 'power' in Budapest reluctantly permitted the congress, with its 600 members, to take place, provided there was no media coverage. I quietly gathered my contacts among the writers, and met them informally to hear about each day's events. Inside the closed hall, things were not going well for the Party.

Earlier in the year, a popular playwright, István Csurka, had been banned from publishing, because of an interview he had given in America, sharply critical of the authorities. Csurka was then attacked by Sándor Fekete, editor of the weekly paper Uj Tükör—New Mirror, for not being sensitive to Hungarian 'realities'—a euphemism for the threat of another Soviet invasion.

'Our soul cannot be a galley-slave on the pirate ship of Hungarian reality,' thundered Csurka in response. At the congress, Csurka told the writers 'the Ecseri marshes are on fire'—taking the example of a real fire, in eastern Hungary, to reflect his vision of the state of Hungarian literature. 'The Ecseri marshes are no longer on fire,' János Berecz replied. 'Last night it rained, and the fire was put out.'

It all made for exciting reporting, and I broadcast every twist and turn on the Hungarian language service of the BBC.

'We must be careful, comrades,' Berecz announced on the last day, 'it seems the BBC is in the room with us.'

Emboldened, I was told, by my reports, the majority supported Csurka against Berecz. The propaganda chief then consulted with his bosses, and came back with an initiative to set up a new, 'loyal' Writers' Union, and sideline the old one. But although the majority of the writers were also members of the Party, they put their loyalty to the Union first, and refused to join the new structure. Only a handful of the 600 Union members had joined it so far, I reported.

The counter-attack against me personally began on my birthday, in February. The phone rang at seven-fifteen in the morning. 'Congratulations,' said Miklós Haraszti, one of the dissident leaders. 'You have been attacked by name in Népszabadság.' My heart sank.

The article was snide, and unsigned. It compared me and Gyula Fekete, one of the writers I had interviewed, to the character of Chichikov in the Russian novelist Nikolai Gogol's story, *Dead Souls*. Chichikov, a landowner, buys the rights to dead serfs for tax purposes. Fekete had said in my interview, that 'only twenty-seven writers had joined the new 'loyal' union,' and of these, 'one has since died.'

I was described, sarcastically, as the BBC's 'diligent reporter'.

Then I was summoned to the Foreign Ministry. I went into the building, which always smelt of pork stew from the canteen on the ground floor, fully expecting to be expelled.

Fierce, bowel-loosening coffees were brought. In the waiting room, there was a long, dark painting of sheep standing, forever patient, on the Great Hungarian Plain. I felt I too was about to be sacrificed. I placed my notebook on the table in front of me with my BBC biro very visibly on top, and faced my accusers on the other side, two men and a woman, who represented the Party organisation within the Ministry.

'It is my understanding,' Lajos Tóth began through his slightly shaded glasses, 'that the job of a foreign reporter is to report for a foreign public. But through your work for the BBC Hungarian section, your reports are. . . . influencing Hungarian events.' His colleague, Gabriella Czimborász, nodded vigorously.

'Are you saying that my reports, including those on the Writers' Union dispute have been inaccurate?' I asked. 'Because, obviously, if they have been, then I and my editors would take that very seriously.'

Not at all, he hurried to reassure me. 'Then I can ask no greater praise,' I said. 'And in the best traditions of the BBC and of British journalism, I will continue to write, fairly and objectively, on all subjects which I and my editors find of interest,' I added.

My remarks would be passed on to the appropriate authorities, Mr Tóth told me wearily. I would be informed of the outcome.

The British ambassador, Len Appleyard, invited me out to coffee and cakes an hour later, in Gerbeaud's, the most elegant café in the city, with its red flocca wallpaper and black and white aproned waitresses. We chose a table right in the middle of the room and ordered large coffees, and larger cakes.

'Of course, if they expel you, the Népszabadság correspondent in London can pack his bags,' the ambassador told me—and everyone who was listening—in a booming voice. Népszabadság was the main

Communist Party paper in Hungary, and the London correspondent doubled as correspondent for MTI, the Hungarian News Agency. If he was thrown out, Hungary would lose her only reporter in Britain, and a big international scandal would develop.

Two weeks later, the British Foreign Secretary, Sir Geoffrey Howe, was due to visit Budapest. When he did, he raised 'the Thorpe case'. For a moment, I felt like a pawn in the Cold War. The Hungarian authorities backed off rapidly, and there were no more attempts to influence my work. Though in a last kick in my general direction, my phone was cut off for six weeks, and the telephone engineers seemed strangely unable to fix it.

Through 1987 and 1988 the pressure for political change in Hungary accelerated. The Writers' Union affair had punctured the Party's claim to unique authority. So had the growing popularity of the Danube Circle, opposing the hydro-electric dam system. More groups now followed. Not to oppose the system as such—that was the prerogative of the dissidents. The new groups rather chose to ignore the Party, and get on with organising their lives independently of it. The fact that Party members, too, took part in these activities added to the sense that the Party was now increasingly irrelevant. A fifteen-year-old girl told me that no-one in her class joined the Young Communist League—they were mocked by their classmates if they tried. But her older sister got into trouble, as the only member of the class who refused to join. Things were moving that fast. The state was retreating as society expanded. My friend Richard, the journalist from HVG, rang me happily to say that we could meet again.

In September 1987, he attended a meeting of what was to prove to be one of the most important of the groups, the Hungarian Democratic Forum. At a farm on the outskirts of Lakitelek on the Great Hungarian Plain, writers, artists, historians and lawyers, university lecturers, sociologists and architects and a token dissident, György Konrád, met to discuss the future of the country.

'There was a big, wedding-tent atmosphere,' one of those present told me later.

There were also Party members. Imre Pozsgay was head of the Patriotic People's Front, a sort of talk-shop, set up when other parties were banned after the communist takeover, to somehow include all those who didn't want to join the Communist Party in the building of socialism. For nearly forty years, the Front had languished in obscurity, mumbling largely to itself. But Pozsgay, a young, bright reformer in the Party, whose other lines of advancement had been blocked by older, less bright Party officials, was turning the Front into a genuine talking shop. He provided an umbrella of respectability for intellectuals deemed 'suspect', 'bourgeois', or 'disloyal' by the hardliners in the Party. Not an alternative power centre—of which he was sometimes accused, but more an alternative discussion centre, where alternative ideas to the single party system could be discussed. Pozsgay was the star guest at Lakitelek.

In front of 150 attendees, he spoke of the need for a new constitution, guaranteeing freedom of association, the right to gather and form political groups, and a Parliament which would be democratically elected and which would take charge of mapping the country's path to democracy.

Others present went further.

'There is a crisis in every sphere of society,' said Mihály Bihari. Full information on the real situation should be made available. Real reform programmes should be worked out for all areas, starting with health, education and welfare, alongside the political reforms proposed by Pozsgay. And a nationwide reform movement should be formed immediately.

At the end of the gathering, a writer, Gyula Fekete, read a poem.

> Don't be sad my friend,
> for those who try to push us aside from the road
> will get nowhere,
> for we are the wheels of the cart . . .
> without us, there is no Hungary, and no revolution.

All of this was faithfully reported to me, by phone, that evening. I rang Pozsgay's office to ask whether or not his speech had been public. He wasn't there, so I left a message with his secretary that I was about to publish extracts from his speech at Lakitelek. Then I wrote my radio report and sent it to the BBC. Ten minutes before it was due to be broadcast, Pozsgay's secretary rang back, and asked me not to broadcast any of it.

Concerned that I was about to become the weapon with which the hardliners destroyed Pozsgay—'the Hungarian Gorbachev', as people were starting to call him—I rang the BBC newsroom to ask them to block my report until I had sorted out what I could broadcast and what I couldn't. An experienced news editor answered the phone. Was I satisfied that I had an accurate version of his words? Yes. Then the report should go ahead, he said. The political consequences of what public figures said in public were not of concern to the BBC as a news organisation. I had to agree he was right.

In the weeks that followed Lakitelek, Pozsgay was attacked from all sides. There were rumours that he was about to be sent off as ambassador to some small African republic. János Kádár reportedly referred to him now as a 'rag man'. 'Whenever I turn on the tap,' he is reported to have told a colleague, 'I hear his voice.'

Pozsgay hit back at his critics. Lakitelek was not, he said in one interview, a meeting of the opposition, but rather of 'citizens who are conscious of their responsibilities, are unprejudiced, ready for action, and willing to prevent a catastrophe.' His only nod in the direction of the Party, was when he said he disagreed with one sentence in the final statement from Lakitelek. That 'our nation has no image of the future that is collectively acceptable'. Socialism, Pozsgay said, was still 'an important part of the national identity.' And Pozsgay lamented that more of his comrades did not regard gatherings like this positively, because if they did, he concluded, 'we would not exclude ourselves from the public life of this country . . .'

The Forum began to hold bi-monthly meetings in the Jurta theatre in Budapest. They discussed the economy, poverty and the growing flood of refugees from Romania.

At this time I first became aware of a peculiar division among opposition intellectuals in Hungary, between so-called 'populists' and 'urbanists'. It was one which was to become more acute through the following years, and continues to harm, even sometimes to paralyse, political discussions to this day. The populists searched for and defended what they saw as national values, attachment to Hungarian tradition, myth, ethnography and history. Attachment to the land, the language and, above all, what they called magyarság, 'Hungarianness'. They were particularly focused on the loss of two thirds of Hungarian territory, and of one third of the Hungarian population, according to the terms of the Treaty of Trianon in 1920, as the Austro-Hungarian Empire was dismantled by the great powers. This was considered an enormous injustice by all Hungarians, but the populist writers went further, and carried it as a kind of national wound. No-one seriously demanded the return of territories—either then or since. That had been the foreign policy of governments between the wars, which had led Hungary into its disastrous alliance with Nazi Germany, and so the idea of redrawing national boundaries was utterly discredited. But the populists wanted international recognition for the injustice of Trianon. And for the injustice of the Beneš decrees, named after the Czechoslovak leader Edvard Beneš, who oversaw the expulsion of Hungarians from Slovakia, and Germans from the Sudetenland, after the war.

In contrast to the populists, the urbanists stressed the modernisation of Hungary above all else as the main plank of their programme. Most of the dissidents around the samizdat journal, Beszélő, belonged to this group. They despised what they saw as the romantic, provincial, petty bourgeois aspirations of the populist group. They felt what Hungary needed most was to be dragged, kicking and screaming, first into the twentieth, then into the twenty-first century. I sympathised with both, but found myself increasingly frustrated by the animosity between them. I could understand the need for roots, the sense of identity and pride of the populists, but at the same time I could see the need for the civic values, the universal human rights of the urbanist group. What I could not understand was the almost compulsory enmity between the two sides, and how even before the political changes, that began to poison public debate.

* * *

At the end of March 1988, several students came to see me in my top floor flat, overlooking the roof of a handsome, seventeenth-century Greek Catholic church, a street away from the Danube. Over tea, Viktor Orbán and his friends told me that they were setting up an Association of Young Democrats, to be called Fidesz.

Their plan was to organise nationwide, and become a rival to the Young Communist League. I made a second pot of tea. Then warned them that, as far as I could tell, that might prove a bridge too far for those in power. I reported the foundation, nonetheless, of their new organisation, and wished them luck.

Within days, they received a court summons, which told them they were under investigation for 'attempting to overthrow the established order'—an anti-terrorist charge. But the case against them was silently dropped.

At about the same time, the first independent trade union was founded, TDDSZ, for scientific workers, in the hall of mirrors of the Arts University.

The delegates' earnest faces were magnified to infinity by the old mirrors on all sides of the room. Just as the voices of the protesters echoed back from the tall buildings when they marched each year on 15 March. But there was no police raid.

A group of journalists formed the Glasnost club, to appeal for the end of censorship. They sometimes found the premises they rented for their meetings locked, but there were no more serious repercussions.

On the eve of 15 March 1988, police raided many houses of known dissidents. Literature and printing equipment was seized, and people detained for a few hours. But the police did not find what they were supposed to be looking for—tens of thousands of leaflets with lists of demands to the government, such as the withdrawal of Soviet troops from Hungary, and withdrawal from the Warsaw Pact.

'The authorities think that if they attack the Democratic Opposition, they can paralyse the centre of discontent,' Gáspár Miklós Tamás told me. 'But we represent only one section of public opinion. There is no centre.'

From the point of view of the Party, the democratic movements in 1988 must have seemed like a virus, an epidemic to the 'doctors' from the Party. And their efforts to eradicate the disease were at best half-hearted.

On 15 March, 7,000 students marched through the centre of the city. For the first time, I heard the protesters chant the slogan 'Multi-Party System.'

'The restoration of the multi-party system would not bring solutions,' János Barabás, a leading Party official with a neatly polished bald head, told me in an interview. 'We are so sure of that, we do not even want to put it to debate.'

'Citizens of Hungary . . .!' thundered the bearded, cigar-smoking philosopher, Gáspár Miklós Tamás, from the plinth of the Kossuth statue, 'the revolutionary aims of 1848, 1918 and 1956 have still not been achieved! Strengthen your backs! Dare to ask! Long live the Opposition! Long live Hungarian Freedom!' This time the opposition loudspeakers were working. There was no rival Party music. And the police loitered in the backstreets, smoking cigarettes, like common criminals.

Party members were ordered to have nothing to do with the Hungarian Democratic Forum. Those who did faced expulsion. Kádár's strategy appeared to be to try to isolate the Forum, as he had tried to do with the Writers' Union. And here, too, that strategy seemed doomed to failure.

At one meeting of the Forum, I noticed a secret policeman who had followed me once, on a Danube Circle march, sitting right behind me. At one point, during the voting, I turned round to see him casting his vote enthusiastically for some radical reform proposal or another. He got his hand in the air before anyone else. Even the secret police are backing the reform now! I thought. More likely he was just ingratiating himself with the crowd, in order to stand out less clearly. At the end of the event, when the crowd applauded, it seemed to me that they were clapping themselves.

One vivid symbol of the new freedom was the 'world passport' issued to Hungarians on 1 January 1988. From now on, they would not need their employers' permission before they travelled abroad. The only remaining condition was that they have a small amount of hard currency each time they travelled to the West. But no-one was going to ask where the hard-currency came from. Traffic thickened markedly on the roads leading west to Austria, especially at weekends. The Austrians arrived in their shiny, modern cars, taking home bootfuls of cheap wine, champagne and children's clothes. In the western town of Sopron, I saw children begging for the first time in Hungary. 'Forint . . .?' they pleaded hopefully, to tourists only too pleased to get rid of all that annoying small change.

And the Hungarians returned from Austria with their small cars weighed down by fridges, washing machines, televisions and other household items that were hard to get, or to get in good quality, in Hungary. In turn, the Austrians booked appointments with excellent, German-speaking Hungarian dentists.

'Not only is it cheap, but the Hungarian women are beautiful,' one customer told me. 'And if I am going to have pain inflicted on me . . .'

If the world passport was a kiss from the state, the kick was the introduction, at the same time, of personal income tax and value added tax. Until now, some forty-five different kinds of tax had been levied by the state on producers, according to a World Bank report. The essence of the economic reforms was to shift some of that burden onto the workers. To encourage prosperous companies to prosper more and to allow loss-making companies rooted in the old system, which had survived on state handouts for years, to go to the wall.

In May 1988, the Party called an emergency conference. To 'renew' itself, in the face of the economic and political challenges of the times.

The economic challenges alone were enormous. Inflation was running at fifteen percent in a country where people were used to zero inflation— apart from a few well-flagged, centrally planned increases. Hungary's foreign debt was now $18 billion—the highest per capita in eastern Europe. Poland's debt was $35 billion, but it had a population nearly four times bigger than Hungary's. Economists were urging the Party leadership to reduce the $6 billion spent on subsidies to industry a year.

They knew how to do it—allow the big loss-making companies, especially coalmining and steel manufacturing, to collapse. But that would mean a huge surge in unemployment—only officially 10,000 in 1987, in a country where to be unemployed was, on paper, illegal.

There was also growing pressure for János Kádár, now seventy-seven, to resign. Right up to the last minute, he was reluctant to go.

It was not only radical reformers like Pozsgay who were pushing him out. Károly Grósz, politically a hardliner, had emerged as an economic 'pragmatist' and had been urging the closure of inefficient factories. Kádár himself seemed increasingly lost in the new political environment. Always a keen chess player, the writer György Konrád once described him as 'the grey king on the chessboard'—neither properly white, nor black, but something in between. And how does one play against a grey king?

By now, however, the king had lost most of his knights and bishops, and all of his pawns. In a last, desperate gesture, he turned to the same people who had put him into power—the Kremlin. On the eve of the May Congress, the message came back from Gorbachev. 'The Communist Party of the Soviet Union thanks you for your services.'

The so-called Sinatra Doctrine was a reality. The satellite states could indeed do it their way.

I heard the news from Miklós Vásárhelyi, father of the dissidents, on the night before the conference, who had just heard it from Rezső Nyers, a former Social Democrat and one of the most approachable people in the Central Committee. Suddenly unsure how to mark such a momentous event in my adopted homeland, I bought a great bunch of flowers and walked home through the streets in the driving rain.

3. Bringing down the Curtain

Now it's your turn, Eastern Europe, know-all East Europe, hero in boots, doing your egg dance,
    Somewhere Europe, once upon a Europe, shedding your blood, and your cartloads of shame,
    Walk, Eastern Europe! There's a dance, Eastern Europe! Dance, because now you're allowed in the game . . .
Tamás Cseh, Hungarian singer

'Look into the flame,' Pastor Géza Németh preached, '. . . and think of those you have left behind.'

Candles were passed among the congregation. A prayerful silence descended, or as close to one that a crowd of several hundred refugees—men, women, and children—can achieve, crammed into a church, overflowing through all its doors, out onto the porch and the grassy slopes around it.

And there were many people to think of, in the candle flame that day.

This was the work of the 'Community of Reconciliation', a protestant church group founded by Pastor Németh at his church in Rákosszentmihály, a far-flung eastern suburb of Budapest, to help the drop-outs—the alcoholics and drug users and homeless and sufferers from other ills which socialism had promised to cure, and now preferred not to admit the existence of. But now the community had a new role—helping some of the tens of thousands of Romanian citizens, most of them from the Hungarian minority in Transylvania, who were flooding across the border, legally and illegally, to escape from Ceauşescu's Romania.

The Hungarian state, at first, was paralysed. 'Socialist unity', spelt out in the treaties of the Warsaw Pact, allowed only that refugees be accepted 'in the cause of social progress.' This had allowed Hungary and other countries in the bloc to accept refugees from Greece in 1949, after the collapse of the communist side in the Greek civil war, and from Chile after the fall of Salvador Allende's government in 1973. But to accept refugees from a fellow Pact member country was unheard of.

As a result, church groups like the one in Rákosszentmihály bore the brunt of caring for the first wave of refugees, in 1987 and 1988.

There were, however, other reasons for the state's reluctance to get involved. If Hungary began granting money for 'foreign' refugees, why was it not spending enough to deal with the problems of the poorest stratum of its own population?

Even the involvement of the churches was problematic. One of the foundation stones of the socialist system had been to exclude the church from all its traditional educational and social roles, including charity. These would all be taken over by the Party in the atheist society. So if the churches' work to help refugees was now to be tolerated, why not tolerate its activities in other fields?

In practice, due to the relatively relaxed attitude of the authorities in Hungary, some charity work was already tolerated. Various orders of nuns had been champing successfully at the bit for years to care for the sick and elderly. But even in the late 1980s, this was still a point of principle for hardliners, another field of life from which they feared that their beloved Party was beating an undignified retreat.

The final worry among dyed-in-the-wool communists, who still made up a solid contingent on the bridge of the great Hungarian ship, was that the influx of ethnic Hungarian refugees, and the sympathy they engendered, was 'fanning the flames of nationalist feeling.' And as every good communist knew, 'nationalism' was the greatest threat to socialism.

'Today, we have a guest from the BBC,' the good pastor announced, on my first visit to his church. To my amazement the whole congregation erupted in applause. Then they sang 'We Shall Overcome' in my honour. For the first time in two years as a reporter in Hungary, I felt myself welcomed back into the bosom of a protest movement. Tears streamed down my face.

Afterwards, people crowded around me. Many knew my name from my broadcasts. I was bombarded with requests I was powerless to fulfil. 'Could I help them get their wives and children out of Romania? Could I get them a visa for Great Britain?'

Their own escape routes varied. Most came legally, 'on holiday', having applied first to their employers, then to the local police station, and finally to the Hungarian consulate for the necessary documents.

In such cases, it was very unusual for a couple, or a whole family, to receive permission at the same time. Some family members were kept behind as 'guarantees' that the one with the visa would return. Or to be punished in their place, in the event that they did not come back. Thus, the vast majority of those who came were single men, and one of the first things on their mind, when they sat down with the pastor's many helpers, was to apply for 'family re-unification'. The Hungarian Red Cross could at least apply to the Romanian Red Cross on their behalf. But there seemed little hope.

Part of the misery of the refugees was that they knew their wives and children, brothers and sisters, mothers and fathers were already being mistreated on their behalf. Jobs and university places were lost, career prospects ruined and freedom to travel limited. The secret police network in Romania was so vast and all-powerful.

In 1987, Romanian citizens crossed the border into Hungary 860,000 times. There were no figures for how many people stayed illegally, but tens of thousands were now living with friends and relatives. We knew from official sources that 10,000 had actually applied for asylum in Hungary. Most were from the Hungarian minority in Transylvania, but a small number, around five percent, were ethnic Romanians who wanted to travel on to another country.

Traffic at Hungary's western border with Austria also increased considerably. At first, according to an Austrian consular official in Budapest, they 'noticed an influx of pretty girls.' They found it easiest of all to persuade young, Hungarian conscript border-guards to let them through. Then others followed. If the Hungarian policy was still written in Warsaw Pact stone, the practice was softening—according to the whims of individual guards.

But there were official moves afoot, as well. In October 1988, Imre Pozsgay, the most reform-minded figure in the Hungarian Politburo, and also Deputy Prime Minister in the government, called an international press conference at Hegyeshalom, on the Austrian border. 'The Iron Curtain is a political and technical anachronism,' he told the astonished reporters. Hungary had decided to take it down.

Pozsgay didn't take the decision alone—Miklós Németh, the Prime Minister, and István Horváth, the Interior Minister, were 'co-decision makers'. But by announcing it when he did, Pozsgay, who had a knack for making things irreversible, used the press skilfully to achieve that effect.

We reported what the other Party leaders were saying as well. Their doubts, their reluctance, their occasional threats to rid themselves of the troublesome reformers. They were, however, increasingly tongue-tied and increasingly demoralised. The reformers were making the running, encouraged by, and encouraging, a great groundswell of public opinion behind them.

In December 1988, Imre Pozsgay got a phone call from an excited border-guard commander on the eastern frontier with the Soviet Union.

The Soviets had started building an Iron Curtain of their own, to keep their own citizens in. Rolls of barbed wire, even an electronic surveillance system like the one the Hungarians had decided to take down, were being installed.

'It was the best possible news I could have received,' said Pozsgay. 'It suggested that the Soviets were going to let us do what we liked.'

Pozsgay and his government's next move on the border issue was to order a technical report from border-guards on the actual, physical state of the Iron Curtain, along the Hungarian-Austrian border. It was in terrible condition, they were pleased to read.

The Iron Curtain represented not just Hungary's western border with the 'hostile' world, but that of the whole block. In 1961, the sudden erection of a wall between East and West Berlin was justified with the following words.

'Through deceit, bribery and blackmail, West German Government bodies and military interests are inducing certain unstable elements in the German Democratic Republic to leave for West Germany. In the face of the aggressive aspirations of the reactionary forces of West Germany and the NATO allies, Warsaw Pact member states must take the necessary steps to guarantee the security of the GDR.'

And those 'necessary steps' were spelt out in a secret protocol to a 1962 agreement between Warsaw Pact members. Citizens of eastern bloc countries should not be allowed to cross the borders of one another's frontiers with the West. East Germany, Czechoslovakia and Hungary, as 'borderland states' along the Iron Curtain, agreed to act as loyal guards to prevent any citizens crossing. Initially it was done with mines, then with 16-volt wire, designed not to kill, but to alert border-guards to get to the scene of any infringement within ten minutes, down a track that ran the whole length of the border.

There was, however, little obstruction to free movement between the eastern bloc countries.

Lake Balaton in western Hungary, central Europe's biggest lake at 100km long, was a favourite meeting place for East and West German tourists. Many were related—cut off for forty years by the Iron Curtain and the Berlin Wall. Others fell in love—with one another, or their hosts. East German blondes were rather popular with Hungarian boys. On the other hand, Hungarian girls had long been famous for their good looks. They were already in great demand in the dance-halls and brothels of St Petersburg long before the Russian Revolution.

In the 1960s and 70s, while west European youth hitch-hiked to France, Greece or Italy for their summer adventures, east European youth hitch-hiked to Lake Balaton in Hungary, to the Black Sea beaches in Romania or Bulgaria, or to the Polish and East German coast for their holidays. Polish jazz music was popular. Critical bards like Tamás Cseh in Hungary, and Vladimír Merta and the Plastic People of the Universe in Czechoslovakia sang plaintive, ironic, Bob Dylan-like words, gently or fiercely mocking the communist authorities. Afraid of creating a scandal, and alienating what little support they still enjoyed among young people, the authorities alternated repression and tolerance. The degree of repression varied. Only in East Germany, Czechoslovakia and Romania were skulls cracked by police truncheons, and did detentions turn into spells in prison.

Spurred by the arrival of so many asylum-seekers from Romania, the Hungarian Parliament began to draw up a new refugee law. Within the Party, Mátyás Szűrös began work on the documentation necessary for Hungary to accede to international treaties on refugees. In Vienna, at the Conference for Security and Cooperation in Europe, Hungary pressed for the condemnation of Romania, and for a reference to the defence of minority rights, in the final document. The Vienna conference ended in January 1989 with a ringing condemnation of Romania's human rights record. Hungary signed the document, while most other eastern bloc countries, including the Soviet Union, abstained. Nicolae Ceaușescu was running out of friends—only China, North Korea and Albania stood by him.

* * *

Soon after I left Brașov in November 1987, I received a phone call from a man saying he was a Romanian dissident, living in Hungary. I was wary at first, afraid that the Securitate might be trying to exact revenge for my visit to Braşov, and my interview with Silviu Brucan. But as he spoke, the man's story seemed more genuine. He was in Budapest with his wife, he said. They had left their children behind. Their aim now was to make contact with Hungarian opposition groups. Could I help?

I agreed to meet them outside the Air India office on the corner of Vörösmarty Square, in the very centre of Budapest.

Over coffee nearby, I decided I could trust them. Unlike other Romanians in Hungary, they were not interested in travelling on to the West. Instead, their plan was to use Hungary as a base for anti-Ceauşescu propaganda. To encourage the much-stifled people of Romania to revolt.

Their first action took place on 1 December 1987. They sprayed the following message in gold paint, through a stencil, onto hundreds of A4 sized pages, and placed them carefully on all the seats of the Budapest to Bucharest train, just before it set out.

'Citizens of Romania. You are requested to protest against the dictatorial power of the Ceauşescu family, by turning out your lights, every evening at 22.00, for three minutes. Signed: Romania Libera.'

There was even a rather garbled Hungarian language version, for Hungarians in the motherland to pass on to the Hungarian minority in Transylvania. 'Hungarians—Only you can help us now! Please pass this message on to your relatives, friends and acquaintances! Turn off lights at 22.00 each evening for at least three minutes! Free Romania thanks you.'

The action was repeated on 6 December, and they wrote to me, in beautiful French, 'In the unfortunate case that we fail today . . . and we fall into the hands of the Hungarian authorities, there is little chance that we will avoid extradition to Romania, where the oppressive apparatus will destroy us.' I was implored to broadcast the contents of their appeal, and publicise their fate.

'In order to do what we are doing here, we had to abandon our two children, aged seven and eight, in the hope that we will be able to rejoin them one day, on one side or other of the Iron Curtain. Millions of Romanian citizens, in hunger and fear, divided against each other, incapable of coordinated action . . . deserve our sacrifice, to help rid them, without violence and bloodshed, of this awful ruling family.'

In his letter to me, Cornel also implored me, in the event of the Romanian authorities dismissing their stunt as another act of 'sabotage' by the Hungarian minority, to emphasize that their action was a purely Romanian one. For the first time in the letter, they told me their real names, addresses, and identity numbers. He was Cornel Rosca, an economist, from Timişoara. She was Doina Rosca, a computer programmer, from Oradea.

They also spray painted the same messages on the inside of the train doors. The doors opened inwards when the Romanian guards came aboard at the border, so they never saw them. But the passengers saw the messages throughout the journey, and at their destination, as they waited to get off.

All this was done clandestinely, and reported by various western news organisations, including the BBC. The airwaves spread the message, faster and wider than the trains could.

The action passed off without a hitch. If the Hungarian secret services knew what they were doing, as they surely did, they chose not to intervene.

'Aren't you afraid of getting people into trouble?' I asked Cornel later. 'If the Securitate see their lights going off?'

'They could never be sure. . . . people have to go to bed at some time anyway. Then maybe they forget something in the bathroom . . .'

The idea was to make people realise they were not alone in their opposition to the regime. I never found out whether the idea caught on.

* * *

In October 1988 in a sports hall in Budapest, Károly Grósz warned Party activists that a 'white terror' was threatening the country—a euphemism taken from the early 1920s in Hungary, when the 'red terror' inflicted by communists when they briefly seized control, was followed by the 'white terror' of the reprisals against them.

'But don't worry comrades,' Grósz had added. 'If it comes to that, we too will be on the streets.'

It is difficult to guess just how far Grósz was willing to go, without Soviet backing, and with only feeble support within his own party. Even his propaganda chief and erstwhile rival for the leadership, János Berecz, began to desert him.

Berecz spoke at a Party meeting in Tatabánya, the day after Grósz's 'white terror' speech. Despite pressure from the hall—everyone was talking about the Party leader's remarks—Berecz deliberately made no reference to them. That evening Grósz rang Berecz, 'Why didn't you speak out in public, in my support?' he asked.

'Because I didn't agree with you,' Berecz told him, simply.

On 28 January 1989, Imre Pozsgay dropped his next bombshell, while Grósz was on an official trip to Switzerland. The previous June, Pozsgay had been commissioned to oversee the work of a committee of historians whose task it was to re-evaluate Hungarian history since 1949. When it finished its work in January, Pozsgay decided to make public its conclusions, without first seeking approval from the Party leadership. He was afraid that they would sit on, shelve, or simply rewrite them. On a Friday afternoon in the corridor of Parliament, Pozsgay accosted a Hungarian radio journalist he knew, and offered an exclusive interview.

The interview led the main evening news at six o'clock the following Monday. Pozsgay had told no-one.

'The first my wife knew about it was when she heard it on the radio,' he told me, long after the event.

'1956 was a popular uprising,' Pozsgay declared.

Hardliners in the Party reacted with fury, and called for Pozsgay's immediate expulsion. A popular uprising was tantamount to a revolution. And if 1956 was a revolution, Károly Grósz is said to have remarked, 'then we would be counter-revolutionaries!'

The whole legitimacy of a Party which came to power on the back of Soviet tanks which crushed the revolution was swept away with a single phrase.

The glass facade of communist power in Hungary, so strong for so many years, had been shattered with a single pebble.

At a meeting of the Central Committee of the Party on 10 February 1989, fifty-two delegates stood up to attack Pozsgay. Very few raised their voices in his defence. But what the Party feared most of all was division in its own ranks. So when Károly Grósz weighed up his options, he decided it would be more dangerous to throw Pozsgay out than to keep him in. The hardliners were not going to storm out and found a new party of their own, but the reformers were already considering it.

As a result, Pozsgay easily won a vote of confidence. The force for change was to come from within the Party itself rather than from the street.

'The Party was paralysed by the 1956 question,' Pozsgay told me, many years later. 'In February 1989 it had to choose between being the Party of a totalitarian state, or joining the side of those pushing for change. It chose the latter.'

By the spring of 1989, at least four tails were wagging the Party dog in Hungary. The first was the economy. The second was the issue of 1956. The third was the controversial Gabčikovo-Nagymaros dam. And the fourth was the fate of the Hungarians in Transylvania.

The dam and the refugee issue woke Hungary's small middle class from decades of Kádár induced political slumber. The rebirth of 1956 as the revolution people had always, in their heart of hearts, known it to be, gave another fillip to their self-esteem. The economic situation gave an urgency to the programmes of political reform being advanced on all sides. But it was the hole punched in the Hungarian stretch of the Iron Curtain, initially by refugees from Romania, and then from East Germans looking for a way out of their own, unreformable paradise, which was to prove Hungary's main contribution to the collapse of the system known as communism.

* * *

Imre Pozsgay didn't waste time with his plans for the Iron Curtain after his October press conference. The National Border Guard was asked to prepare a study of its physical state. Forty years after it was first drawn across the continent, it was still formidable, but not in good shape.

In its youth, the iron in the curtain was composed mostly of mines, rather than wires. There were two kinds, both Soviet, and about three million in all, stretching from Tornyiszentmiklós in the south-west corner of Hungary, 243km north to Rajka in the north-west. A watchtower stood every 5km, manned twenty-four hours a day.

The mines were half a metre high and connected by trip wires. They were both a physical obstacle, and a visible deterrent. There was also a thick barbed wire fence.

In February 1956, in his 'secret speech' to the Soviet Communist Party, its leader Nikita Khrushchev lambasted the crimes of Josef Stalin, three years after his death. That speech ushered in a thaw in Cold War relations with the West, and in the spring of that year, the Hungarians were told to start lifting the mines along their border.

That was to prove the extraordinary good fortune of the quarter of a million Hungarians who fled across it that winter, after their revolution was crushed on 4 November. In spring 1957, János Kádár ordered the rebuilding of the curtain. Initially mines were re-laid. Then between 1965 and 1967, they were replaced by iron, once again, but of a different kind.

Closely following Soviet instructions, an elaborate system of barbed wire and electronic surveillance fences were erected. First the main fence, strung between concrete posts, four metres high, with 16 volts of current running through it. Their duty was to patrol the fence every fifteen minutes, day and night. Just inside was a carefully raked strip, several metres wide, which would clearly show the footprints of anyone who tried to approach the fence. Beyond that, the gravelled road used by the border-guard jeeps. Then more strips of barbed wire.

The curtain did not exactly follow the physical border, but rather the contours of the land, including hill-tops, sometimes as far as 10km from the real border. As a result, some thirty-six villages or small settlements were actually sealed off, on the wrong side of the Iron Curtain, but still in Hungary. The population was strictly controlled, both in terms of who could go near the border, and for those living in the cut-off villages. To reach the physical border, you had to go through five checkpoints. Local farmers had to register in a book when they went out to tend to their cows, or their vines. There were occasional attempts to cross, but few succeeded.

One success story was that of three Gypsy boys from Sopron, in November 1978. Three strands of barbed wire extended under the soil. The boys dug down beneath the last wire, and wriggled to safety. When their escape was discovered, with the stick left resting guiltily in the hole, senior officers arrived from the city to investigate. The next day they returned with conscripts, to perform an experiment. Was it really possible to dig a hole in such a short time—the fifteen minutes between patrols? The conscripts took thirty minutes to dig the hole. The border-guards who were supposed to be on duty that night each received three year prison sentences, and their commanding officer was demoted.

In 1978, the order to open fire on all who tried to escape was rescinded, to be replaced with a softer version which allowed border-guards to open fire only if they felt physically threatened. But that left considerable room for interpretation by zealous guards. Between 1957 and 1989, 105 people died on the border. Sixty-five of them were border-guards, killed in accidents laying or lifting mines, or shot by their fellow officers when they tried themselves to escape.

By 1989 the electronic system was falling apart. More than ninety per cent of signals were false alarms—caused by deer or wild boar wandering too close to the fence, or simply short-circuits caused by the wind, snow or rain.

In response to the government query, the commander of the border-guard dutifully reported back to the Hungarian government, which mournfully announced to its Iron Curtain allies that the fence was, unfortunately, irreparable, so they were going to have to take it down.

On 2 May 1989 at eight o'clock in the morning, the men who had been responsible for the maintenance of the fence assembled at Hungary's four main border crossings into Austria. Using tractors, lorries and cranes, they began to dismantle the fence and surveillance system exactly 1km either side of the main road. It was both a symbolic breach, designed to impress upon sceptical western leaders that Hungary was serious about its commitments. While at the same time, to further test the waters with Moscow.

'It all worked like clockwork,' said Lt. Colonel Árpád Bella, the forty-one-year-old commander of the crossing north-west of Sopron. 'First the concrete pillars were lifted, by crane, onto the back of the trucks. Then another vehicle with barbed wire coiling equipment set to work.' The Iron Curtain had been breached, but it was still not open.

For the first time, the East German Communist Party leadership panicked. Erich Honecker, the leader, immediately accused Hungary of treachery at a Politburo meeting on the same day, 2 May. On 4 May, his Defence Minister, Horst Kessler, arrived in Budapest, demanding an explanation. He found it hard to believe the Hungarian response that the fence was in such poor condition it could not be repaired.

The Hungarians endeavoured to reassure him. The border would be patrolled as strictly as before, he was told. And after two warnings, any East German found trying to cross it illegally would be handed back to East German police.

At Sopron, near the border, Árpád Bella experienced the consequences of Kessler's visit like a cold shower. Just as the East German Minister had been informed, he was told to control the border as diligently as before. 'It was unworkable,' he said. The bird had not yet flown, but it was exercising its wings.

In 1988, according to official figures, out of 1300 attempts to cross the border illegally, only thirty-five succeeded.

With the job of dismantling the curtain underway, and his officers demoralised, there was no way the order could be fulfilled.

Over the following three months, 6,000 East Germans, and 2,000 Romanians were turned back. A further 6,000 East Germans, according to figures from the West German embassy in Vienna, crossed successfully, and were helped to travel on to West Germany.

Another detail that Horst Kessler had not been told was that attempting to cross the border illegally had been redefined under Hungarian law as an 'infringement', not a criminal offence. Those caught were no longer arrested, or worse still, sent back to Berlin or Bucharest, as they had been in the past. They were simply dumped at the nearest railway station. From which they invariably tried to cross the border again, on another route.

Then came the summer, and hundreds of thousands of East Germans flooded into Hungary, as usual, for their summer holidays. Some had chosen Hungary as that year's destination simply to test the news that it might be possible to cross to the West without the right papers.

There had been rumours all spring that the East German government was going to restrict travel to Hungary. Many set out just in case a new Iron Curtain was about to appear to prevent East Germans leaving their own country. No-one knew either whether or not pressure on Budapest might persuade the Hungarian authorities to change their minds. All of which helped to speed up the westward migration of peoples.

Then, in an ultimately misguided move to make staying in the East more attractive, the East German authorities even sold 15,000 Wartburg cars with the new Volkswagen engine to Hungary in spring 1989—despite the fact that there was a several-year waiting list for the same cars for East German citizens—for which the Hungarians paid in forints. The money was made available to East German holidaymakers planning to play volleyball under the willows and poplars along the shores of Lake Balaton. Little suspecting that they might spend it on sandwiches on the sun-drenched road to Vienna.

4. The Miracles Begin

> As a soldier . . . I knew it was not my job to use my weapon against women and children, against civilians, young and old.
> Lt. Colonel Árpád Bella, Hungarian border guard

In 1985, a year before I moved to live in eastern Europe, I was offered a lift in a truck from Bradford, in the north of England, to Budapest. The route the driver had taken was through Germany, across into Czechoslovakia, then down the highway to Bratislava, then Budapest. Knowing my bags would be searched on the West German-Czech border, at Waidhaus, I took the precaution of placing a copy of Fyodor Dostoyevsky's novel *The Idiot* on top of the clothes in my rucksack.

We reached the border-crossing at noon, and the ruse worked perfectly. I climbed down from the cab, and placed my humble possessions on the road. A young border-guard was assigned to deal with me.

'Open the bag please!' He barked in loud, nervous English.

'Ahh, Dostoyevsky!'

A lively conversation about literature ensued, and the rest of the contents of my bag remained undisturbed. He was a student of American and English Literature, and Geography. Who was my favourite author? What about Hemingway? Hemingway is my favourite! He then eagerly listed all the books he had read. The young conscript had even learnt English from Hemingway, it seemed. He spoke like *The Old Man and the Sea*.

'But . . .' he lamented, as the other border-guards began to give us funny looks, and even my truck driver had finished his laborious paperwork, 'I am not a go-getter . . . when I end my military service, I will work here, in the fields.'

We bade each other a fond farewell, then I was driven on, down avenues of horse chestnuts, the top of our vast vehicle brushing the lower branches of the trees, the grey, frozen mists of Bohemia unfolding reluctantly before us.

My next visit to Czechoslovakia was by train from Budapest to Prague in the late autumn of 1987. I went not as a journalist, but simply as a tourist, with a Danish friend, Marlene, to explore the city for the weekend.

Prague seemed deserted. Rain turned to sleet as we crossed the Charles Bridge. The statues were blackened by age and air pollution. We slept in an ugly tower block which a tourist agency had arranged for us, on uncomfortable beds in someone's living room. We drank cold coffee, and ate unnecessarily sweet cakes, in smoke-filled cafés. Everything was a shade of grey. The people only grunted when we spoke to them, and seemed lost in their own troubles. My strongest memory of the trip was Marlene setting off down the carriage on the way back, after announcing 'I'm going to look for kinky sex!' Even that hope was disappointed. She returned, disgruntled, soon afterwards. I buried myself in my book.

'In the nineteenth century, we looked to Vienna for new ideas,' Imre Pozsgay, the leading reformer in the Hungarian Communist Party commented wryly, from the steps of the Hungarian National Museum in Budapest, on 15 March 1988. 'Now we look to Moscow.' It was a joke, but it went down well with the Hungarian crowd.

In Prague, however, the riot police didn't think it was funny.

The fifteenth of January 1989 was the twentieth anniversary of the suicide of Jan Palach. Several thousand brave protesters gathered at the foot of the statue of Good King Wenceslas, at the top of Wenceslas Square—the very spot where the young student had burnt himself to death in protest against the Soviet-led invasion in 1968.

Terribly burnt, the twenty-year-old Palach was still alive when they got him to hospital. Did they find the letter? he whispered. Yes, they found the letter. He attempted a smile, and shut his eyes. Three days later, he died of his injuries. The previous August, a flowering of free thought and free speech, known as the Prague Spring, had been crushed by Soviet tanks, as thoroughly as the Hungarian uprising twelve years earlier. Unlike the Hungarians in 1956, the Czechs didn't fight. They photographed, and they fled.

In the film version of Milan Kundera's novel, *The Unbearable Lightness of Being,* you hear the rumble of tank tracks on the cobbles, just before Teresa runs out into the street, armed with her camera.

Through her lens, you see the joy of the revolution on the faces of the students turn to fear as the tanks swing round the corner.

'It is better to die standing,' wrote Jan Palach, 'than to live on your knees.' Thousands attended his funeral, then went home and continued their lives. But his message incubated, and hatched in 1989.

'I am Jan Palach,' the Lithuanian-Polish performance artist, Wiktor Szostalo, wrote in 1983, on a placard around his neck in St Louis, Missouri. 'I'm a Czech, a Pole, a Lithuanian, a Vietnamese, an Afghan, a betrayed you. After I've burnt myself a thousand times, perhaps we'll win.'

A man called Miloš Jakeš organised the repercussions after 1968: the arrests, and the expulsion from the Party of nearly half a million reform-minded people.

In 1989, Jakeš was still Communist Party leader and Gustáv Husák was President. Jan Fojtík, the head of Agitation and Propaganda in the Party, like his counterpart János Berecz in Hungary, was a sworn opponent of meaningful reforms. And while Hungary and Poland edged ahead, ignored or encouraged by Moscow, East Berlin and Prague were the anchors of the Soviet camp, fixing the rusting hulk firmly to the bottom of the Marxist-Leninist harbour.

The people, the intellectuals at least, were growing restless.

The pro-Palach protest in 1989 was violently broken up—as its participants knew it would be—by riot police wielding their distinctive white batons. In the photographs plastered across the pages of the western press the next day, the batons looked like an alphabet of repression, outlined on the black of the riot police uniforms. The protests lasted several days in the centre of Prague, and the police swooped each time, with such violence that the US Secretary of State, James Shultz, speaking in Vienna at the closing meeting of the Conference on Security and Cooperation in Europe, condemned the Czech authorities.

'We saw big Soviet planes overhead and shouted, "Gorbachev is in Prague,"' Karel Srp, of the dissident Czech group, the Jazz Section, and one of the organisers of the protests, told a western reporter. 'Gorbachev is watching, Gorbachev is watching,' chanted the crowd, as the riot police attacked. 'Gorbachev' had become a tool in the hands, a slogan in the mouths of the kids on the street, as they confronted the might of the one-party state. And the one-party state was nonplussed. When he visited Hungary in 1986, the distinctive birth-mark on the Soviet leader's forehead was airbrushed out. As they grappled to cope with his impact,

the best the grey men in power seemed able to do was to try to tidy
him up for public consumption. But the Czech protestors wanted him,
warts and all.

On 19 January, even as the Czech police were still mopping up the
protesters, Erich Honecker, leader of the East German communists,
commented that the Berlin Wall would stand 'for fifty, perhaps even a
hundred years', because the reasons for its construction were still valid.
The very same day, Mikhail Gorbachev announced a fourteen per cent
cut in the Soviet military budget. The real reason for the existence of the
Wall had always been the communist fear that their own people would
flee West, if they could. That reasoning might still be valid, but the troops
who would defend the Wall were no longer there.

* * *

Dissident groups in each socialist country developed in different ways,
like trees trying to grow in the wrong soil.

In Czechoslovakia, Václav Havel was the best known figure. At fifty-
three, the same age as Gorbachev when he came to power, Havel was
an unlikely revolutionary. The child of well-off, middle class parents, his
family background disqualified him from university. The communist
system favoured the offspring of workers and peasants, and disliked or
disqualified the previous elite. Instead, he got work as a stage-hand at
Prague's Theatre on the Balustrade in 1960, and began writing plays of
his own soon afterwards.

In 1975, the Helsinki Final Act was signed in the Finnish capital. The
'Declaration on Principles Guiding Relations between Participating
States' included ten points, number seven of which was 'respect for
human rights and fundamental freedoms, including the freedom of
thought, conscience, religion or belief'. The document was a triumph for
the then Soviet leader, Leonid Brezhnev, because it appeared to
consolidate Soviet gains in the Baltic Republics and eastern Europe during
and immediately after the Second World War. The sacrifice of the lives
of so many Red Army soldiers, including the death of 70,000 in 1944–5
in the conquest of Hungary alone, had won international recognition,
in Russian eyes.

Article 7, however vaguely worded, was to have a deeply subversive effect on the communist countries. From the perspective of
1989, the list of signatories reads like the seeds of their own undoing:

Gustáv Husák, Nicolae Ceauşescu, János Kádár, Todor Zhivkov and Erich Honecker.

Only Enver Hoxha, the Stalinist leader of Albania, stayed away. The agreement was strongly criticised by some commentators for the absence of a mechanism to enforce the promises made. The wording was too vague, they lamented, and gave much longed-for legitimacy to the post-Stalinist regimes of eastern Europe, but had no teeth to bite them if they transgressed its provisions. That may have been the aim of Prague and East Berlin, Budapest and Bucharest, but it was not the way it happened. 'Helsinki' became a word to hurl at the oppressor, long before the advent of Gorbachev.

In Czechoslovakia, less than two years later in January 1977, Charter 77 was born. Signed by 240 people, it set out to hold the Czechoslovak government to Article 7, and other international human rights documents. The Party, predictably, reacted with fury. Václav Havel and the others were arrested and hounded. The StB, the secret services, dismissed the Charter as 'a crude attack by hostile elements', and the Party newspaper, Rudé Právo, commented ominously that 'those who lie down on the tracks of history can expect to get their legs cut off.'

Similar dissident groups in the Soviet Union, in Hungary, and other eastern bloc countries, followed the Czech lead. The Helsinki Accords became a raft, a piece of dry wood to cling to, for 'those who thought differently' to the ruling regimes in eastern Europe.

Havel, in 1989, proved himself as the kind of unifying leader which the Hungarians lacked. It was a quality he shared with the down-to-earth, working class and, in most ways, very different figure of Lech Wałęsa in Poland. Havel's wry, central European sense of humour gave Charter 77 a sharp, intellectual edge over the grey, glum, and often dumb figures in the Party leadership.

'It seems that in our central European context what is most earnest has a way of blending in a particularly tense manner with what is most comic,' he wrote.

'Only the Czechs can save Soviet Communism now' ran the Prague joke. How? 'By sending the tanks into Moscow.'

In February 1989, Havel was sent back to prison, his third spell in ten years, this time for nine months for his role in organising the January protests. Alexander Dubček, the leader of the 1968 Prague Spring, was half-forgotten in exile in the Slovak Forestry Commission, and the tall, gangly Catholic dissident, Ján Carnogurský, was on trial on sedition charges in Bratislava. The Czech Party leadership should have had little to worry about. Bu the signs from Moscow were looking very bad indeed.

On 8 January, Mikhail Gorbachev announced that the Soviet Union's economic problems were so bad that defence spending would be cut by fourteen per cent. He criticised those domestic critics who attacked him 'from both the left and the right'.

Even worse from the point of view of the hardliners in east European capitals, on 22 January Gorbachev spoke positively for the first time about the multi-party system. The practice of power, he said, needed to be publicly controlled. It was as if the froth at the top of their beer tankards cleared, and the comrades in Prague suddenly caught a glimpse of their own reflection. It was not a pretty sight.

The signals from Warsaw and Budapest were equally alarming, where they saw the Party putting Gorbachev's rather abstract words into practice and making incomprehensible concessions.

The loss of confidence within the ruling Party was most visible in Hungary and in Poland. In Poland, the country's growing economic crisis was largely to blame.

As in Hungary in the 1960s, so in Poland in the 1980s, unpopular communist authorities tried to buy off the workers with consumer comforts the country could little afford, plunging it deeper and deeper into debt. But the Poles were not so easily bought off. Solidarity had been allowed to continue, underground, backed by the powerful Catholic Church, in a way which would have been completely impossible in Hungary after the crushing of the 1956 Revolution.

Workers in Poland had a recent memory of flexing their muscles, and while they might have put aside their political demands during the 1980s, their economic demands remained the same. When the government, in this centrally planned economy, attempted to put up the price of one of the staples of the Polish diet, sour cream, in March 1987, the workers at several coalmines walked out in protest. By evening, the price increase had been cancelled.

The same month, the Polish Communist Party leader, General Jaruzelski, held a referendum on a programme of radical economic reform, which included steep price rises, but also some cautious political reform.

By holding the referendum, Jaruzelski was attempting to portray his party in a more democratic light than the popular movement he had suppressed. The vote went in favour of both economic and political reform, but because only two thirds of the public took part, the end result showed that less than fifty per cent of the actual electorate voted in favour, so the result was not valid. As an exercise in democracy, it was an interesting experiment—a dictatorship appearing to consult its people for the first time.

Undeterred, Jaruzelski said he would go-ahead and introduce the reforms anyway.

The Polish economy needed strong medicine. Inflation was rampant, and there were shortages of basic goods. One opinion poll showed that between twenty and thirty per cent of the population would like to emigrate.

In the spring of 1988, a wave of strikes began at the shipyards on the north coast, then spread to the vast Nowa Huta steelworks as they swept across the country.

At this moment, Lech Wałęsa, the canny electrician who had led the Solidarity movement from 1980, weary of the strike tool, and worried by the state of the country, announced a change in tactics—away from confrontation with the authorities, and towards compromise—in the national interest.

'We are in the same country. Therefore we are in the same camp,' he announced.

From its side, the Party leadership was willing to recognise that it had failed to crush Solidarity, and that it was time to talk. Jaruzelski, his Prime Minister Mieczysław Rakowski, and the Interior Minister Czesław Kiszczak, initiated the discussions. Kiszczak, also the head of the secret police, found himself in the strange position of both bad cop and good cop, responsible for a service which had murdered Father Jerzy Popiełuszko in 1984, yet now wished to cut a deal with his fellow-believers.

In January 1989, as the Czech police were cracking down on the students of Prague, and the Hungarian Party was preparing to undermine its own legitimacy, and President Ceaușescu was celebrating what would prove to be his last birthday, the Polish United Workers' Party (PUWP) declared that it was willing to lift the ban on independent trade unions.

Round-table discussions between the government, Solidarity and the Catholic Church began on 5 February. Observers in the rest of eastern Europe and the Soviet Union held their breath. For the first time in forty years, a ruling communist party was searching for ways to share power with the rest of society. This was no longer an attempt to 'put a human face' on socialism, to reform it while keeping its mainstay, the leading role of the Communist Party, intact. It was an attempt to map a path from single party to multi-party rule.

Over the next eight weeks, 128 negotiators and fourteen outside experts took part. On 5 April a historic agreement was signed. Solidarity was to be legalised, and trade unions granted the right to strike. Acknowledging for the first time the central role of the countryside in Poland, a trade union representing farm workers, Rural Solidarity, was also legalised. Elections would be held on 4 June, in which a new upper house of Parliament, the Senate, would be freely elected. In the Lower House, the Sejm, only one-third of seats could be contested by the opposition, leaving the Party and its allies with a comfortable majority in the main legislative chamber. A so-called 'National List' of communists who had taken part in the Round-Table, was also drawn up, with candidates on it to be elected if they won more than fifty per cent of the votes cast.

Hardline officials in the Party opposed what they saw as an unacceptable dilution of the Party's central role. Within Solidarity, the more radically minded saw the agreement as a betrayal, the manipulation of their transformation into a tool for allowing the communists to stay in power, while sharing responsibility for the disastrous state of the economy and the inevitably unpopular measures needed to address it.

In the end the sceptics on both sides were resoundingly defeated. Solidarity won everywhere—99 out of 100 seats in the Senate, and all 161 of the seats available to the opposition in the Sejm, the lower house. On the National List, only two of the thirty-five candidates were elected, despite last minute efforts by Solidarity to persuade its supporters to vote for 'good' communists.

The PUWP defeat was as big as the Solidarity victory. Prominent communists like the Prime Minister, the Interior Minister and the government spokesman lost their parliamentary seats. A deafening silence fell on Poland as the scale of what had happened sank in.

In a private telephone call, Gorbachev made it clear to Jaruzelski that the election results must be respected. The problem was that while it had left the PUWP without the legitimacy to continue ruling, Solidarity was without the means to govern since it only held one third of the seats in the main chamber of Parliament. The infrastructure of the state was also permeated through and through by the Communist Party, and could hardly be expected to comfortably execute the orders of an anti-communist movement. Nor was Solidarity in a position to take power. Change overtook even the prime mover for change. Solidarity was still essentially a trade union, supporting a broader, scattered movement, with a vast diversity of views, from westward leaning liberals and atheist fundamentalists, to Catholic fundamentalists, conservatives and social democrats. In the confusion, it was left to the various strongmen on the stage to try to restore order.

The seventeen-member Politburo was still in place and, in theory, according to the existing constitution, ran the country. The Party General Secretary, General Jaruzelski, was elected to the new post of Polish President in July, with the reluctant support of Solidarity deputies. He tried to form a communist-led government, with Solidarity as a junior coalition partner. Lech Wałęsa wisely refused.

In August, without first consulting with other Solidarity leaders, Wałęsa invited the leaders of two other parties, which had until that time been little more than communist puppets, the Peasants' Party and the Democratic Party, to discuss the possibility of joining a coalition. Grateful for the chance to begin to undo four decades of subservience to the PUWP, they agreed immediately to form a government with Solidarity. Wałęsa met Jaruzelski and offered to select the Defence and Interior Ministers of his new government from the PUWP, in a nod of acknowledgement to Jaruzelski's fears that the new government would be unbearable for Poland's Warsaw Pact allies. Wałęsa also agreed that Poland should stay in the Warsaw Pact.

It had been widely assumed, in Poland and abroad, that Lech Wałęsa would be Prime Minister, but he refused outright. The Solidarity choice fell on Bronisław Geremek, a professor of medieval history. He seemed the ideal choice. He was not only the editor of the weekly Solidarity newspaper, but also a Catholic intellectual with strong opposition credentials—he had spent a year in prison—and was a moderate who could be expected to deal fairly with the communists.

On 24 August, Geremek was elected the first non-communist Prime Minister of any country in the Soviet bloc.

'The monopoly of the Party which ruled Poland against the will of the people has been broken,' said Geremek. Only five of his twenty-three ministers were from the PUWP.

At home in Moscow, Gorbachev was moving, but more ponderously. On 19 September, at a meeting of the Central Committee of the Communist Party, he proposed that it be divided on federal lines. It was a rather belated effort to head off the already advanced aspirations of many peoples in the Soviet Union for a restoration of national sovereignty.

Elsewhere in eastern Europe, events were moving fast, and the brake pedal appeared broken. In Hungary, political parties and associations had been forming at breathtaking speed—by the end of 1988 there were already twenty-one. Several, like the Hungarian Democratic Forum and the Network of Free Initiatives, looked more like the seed-beds from which yet more parties would spring than parties in their own right.

On 1 May 1988, I attended the founding meeting of the Network, in a smoky restaurant near the East Station. The aim was to set up a rival, more urban-based alternative to the somewhat provincial Hungarian Democratic Forum, with its emphasis on Hungarian values and the glories of Hungarian history. The Network was to be solidly liberal—but even the liberals found it hard to agree. Tempers frayed, and the meeting degenerated at times into a shouting match, but the roots of two liberal parties, the Association of Free Democrats, and the Young Democrats—Fidesz—were placed in firmer soil. The Free Democrats became a party in November of the same year. Almost before it was established, the dissident philosopher, Gáspár Miklós Tamás, would refer to it as 'my abominable party.' Were there not two people in this country, I wondered, who could agree on anything at all?

For the first time, 15 March 1989 was celebrated legally with a rally of up to one hundred thousand people in front of Parliament. This time the riot police were not even loitering in the side streets. They had been given the day off. There was a carnival atmosphere. In the middle of the crowd I bumped into an old friend, Ágota Ruzsa.

'Just imagine,' Ágota shouted to me excitedly amid the din of the speeches, 'no-one trod on the flowers!'

At that time there were still rose-beds in the gardens in front of Parliament, and despite the crush, people had managed somehow not to trample over them.

A few days later an opposition round-table convened, to prepare for talks with the Party on the peaceful transition to democracy. Disagreement between them ran deep, but more moderate voices won the day. Attempts by party hardliners like Károly Grósz, to divide the members among themselves, came to nothing. The new opposition was finally sitting under one roof, thrashing out a common programme and timetable to take to the Party.

There were disagreements from the start about just what should be on the table for discussion. The Party wanted a broader agenda, to include the deep economic and social crisis facing the country. The opposition argued that neither side had the necessary popular mandate to address such issues—that would be the task of the first democratically elected government. What the opposition wanted to discuss were the mechanics of change: amendments to the 1949 Constitution, an election law, a law on the President of the Republic and changes to the criminal code. The opposition also wanted all talks to take place in public, while the Party argued for sessions behind closed doors. In the end, there was compromise on all fronts.

Swept along on the wave, Károly Grósz told the Central Committee of his party in March 1989, that 'there have been few instances in the history of politics that a party voluntarily surrendered its monopoly position while still in the possession of the means with which to prevent it.'

Grósz was, however, hesitating, and part of his hesitation involved conversations with army generals. Could the whole process actually be stopped, if he decided it was necessary? When Imre Pozsgay heard that Grósz had been talking with the army, he went to see him. 'I don't know how well you know your Hungarian history . . .' Pozsgay told his boss, '. . . but this is not Latin America. A Hungarian soldier does one of two things when he is ordered to shoot into the crowd. He either shoots his own commanding officers. Or he goes home to his mother. Is that what you are trying to achieve?'

Károly Grósz was more pragmatic in his other role as Prime Minister. In communist countries, power had traditionally been wielded by the Politburo of the Party, and especially by the head of each Politburo, the General Secretary. In Budapest, the Politburo—ten, rather portly men— often met at the mineral baths of the Gellért Hotel. The baths would then be strictly closed to the public, as well as to hotel guests. In a small, steamy hot bath at one end of the indoor pool, overseen by mermaids and dolphins, the Party leaders would then debate the fate of their country. At that time, the government itself was little more than a rubber stamp. From 1986 to 1988, it didn't even have a spokesman, or not one that I could find.

But from May 1988, one of the biggest changes was the ebbing of the power from the Party, and the strengthening of the government as the main instrument of policy.

'A strong central government, with an awareness of civil liberties, could be a good solution,' the sociologist Elemér Hankiss told me in late 1988.

'There will be a fierce fight, between the new ruling class and a society trying to protect themselves against them. The major hope now is that the new elite realises that without the help of society, it can't solve the problems.'

The new pragmatism of the government was costing jobs.

'We feel like poultry in a farmyard, waiting for the kestrel to swoop,' a coalminer told me at the appropriately named Farkaslyuk—Wolf's Lair mine in north-east Hungary. By then, they had been told that the mine would certainly close in 1990. It had been open since 1914. In 1988, 70,000 people still worked in the mining industry in Hungary. Most would lose their jobs in the 'change of system'.

*   *   *

In April 1989, the exhumation of Imre Nagy and his companions in the leadership of the 1956 Revolution, finally got underway in that gloomy corner of the city cemetery. As the weeds and soil were removed, and the diggers uncovered the pitiful traces of men executed thirty-one years earlier, there was another shock in store.

The Hungarian Prime Minister had been buried face downwards, wrapped in tar paper. In the film shot of the exhumation, his skull comes away from his body, into the gloved hand of the man who is excavating the grave. His thin bones protrude from his heavy, prison boots. Now these men were at last to receive a proper burial, in wooden coffins, with all the honour the state could muster. And with their reburial, communism in Hungary would be laid to rest.

On 4 June, at a Warsaw Pact summit in Bucharest, the East German and Romanian leaders proposed military intervention in Poland and Hungary. Gorbachev refused, and the others were hardly going to organise their own invasion forces without the Soviets.

Then, from Beijing came the news that Chinese security forces had massacred the students in Tiananmen Square. It was a lesson which gave even the most hardline communist pause for thought.

On 13 June, after several false starts, the Hungarian 'Triangular' Table Talks started, with the united opposition on one side, the Party on the other and official organisations including the trade unions on the third.

'We don't want to share power,' said the lawyer and opposition spokesman, Imre Konya. 'We want the people to decide who runs the country.'

The main negotiators on the Party side were Imre Pozsgay and Rezső Nyers, both prominent reformers. The hardliners had, to all extents and purposes, crawled off into the shadows with their tails between their legs. Unlike in the Polish round-table talks, the power had crumbled before the talks even started.

On 16 June, six coffins were arrayed, draped with the national flag, on the steps of the Palace of Arts in Heroes' Square in Budapest. Five contained bodies—those of Imre Nagy who had been Prime Minister in 1956, Pál Maléter his Defence Minister, Miklós Gimes, the editor of Magyar Szabadság—Hungarian Freedom—Géza Losonczy, the Minister of Information, and József Szilágyi, his chief political secretary. The sixth coffin at the reburial was empty. True to the drama of Hungarian history, it was said to contain the body of the unknown revolutionary— to represent all the others who had died fighting for Hungary during those thirteen days.

Up to half a million people gathered in Heroes' Square for the ceremony. All the faces of Hungary seemed to be there. Old men with crooked noses and crooked backs who might have spent their youth as shepherds on the Puszta, the great plain between the Danube and Tisza rivers. Young women who could have walked off with the prize at any beauty competition in the world, yet worked humbly selling newspapers or popcorn in underground passages. Broad shouldered workers from Csepel. Gypsies from the workers' hostels, or the hovels of the 8th district. Respectable lawyers and doctors.

The most radical speech of the day came from the young firebrand for whom I had made tea in my flat barely a year earlier, and told that I didn't believe he would succeed—Viktor Orbán, leader of the Federation of Young Democrats, Fidesz.

'Fellow citizens. Today, thirty-three years after the Hungarian revolution, and thirty-one years after the execution of the last responsible Hungarian Prime Minister, we have an opportunity to achieve in a peaceful way everything which the revolutionaries of 1956 achieved for the nation in bloody struggle, if only for a few days. If we believe in our own strength, we will be able to put an end to the communist dictatorship; if we are determined enough, we can call on the ruling Party to allow free elections; and if we remain true to the spirit of 1956, we will be able to choose such a government which launches immediate negotiations for the urgent withdrawal of Russian troops . . .'

'I don't think you should have said that,' the more cautious Adam Michnik of the Solidarity movement, told him in the car afterwards. But he did, and they did too, within a year.

The martyrs of the revolution were reburied with honour in the same ground in the same cemetery on the edge of the city from which they had been exhumed. But Plot 301 was now completely unrecognisable. It had been landscaped, trees had been planted, grass sown, a bell-tower erected and the names of the dead proudly displayed at last. A great chunk of limestone, several hundred thousand years old, was brought on a trailer from the quarries of southern Hungary, and placed on the grass—a reminder of how tiny human endeavours are, measured on the scale of geological time.

* * *

Three weeks later, on 6 July 1989, János Kádár died, aged seventy-seven. In one of his last, long rambling speeches to the Central Committee of his Party in April 1989, he referred at length to the revolution he had at first joined, then played a central role in defeating.

'Day and night my brain turns over feverishly, and that alone requires a lot of energy. Going over the things that I am responsible for . . .' Then, muddled together with comments about his own current ailments, especially the paralysis of his right hand, he appeared close to apologising for the execution of Imre Nagy and his associates. If only they had admitted their mistake, he suggested, everything might have been alright. 'The main charge against me,' Kádár continued, 'was that I was a Soviet agent. But I was not a Soviet agent! And what is more, I can prove it to you!'

'As I lived my life, I will answer, in turn, the most burning questions,' he concluded, 'whatever seems pressing now, and what torments me still.'

Several tens of thousands attended Kádár's funeral in the Kerepesi Cemetery, close to the East Station, and the race track.

The hours of the clock were turning just as fast on the Hungarian-Austrian border as they were in the capital. On 2 May, approximately 8km of the Iron Curtain had been dismantled; 2km each at four border crossings. The plan, as announced then, had been to dismantle all 243km of it in Hungary by 1 January 1991. No decision had yet been taken to actually open the border to the East Germans and Romanians who were beginning to flood into the country. On the one hand, the Hungarian authorities were constrained by legality—the new law on freedom of movement, in the spirit of the January 1989 meeting of the Conference on Security and Cooperation in Europe, would not be ready till the autumn. The Soviet Union had proven deaf to the entreaties of the East German and Romanian governments to 'do something' about Hungary. But what if Gorbachev were to fall, and his successor sent in the tanks?

In June, Gyula Horn, the Hungarian Foreign Minister, held a highly publicised meeting with Alois Mock, his Austrian counterpart, on a small hill near the border. The fence had already been removed from the spot, so they had to rustle up a piece of barbed wire from somewhere else so that the two Foreign Ministers could stand, somewhat sheepishly, with their wire-cutters before the photographers and television cameras. But the stage-managed performance concealed a serious message. Hungary's reform government, led by the Prime Minister Miklós Németh, the Deputy Prime Minister Imre Pozsgay, and the Foreign Minister Gyula Horn, had taken the political plunge that was only theirs to take. Another government might have prevaricated even more, or stayed on the springboard. The Hungarians were, for better or for worse, already in the water.

On 19 August, five 'opposition' groups, led by a branch of the Hungarian Democratic Forum from Debrecen in eastern Hungary, decided to organise a picnic on the site of the old Iron Curtain, a 'Pan-European picnic' as they called it, to further encourage their leaders to heal a still divided Europe. They took the precaution of inviting two leading personalities, Imre Pozsgay from Hungary, and Otto von Habsburg, a member of the European Parliament and heir to the defunct Austro-Hungarian throne, to act as sponsors of the event. Both gave it their blessing, and then decided not to actually come in person. For the sometimes radical, sometimes cautious, Pozsgay, it seemed a bridge too far. He saw himself being used as a fig-leaf to cover an otherwise wholly 'oppositional' event. He had so far proved a masterful strategist in judging just what he could get away with. So he stayed at home.

By this point in the summer, East German tourists were queuing up to leave Hungary for the West. They were camped in their thousands in the grounds of the West German embassy in Budapest, on fields beside churches, and in hastily arranged accommodation at the tourist resort at Zánka, beside Lake Balaton. Some saw the posters advertising the picnic, and made their way to Sopronpuszta, in the peaceful meadows just north-east of Sopron.

Lt. Colonel Árpád Bella was in charge of the border-guard that day, just as he had been at the road crossing nearby on 2 May.

At five to three, he was expecting the arrival of the official delegation, which had requested, and received permission, to cross the border, spend an hour or so on the Austrian side, then return to Hungary. The whole event was planned as one of those symbolic 'happenings' which was gradually bridging the divide, a few temporary planks across the moat from the fortress which eastern Europe had traditionally been under communist rule.

'A big group of several hundred people appeared. My first thought was—typical Hungarian bad luck! It must be the official delegation, but their bus has broken down. But as they got closer, I realised they were East Germans, running towards us, bent on crossing the border with Austria, if necessary using force.'

Árpád Bella had about ten seconds to decide what to do. His men were looking at him nervously, waiting for instructions. Under the 1978 review, they were not allowed to actually open fire at those suspected of attempting an illegal crossing, but they were supposed to shout a verbal command to stop, and if that was not obeyed, to shoot, using live ammunition, over the heads of the suspects.

'I knew there would be a huge scandal, of international proportions, if we followed our own rules,' Árpád Bella told me, years later. 'If we had started shooting, anything might have happened . . .'

Instead, he gestured to his men to stay calm, and to stand aside.

Several hundred East Germans ran past them, literally brushing their uniforms—men, women and children. Many wept as they ran, others laughed, some fainted with emotion as they realised they had reached Austrian territory.

Why had he not followed his orders? I asked Bella, on the twentieth anniversary of the picnic.

'If I regarded myself as a soldier, as I did, then I knew it was not my job to use my weapon against women and children, against civilians, young and old. We lived in such a disturbed world then, and I found myself in such a disturbed situation. What I did was the only thing I could do, as a human being.'

As reinforcements arrived, Bella confessed to his 'crime'. Disciplinary action was started against him. 'I knew the East Germans were safe. But I thought my own career was over.'

Only two days later, a tragic event proved to him that it wasn't. Kurt-Werner Schultz, a thirty-five-year-old architect from Weimar, his girlfriend Gundula, and their six-year-old son Johannes were in Hungary, and had already tried and failed to cross the frontier once. Not all the border-guards were as kind as Árpád Bella. They tried again on the night of 21 August, near the town of Köszeg. Once again, two border-guards, aged nineteen and twenty, spotted them. They fired a flare, and warning shots. Gundula and the little Johannes went first, through a hole in the fence, but Kurt was caught. As he wrestled with one of the border-guards, his bag hit the pistol in his hand. It went off, at a range of only ten centimetres, and the bullet hit Kurt in the head, killing him instantly. The border-guard tried to resuscitate him, but in vain. Gundula and Johannes were caught. They were given the option of returning to East Germany, or travelling on to Austria. Two days later, in an act of remorse, the Hungarian border-guards personally drove the two survivors across the border, and handed them over to the Austrian authorities.

'When I saw it had come to this, that we were escorting Germans across, I knew I wouldn't get into too much trouble,' Árpád Bella remembers. Though he has never received written confirmation to this day that the proceedings against him were suspended.

Kurt was the last victim of the Iron Curtain.

'We never regretted the decision to flee, despite what happened,' Johannes said, twenty years later, to the Austrian Kurier newspaper. 'My parents did not want their son to grow up in a system which just imposed restrictions.'

'The death on the border shed light on two facts' wrote the Swiss-Hungarian journalist, Andreas Oplatka. 'Firstly that Hungary, which had won high praise for its humane treatment at the Sopron picnic, was now in danger of being dismissed as a country which opened fire on refugees. Secondly, that it was not fair to expect young soldiers and officers, day in and day out, to resolve such situations by themselves.'

On 11 September, Hungary accepted the fait accompli that it had itself created, and opened the border to whoever wanted to cross, once and for all. East Germany protested in vain.

The dominoes were falling. Hungarian politicians queued to confess their past sins, and pledge their loyalty to a multi-party system.

On 7 October, the Hungarian Socialist Workers' Party, which Kádár had founded and led, dissolved itself at an emergency Congress, and the Hungarian Socialist Party emerged from its ruins. By doing so, it became a pioneer among all the old communist parties of the region, trying to repaint itself in Social-Democratic colours—as if they had always really been there, beneath the red paint.

On 23 October, the anniversary of the outbreak of the 1956 revolution, Hungary was proclaimed a republic. On the same day, police raided the barracks of the Workers' Militia, which had been set up in 1957 to defend the Party's hold on power. No one thought by then that they were preparing a coup, but the new authorities had decided that 60,000 Kalashnikovs, 53,000 pistols and 5,300 machine guns should be in safer hands.

A British diplomat, Jonathan Stoneman, summed up the new situation rather succinctly. 'There is now quite a tailback on the road to Damascus.'

5. The Miracles Continue

> The crowd were chanting 'Gorbi help us! Gorbi help us!' And 'No violence.' For myself, I felt like shouting at the top of my voice. 'What have you up there done with our people?' And I put the question to myself: what can I do for the People, with the People?
>
> Helmut Neubert, Markkleeberg, quoted in the
> Leipziger Volkszeiting, 30/31 December 1989

In the summer of 1989, I drove through Scandinavia, from Norway to Finland and on to Leningrad, and from there back along the Baltic coast to Poland. It was an environmental trip, studying the harm to the fisheries off the Lofoten Islands, the state of the reindeer herds in Lapland and the fragile ecology of the Baltic Sea, threatened above all from the south—from the Soviet empire. Nearly two thirds of the waste reaching the Baltic came from Poland, confessed Professor Wojchiech Dąbrowski. More than a third of the waters of the great Vistula River, which enters the Baltic at Gdańsk, were so bad they were 'beyond classification'.

In the Baltic States, the drive to clean up the environment went hand in hand with the new Popular Front movements to restore sovereignty to countries which had been incorporated in the Soviet Union under the Molotov-Ribbentrop Pact of August 1939, and the invasion of June 1940. There was also common ground, nonetheless, between ecologists. The twenty-three million tonnes of oil-shale burnt each year in the power-stations of Narva, in north-east Estonia, spread sulphurous ash far beyond the boundaries of little Estonia, and harmed the ethnic Russians who had been brought into the region from elsewhere in the USSR just as much as their Estonian neighbours.

'This is a colonial situation. The power is transported away, but the waste remains here,' Toomas Frey, a leader of the Estonian Greens told me.

'A substantial part of the marshlands of Northern Estonia are dying,' said Tamara Ivanova, a Russian ecologist from Estonia. 'In May 1988, the coast was white with dead fish.'

One of the fruits of glasnost in the whole Soviet Union was a new openness about environmental problems, and the emergence of small pressure groups, independent of the state. Ivan Blokov, an activist from Leningrad, reckoned there were thirty groups in Leningrad alone, with up to 5,000 people involved. One of their biggest campaigns was against the construction of a barrage across the mouth of the River Neva, which they said would further harm the environment of a city sinking into the swamp on which its founder, Peter the Great, had built it at such huge human cost.

In Estonia, we drove one afternoon from a meeting with Toomas Frey at the University of Tartu back to Tallinn down a road bordered on both sides with rye fields, specked with blue cornflowers. The sky was spectacular—huge white and black clouds on deep blue, and I realised suddenly where the Estonian flag—these same colours—originated. Swallows mocked my old Swedish car, dive-bombing the windscreen, but never quite colliding, as we drove back towards the coast. On the backseat, two hitch-hikers chattered like sparrows.

'You can say and write anything you want now,' the boy said, 'but nothing else has actually changed. If anything, there is even less in the shops.'

Occasionally outside factories we saw the red flags of the Interfront, a rival organisation to the popular fronts, set up to defend the rights of the 600,000 Russians living in Estonia. The Estonian flag had only been hoisted above the Toompea, the Parliament, in February, on the anniversary of the foundation of the first republic in 1920. The red flag which used to fly there had been relegated to the History Museum, on Pikk Street.

The struggle for independence in Estonia was also taking place in the countryside. There were already 500 private farmers. In the town square in Tartu we saw activists from the Popular Front collecting signatures for independence.

'We, the undersigned, believe that the declaration of 22 July 1940 under which Estonia was incorporated into the Soviet Union was not the free will of the Estonian people. . . . we demand compensation for what we have suffered, and the juridical and political guarantees for the peaceful re-establishment of the Estonian state.'

The same petition was laid out for signatures in the Museum of Local Painters in Tartu. Visitors were invited to sign it as they bought their tickets. 'We've got 200 signatures in four days,' said the elderly lady behind the desk, proudly. But what should she say to the Ukrainians and

Russians who want to sign it? 'Give them a separate sheet,' our guide suggested.

In the fortress, on one of the fat round towers of old Tallinn, a group of blind students pressed their camera into my hand, and asked me to take their photograph. Then carried cheerfully on, on their sight-hearing, sound-smelling tour of the old town, their sticks clicking on the cobbles and their arms tight around each other for safety, laughing uproariously as they went. Only after they had gone did I grasp the enormity of what had just happened.

Estonia was in the grip of what was known as 'the singing revolution'.

People sang in the squares, in the streets, and for all one knew, in their homes, for the restoration of the independence lost since 1940. In November 1988, the Estonian Parliament issued a symbolic declaration of independence. The Russians, immigrants brought in during the past decades to industrialise the country, or officers from the Red Army who had retired to spend their last years enjoying the climate of the Baltic coast, were afraid of becoming second class citizens.

In the basement of an old stone house in the suburbs of Tallinn, I drank honeyed-water with Peeter Liiv of the Estonian Green Movement, in the first wholefood restaurant in Estonia, possibly in the Soviet Union. Peeter was the only Estonian I met who didn't stress the immediate necessity of independence.

'The important changes have to take place inside us, in our spiritual development,' he said.

As the sun set over the cranes and spires and smoke-stacks of Tallinn, the lights on the trawlers anchored off-shore grew brighter. Searching the poor, polluted Baltic for the last few herring.

As I travelled on, through Latvia and Lithuania, it was a similar story.

Ecologists, united in their struggle for a cleaner world, agonised over the political forms under which it might be established.

'Independence is a pre-condition for cooperation, sovereignty is the basis of everything,' Anda Anspoka of the Latvian Green Movement argued in the kitchen of her pale wooden house, close to the amber-lined, fir-treed shore. 'Please don't leave, or at least, not for another ten years,' pleaded her friend, Jelena from the Leningrad Greens. 'The Baltic States have the living memory of democracy, and democratic institutions, which most parts of the Soviet Union never had.'

*   *   *

In 1989, Poland led the way for the rest of eastern Europe to follow, only to be overtaken in the autumn, like a long-distance runner who has led the race for so long that he almost forgets there are other competitors.

Hardliners in Prague, Berlin and Bucharest began looking over Gorbachev's shoulder, towards those in the Soviet Party who might protect them. Igor Ligachov, the number two, seemed to be the man. Throughout the summer and early autumn of 1989, the hardliners across eastern Europe hoped for a coup which would topple Gorbachev.

In August 1989, the Czech protesters who had been beaten and arrested in January gathered again, with the same result. There was no softening of the white batons. But the exodus of East Germans through Hungary was fatally undermining the self-confidence and the grip on power of the East German Party.

'It has been said that the people have betrayed the trust the Party placed in them,' wrote the East German playwright, Bertold Brecht, in 1953 in his poem *Stalinallee*. 'Perhaps the Party should dismiss the people, and elect a new one.'

In May 1989, local elections were held in East Germany, in which voters were given the chance to choose just one candidate on the list. As a democratic exercise, it was as hollow as the country's name, the 'German Democratic Republic.'

In October, the leadership of the communists, known in East Germany as the Socialist Unity Party (SED), awaited Mikhail Gorbachev's visit for the celebrations of the fortieth anniversary of their state. And they waited with some trepidation.

Leipzig, like all big cities in the country, had been badly hit by the exodus of workers to the West, via Hungary. The exodus from the East by people who saw no hope of reform in their own country was to prove instrumental in the collapse of the old regime at home. Soon those who fled would be thinking of coming back.

As in Poland, the church served as a focal point for those who stayed behind. One sixth of the population of Leipzig had left in the past five years, initially at least for other parts of the GDR. The Protestant church in cities like Leipzig provided an umbrella of limited safety for young German pacifists. Like the Dialógus group I had first travelled to Hungary to meet, young East Germans were looking for ways to oppose both nuclear weapons, and the destruction of their environment.

East German factory chimneys pumped five million tonnes of sulphur dioxide into the atmosphere each year. To visit the country, especially in winter, was to travel through a black and white world, with all the sharp outlines, the shades of grey, to which colour usually blinds the traveller. One of my strongest images from that autumn was of the clotheslines of East Germany—white bed linen, white underwear big enough to fit a whole family, billowing like angels in a stiff breeze in an otherwise dark world. I had no camera with me, but sought out clotheslines wherever I went. They still dominate the mental photo album called 'East Germany'.

Pollution from the lignite mines in the Leipzig and Lausitz regions was especially bad. The two-stroke engines of East German cars like Trabants and Wartburgs made the situation even worse in the cities. One of the main demands of church groups was to publish complete data on the true extent of air pollution, and its impact on human health.

East Germans had paid a high price to become the most 'successful' industrial state in eastern Europe, the 'powerhouse' of the East. Fifty million tonnes of chemical fertiliser a year were spread on the fields, to keep them lining the shelves of East German shops. The country's leadership prided itself on the sheer quantity of goods, compared to the shortages of Poland, Romania and even, sometimes, Hungary.

Much of the fertiliser poured into the river system, and eventually into the mighty Elbe. By the time it reached Dresden, according to the young environmentalists, the Elbe contained twenty substances only available on prescription.

In Leipzig, young environmentalists and pacifists worked from the shelter of the church of St Nicholas, one of the oldest in the city, where they had outspoken champions in the pastors Christian Führer and Christoph Wonneberger. Since 1982, prayers for peace had been held in the church, in emulation of the massive anti-nuclear protests in West Germany.

'The only chance we had to discuss and reflect on this burning issue was at meetings held within churches,' wrote Führer. 'It was a young congregation in the eastern part of Leipzig which decided to hold these peace prayer services week after week, resulting in the regularly scheduled Monday evening services. Later the responsibility for conducting the peace prayer services was transferred by peace groups comprised of former "Bausoldaten" (people who rendered their compulsory military service by serving in special, unarmed units), environmental activists and people interested in third world issues. Together they sought to stir the public's conscience and encourage action.'

The interior of the church was a dazzling white. Lit mainly by candle-light, there was a strange vibrancy, an excitement in the air; many of those present would not have described themselves as religious at all. There was a sense of the church as the flagship of the protest, in the grey ocean of the German Democratic Republic, which drew them there. As the momentum of change built up through eastern Europe, the church groups grew too, both in size and in confidence. By the summer of 1989, the sense of claustrophobia in the country was enormous, even compared to other east bloc states. At the 'Our Common Baltic Sea' conference I attended in Kotka, on the Finnish shore east of Helsinki, in July, only the East German environmental activists were refused permission by their authorities to attend. The conference was full of Russians, Poles, Estonians, Latvians, Lithuanians and others.

On 18 September the authorities in Leipzig finally lost patience with the church-sponsored group. Uniformed and plain clothes police-men broke up a meeting, arrested around a hundred participants and packed them into military trucks. A crowd gathered outside the church and tried to stop them driving away. The drivers panicked, and drove straight into the crowd, badly injuring several people. A large protest demonstration was called for Monday 2 October—just days before Mikhail Gorbachev was due to arrive in East Berlin for the official celebrations on 7 October.

On 2 October, 20,000 people gathered outside St Nicholas' church for what turned into the biggest demonstration in East Germany since 1953.

From the church, the demonstrators marched to Karl Marx Square, chanting 'Gorbi, Gorbi' in emulation of the crowds in Prague. As the riot police intervened with water cannons and tear gas, some protesters took refuge in the church of St Thomas, where Johann Sebastian Bach is buried.

The next day the crowd returned. For three consecutive nights, similar scenes were repeated on the streets of Leipzig. Václav Havel's wry, central European humour spread here as well. 'A revolution is of no value, unless it is able to defend itself—V.I. Lenin,' someone painted on the walls of the secret police headquarters. And the people, with their sheer numbers, were now doing just that.

On 7 October, Mikhail and Raisa Gorbachev's plane touched down on the runway at Schonefeld airport in East Berlin. From the start, their visit was censored by the East German press—no footage of their arrival was shown on state television, in a clear break with tradition.

'I think that dangers only exist for those who don't grasp the situation, who don't react to life,' Gorbachev said, in public. In private, he urged Erich Honecker, now seventy-five, to step down.

That evening in Leipzig, the riot police blocked Nikolaistrasse (St. Nicholas Street) in front of the church for the fifth night in a row, but they also began fraternising with the crowd. Moments later, the order to clear the street was given, and obeyed with the customary brutality. Police hearts were, however, beginning to soften. The sheer persistence of the people on the streets was winning them over.

'On Monday 9 October, we were supposed to crush the demonstration, once and for all,' Jörg Schlegel, a member of a special police commando unit remembered.

'A stone fell from my heart when I saw 100,000 people marching towards us, among them, my own fiancée. 'Wir sind das Volk' they chanted, 'We are the people'.'

Police units had been issued with live ammunition. Extra beds had been made available in the hospitals. Blood and drug supplies had arrived from Berlin. 'Fortunately, the order to attack them never came. I will never forget that day,' said Schlegel.

'The prayers for peace ended with the bishop's blessing and the urgent call for non-violence,' wrote Christian Führer. 'More than 2,000 people leaving the church were welcomed by tens of thousands waiting outside with candles in their hands—an unforgettable moment. Two hands are necessary to carry a candle and to protect it from extinguishing so that you can not carry stones or clubs at the same time. The miracle occurred. Jesus' spirit of non-violence seized the masses and became a material, peaceful power. 'Troops, military brigade groups and the police were drawn in, became engaged in conversations and then withdrew. It was an evening in the spirit of our Lord Jesus for there were no winners and no defeated, nobody triumphed over the other, nobody lost face. There was just a tremendous feeling of relief . . .' the vicar said, describing the events many years later.

'I stood there on the street, trembling, tears pouring down my face,' another man told the local newspaper, when it was all over.

'The crowd were chanting 'Gorbi help us! Gorbi help us!' And 'No violence.' For myself, I felt like shouting at the top of my voice. 'What have you up there done with our people?' And I put the question to myself: what can I do for the People, with the People?'

Prominent local people, including party officials, came over to the side of the people. Kurt Masur, the well-known conductor of the Gewandhaus orchestra, spoke alongside SED officials on a stage set up by the demonstrators, and called for 'basic changes'. Events in Leipzig began to spread to the capital, and elsewhere in the country.

'We had planned for every eventuality,' Horst Sindermann, a member of the Central Committee of the East German Communist Party would say in an interview before his death, 'but we were not prepared for candles and prayers.'

In Berlin, rock and jazz musicians organised a concert against violence. The Writers' Union called for revolutionary reforms. For the message to spread, the media had to carry it, and a part of the media now began to do just that. Meanwhile in Leipzig, the organisers of the daily demonstrations agreed to focus on one main day a week to concentrate their strength: the same day that it had all started, a Monday.

The rally in Leipzig on Monday 16 October, the Monday demonstration, in which 100,000 people took part, was mentioned for the first time in the state media.

Erich Honecker, the Party leader, in ill-health even before the excitements of the autumn, resigned on 18 October. He was replaced by the youngest member of the Politburo, Egon Krenz.

Krenz promised change, but no change in the 'leading role' of the Party, something which communists in Hungary and Poland had already abandoned. In the eyes of the East German street, his position was already undermined by his support for the crushing of the protests in Tiananmen Square in June. On his first day in office, 2,000 East Germans left the country for the West.

'There is a time for every season under heaven,' the pastor preached, in St Nicholas' church in Leipzig. And this was the season of protest, he told them, in one sermon I attended. He called for the restoration of democracy, and the re-unification of Germany. By now I was growing used to clapping in church.

On the streets and in the corridors of power, the ferment continued. On 7 November the government resigned, and on the 8th, the entire Politburo. That day, up to a million people gathered on Alexanderplatz in East Berlin to demand far-reaching change.

By then, 225,000 East Germans had left, mostly through Hungary, but a smaller number across the Czechoslovak-West German border, which was also softening by the day. Most were from the most physically active part of the population, workers which the East German industrial machine could little afford to lose.

Unable to stem the tide to the West, the East German leadership decided it was time to prove it was not immune to the times. Gunther Schabowski, head of the SED in East Berlin, made the stunning announcement on 8 November. From the next day, the entire border with West Germany would be open for people to leave, or come back.

Few people went home that evening. They stayed on the streets, celebrating and waiting for a moment few had ever thought would come in their lifetimes. Schabowski had not mentioned the exact time the borders would open, so people took it to mean at one second past midnight. Drinking champagne and dancing in the streets, the crowds began chanting *Tor auf! Tor Auf!*—Open the Gate!

And at midnight, the gate came down. There seemed little point in waiting for morning. East Berlin invaded West Berlin, and East Germany invaded West Germany, not with guns, but with laughter.

Children sat on their parents' shoulders with little signs, 'Welcome to West Berlin . . .'

'My most vivid recollection is of going into a car showroom near the Ku'Damm, a famous shopping street in West Berlin, and seeing the astonished look on the faces of East Berliners sitting behind the wheels of glittering new red BMW convertibles. The joy on their faces was matched by that on the faces of the showroom assistants. They laughed, they pinched themselves. And on the lips of everyone there was just one word: Wahnsinn —Madness!' wrote the British reporter, Adrian Bridge.

'East Berliners were joined by scores of fellow East Germans swarming into the western part of the city that day, anxious to catch it just in case somebody said it had all been a misunderstanding and the Wall would be going back up. But deep down we all knew it was too late for that. At the Wall itself the Mauerspecte (Wallpeckers) armed with their hammers and chisels had already begun complementing the work of the bulldozers being sent in to remove the slabs one by one' wrote Adrian.

Days later in Berlin, now a miraculously re-united city, I met an East German film director, searching in vain for models. He explained, with hardly a trace of humour, that it was now impossible to find East German girls willing to undress on camera. 'They've all gone to the West, where they will be paid more,' he lamented.

'What the hell, let's have a drink anyway.' I felt sorry for him, so accepted his invitation. We drank champagne in the first bar we found, for no better reason than it was the main drink on offer.

In the street near the Brandenburg Gate I met a man who had last visited West Berlin as a child holding his father's hand, and had just been for a walk on 'the other side' for the first time. He seemed moonstruck. Noticing a small package in his hand, I asked what he had bought. 'This, to read to my children,' he said, proudly showing me George Orwell's *Animal Farm* in German. 'So that I can begin to explain to them what it was like to live here, all these years.'

'And this, for myself,' and he beamed as he showed me a packet of Dutch tulip bulbs, to plant in his allotment. Dutch tulips, he was convinced, were going to be much more beautiful than the flowers he had planted up till now.

That evening I watched the Berlin sun sink behind the remains of the Berlin Wall, as leaves swirled in crazy circles around the foot of the Brandenburg Gate. At the end of the day, that was why the Wall had to go, I thought—because it obstructed an old human need to watch the sun slip down, beneath the horizon.

* * *

The collapse of the Wall, the Iron Curtain and the East German Communist Party, left the Czechoslovak leadership dangerously exposed. They could hardly see Ceaușescu's aberrant regime in Romania as a serious ally. And the demonstrations were building on their own streets. The youth of Prague were determined not to be left behind by the tide of history.

'There were so many changes taking place all around us,' said Hana Fialová, a twenty-one-year-old student at Charles University. 'We all sensed that something was going to happen here too. We just didn't know what, or when.'

The seventeenth of November 1989 was a Friday, and the students of Prague had applied for and received permission to hold a rally on the fiftieth anniversary of the death of Jan Opletal, a student killed in a protest against the Nazi annexation of Czechoslovakia in 1939.

From the start of the rally, it was clear that the 20,000 or so students who gathered at Prague's Medical University had contemporary events on their minds. If there was a parallel, it was that communism, like fascism, seemed to belong in the same historical dustbin. Meanwhile Jan Fojtik, the party secretary in charge of ideology, repeated the hardline mantra, 'There can be no dialogue with those who set out to destroy our society.'

As in Leipzig with Johann Sebastian Bach, and Budapest with Zoltán Kodály, classical composers in Prague somehow became entangled in the uprising. At the Vyšehrad Cemetery, on their way to Jan Opletal's grave, the marchers passed the graves of Smetana and Dvořák. According to the permission received by the organisers, the march should have ended there, at about three o'clock.

About 3,000 students set off, back into town, to try to reach Wenceslas Square. In Národni—National—Street, they were stopped in their tracks by a wall of riot police—their sparring partners from the demonstrations in August and January. For two hours, there was a tense stand-off. The crowd clapping loudly, in ironic applause of the police, the clapping echoing off the walls of the Opera and down the arcades of shops on either side of the road. There were attempts to fraternise with the police, and with the police dogs. 'You are the same as us, don't use violence against us,' they chanted.

The students held their arms in the air, as if in surrender. 'We have no weapons,' they shouted. One banner read simply *Milso*—the name of the Party leader, Miloš Jakeš, spelt wrongly. This was a joke on his alleged stupidity—a month earlier, a video-tape of Jakeš addressing the Politburo had circulated on the black market.

'Comrades, yes, this bloke made a mistake, each one of us made a mistake, but whose government is this?' Jakeš says in poor Czech. 'It's a communist government, always was and always will be, and it does not matter who is standing on what positions . . .' The tape became the talk of the town.

The students sat down in the road and started singing anything they could remember. Old hymns, protest songs by banned musicians, even Beatles songs.

The police commanders responded with the more monosyllabic, 'Go home!'—bellowed through loudhailers. As darkness fell, the students lit candles.

Meanwhile, more riot police had come up behind the students. They were now trapped—like the much smaller group three years earlier, on the Chain Bridge in Budapest.

Then a police car drove into the crowd for no apparent reason and people began to panic and run away. The police started laying into them from both sides with their white batons. They would grumble later that they slipped on the wax from the burning candles.

The brutality of the police was unprecedented, even by the standards of previous Prague demonstrations. 'You could literally hear the bones cracking,' said Martin Polách, a student from the Art Academy. Wherever the students ran through the narrow arcades beside Národni Street, the police pursued them.

There were not just riot police, but 'red berets' present too—police special troops, or commandos. Three of them grabbed a young woman by the hair, banged her head against a wall, then continued to kick and beat her as she lay, slumped on the ground. And as they beat her, they laughed.

Pavlina Rousová and Otto Urban, students from the Charles University, took refuge in a courtyard of Mikulandská Street. Then squeezed, with several dozen others, into a friend's apartment. The terrified students, many bleeding from their injuries, kept the lights turned off and hardly dared breathe. From close by, they heard the bellowing of the riot police, 'Hands up, you whore!', and then the screaming of a female student.

Later that night, they slipped home, in ones and twos through the deserted streets, a defeated rabble.

'Police were called in to preserve order in the city centre' ran the short account in the following morning's edition of Rudé Právo, the Party paper. 'They checked the identity of the demonstrators, and about 100 were detained.' And that was all the start of the revolution got.

The next day, a Saturday, it seemed that the whole of Prague was talking about the protest. Such had been the violence of the police that people began to call the events 'a massacre'. Wild rumours circulated about at least one death. And the 'dead' student was soon given a name— Martin Schmid. Police had allegedly told his girlfriend, Drahomira, that they had 'finished him off' when she begged them to tell him where he was after they had dragged him away.

News of the 'death' was handed out liberally by Petr Uhl, an activist from Charter 77, who specialised in contacts with the foreign press. Soon both Radio Free Europe and Voice of America were reporting a death. That, and the free use of the word 'massacre', brought the people back onto the streets. Anyone who had witnessed the degree of police brutality would have found it hard to believe that some demonstrators had not been killed.

Flowers were laid and candles lit all the way along Národni Street, in the places where the students had been beaten. To the amazement of passers-by, two young Soviet soldiers were spotted, lighting their own candles at one spot.

Over the following days, layer after layer of coloured wax piled up at these makeshift shrines. The underground printing presses of the city went into overdrive, producing leaflets, demanding an independent enquiry into the police action and resignations.

The secret police, the StB, began work to discount the rumours, and tracked down no less than two Martin Schmids, both in the bloom of health. One had taken part in the protest, but had escaped without injury. The other had nothing to do with it. In the meantime, with all the traditional clumsiness of the state bureaucracy, they arrested all the people with any apparent connection to the case, including Petr Uhl, Martin's girlfriend Drahomira, and other spokesmen of Charter 77.

On Saturday, the students regrouped, and declared that they were going on strike. The actors of the National Theatre held a meeting in solidarity, and announced that they were joining them. Other theatres did the same. The Film and Theatre Faculty of the university set up a production line of darkrooms, just as individual photographers had done in 1968. A5-size, black and white prints of the protest and of the police violence on 17 November were produced first in their thousands, then in their tens of thousands. With no access to official media, the only way available to the students of getting the news out about what had happened in Prague was to take it out themselves.

In groups of two or three, hundreds now set out for provincial towns and cities, carrying hastily printed leaflets and the precious photographs —the proof of the uprising. Many who studied in Prague went to their home towns and villages, where people might know them and trust their word. On the Saturday afternoon, two female students from the Faculty of Journalism even went to the home of Prime Minister, Ladislav Adamec, a relatively mild figure by the standards of the current Communist Party leadership. He had been told by telephone that the police intervention had been 'mild', he informed them. He then listened sympathetically as the students disabused him of that notion.

'Whose fault is the crisis in the country?' the students asked him, bravely.

'Ours,' he confessed, after some hesitation.

On Sunday, Václav Havel, who had been released from prison during the summer, sat down with his friends from Charter 77 and student representatives at the Magic Lantern Theatre, and founded the Civic

Forum, 'On behalf of that part of the Czechoslovak public which is increasingly critical of the present Czechoslovak leadership, and which in recent days has been profoundly shaken by the brutal massacre of peacefully protesting students.' The declaration demanded the immediate resignation of the Party First Secretary, Miloš Jakeš, the Interior Minister and other communist leaders, and the setting up of a Commission of Inquiry into the police action on 17 November.

On Monday night, 20 November, 200,000 people took to the streets. This was the moment, perhaps, when the revolution became unstoppable. The state media began to report the protests, as journalists and their editors shook off a long tradition of censorship. The same day, smaller demonstrations took place in the Slovak capital Bratislava, in Brno, the capital of Moravia and other cities. In the northern town of Teplice, an already scheduled protest against air pollution from the brown coal strip-mines and local power stations, turned into an anti-regime protest as well.

Like in East Germany, Hungary and Poland, once the crowds began to formulate their anger, the appalling state of the natural environment was high on their agenda. The crowds demanded the release of health statistics, and an end to the wanton destruction of the environment.

To participate in the demonstrations was to experience the sheer creativity of a crowd, the essence of a revolutionary situation. There was a pun on the name 'Jakeš'—which means 'gander' in Czech. Anything that rhymed was repeated with delight. At first by groups of two or three seconds later and then, for the best examples, by thousands, then tens of thousands. Some were written on boards for future occasions. It was like an outburst of popular poetry. Pasted on shop windows, on hoardings, anywhere where glue would stick and people might pause to read, the papers multiplied.

One popular one was called 'The Eight Rules of Dialogue', which underlined the non-violent nature of the movement, and the sense of the street as a kind of university of democracy. I reproduce it in full.

1. Your opponent is not your enemy, but your partner in the search for Truth. We are not engaged in an intellectual competition, but in the search for the Truth. To take part in dialogue, there are three pre-conditions: respect for the Truth, for the other, and for oneself.
2. Try to grasp what the other is saying. If you cannot understand their point of view, you can neither accept nor reject his

statements. Repeat his statements yourself, to make clear that you have understood them.

3. Statements for which no proof is offered are not valid as arguments.

4. Do not stray from the point. Do not try to dodge uncomfortable questions or arguments by steering the discussion in another direction.

5. Don't fight to always have the last word. A great flood of words will never replace a missing line of argument. If you reduce your opponent to silence it neither means that you have defeated his point of view, nor succeeded in changing it.

6. Never devalue the worth of your opponent. Whoever attacks the personality of his opponent loses the right to participate in dialogue.

7. Never forget that dialogue demands discipline. We should formulate our thoughts and conclusions in a reasonable, not an emotional way. Whoever is incapable of controlling his feelings and passions cannot conduct a thoughtful conversation with another person.

8. Do not confuse a dialogue with a monologue. Everyone has the same right to express their opinions. Don't lose yourself in irrelevant details. Prove your respect for others by using the time economically.

Václav Havel proved a master tactician. As overtures reached him from a Party leadership in obvious and increasing panic, he relayed them to the crowd from his balcony overlooking the river, or from the balcony of a newspaper overlooking Wenceslas Square.

Aware of the tricks of the authorities, he turned down the offer of a visa to Sweden to receive the alternative Nobel Peace prize, awarded to him months earlier, while he was still in prison.

A crucial moment was the arrival of a message from the coal miners of North Bohemia, declaring their willingness to strike in solidarity with the students.

On Monday 20 November, the biggest roar of approval at the demonstration was awarded to a delegation from the ČKD locomotive factory, arriving to join the protest. But the number of workers participating was small at first.

To succeed, the crowd knew it would need the workers on its side, but the workers, used to the comforts of a regime which provided them with better conditions and food than many in the population enjoyed, hesitated to lay down their tools.

The posters and fliers multiplied, in Prague and other cities. Communist Party activists and secret policemen initially tried to tear them down, but were soon overwhelmed by the sheer numbers, and the speed at which more were printed.

'End the One Party System! End the Communist Party monopoly of Power! The Civic Forum opposes all forms of violence!'

Appeals were printed to the citizens, and especially the students of other countries.

'Our country is in deep moral, spiritual, ecological, social and political crisis,' the Programme of the Civic Forum, began. Events were moving so fast that each proclamation was given not only a date, but a time of day.

At six o'clock on 26 November, the day of the general strike, the Party leadership and government were given a deadline by the Civic Forum: resign by 3 December.

'The political monopoly of appointments to all important positions maintained by the Communist Party has given rise to a system based on injustice and subservience which paralyses our entire society,' the proclamation continued. Fundamental changes were needed in the law, the political system, foreign policy, social justice, the environment, national economy and culture. On the same day, 26 November, the names of 500 factories which had joined the uprising and sent representatives were read out to deafening applause.

The protests gathered momentum each day, despite a freezing fog settling on the city—a regular feature of Prague's polluted winters. The coughing at the demonstrations was sometimes almost as loud as the applause. The illness was even given a revolutionary title—'liberation flu'.

Václav Havel's voice became more and more hoarse at demonstrations.

As the crowd chanted his name, beside that of Alexander Dubček, the leader of the 1968 Prague Spring, the two men embraced clumsily on the balcony overlooking Wenceslas Square. In archive film of the moment, they appear to be dancing. In fact, they are jumping up and down, to keep warm.

When people could barely speak anymore because of the pain in their throats, they rattled their keys—a gesture to the Communist Party authorities that it was time to leave the palaces of power.

There were now several 'engines' to the unrest. One was the demand for a full enquiry into the events of 17 November. Another was the demand for the resignation of top officials. A third rapidly became the increasingly well-articulated demands of the Civic Form, which gave shape and focus to what would otherwise have been an amorphous and potentially confused mass of people.

At one point, the secret services changed tactics, and instead of trying to tear down the posters and leaflets covering every wall and window, they began putting up posters of their own, calling for violence.

The Eight Rules of Dialogue helped make sure that had little effect.

Struggle for control of the mass media became another important battlefield. At the state television, 4,900 staff voted to cover the demonstrations and to broadcast footage of the 17 November protest, with 300 against. On 23 November, the secret police moved in, sacking the top staff and imposing their own stooges.

Then footballers came out on strike in support of the students, and all matches in the national league the following Saturday were cancelled.

The senior command of the army issued a statement in support of the government.

'We reject the anarchy which is spread by external and internal anti-socialist forces,' read their statement. But at the daily demonstrations, soldiers in uniform cheering with the rest of the crowd, and carried on their shoulders, were increasingly visible. There were reports of riot police units refusing to obey orders. Two student got into the riot police barracks and interviewed some of those responsible for the violence on 17 November.

'There are parts of the body we shouldn't hit,' said one 'but then something happens and, without you intending it, you hit his head.'

The Church, too, began to get involved, as in East Germany and Poland, and even in Hungary. On 21 November, the elderly Cardinal Tomášek told the crowd, 'We are with you.' Most important of all, with the airwaves still partly controlled by the state, he mentioned the situation in a televised mass, being held to celebrate the canonisation of Saint Anna of Bohemia.

'In this historic moment in the fight for truth and justice,' the ninety-year-old Cardinal said, 'I and the Catholic Church are on the side of the people.' Large numbers of church-goers walked down the hill from St Vitus' cathedral to join the protests.

In the wake of the Civic Forum, all kinds of other civic initiatives sprang up like mushrooms in the damp, freezing, polluted Prague autumn.

An advice bureau for citizens, a sort of Czech equivalent of Citizens' Advice Bureaux in Britain, but entirely spontaneous, was set up in central Prague by students from the Psychology Faculty. One of their first visitors was a man who claimed that 'the Central Committee of the Communist Party has planted a controlling device in my brain'. The Party frequently took control of him, and he had no power to resist, he explained. He asked the students to remove the device.

One morning I went with Hana Fialová and Mirek Boháč to the State library, where 960,000 books were currently banned, we were told, and had been shipped out, box load by box load since 1968, to a small town 30km from Prague. The librarian told us he was ashamed about the restrictions his library had suffered, and offered to get us any book we wanted within twenty-four hours.

Each evening the National Opera just off Národni Street played host to the revolution. There were songs and speeches. Many concerned historic injustices.

A friend of Jan Palach described his last trip to the capital, and the death mask which was made in his honour. He finished his account with the words. 'It's hard to say how we felt. We just didn't know what to do. The event was too big for us.'

Many speeches dealt with what to do next. There was a touching jumble of local and national issues. The students, among other things, wanted the right to choose fewer subjects at school.

Each time the authorities appeared to satisfy one demand, the revolution asked for more. Miloš Jakeš and the entire Politburo resigned on 24 November—only a week after the 'massacre' of students. Not enough, thundered the crowd, and the general strike went ahead two days later.

As the days passed, the number of workers joining the demonstrations grew, turning what began as a protest of students and intellectuals into a movement which the Party, claiming to represent the working people, could no longer resist.

The new government, announced on 3 December, looked much like the previous one. Only five of the twenty ministers were non-communists. The next day 300,000 people gathered on Wenceslas Square, and the new government resigned as well.

On 6 December, Saint Nicholas' day, children who had behaved well during the year were traditionally given sugar lumps in Czechoslovakia, while naughty children received lumps of coal. Early that morning, a small group of students wheeled a barrow-load of coal through the streets of the city, and tipped its contents unceremoniously onto the steps of Party headquarters.

There were also bizarre, even frightening moments. As I came out of the Hotel Alcron, just off Wenceslas Square, in broad daylight, a rock crashed onto the pavement just in front of me, passing so close I felt its wind on my face. If it had landed on my head, I doubt I would have lived. I was on my way to send the translation of several days' work—eye witness accounts of the exact events of 17 November, as published in the newspaper Mladý Svět—Young World —to the Observer foreign desk in London. Was someone trying to kill me?

I woke at four in the morning to hear somebody trying to get into my room at the Hotel Europa, a crumbling beauty of a building, half-way down Wenceslas Square. Then couldn't get back to sleep because of the intensity of love-making in the next room. In the common toilet at the end of the corridor—I had taken one of the cheaper rooms—I found hundreds of bank-notes, torn to shreds in the bowl.

In the opera one night, I listened spellbound with Hana and Mirek, as the orchestra played Beethoven's *Spring Sonata*. 'It is a sonata for lovers,' Hana explained. 'Because we are all in love with the students.'

Mirek recounted how an elderly lady had arrived at the Faculty of Arts as he sat in the canteen one morning, and handed him 500 crowns. She had just bought a second hand coat for herself, she said, saving herself a lot of money compared to buying it new. She wanted to give the difference to the students.

On the streets, hot food arrived at the demonstrations, provided free by some of the hotels of the city. Everywhere we went there was hot red spiced wine. That was the fuel of the revolution.

On 10 December, a new government was finally formed with a majority of non-communists. The Foreign Minister was Jiří Dienstbier, an old friend of Václav Havel and central figure in Charter 77. The new Interior Minister was the Slovak, Ján Carnogurský. Only ten days earlier, he had been in prison in Bratislava, awaiting trial on charges of sedition.

Czechoslovakia and East Germany were in a sense 'classical' revolutions, in which the street overthrows the power of the state.

Hungary was a much more controlled affair, inspired by the ferment below, but settled in the corridors of power. Poland was somewhere in-between, based on the power of Solidarity in the work-place and in the squares, but decided at the round-table, and the ballot box. But the fiercest and bloodiest revolution of all was to follow, in Romania.

6. Romania—the pudding which exploded

'Why don't we go and demonstrate too?' Lorin's thirteen-year-old
daughter asked.
  'If something happened to us, who would look after you?' he
replied.
  'Don't the people who are on the streets now have children too?'
she asked.

Lorin Fortuna, Timişoara

And imagine, a Gypsy brought us our food on the barricades! A Gypsy!

Harald Binder, Sibiu

I heard the news of the uprising in the western Romanian city of
Timişoara on my radio, lying in bed in East Berlin. On Christmas Day,
the BBC asked me to go to Romania the next day. Nicolae Ceauşescu
had just been executed.

On Boxing Day, 26 December 1989, I sat in front of a television set
in the Intercontinental Hotel in Budapest. It was snowing outside, and
minus 5°C. Only George Fodor and I were in the room. George was a
soft-spoken Transylvanian-Hungarian-Romanian-Jewish-English friend
who sometimes reshuffled the order of his identity, but had the sharpest
eye for the nuances of east European politics. While another BBC team
was covering events in the capital, Bucharest, we were due to tour
Transylvania, birthplace of the revolution.

We were watching a poorly filmed, bootleg video of Pastor László
Tökés, a Hungarian priest from Timişoara, whose defiance had sparked
the uprising.

The film had been smuggled out of Romania and showed him
preaching from the pulpit in his church. His deep, Biblical voice passed
right through us.

'He speaks like God,' George whispered.

Crossing the Hungarian-Romanian border the next day in our
convoy of hired vehicles, the Romanian border-guard grinned when he

looked up from my passport. 'Planning to visit Braşov, Mr Thorpe?' he asked.

Definitely! All the flags at the border-crossing had a hole cut in the centre—where the communist emblem used to be. 'Welcome to Romania!'

It was nice to know the old police records still existed. They might be useful one day, I thought, to jog my memory.

Another border-guard offered us a drink from a bottle of plum brandy, the only antidote to the bitter cold. We swigged from it and then passed it around our small group of journalists, border-guards and policemen. This was turning into one of my weirdest border-crossings ever.

Suitably warmed, we shook hands and said our goodbyes. I had only learnt to drive a few months before, and this was my first experience of driving in snow. The rented Volvo skidded on the pot-holed, icy road, then recovered.

People lined the roadside in each town and village with wonder in their eyes, poor clothes on their backs and frozen mud and snow beneath their feet, waving and shouting 'Libertate! 'Freedom!' and giving the V-for-victory sign. The Romanian flag with the middle cut out was everywhere. It was like Hungary must have been, during the heady days of October 1956.

Our convoy of three cars swept down tree-lined avenues between snow-covered fields. Sometimes a horse and cart passed, loaded with fire-wood. In one place, sheep sheltered beneath a roadside tree, their shaggy coats yellow against the snow. In each town and village, people came out to cheer, as though it was our revolution, not theirs. At least twice, we were stopped at rough barricades across main roads by bearded, heavily armed men determined to either shoot us, or drink with us. Our explanations rapidly accepted, we settled for the second option each time. It would have been rude, and extremely unrevolutionary, to refuse.

A few hours later, we were in Timişoara, birthplace of the Romanian revolution.

I had heard of Pastor Tőkés before. The previous September, the Hungarian television news programme Panoráma had broadcast a forty-five minute film about him.

At thirty-seven he already had the reputation among the Romanian authorities as a 'troublesome priest' for the power of his sermons, and his uncompromising attitude to human rights in general, in particularly the rights of the minority Hungarians in Transylvania. He had been placed in Timişoara the previous year, as assistant to another priest who was notoriously subservient to the Ceauşescu regime who could be certain to keep an eagle eye on him. To the dismay of the authorities, the other priest had died from overwork, after refusing to allow Tökés to take any of it on.

Pastor Tökés found himself with a parish all of his own, and a church to set about reviving after the lost years of the previous priest's tenure. He set about the work with a vengeance, and rapidly earned a series of reprimands.

On 4 September, his bishop, a lackey of the regime, suspended him from his post and ordered him and his family out of their flat within ten days. He refused to go, and throughout the autumn of 1989, he expected to be forcefully evicted from his small vicarage with Edit, his wife, who was heavily pregnant, and their three-year-old son.

The Securitate threatened his life, and that of his family. Human rights groups in Hungary expressed concerns for his safety. Several other 'troublesome priests' with ethnic Hungarian backgrounds, Imre Tempfli, Géza Pálfy and Ernő Újvárosi, had been killed or died in detention.

The only question seemed to be when the Securitate would make their move against him.

The turmoil in the rest of eastern Europe—the collapse of one communist regime after another—seemed to be having no effect, on the surface at least, on the survival of the Ceauşescu dynasty in Romania. Tökés was finally informed, politely but firmly, that he was to be evicted from his home on Friday 15 December. The windows of his first floor apartment had been broken by the Securitate weeks before and were now boarded up.

'Dear Brothers and Sisters in Christ,' he had begun his sermon the previous Sunday, 'I have been issued with a summons of eviction. I will not accept it, so I will be taken from you by force next Friday. Please come and be witnesses of what will happen. Come, be peaceful, but be witnesses.'

The sense of the importance of witnessing a crime, an aberration, the lack of a basic right, was felt very strongly among the dissidents of eastern Europe. The samizdat or underground press in Czechoslovakia and Hungary were renowned for their criticism of their own regimes but, on another level, they were simply witnesses, the corpse at the bottom of the pile, feigning death to miraculously survive to tell the tale.

Tökés knew it was quite possible that he would be killed. If not that day, then another. Like Jan Palach, who took his own life in January 1969, he wanted his story to be told.

When he pulled aside one of the boards to let some fresh air into his room on the morning of 15 December, László Tökés discovered several dozen parishioners already waiting outside in the cold. He could also see plain-clothes men he did not recognise, obviously Securitate, loitering on the edge of the crowd.

'We are safe, no one has tried to evict us . . . perhaps you should all go home,' he told the crowd.

But they refused, and through the day the crowds outside his window grew and grew. In the early afternoon, the Securitate drove away a car they had parked outside so that officers watching Tökés could keep warm. The crowd welcomed it as their first, minor victory.

As the day wore on, the number of Romanians in the crowd soon outnumbered the ethnic Hungarian members of his congregation. At first, the Hungarians assumed that these were agent provocateurs—preparing an incident to give the militia a chance to move in and break up what was rapidly taking on the characteristics of an anti-government demonstration.

Every half an hour, Tökés would appear at the window, and try to persuade the crowd to go home. He was getting increasingly worried about his pregnant wife, Edit, and their unborn child. Their first child was away, staying with relatives. Neither of them had been able to sleep properly for days, and now he worried that the strain would be too much for her.

But the crowd would not listen to his pleas. Even when the mayor arrived, pushed his way through and persuaded Tökés to appear with him once more at the window. The mayor even promised that the broken windows would be repaired, if everyone would just go home, and that his wife would be allowed to see a doctor—something she had been denied for weeks. It was no use, the crowd would not budge.

'Don't believe him, he's a liar!' they shouted. 'A lying communist!'

And as the evening lengthened, the crowd chanted Tökés' name incessantly.

When Tökés looked out now, the street was full of candles which stretched in both directions, as far as he could see. Below him was a sea of faces of his fellow Hungarians and Romanians. Unable to influence the crowd any more, he and his wife sat down to eat the last of the food they had in the house with a few friends.

The next day the mayor, true to his promise, arrived with workmen to fix the windows. Then with not just one doctor, but a team of them.

After examining Edit, they said she should be moved to hospital immediately.

Tökés, suspecting a trick to divide them, refused. Their own doctor had managed to get in to see her just before, and told her that all she needed was rest.

'There is no need whatsoever for Mrs Tökés to be moved,' he defied the 'official' doctors. 'It would be most harmful for her.' The mayor was furious but, for the time being, powerless.

The day developed in much the same way as the previous one. The mayor promised to bring back a document cancelling the eviction order. And then failed to deliver. By nightfall on Saturday 16 December, the crowd stretched all the way from Tökés' house to the Opera Square and the steps of the Orthodox Cathedral, in the centre of Timişoara.

Sometimes the crowd chanted Tökés' name. Sometimes they sang the banned anthem, 'Awake, Romanian', which had been sung in Braşov in November 1987.

Then at about seven o'clock on the Saturday evening, a young man jumped up onto one of the trams which was stuck in the midst of the crowd at the far end of the street.

'I am Mihai Zaganescu!' he shouted. 'And I am not afraid of the Securitate any more! All people ... shout with me: "Down with Ceauşescu!" "Free Romania!" "Now or Never!" "We want the Truth!" "Timişoara!"' And like the conductor of an orchestra, he chanted with the crowd, teaching them their lines.

Now the crowd finally did start leaving the street in front of Tökés' house, but they did not head as either he, nor the authorities had imagined, to the safety of their own homes. They marched on the Party headquarters, tearing down the Party emblem from the front. They then began smashing the windows, and forced their way inside.

At nine o'clock, the shock police arrived and charged the protesters. A fire engine, used by the police to spray water into the crowd, was taken over by the demonstrators and used against the militia, who retreated, briefly. The demonstrators, swollen by now to about 30,000 by the arrival of students from the university, regrouped, but so did the security forces. Now the ominous rumble of tanks and armoured vehicles could be heard on the old cobbles of the medieval town. And the shooting started.

At three in the morning, the street outside his flat now empty, the Securitate came for Tökés. He and his wife and those still in the flat managed to get into the church upstairs, and barricaded themselves inside, but the militia soon broke down the doors.

Standing by the altar, a uniformed security officer Tökés knew, known as Veverka, came up to the priest and punched him hard, first in the stomach, then in the face. He was dragged to his own office, beaten all the way. Out of the corner of his eye, he saw his wife being roughly taken away, and his closest friends being kicked and beaten.

First of all, he was taken to Securitate headquarters.

'The scene was like an old engraving of the gates of Hell,' he would write, later. 'Or a scene from Gestapo headquarters in a war film.'

'Cars roared in and out at great speed, and soldiers were running in all directions at the command of officers who appeared from the main building shouting orders ... People were standing in isolated groups; some were weeping. At the front of the building, partly covered, was a row of dead bodies. There were dead bodies everywhere.'

It was the nightmare scenario which everyone in eastern Europe—in Poland, the Baltic States, Hungary, Czechoslovakia and East Germany, from both sides of the spectrum, pro-communist and anti-communist, pro-reform and anti-reform—had tried so hard, and succeeded so far in avoiding.

The Romanian revolution was to be drowned in blood.

* * *

Tökés and his wife were taken, to their relief, to the little village of Mineu in the north of the country, exactly the parish to which he had been informed by his bishop he would be sent. A fence was erected around their new, dusty home, as they were forbidden contact with parishioners except on Sundays during the service, and the new fence was patrolled day and night by the Securitate. But they were still alive.

Back in Timişoara, the demonstrations began again early on the Sunday afternoon. Soon Molotov cocktails were flying at the tanks. Several people were killed as the Soviet-built tanks, manoeuvring wildly in the streets and squares billowing black smoke, ran them over by accident.

The crowd, largely made up of students and young workers, responded by jamming iron bars into their tracks, and trying to set fire to the fuel drums on their backs after hacking them open first with axes.

Imre Borbély, a friend of László Tökés, watched as one man was shot at point blank range by a tank. He saw more people die on the steps of the Catholic Church in the industrial part of the city. The demonstrations ended around half past four in the afternoon, but the shooting continued.

Borbély went home and started ringing everyone he knew in other towns in Romania; in Bucharest and in other cities in Transylvania. It was a lesson people had learnt from the protests in Braşov two years earlier. They knew that at any moment communication with the outside world might be cut off. News of the Timişoara uprising had to be spread, before it was too late!

Borbély also spoke to a doctor he knew at the hospital, who estimated that there were 450 dead.

That night at ten-thirty, at least 2–3,000 demonstrators gathered in front of the Orthodox Cathedral, many praying on their knees, others trying to warm their hands on the candles they held in the bitter cold. Again, the army opened fire. Eyewitnesses described the soldiers packing the bodies—dead and injured—into army trucks, and driving off at speed. According to some stories, they were buried in mass graves in the paupers' cemetery. Other rumours suggested they had been driven out of Timişoara, on the road towards Sacalas.

'The revolution was made by the youth and children,' said Dubra Andreics, an actress from the German theatre in Timişoara. 'By the children of the decree.' She was referring to the decree that Ceauşescu had passed in 1968 banning contraception and abortion. Each family should have at least five children, Ceauşescu suggested. 'Everything he did then, is coming back to haunt him now,' she said. 'He was brought down by the generation he created.'

In the bloody anarchy of Timişoara, there was an urgent need for leadership.

Claudiu Iordache, a banned local playwright, and Lorin Fortuna helped to provide it.

Fortuna had been in the crowd outside the Tökés' house on the Saturday, as well as in the crowd who ransacked Party headquarters later that night.

'I threw stones like everyone else,' he said.

The next morning, he told his family what had happened.

'Why don't we go and demonstrate too?' Lorin's thirteen-year-old daughter asked.

'If something happened to us, who would look after you?' he replied.

'Don't the people who are on the streets now have children too?' she asked.

'You're afraid, that's really why you are not going out.'

'So, I'm leaving . . .' he told her.

He was on the streets all day on Sunday, pleading with the soldiers not to shoot. On Monday he drove to a factory which he had heard might go on strike.

'Form a strike committee,' he advised them. Then he went with a column of workers to another factory to spread the word.

Back at the university there was a meeting of students and teachers. Together they made placards to carry at the next demonstration:

'Today Timişoara, tomorrow—the whole country!'

'Bring us back our dead!'—a reference to the disappearance of the bodies of those killed during the revolution.

Seeing the crowd in front of the Opera, Fortuna smashed a window at the back to get in, and went out onto the balcony to address the crowd. Iordache and other local people, including Petru Iliesu, a local poet, joined them. Together, they formed what they called 'the Democratic Front of Romania.'

Timişoara was still the only city in Romania in open revolt, but news of what was happening had spread throughout the country. The fortunes of the revolt were tipping on a knife edge.

But then the army changed sides and joined the revolution. Twenty years later, there are still disputes about the exact hour, and the exact way that this happened.

'The people, not the army, began this revolution,' the commander in chief of the garrison in Timişoara, Major General Gheorghe Popescu explained to the international press. 'Although we were ordered to act against the people, we refused to obey the Ceauşescu clique. The allegations that the army opened fire are simply not true.'

How could he then explain hundreds of dead, and the eyewitness reports of thousands? So-called anti-terrorist units, dressed in army uniforms, but without badges, and loyal to the President were responsible, he said. They would be tried by a military prosecutor.

About 300 such 'terrorists' had been detained, he said, and military investigators were working to discover their identity.

Yet, however it happened, no-one disputes the fact that from Monday 18 December the army joined the protests in Timişoara.

Sibiu, 200km south of Timişoara, was the next town to join the revolution.

Harald Binder, a local barber, first heard about the events in Timişoara on the Romanian language service of the BBC and Radio Free Europe. An ethnic German, like many in Sibiu, he was visited by a painter friend on the Tuesday evening, who wanted to organise a demonstration in the town.

'Can we count on the Germans?' his friend asked. Binder said yes, and word spread through the town to gather the next evening at nine o'clock, carrying candles to commemorate the dead of Timişoara. But the next morning, the Wednesday, he heard that people were already gathering in the main square, and set out to join them. There were soldiers everywhere, one of the cars of the militia was on fire, and the demonstrators were chanting at the soldiers, 'No violence'. At that moment he heard shots, and the window of a bank nearby shattered. Assuming that the man next to him had thrown a stone, he turned to him angrily,' I thought we said 'No violence'?'

'Look closer' the man replied, 'that was a bullet.'

A woman working inside the bank was injured.

He found out later that the militia car had been set on fire after it had run over—and killed—a child. The other militiamen, beaten by the crowd, had run away. For a while there was no more shooting. People remonstrated with the soldiers, 'You have wives and children too . . .'

A delegation of students from Timişoara arrived and, from the plinth of a statue, began to tell the people what had happened in their city.

Some of the crowd had gone to the larger factories on the edge of the city and now began to return, accompanied by crowds of workers. The soldiers tried to prevent them reaching the square, but were pushed aside.

The crowd were chanting, 'Down with Ceauşescu', 'No violence!' and, no doubt inspired by the new situation in Timişoara, 'The army is with us!' There were even confused chants of 'Nicu is with us'. Nicu Ceauşescu was one of the spoilt children of Nicolae and Elena Ceauşescu, who ran the Communist Party apparatus in Sibiu, and the whole city, as his own fiefdom. He was known for his playboy lifestyle, his generosity to his friends and his cruelty to his enemies.

Some in the crowd smashed the windows of a bookshop in Nicolae Bălcescu Street, where books by the Ceauşescu couple were prominently displayed, and set fire to a pile of them in the street. 'Down with the cobbler!' they shouted—a reference to Ceauşescu's humble origins. 'Today Sibiu and Timişoara, tomorrow, the whole country.' Some students stayed on the square all night, nursing candles. So did the army, nursing their rifles, but there were no more clashes.

On Friday morning, a large crowd gathered again. The soldiers told them they had been told by their commanders that they were there to fight 'foreign mercenaries' and that 'Romania was under attack from Hungary!'

'My wife made a big jug of coffee, from a supply that we had been sent by relatives in West Germany,' said Harald Binder. 'And I took packets of cigarettes that I had bought on the black market. Then, with all three of my children, we went back down to the square. My youngest child is four, and his foot was in plaster. I pinned a poster on his back, with the words, "We children want to live too!" As we left the house he asked me, "Do we have to die, Papa? Do they shoot children?"'

'Then we started pouring cups of coffee for the soldiers and distributing the cigarettes. At one point I saw an army officer I knew, a major.'

'Are you going to shoot us, Ovidiu?' I asked him.

'We have orders from the commander of the garrison not to shoot into the crowds,' he replied.

Then the major pointed to the top windows of one of the buildings overlooking the square. 'You'd better watch out, the Securitate have taken up position there,' he said. As we watched, I could see figures moving at a window.'

'It was our great luck—mine and my children's—that the coffee ran out just then,' Binder explained. 'We went back to our flat, nearby, to refill the jug. Then we heard the sound of shooting from the square.'

He left his children at home this time and went back to the square alone. People were fleeing in all directions. Some lay lifeless on the ground. The shooting continued. For the rest of the day, he transported the injured to hospital in his car, or in others which he flagged down. At some point, on the television, he saw the announcement that Ceauşescu had fled Bucharest.

The shooting and the chaos continued in Sibiu for two days. Masked 'terrorists', as the Securitate were known, even went into the hospital to shoot the injured.

Soldiers and civilians set up barricades together, and the army started firing at the Securitate positions. Some of the snipers had been captured as well, Binder explained, and were being held in an empty swimming pool at the military barracks. Some of the injured were soldiers, shot by the secret police.

'At one point on the barricades, a Gypsy brought us food,' Binder commented, in amazement. 'Can you imagine, a Gypsy?'

'I am afraid of walking home at midnight alone', the girl at the reception desk of our hotel in Sibiu told me. The nineteen-year-old was afraid of snipers' bullets, not rapists. Physical violence almost disappeared from the streets under the communist regimes of eastern Europe.

It was true that Ceauşescu was now on the run. He was on an official visit to Iran when the uprising began in Timişoara, but hurried back to take control of the situation.

On Wednesday 20 December, he appeared on television, describing the demonstrators as 'foreign agents, hooligans, fascists and traitors'.

But his cardinal error was to organise a gathering of Party stalwarts in Bucharest, in front of Party headquarters, the next day, 21 December, and address them himself from the balcony, in a news item carried live on state television. The same day, the country was awash with rumours, which later proved true, that the Defence Minister, Vasile Milea, had committed suicide.

The crowd, bussed in from factories around the capital, began chanting 'Timişoara'. Then 'murderer'. The seventy-one-year-old dictator looked puzzled. In unchallenged control of his country for twenty-four years, and the subject of an ever-growing personality cult, he just couldn't understand what was happening. He tried to carry on speaking. He waved, as if the shouts were in support of him and his enlightened policies. Then two bodyguards ushered the bewildered, broken man inside.

Television screens across Romania went blank. The crowd began to trample their pro-Ceauşescu banners underfoot.

It was midday in Bucharest. No-one seemed to know what to do next. Huge crowds wandered aimlessly through the streets. Then the shooting started there, too.

It was Ceauşescu's revenge. Securitate forces who had taken up positions at windows overlooking University Square opened fire into the crowds below. There were even officers who ran into the throng, with bayonets fixed. Eighty-five people were taken to hospital. Many, doctors said, had been shot in the back as they fled.

As in Timişoara, the bodies of the dead were piled into the back of military trucks and driven away.

The revolution in Bucharest was fought and won on Friday 22 December. As the tanks drove down one of the wide boulevards of 'the Paris of the East', the crowd, made up largely of students, waited patiently for them. 'We stood in the square and waited to die,' one student recalled.

Then a soldier stood up on the top of his tank, in full view of the crowd, and removed the magazine from his Kalashnikov assault rifle. Other soldiers did the same, and the crowd embraced them. A new chant spread through the capital, like thunder breaking, 'The army is with us!'

At Party headquarters, officials tried to burn or throw away documents as the crowd broke in on all sides. The students rushed from room to room. Meanwhile, on the roof, the rotor blades of a helicopter began to turn. Elena and Nicolae Ceauşescu were fleeing, with a bodyguard who was pointing a pistol at the pilot's head. As the first protesters reached the roof, the helicopter took off. It landed at one of the Ceauşescu homes, where the dictator and his wife quickly packed their bags, then took off again, for a military airport. It was later believed that they intended to try to flee to China. But the helicopter landed a short time afterwards. Ceauşescu apparently panicked, afraid of the loyalty of the soldiers at the airport.

A passing car was commandeered, and the couple set out in a red Lada, eastwards, in the general direction of the Soviet border. They were stopped a short time afterwards.

In the meantime, in the capital, a National Salvation Front had been formed, led by, among others, my old friend Silviu Brucan, who had spilt the beans about the riot in Braşov and prepared his famous statement two years earlier. Another key figure in the Front was Ion Iliescu, a former Ceauşescu favourite and bright young communist from Iaşi, in the east, who had once played tennis with Ceauşescu, then fallen foul of him. On one of my earlier trips to the country, in the spring of 1987, I had asked if there was any hope of 'a Romanian Gorbachev'. 'Perhaps Iliescu . . .' an elderly man, a former leader of the Peasant Party, had whispered to me. Another man invited to join the Front, although he didn't know it yet, was Pastor László Tökés from Timişoara, now locked in his dusty vicarage by secret service officers who were themselves only now receiving rumours that Ceauşescu had fallen. Another figure was Doina Cornea, a brave dissident woman writer in another Transylvanian city, Cluj.

One wing of the Securitate broke away and joined the revolution. But another hardline faction kept shooting for three days.

In Bucharest, and cities and towns across the country, especially in Transylvania, Securitate units took over official buildings, and opened fire with sniper rifles and machine guns on the furious crowds. Bolstered by the army, civilians set up barricades. From the poor shelter of parked cars down the streets of the capital, foot soldiers shot back at the top windows of buildings, where the secret policemen still ruled. In railway stations and hospitals, hotels and Party buildings, the battles raged. The only strategy of the secret police appeared to be to kill as many people, to sow as much terror, as possible.

The Front set up its headquarters in the building of the national television, close to the cameras. Across Romania, the astonished population saw them standing, shoulder to shoulder, in a line. They appealed for financial help, food and military aid, to the West and East alike. An emergency meeting of the Warsaw Pact in Moscow, chaired by Mikhail Gorbachev, called for an end to the fighting, but refused to offer assistance. Lorry and car loads of food, organised spontaneously by Hungarians, began pouring in across the border.

The people of Bucharest, as before in Timişoara and Sibiu, risked their lives to take food and drink to their own soldiers and revolutionaries.

It was still far from certain that the revolution was going to succeed, though the reported capture of the Ceauşescus gave many people hope.

'If Nicolae Ceauşescu could have taken command of state security, Romania would have become a bloodbath with hundreds of thousands of dead,' Silviu Brucan said. In fact, just over a thousand died, the largest number in Timişoara.

On Christmas Day 1989, Nicolae and Elena Ceauşescu faced a military court martial.

'They acted in a despotic and criminal way. They destroyed the people whose leaders they claim to be ... I plead, on behalf of the victims of these two tyrants, for the death sentence,' said the prosecutor.

'I refuse to answer,' replied Nicolae Ceauşescu. 'I will only answer questions before the Grand National Assembly. I do not recognise this court. The charges are incorrect, and I will not answer a single question here,' he concluded.

'Did you know about the genocide in Timişoara?' Elena was asked.

'What genocide?' she replied. 'I will not answer any more questions.'

In dark overcoat and tie, and wrapped up in a winter scarf, Nicolae Ceauşescu was executed by firing squad, and Elena with him. 'I was like a mother to you all,' were her last recorded words.

Later on Christmas Day, a video of the execution was released to an astonished world. After all the revolutions of the autumn, this had been the classic event. The real thing. In the tradition of the French and Russian revolutions before it. The revolution had executed the tyrant, the oppressor.

123

To drive through Romania in the days after the revolution was to experience the euphoria and ecstasy of a people freed from the rule of the dragon—and to witness the appalling poverty and suffering to which his rule had reduced his people.

In Timişoara, rats ran through my hotel room, demolishing the food I had brought with me from Hungary. The toilets of the Democratic Front were as bad as any I had experienced in Africa.

We drove from town to town, talking to Doina Cornea in Cluj, and to fighters at roadblocks everywhere.

When we said we were from the BBC their faces lit up, and they insisted that we drink their brandy with them, to toast their revolution. In Tirgu Mureş, we stayed three nights in the best hotel in town, and were given tricolour, Romanian armbands to wear 'to show we were not terrorists'.

When we set out to leave, the hotel refused to let us pay. 'You are guests of the revolution,' the manager insisted. There was a surreal standoff in the lobby. 'But we are the BBC. We are rich!' Julian O'Halloran, the Newsnight reporter, pleaded.

The centres of every town became shrines to the dead, and to the bravery of the living. Little icons of Saints and of the Virgin Mary were lain with flowers and candles that seemed to burn day and night, and spread their wax in growing puddles, many layers thick, in all directions. Romania was like Prague, but with casualties. And there had been many casualties in many towns. The execution of the ruling couple had taken the wind out of the sails of most of the secret police, but there was still some sporadic shooting.

On New Year's Eve in Timişoara, graffiti appeared on the walls in prominent places. ' Timişoara, hero town, tonight you will breathe your last,' it read.

Many people took it to be a threat of some new atrocity, even of an attempt by the secret police to seize back control. Rumours spread of bombs and booby-traps, laid throughout the city, of a mad scheme to blow the whole place to smithereens. In my hotel room, the glass shattered with bullet holes from the fighting a week earlier, I arranged my tape recorder and microphone on the window ledge, pressed 'record', and waited for midnight.

The bells of the cathedral began chiming, and the shooting started. Bursts of machine gun fire. Then shouts of joy, and relief. The soldiers and their allies were shooting in the air. The revolution had succeeded.

7. The Morning After

There should be roses blooming here
I dig my own grave with my fingernails, inside myself
[. . .]
At the last moment I see someone
He's like me . . . he's silent—and sings
—What are you doing to me? I don't want to be split!
A grey piece of cement is hardening in my head
–And the voice behind the glass orders—Disconnect!—
End of the song . . .
End of the singer . . .
End of the experiment'

Vladimír Merta, Czech singer-songwriter

The first of January 1990 was a Monday. That morning, people stared out from the windows of the tower blocks in which one fifth of the people of eastern Europe lived, at a new world.

The most glaring absence from the political landscape was the Communist Party itself. In October 1989, the Hungarian Socialist Workers' Party had transformed itself into the Hungarian Socialist Party. Everyone was going to be middle-class now, so the 'workers' had to go. The red stars had been taken down from the pinnacles of parliaments, the tops of post-offices and the metal gates of agricultural co-operatives and state farms. The smaller ones were sold by the bag-full at the Ecseri flea market in Budapest, beside brightly-coloured pleated gypsy skirts, milk-bottles from the 1930s and pornographic magazines from the 1970s in which the girls sported astonishingly tall hairstyles but not much else. Or at the stalls that radiated out from the Nevsky Cathedral in Sofia, alongside old watches, penknives, coins and bric-a-brac from the old empire, or the war years.

There were ice-floes on the Danube, the same as every January. The sixteenth of the month was traditionally the coldest day of the year. The pieces changed shape gradually as they broke against one another, from the large, irregular, jagged floes to the smaller, more rounded ones. You could stand on the bridges of Budapest for ages and watch them pass below. Some things didn't change, but the Party had become just a party, and had to take its place among dozens of others, competing humbly in the first free parliamentary elections for more than forty years. The red star was traded for the red rose. Its sharp edges would no longer dig into our flesh, but we would still prick our fingers on its thorns.

Through the first months of 1990, the statues with which the Party had reminded people of its importance were dismantled in many countries. Some were destroyed, others preserved for posterity as peculiar souvenirs.

The Lenin statue which once stood on the edge of Heroes' Square had been conveniently removed for 'cleaning' the previous year, and was one of the first exhibits in a new 'statue park' in a leafy Budapest suburb.

'We treat the exhibits with all the respect they deserve, as works of art,' said András Szilágyi, the man in charge of constructing the park.

'We are not building a park of shame, but attempting to show in a fair way the ideology of an era.'

The giant Lenin statue in Nowa Huta in Poland had been removed 'for repairs' in December 1989, after three failed attempts by young people to destroy it. The Lenin in front of the old Agerpress offices in Bucharest, where Pat Koza and I saw a rat in November 1987, was taken down in March 1990. The Lenin in Lenin Square in Sofia survived until early summer 1990, then disappeared. 'I hear it was buried somewhere in the woods,' its sculptor, Lev Kerbel, told the New York Times. Kerbel produced hundreds of Lenins and Marxs in his time. 'Brezhnev ordered ten Lenins like this, and whenever he went somewhere, he would give one away,' he told the same interviewer. Only a few have survived.

The Polish United Workers' Party was on its deathbed, and voted to disband itself on 6 January. In Romania, the National Salvation Front included many former 'second rank' communists, but the old Romanian Communist Party, with its three to four million members, was no more. In East Germany, the Party of Democratic Unity turned into the Party of Democratic Socialism—as if to underline that there was not much unity left, but still a hankering for socialism, whatever that might mean in the future. In Bulgaria, the Bulgarian Socialist Party was emerging from the communist ruins. Only in Albania did communism still hold firm, for the time being. To report from eastern Europe for a British public sometimes felt like being a messenger from an ancient empire, the existence of which people no longer believed in. Were there really such places as Albania, Moldova, Latvia, Lithuania and Estonia? people wondered. Or was I making it up? The Iron Curtain had been more effective than its founders had ever dreamed.

The all-powerful Party had been home to so many people for so long. Even for those for whom it had not provided shelter, it had been a landmark or a useful whipping boy for everything which went wrong in one's life. With the Party gone, people felt disoriented. Now there would be no-one to blame.

Communism had been very different in each country, and so too was its legacy.

Hungary had had private enterprises, commercial banks and foreign investment, albeit in a rather restricted form, for several years. It was now in a good position to accelerate away from the starting line and put factory after factory up for sale. Personal income tax and value added tax already existed. Hungarians had passports, valid for travel to most countries in the world. A friend of mine had a 'Kiss me, I am Hungarian' badge pinned to the curtains in her bedroom. The Hungarians were at their happiest, and most self-confident.

The country was, however, also deep in debt—$21 billion, to be precise, the highest per capita in eastern Europe. Some hoped for at least part of that debt to be cancelled. Margaret Thatcher dodged the question at a press conference when she visited in the summer, but bought a string of garlic in the big covered market by the Danube as a consolation. Others were more realistic.

'Western readiness to help—out of a mixture of solidarity, and bad conscience—is not unlimited,' wrote a columnist in the Hungarian weekly, HVG. 'Many fear that the country will be sold out. I personally feel the presence of foreigners will not be big enough.'

Poland had the advantage of the national pride and unity created by the Solidarity movement and the Catholic Church led by a charismatic Polish Pope. That unity, like that of the former opponents of the communist system, would soon be broken, but it provided a valuable launching pad. Czechoslovakia had Václav Havel and the Civic Forum in the Czech lands, and Public Against Violence in Slovakia. In the whole of eastern Europe, the first few months of 1990 were calmest in Czechoslovakia.

I rented a flat in the Smíchov district of Prague, just up the hill from the brewery. The metro station at the foot of the hill lost its old name, Moskevská, and was renamed Anděl—the Angel. The old murals remained, but were now nicely set off by a statue of an angel in the hallway. In the church round the corner, a young priest who had been active in the opposition, Václav Malý, served the blood as well as the body of Christ to believers. A pink tank took up position in the Malá Strana district, to protect the city from too much seriousness. It was a time of love, and heresy. Not only had the revolution been velvet, the preparations for the first democratic election since 1938 proved surprisingly smooth as well. In the Magic Lantern theatre, where the Civic Forum had been formed in the heady days of the previous November, I watched a performance of a play based on Homer's *Odyssey*. It began and ended with the happy couple, Odysseus and Penelope, 'deeply engrossed in one another'. Society however 'cannot bear the sight of their happiness and divides them'. Everything read like a parable for the times just past, or a prophesy for the times ahead.

* * *

It wasn't just society that needed mending. Ruthless industrialisation formed the backbone of the communist experiment in eastern Europe, and the landscape was deeply scarred.

In Copşa Mică in Romania, black sheep followed a shepherd down a street of single storey peasant homes. The horror of it was that the sheep should actually have been white—their coats were stained black by pollution from the Carbosin factory, which produced rubber tires for Dacia cars, and the IMMN factory, which smelted lead, cadmium and zinc from ore brought from Baia Mare in the north.

Many of the original seven thousand inhabitants fled the area, because of the pollution. Children were found to have double the permitted level of lead in their blood, and to be suffering brain damage because of the heavy metals. Farm produce within a 30km radius was declared unfit for human consumption. Workers were brought in from outside, to work shorter shifts, because of the appalling conditions. Respiratory diseases and eye infections were two to three times more frequent than the Romanian average. The end of communism meant that Copşa Mică could finally be declared what its people had long known it to be, a disaster area. It was the most spectacular example, but the attitude to nature, as an object to be changed and manipulated at will, was true throughout the region. Only the borderlands, and strips of land which the big machinery of the state farms and cooperatives could not reach, became oases of wildlife in otherwise battered landscapes.

Environmental activists had played an important role in toppling the communist regimes—Ecoglasnost in Bulgaria, the 'Basis groups' of the Protestant church in East Germany, the Danube Circle in Hungary—but no magic wand could be found to heal the destruction wrought. As a former activist myself, I had tried to draw attention to threats to the environment in Britain, but what I witnessed in eastern Europe was on another scale altogether.

The forests of Germany were dying. The wooden rocking horses, made by the craftsmen in Seiffen, high in the Ore Mountains between East Germany and Bohemia, might crack when a child sat on them. 'The wood has lost its strength,' the carvers complained. The evergreens were more susceptible to pollution than deciduous trees, because they only shed their needles every three years, allowing the poisons to build up for longer.

Larches planted in the hills, the carvers told me, rarely last more than fifteen years. In 1989 the craftsmen watched the revolution unfolding on the plain below them with jaundiced eyes. They knew their beautifully carved and painted carousels, Bethlehems, and hunting scenes were sold for a fortune at the Christmas markets in West Germany, but they only received a pittance. Might they receive more for their work under a capitalist system, they wondered? Their peasant common sense told them that the middle man always got rich, and the workers always stayed poor, whether the middle-man was the socialist state, or a capitalist from the city.

Long stretches of the River Vistula in Poland, the Elbe in Germany, the Vltava in Czechoslovakia and the Danube as it flowed through eight countries to the Black Sea, were vast sewage outlets. Nitrates from agriculture, untreated human waste from cities and industrial effluents from factories made the water froth and simmer.

'The toxins concentrate near the backbone,' a Polish fishermen explained to me, beside the Vistula in the summer of 1989, expertly slicing a fish from end to end. 'And so it's OK to eat, so long as you don't eat the flesh just there . . .' and he pointed with the tip of his knife. I wondered whether his children clamouring for more supper had received the same lecture.

The nuclear power industry, secretive in every country, had been in trouble since the accident at Chernobyl in Ukraine in 1986. Only the reactors at the Ignalina nuclear plant in Lithuania were of the same, RBMK design as those at Chernobyl, but many of the pressurised water VVER reactors elsewhere were getting old, and had safety issues.

There were plans in several countries—Czechoslovakia and Bulgaria, in particular—to build new VVERs. The nuclear lobby, backed by Moscow, was strong in each country, and isolated anti-nuclear protests had been little tolerated by the regimes.

I found Heinz Märchner in an armchair in his attic room in a flat above a toyshop in the town of Wismut, East Germany. His wife let me in. From the wrinkles on his face, he could have been ninety. In fact, he was sixty-five. The twentieth century had not been kind to him. Fifteen-years-old at the outbreak of the Second World War, he had been forced to enrol in the Hitler Youth. In 1945 he became a uranium miner in his home town. For the next twenty-eight years he worked underground, first for the Soviet nuclear missile programme, then for its offspring, the East German nuclear energy programme. At the age of fifty he was forced to retire due to ill-health. When I met him, in early 1990, he had just been diagnosed with cancer. He smiled at the small turtles, crawling surprisingly fast across the floorboards towards him. He smiled at the gladioli seeds his wife had brought him from West Germany. His window faced south, over a cobbled street, a railway siding and a wide stream.

'I'm making a film about Wismut, and uranium mining . . .' I began.

'Close it all down!' he interrupted, with unexpected firmness. At least now he could say that, without fear of retribution.

The mines ran for many kilometres underground, a network that radiated out on both sides of the East German-Czechoslovak border. In the works canteen, you got double portions of meat if you worked underground. 'Where do *you* work then, in the sky?' asked the woman serving the food when I asked for a helping without any meat at all.

The workers and managers alike were worried in the spring of 1990. The uranium was running out and their health was running out. There was no likelihood of investment in the mines. To confound their problems, a glut on the world market meant that nobody seemed to want what they had ruined their lives trying to extract.

The slag heaps of uranium tailings near the Wismut mines were overgrown with spindly silver birch trees. I was surprised to see local people picking mushrooms there. 'They sell them to the smart hotels,' someone told me. 'The West German guests don't know where they come from.'

Just the other side of the border, at Tachov in Czechoslovakia, another uranium miner, forty-four-year-old Jan Vácha, told horror stories about the lack of respect with which the communist management had treated the workers; how radiation checks were carried out regularly in the mines, but only at places where they knew there was low radiation; how the giant ventilators which were supposed to keep a steady flow of fresh air through the tunnels were regularly turned off to save power.

Jan was forced to quit mining because of ill-health in 1987, but was told by doctors that his illness was not related to his many years down the mine. He didn't believe them, and began to research the health conditions of the eight thousand uranium miners still working underground, and of those like himself, who no longer could. He had another, personal reason to do so. His baby son had died, he believed, from a genetic weakness, inherited from him.

The authorities actively discouraged him from collecting data but even before the revolution, Jan had made progress uncovering the facts. And since the revolution, the records had been properly opened, and what he discovered was appalling.

Life expectancy for uranium miners in Czechoslovakia was forty-seven—twenty years below the national average for men. The miners died from a combination of cancers.

By the time the radiation damage was diagnosed, it was usually too late to treat. Even when the ventilation in the mines was improved, carcinogenic microtoxins remained, concentrated in the fungi which flourished on the hot, damp walls of the tunnels, and the poisonous air flowed out through vents into the villages. In Löbichau, I found a vent next to a kindergarten. The radiation itself was not the main cause of death among the miners, Jan discovered, but only an indirect one—as a catalyst for the production of microtoxins. He showed me photographs he had taken of long, evil-looking fungi growing deep in the mines, where he believed the radiation was most concentrated.

On the basis of his research, he recommended that miners wear special masks, and be given extra vitamins to boost their immunity. But the real damage was already done, he felt. The mines simply had to close. After three years as an outcast, the officials were finally starting to listen to him. A parliamentary commission was formed to study the health conditions in the uranium mines.

Not far away in the same, northern Bohemian region, Jaroslav Marek, a local geologist, stretched out his arm. We were standing in front of the fourteenth century castle at Jezeří, near the city of Most, balanced precariously on the edge of man-made cliffs. Behind it, the densely wooded slopes of the Ore Mountains stretched north, over the border into eastern Germany. Just in front of the castle he pointed into a vast cavity, 300m deep, 10km wide and 50km long. Here and there, smoke wound upwards from spontaneous fires. So eager to be burnt, the lignite sometimes caught fire by itself. The biggest brown coal strip mine in Czechoslovakia stretched before us.

'From November to February, we barely dare go outside,' a local woman said. 'The air is so thick with dust from the mine, and sulphur dioxide from local industry.'

Jaroslav had fought the spread of the strip mine for twenty years. The revolution came just in time to stop it moving further east, and sweeping away the lone castle on its outcrop of rock, and what was left of the 'English Park'; the ornamental woodland in front of it. Many villages had already disappeared into the hole.

Jiřína Rydvanová lived in a second-floor flat, overlooking the ring road in Most. She had been evacuated ten years earlier, with her husband, her children and grandchildren from the village of Albrechtice, close to Jezeří, to make way for the expanding mine. The children were not even allowed to finish their term in the village school. 'It was the most beautiful village in the valley,' she said. In Most it was easy to identify those who had been evicted from the villages—they were the only ones who went to the trouble of putting flowers on their balconies and in the stairwells of the blocks of flats where they now lived. In an overwhelmingly industrial landscape, they retained the proud dignity of villagers. Jiřína was too sad to go back to see where her village once stood, or even to walk in those oak and beech woods which still survived, behind the castle at Jezeří, where she used to take her children after nursery school. Nearby, in Janov, streets were named after the villages from which the people had been moved.

The park or arboretum at Jezeří had once been famous all over Europe for its seedlings. They even grew orange trees there. Now, only about a third of the trees in the arboretum remained, including an 800-year-old oak.

The sound from the hole was unearthly, resembling something between a dungeon and a slaughterhouse—the groaning of machinery, stripping the poor-quality coal from the bowels of the earth far below.

'They call me 'catastrophe Marek' at the mine,' Jan laughed 'because I have been warning them for years that if they carry on like this, the hills themselves will collapse on top of them.'

Studies of the health of the local population showed mostly respiratory and digestive diseases, especially asthma. Peoples' immune systems were eroded. Depression was a huge problem. The region had the second highest divorce rate and one of the highest for youth suicides in the whole country.

'If we save the arboretum, the mines can work for ten more years,' he said. 'If we can't, they can work for thirty.'

Though coal had been mined underground here since the 1880s, the communists favoured strip mining, which meant that up to 150m of soil which lay on top of the coal seams had to be removed first.

'In communist times, mining was always the priority. Now we should put people, villages and trees first,' he said.

Above our heads, the wind tugged at the surviving stands of beech and oak on the hillside. The winds had become another threat to the woods, gathering strength in the vast open spaces of the mine to whip through the trees on the slopes above.

Part of northern Bohemia was known as the Sudetenland before the war. In 1938, it was annexed by Hitler, as part of the agreement struck by the German leader and the British Prime Minister, Neville Chamberlain, in Munich.

After the war, the Sudeten Germans were expelled, and the new Czech population brought in in their place had no ties to the land. Grateful to the communists for their new homes, and with little knowledge of the local ecology, they were the least likely to protest against its destruction.

The region was assigned the role of powerhouse of the industrialisation of Czechoslovakia, and it was a process which took no prisoners. It proved easier for people to destroy a landscape to which they had few historic or emotional ties. There was a similar story in western Poland, which had been ethnically cleansed of Germans after the Second World War and re-populated with deportees from the East—those parts of Poland now absorbed in the Soviet Union.

In the 1980s, researchers began to clear some of the undergrowth from old German cemeteries in Bohemia, while young men and women arrived from Israel to clean up neglected Jewish cemeteries. The Jews and their persecutors, the Germans, were both peoples who had played a central role in the building of eastern Europe. Now, with the exception of study tours, they were both strangely absent. During the last years of the 1980s, a book of black and white photographs was published in Germany and smuggled into Czechoslovakia. It was called *Verlorene Geschichte* or *Lost History*.

In Hungary, efforts to stop the massive Gabčikovo-Nagymaros hydroelectric project on the Danube were only partially successful. The Hungarian government unilaterally suspended construction of the Nagymaros section at the Danube Bend in Hungary, in May 1989. The Slovaks pressed ahead and drew up plans—the so-called C variant—to make the project work even if the Hungarians pulled out completely. While the stopping of the dam was seen as one of the first fruits of democracy in Hungary, the completion of it became a matter of national pride in Slovakia, especially at a time when Slovakia was defining itself more and more against both the Czechs on one side, and the Hungarians on the other. Gabčikovo became a matter of national prestige.

The centre-piece of the Gabčikovo project was a 27km long, over-ground canal, into which the main stream of the Danube would be diverted. Just a trickle would be left in the original bed.

In October 1992, despite the vehement protest of the Hungarian government, Slovakia went ahead and diverted the river.

In his garden near Dunajská Streda in Slovakia, Ferenc Zsemlovics showed me a black plastic bucket, with flecks of gold floating on the surface. Real gold. His father had been the last gold-washer on this stretch of the Danube, where the River Váh brought the precious dust down from the mountains. This was the last bucketful his father was working on when he died. Ferenc kept it in his memory. He remembered as a child going proudly to the bank with his father with an ingot of gold, which they exchanged for enough money to buy the first family car.

There would be no more gold-washing without a river, he lamented. He had made plans to set up an ostrich farm.

* * *

The Party might have disappeared, but one of its creations—'the intelligentsia'—remained.

Under communism, intellectuals had come to represent something like a new 'class', complementing the workers and peasants. Under the

Stalinist system in the late 1940s and 1950s, the state bureaucracy was in undisputed control, with the blunt weapon of the secret police to beat anyone's fingers, or sometimes their heads, if they stepped out of line. But in the 'post-Stalinist' world of the 1960s, 70s and 80s, the intellectuals had become rather useful.

'The bureaucracy had lost legitimacy, and needed intellectuals who could, through their professional knowledge, legitimise the existing system, and strengthen the basis of bureaucratic knowledge,' wrote András Bozoki, a Hungarian sociologist.

Liberal intellectuals, often rooted in the dissident movement, or in the circles of sociologists and economists who fed it, came into their own during the transition. Now they set up liberal parties to continue their work. In the campaign for the March-April 1990 elections in Hungary, the Free Democrats campaigned with the slogan, 'We know, we dare, we are able'. They came a respectable second, after the centre-right Hungarian Democratic Forum, with twenty-one per cent of the vote. Some lamented that the 'change of system', as it was already known in Hungary, would now continue without their presence in government. Others pointed out that a liberal party had never before in Hungarian history mustered so many votes. The Socialists claimed credit for giving up power in such a gentlemanly fashion, and won twelve per cent in Hungary. The new Prime Minister, József Antall, was a former museum director, whose father had been an important figure in the Peasants' Party after the war. Antall had begun to shine during the opposition round-table talks the previous year and, in a field with few natural statesmen, rose quickly to the top of his own party, then his own state. His presence was balanced by the election of Árpád Göncz, a writer and veteran of the 1956 revolution, as President. Göncz spent much of the night before his inauguration helping a friend redecorate her flat. While some of the new politicians quickly got a taste for the trappings of office, others remained refreshingly human and humble.

In Czechoslovakia, the movements which led the revolution, Civic Forum and Public Against Violence, won landslide victories in the June elections.

In Bulgaria and Romania, however, successor parties to the communists won office.

After the execution of Nicolae and Elena Ceauşescu on Christmas Day 1989, the new National Salvation Front moved fast to take control of the country. It secured the allegiance of the army, the secret police and the civil police, and began the preparations for new elections. From the start, the exact circumstances of the overthrow of the regime, the identity of those who shot into the crowds and killed just over a thousand people, cast a long shadow over the triumph of the people.

'The revolution was a coup d'état,' said Doina Cornea, a brave, diminutive opponent of Ceauşescu, who had suffered years of persecution under the old regime. We met several times over the following years in her house in Cluj, Transylvania, and her view of what had happened never wavered. She spoke beautiful French, like many Romanian intellectuals. 'We, naive innocents, walked out onto the streets, into a spray of bullets!' Her voice raise to a high pitch, and the silver cat on her shoulder, the colour of her hair, leapt onto the sofa, and sharpened her claws on the upholstery, as if to emphasise the point.

The Front and, in particular, its leader, Ion Iliescu, had 'profited from the situation, to seize power,' she said.

Doina Cornea had been invited to join the Front, but had never made it to Bucharest, 'because of the fog,' she said—Cluj felt a million miles from Bucharest, at the best of times. A practising Catholic, she hoped for a restoration of the monarchy in Romania, and the return of King Michael from exile on the shores of Lake Geneva. I asked her once about her faith. 'If people believe in something, or someone higher than themselves, they will be humbler, more gentle in their dealings with one another,' she explained. And that was exactly her trouble with the new government. They were continuing a tradition in which those in authority felt answerable to no-one, and the humble citizens expected those in authority to be arrogant and corrupt. For the past twenty years, opinion polls in Romania have consistently shown that people trust the Orthodox church and the army the most, and politicians the least.

Through January and February 1990, a war of words flared up between the Front on one side, and Hungarian intellectuals in Transylvania and the Hungarian government on the other. Up to two million Hungarians lived in Transylvania, and they saw the Romanian revolution and, in particular, Pastor László Tökés's role in starting it, as a chance to reassert their identity within what they hoped would be a democratic Romania.

Communism under Ceauşescu had been a peculiar brew of 'National Communism'—unlike the 'communist internationalism' preached elsewhere. Romanian peasants in traditional costumes were drilled in football stadiums. Everywhere one went, the glorious past of the

Romanians, as descendants of a union between the occupying Romans, in the first century AD, and the local population, was underlined. The Romanian language itself, with its close relationship to Latin, was held up as proof.

The Hungarians, who regarded Transylvania as their own heartland, argued that the Romanians were Vlach shepherds who wandered down from the mountains many centuries after the Roman occupiers had gone home. And long after they, and their Saxon neighbours, had built a prosperous and independent-minded Transylvania—Siebenburgen as the Germans called it—'seven castles'.

There was so much historical baggage to digest that it was hardly surprising so many people got indigestion. Romanians had often been ignored or ill-treated during the years of Hungarian rule in Transylvania, which ended in 1918, and the Hungarians felt they had been ill-treated since. Ceaușescu had re-populated Transylvania with Romanians, to reduce the Hungarians to a smaller and smaller minority. Now, while the Hungarians saw the revolution as an opportunity to end the threat of their own assimilation, many Romanians saw the Hungarians as fifth-columnists, intent on re-annexing Transylvania to Hungary. Vatra Românească, the 'Romanian Hearth' organisation, was born, to define 'Romanian-ness' in the post-communist era, and to defend Romania from what was seen as a Hungarian threat. In Slovakia, Matica Slovenská, in Croatia, Matica Hrvatska, and in each country throughout the region, cultural organisations were set up with clear visions of 'national enemies' intent on rolling back their achievements.

The Second World War left as many wounds on the map as on the body. Hungarian foreign policy from 1920 to 1945 had been openly focused on one goal; to win back some of the lands lost after the First World War. That was what led Hungary into its disastrous alliance with Hitler—he was the only one offering border changes in exchange for support. So Hungary briefly re-occupied parts of Transylvania, northern Serbia and southern Slovakia, and then lost them again four years later. Romania began the war on Hitler's side, but then switched at the last moment to join the Allies. Bulgaria was nominally an axis power, but refused outright to deport its Jews. Jozef Tiso ruled as a fascist puppet in Slovakia, after Hitler encouraged him to declare independence from the Czechs, as German troops entered Bohemia. The Czechs lost their most developed region, North Bohemia, without a fight. Immediately after the war, under the Beneš decrees, they expelled up to three million

Germans from the same territories. Poland lost great swathes of land in the east, but gained others in the west. The advance of the Red Army in 1945, followed by the imposition of communist rule in the following years, froze all these border disputes, and national hurts and losses.

History teaching was very selective for the next four decades. There were many taboos, but when the rusty old Iron Curtain fell, all this unfroze.

The roads and fields of eastern Europe were re-populated by ghosts. The dream of a united Europe was shared by most. No-one in their right mind wanted a return to war, or to forcible border changes. But everyone wanted at least a chance to lay down their own version of what had actually happened. To read the more national-minded press of each country in the early 1990s was to mine a rich seam of suffering. And each people claimed they had suffered more than their neighbours.

'They are like characters from one's distant youth, or from a play seen long ago and barely remembered,' wrote Mark Frankland in *The Patriots' Revolution*. 'There is the Pole, devout in the defence of national honour; the moody Hungarian, preoccupied with the survival of his culture and his race; the Czech democrat, straightforward yet with a knack for slyness. The traveller in east Europe rubs his eyes. How can such figures from the past reappear in countries that half a century ago were mangled in Hitler's war, then swamped by the Soviet flood?'

There were also striking contrasts between and within different countries. An idle shopper in Váci Street in Budapest might for a moment think they were in Vienna—only the queue outside the Adidas shop would remind them that they were somewhere else. In Romania, Gypsy children went barefoot in many villages, even in winter, as they ran and fought around the village tap. Communism had come up with some rather crude solutions to health care. On one visit to an orphanage, I asked why all the children limped. 'Because of all the injections,' I was told. In order to support the domestic pharmaceutical industry, antibiotics were all distributed in injectable form, rather than in tablets or capsules. The poor children had needles jabbed into them for the slightest ailment. The most tragic result was in the number of children with HIV/AIDS. A shortage of needles meant the same ones were used, again and again, even by health workers.

National passions came to a head in the Transylvanian city of Tirgu Mureş in March. As Hungarians set out to celebrate their first 15 March in freedom, Vatra Românească supporters attacked them with wooden sticks and iron bars. Some of the Hungarians took refuge in the town hall. A crowd gathered outside, baying for their blood. The police eventually assured them a safe passage, but when they left the building, they were badly beaten by the crowd while the police stood by and watched. The well-known Hungarian writer, András Sütő, lost the sight in one eye. Roma from nearby villages arrived, armed with sticks and stones, chanting, 'ne féljetek magyarok, itt vannak a cigányok!'—don't be scared Hungarians, the gypsies are here to help you!' Four people died in the fracas. The Romanian courts found only Hungarians guilty.

At a stroke, Romania's reputation as the darling of Europe, Ceauşescu's pitiful orphan, was shattered. The world press changed its tone. Was communism going to be followed by ethnic war, between Hungarians and Romanians in the eastern Balkans, between Serbs and Croats in the west?

'In my opinion, there is no basic tension between Hungarians and Romanians,' Doina Cornea told me. 'Romanians lost their identity under Ceauşescu too. We couldn't speak our own language, we could only speak the wooden language of the communists . . .' She reminded me of the Romanians who went to Pastor Tökés's house in Timişoara, to defend him. 'The problem between Romanians and Hungarians is a false one, created by those in power . . .' The solution was for the majority, in any situation, to respect the fear of the minority, of disappearing, she said.

Ethnic tensions in Transylvania were seen in the light of tensions elsewhere, where the picture was even uglier. In Yugoslavia, what was known as the 'anti-bureaucratic revolution' had raged from 1988 to 1990, with a strong ethnic component.

Slobodan Milošević and his allies saw the autonomy of Kosovo in the south of Serbia and Vojvodina in the north of Yugoslavia as mortal insults to the unity of Serbia. Ever-larger rallies were held by Serb nationalists in Belgrade, in Kosovo Polje, and in Novi Sad, demanding the 'equality' of Serbs within Yugoslavia, after what was increasingly seen as their 'suppression' in the past forty years. Other nations in Yugoslavia, especially the Croats and Slovenes, saw such developments as a direct threat to them, and intensified their own efforts to break free of Yugoslavia completely. Young men of all nationalities still served shoulder to shoulder in the Yugoslav National Army (JNA), but there were growing conflicts there as well. Young Albanian conscripts from Kosovo might be picked on by Serb soldiers one day. On the next, the

Albanians (the only people the Serbs actually feared, according to a Hungarian friend who served in one such unit) wrought a terrible revenge on the Serbs. Many such incidents ended in physical injury, and there were a number of deaths. The arrival of body-bags from JNA barracks in a country supposedly at peace further embittered the majority Albanian population in Kosovo against the Serbs. No-one knew just how much ethnic conflicts might escalate in post-communist eastern Europe—but there was no shortage of prophets of new wars.

In May 1990, Ion Iliescu was elected President of Romania with eighty per cent of the vote, and the National Salvation Front (NSF) won a landslide victory in the parliamentary election with seventy per cent.

Like the Civic Forum and Public Against Violence in Czechoslovakia, the NSF had initially declared itself a revolutionary organisation which would disband itself after organising free elections. In each case, the sense of being indispensable to the future of democracy prevented that happening. Apart from that, the NSF and Civic Forum could hardly have been more different.

Iliescu himself had joined the Communist Party in 1953. Václav Havel had been jailed three times by it. Iliescu had been a rising star in the Party, in charge of propaganda, then of youth policy, and had even been tipped as a potential successor to Ceauşescu. The dictator became jealous, and Iliescu fell suddenly from grace in 1971 and was exiled to the provinces. In 1984, he was expelled from the Central Committee of the Communist Party, and became editor of a publishing house.

'Iliescu is a very astute politician, head and shoulders above the others,' Silviu Brucan told me. Did he betray the revolution? I asked.

'That is partly true,' replied the wily professor, himself a former devout communist. 'But I think the issue of communism is no longer relevant. It is quite natural,' (to find former communists in leading positions after the revolution) Brucan argued, 'because under communism no political leaders could get experience . . .'

Romania abounded with rumours that Iliescu was Moscow's man, and even a former KGB agent, as Vladimir Bukovsky, a former Soviet dissident, alleged. The same theory, in a season of conspiracy theories, maintained that the whole Romanian revolution was a KGB plot to bring Romania back into the Soviet or Russian sphere of influence, from which it had gone astray under Ceauşescu's 'national communism'.

One apparent proof that this was not actually the case came as Iliescu cautiously steered Romania towards NATO membership. What was certainly true was that he was no friend of the free market, human rights or participatory democracy. Broadcast media, especially state television, were used as mouthpieces for the government. The secret services were a tool in the government's hands, albeit an authoritarian, not a totalitarian tool. Some observers argued that, stumbling blind from the darkness of Ceauşescu's tunnel into the bright light of day, Romania could only stay upright if it had a strong hand to guide it. Others countered that it was just this strong hand that was physically preventing Romanian society from growing up.

After the 1990 election, the Romanian opposition was reduced to a handful of 'historical' parties, like the Peasants' Party, a small group of liberal intellectuals and students from the main universities. The elections proved that Romanians wanted 'liniste'—peace and quiet, law and order—and Iliescu was the man who could deliver. Ideas like 'justice', 'truth' or 'revenge' for the years of oppression, were either too abstract, or too frightening. Life remained for a long time a matter of everyday survival.

There were severe shortages of basic goods. Butter, sugar, grain and oil all had to be imported into a country which was known in the 1930s as the 'bread-basket' of Europe. Donations of clothes were delivered by the lorry load from many countries, including Hungary. Driving north from Bucharest soon after the election, I picked up a couple hitch-hikers. They had never seen a one-and-a-half litre plastic bottle before, and were so delighted by the one I kept my drinking water in that they offered me several pairs of nylon socks from the factory where they worked in exchange for it.

An American photographer I met, who had photographed wars and famines all over the world, told me he had never been in a country like this before, where even children would not look into his lens. The whole people appeared cowed, he said.

Student protests continued, intensified even, after Iliescu and the NSF's sweeping electoral victories. The rumour mill worked overtime. Everyone had their own theory about where the missing bodies of those killed in the uprising had gone, and what had happened on each day of the revolution. I went to see *Mad Forest* by the British playwright Caryl Churchill at the Royal Court theatre in London. It was a brilliant portrayal of just this—the endless, maddening whispering among the trees, about just what had happened, who was responsible and when.

By June 1990, Iliescu had had enough of a protest which blamed him, personally, for the 'theft' of the revolution. The opposition went so far as to say that he had even more blood on his hands than Ceauşescu.

At dawn on 13 June, the police broke up a long-standing anti-government protest camp in University Square in Bucharest. In the riots which followed, troops opened fire on the crowd outside the Interior Ministry, killing four people.

The same day, President Iliescu invited the miners of the Jiu Valley in western Romania to come to Bucharest and 'restore order'. It was an astonishing, appalling act from a head of state. About 5,000 miners arrived on trains, specially laid on for them. Their faces blackened with coal dust, dressed in their black miners' overalls, wearing spotlights on their heads and carrying lengths of wood or metal piping in their hands, they were a terrifying sight. They rampaged through the streets, beating students or anyone else they considered 'hooligans' or 'vermin'. The offices of opposition parties and newspapers were ransacked. The police followed in their wake, arresting the injured. Some of those under attack fought back. Shop windows were smashed and goods looted. For three days, anarchy ruled in the Romanian capital, and the country's reputation as a place of miracles was shattered.

I asked for an interview with the miners' leaders, and was directed to the coal-face underground, in the Liveanu shaft near the town of Petroşani. The miners would only speak, they said, if we were willing first of all to see the conditions in which they worked.

Arriving in Petroşani in mid-summer, the word Pace!—Peace!— screamed from roadside hoardings, on posters left over from the Ceauşescu era. The miners passed them on their way to Bucharest.

'I tried to stop them going,' said Traian Iordache, the general manager of the mines. 'So they got hold of me, and took me with them.'

We stumbled and tripped for what felt like hours ever deeper into the hillside, over an obstacle course of broken, abandoned machinery, coal wagons and dangling power-cables, past miners who had to carry their equipment to the coal-face by hand. In places, the tunnels were so narrow that we had to crawl on our hands and knees. The greatest danger, our guide explained, was from falling rocks. Ninety people had died in accidents in the Jiu valley mines in 1988. The greatest risk was of explosions from the lethal mix of coal dust and methane. As we finally reached the coal-face, one of my companions, a female journalist, fainted from heat and exhaustion.

Her plight broke the ice with the miners, who seized the opportunity to prove their gallantry, and that they were not simply the thugs they had been portrayed as in the world media.

'Down here our decisions are a matter of life and death,' said one. 'That was why we went to Bucharest. The government was in danger, so we rescued it.'

'We don't hate students,' said Horea Puiu, chief of sector 2 of the Liveni mine, 'we hate people who don't work.' And he and his comrades went on to list the categories of people they had in mind: 'businessmen, prostitutes, Gypsies and drug addicts'.

So soon after the revolution, 'business' was still a dirty word in their country. It was indistinguishable from 'black-marketeer'.

A few of the miners we spoke to admitted that they had used unnecessary force, but said they would visit the capital again if they were invited or, perhaps, even if they were not.

From Petroşani, I went to Timişoara. The Timişoara Society had been founded there by those who had fought in the revolution, or who still supported its aims. Its members were afraid that the miners would try to 'restore order' there next. Wild rumours circulated that they were already on their way. Several hundred students took to the streets chanting, 'Bucharest is dying, Timişoara is sleeping.'

Timişoara was the only city where former members of the nomenclatura had been removed from power. The society called a meeting of all opposition groups in the country, to discuss a new strategy with which to challenge the government. Were the miners the 'Jacobins' of the Romanian revolution? we wondered. Was the violence about to begin again? Was Marion Cosma, the miners' leader, another Robespierre?

The Timişoara Society released a statement. 'We condemn in the strongest terms the barbarian aggression of the Bucharest police on the morning of 13 June, which targeted the hunger-strikers . . .' And they called for the resignation of the Interior Minister and a new enquiry into those responsible for ordering and carrying out the violence. Their protest against the government would continue, they stressed, but only in a non-violent way.

*   *   *

'Since the disappearance of the Iron Carpet,' a nervous interpreter once misinterpreted the 'Iron Curtain' to me—but the image was perhaps as good or better than Winston Churchill's. It gave a sense of the harm done. The squashed yellowing grass, the greyness and the wasted lives. The iron carpet rusted, and fell apart in many places, before it was thrown aside. And when it did, stories which had been kept silent for years could finally be told.

The Hungarian poet, Sándor Csoóri, told me once that an old man had recently been to see him, a Hungarian from sub-Carpathian Ukraine, just across the border. He and his brother had tried to flee to Hungary during the worst times in the 1950s, by swimming at night across the fast-flowing Tisza river, which forms part of the border. The escape was successful, and they fell asleep in a hay-rick on the Hungarian side. But in the morning they were caught, and the Hungarian authorities, following to the letter the rules of 'socialist solidarity' between the two countries, handed them back. As a punishment, they were sent to a work-camp in Siberia, where his brother died. In the camp, political prisoners were incarcerated alongside violent criminals, who ran a gambling racket. Everyone had to gamble, and when your money ran out, you had to gamble with your life. Those who lost would either be killed themselves, or have to murder another prisoner. It was just one example of the brutality of the past and of the memories carried by some of the people sitting opposite the innocent western visitor on the tram.

The most urgent task, for the newly-elected governments of each country, was to reorganise the state according to democratic rules. The new rulers had the political legitimacy to set to work.

'We will govern for you, but without you,' János Kádár had said.

The hope in 1990 was that those who won the elections would set out to govern both 'with us and for us'. But this was to prove to be not as simple as it sounded. The communist regime had inculcated in the people a sense that 'power' is something absolute. Either you have it, or you don't. And once you get it, you hang onto it. To lose power would be almost too humiliating to bear.

'Everyone knows who lost, but who won?' the Polish journalist Konstanty Gebert asked in the summer of 1990. And he set out to answer his own question.

The man in the street would argue that 'the nation' had won, reaffirming national and religious identity. That was certainly the argument of the Hungarian Democratic Forum, which won the Hungarian elections in April 1990.

The freezer has broken down, Gebert explained, and all the people and emotions which the communists froze when they came to power had now come crawling out.

It was important not just to see the traditionalists as anachronistic, he said, but to understand their genuine fear of modernity and the consumer society.

High in his new office in the castle in Prague, I interviewed Václav Havel. He grumbled a bit about having to wear a tie every day instead of his favourite jumper.

He didn't like having to smile all the time either. As we spoke, he dismantled two unlit cigarettes between his fingers in half an hour—he was under strict doctor's orders to cut down. He missed making his own coffee, driving his own car and 'scrubbing my own back', he joked. But he expressed alarm, at the same time, about the seduction of power, which he could already feel tugging at him.

He hadn't changed his views, he said, about 'the crisis of global civilisation, and the crisis of consumer society.' He disliked 'television advertisements and other forms of manipulation' just as much as before. But when he spoke now, he had to remember constantly that he spoke as the representative of his people, not as a private citizen.

He agreed with my assessment that communism and the Soviet presence had, inadvertently, preserved something of value in the East.

'The long years of totalitarian rule paradoxically enriched the human mind. They uncovered the meaning of certain moral values. They created a certain sense of solidarity. They made people more extrovert, broadened their horizons. And even though most people served the system, they also knew that they ought not to, that they had dirtied their hands.'

What he called 'the central European tradition of black humour, self mockery and scepticism' provided useful tools, he suggested. But the trick now would be to find ways of using this constructively, in the new situation.

In mid-July 1990, I was invited on a camping trip in south Bohemia.

Hornosin, the name of the camp, was tucked away on a gentle slope behind fir trees, among rolling hills miles from the nearest town. There was even a flag on a pole, not the Czech red, white and blue, but orange and green batik, a hippie emblem made by the campers years before, frayed from use. Most of the campers were psychiatrists, one particular group among Havel's friends, some of whom had been active dissidents with him in Charter 77.

145

There were wild raspberries growing in the bushes on the edge of an oak wood, wildflowers in the grass, butterflies everywhere and a long wooden hut where dishes could be washed and food prepared. The camp was full of children, dogs and long-haired, laughing people.

A few hours after us, the President himself arrived with his girlfriend, in a black limousine, followed by an identical car with his bodyguards. Bouncing over the rough track, the cars were like giant shiny beetles which had just crawled out of the woods. Havel got out of the car wearing jeans and a chequered shirt, and went around shyly shaking hands and hugging people as though he had just got out of jail.

The children made pancakes in his honour. I went off into the woods with Ján Langos, a Slovak mathematician and former colleague of Havel's in the underground, who was now Interior Minister, to gather firewood. Langos had been famous for many years at the camp for his wood gathering zeal, and just because he now wore a suit and had to comb his long black hair on weekdays, he didn't want to lose his reputation.

Late at night, around the fire, when the children were asleep, the grown-ups talked politics, but most of all morality—about the nature of change, and loyalty and truth. We passed around bottles of beer, and bitter, dark Czech liquors flavoured with herbs, till the early hours. Vladimír Merta, a Czech guitarist who had been alternately banned and tolerated by the old regime, played and everyone sang.

One of his most popular songs was *Konec Experimentu*—the end of experiments—because that was the experience of communism which many people had gone through—as guinea-pigs, experimented on by the Party doctors. And this was what they hoped was over, once and for all.

By about three in the morning, there were only a few of us left by the fire. Václav Havel suddenly remembered he had forgotten to bring any bedding. Did anyone have a spare blanket? I had a beautiful green sleeping bag, almost new, stuffed with goose down. I surrendered it immediately to the needy President. My contribution to his presidency.

The next morning, the psychiatrists and hangers-on like myself, challenged Havel's bodyguards to a volleyball match. We won by a single point. We hoped they were more skilled in their professional lives.

Meanwhile, the children kidnapped their leader and suddenly appeared with him sitting precariously in a wheelbarrow, as they whooped with laughter, sprinting through the camp, pursued by more children shouting 'make way for the President, make way, make way!'

Then he was gone, back to his desk job, and I got my sleeping bag back.

Later that month, Havel spoke at the Salzburg Festival in Austria about a strange paralysis which had afflicted him and his colleagues after they had taken over the reins of power. 'It was an extremely odd sensation, comparable to a bad hangover after some wild binge, from awakening from a pleasant dream to the ugly reality of cold daylight, to the shock of a man in love discovering his sweetheart's treachery. . . . what Sisyphus might have felt if one fine day his boulder stopped, rested on the hilltop, and failed to roll back down.'

*   *   *

In December 1990, I went back to Timişoara for the first anniversary of the revolution.

Colonel Not was regional controller of the new Romanian secret police, the RIS. His building was the same as that of the old Securitate, the 'other door' of the police station. There was no insignia outside, no flag flying, no light in the window. The door swung open easily when pushed. A pleasant-faced young man in everyday clothes jumped up hurriedly from a bed where he was reading a pro-government newspaper, and came over to the little window of his booth, inside the entrance hall. He slid the window aside, took down my details, picked up the phone in one hand and then turned his back, as though he didn't want me to see the number. After a while the colonel appeared; he had a cadaverously thin face, lightened somewhat by a genuine, if ironic, smile, gold teeth and a red tie. We sat down at a table and he lit a black market cigarette.

'No-one is afraid today in Romania,' the colonel insisted, as I picked through my long list of concerns. 'They have nothing to be afraid of.'

The room in which we were sitting had armchairs upholstered in green velvet. Nationwide, I had been told, around a quarter of the staff of the new body worked in the Securitate. I had also seen higher figures.

The task of his organisation, he explained earnestly, was to investigate the present and the future, not the past. I mentioned Nuremberg, and the trials of top Nazis after the Second World War. Wouldn't it be useful to hold such a trial in Romania, I asked, where as much of the truth about the Ceauşescu era in Romania could be unveiled as possible?

His grin faded. 'Trials are taking place . . .' he said quietly.

'But the numbers are tiny, and the accused say they are innocent,' I countered.

'Romania needs a second revolution,' said László Tökés, at a press conference on 16 December 1990 to celebrate the anniversary of the start of the first.

'We need peaceful change, with peaceful means. The former regime still exists in ourselves, in our relations with one another, in every aspect of our lives . . .'

'Ethnic divisions are being used for political purpose, to incite people against each other, on every national holiday.'

At the 17 December Association for Victims and Bereaved Families, Traian Orban walked painfully with a crutch, the consequence of a serious thigh wound which he received during the revolution. He picked up the papers from his desk.

'Forty-three bodies are still missing,' he said, at the end of a long list of numbers of dead and injured.

'Are you getting any closer to finding out the truth about what happened?'

He shook his head. 'We're getting further away.'

From the Association's bank account, he distributed money—$200–$800 for the injured, and $1400 for the families of the dead.

The Association collected written evidence against Securitate officers it alleged had personally killed civilians during the revolution. On the basis of their research, they were convinced that many still worked for its successor organisation.

Twenty-one men were still being held on suspicion of taking part in the shooting. Their photographs appeared in a local newspaper.

'These are the accused, but where are the guilty?' screamed the headline.

The students of Timişoara, ever militant, called for a general strike, and workers from several factories—including Electrobanat, and the UMT heavy machinery works—joined them. An ecumenical mass was held on the steps of the Orthodox Cathedral to mark the anniversary. There were banners and slogans, and the sun even came out, briefly, in the cold. But the strike did not spread to other cities. The desire of the people for justice was smaller, at odds even, with their hunger for food, and security.

8. Lonely Russians

Then I grasped it was a wishbone—
'Gorbachev' I shouted
I watched him stumble
'Pull it Michael, pull it!'
He looked distracted,
His fingers froze on the battlefield
I wanted to have children
I wanted to have planet
A big blue wishbone
In the sky over the Caucasus
Wind over Wilverley
Gales in the Atlantic

March 1990

Captain Alexander Krylov of the Soviet Southern Army breathed a long sigh.

'I've got mixed feelings about leaving here,' he said. His daughter was born in Hungary. His wife liked the shops. The standard of living was higher than at home. He'd even bought two dogs for himself during his three years here—Neapolitan mastiffs. He came from Volgograd, the former Stalingrad—'it's twinned with Coventry.' Above all, as his army prepared to leave Hungary, he was worried about the state of the Soviet Union, about the economic and social problems at home and the fact that he, like many of the officers in the middle of their five-year term of service abroad, owned no flat at home. 'I'd like to go to Kiev,' he said. In four to five years, he could expect to be promoted to lieutenant. A career officer served a minimum of twenty-five years in the Red Army. As first the Soviet Empire, then the Soviet Union fell apart, he was running out of places to complete his service.

We were walking across the hardened tarmac of the Southern Army base at Mátyásföld, on the eastern edge of Budapest. It was February 1991, and the last Soviet soldier was due to leave the base by May.

149

Plastered across Hungary, the Young Democrat Association, Fidesz, had put up posters with the words *Tovarishch Konets!*—'The end, Comrade!' and an extremely unsympathetic portrayal of the back of the head of a Soviet officer, with rolls of fat and protruding ears.

'I don't like the posters,' Captain Krylov admitted, 'I prefer our own . . .'—waving, laughing soldiers, with bunches of carnations on their arms, framed by bugle players, lingering over the notes of the 'last post'.

They might be withdrawing without a fight, but there had not been much opportunity to fraternise with the Hungarians either. He knew of only ten soldiers, out of 72,000 in Hungary who had actually married Hungarian girls. Rather surprisingly, to me, he felt the Soviet withdrawal was a fair demand from the Hungarians. 'We have to leave . . . armies should normally serve on their own territory . . .'

Then we moved on to politics.

'Gorbachev must have much greater power than he has now, to create discipline and stability. We have enough democracy now.'

1990 had not been an easy year for the Soviet leader, and 1991 was promising to be worse. As a direct consequence of the policies he had introduced, the Soviet Union was now breaking apart, and his critics were demanding tough measures to halt the process.

In January 1990, Gorbachev had visited the Baltic republic of Lithuania, the first leader to do so since the country was annexed by the Soviet Union in 1940. There he announced that the Soviet Union was working on a law which would lay down the legal mechanism for republics to leave the Union. At the same time, he pleaded with the Lithuanians, the Estonians, the Latvians and all other peoples who were straining at the leash, to seriously consider their options before they opted for independence.

While there were rumblings around the Soviet shoulders, open warfare had broken out down by the Soviet belly, in the Caucasus. The autonomous republic of Nagorno-Karabakh declared independence from Azerbaijan, backed by Armenia, and requested economic aid from Turkey and Iran. The Soviet Army was sent in to restore order. Armenian refugees fled from Azerbaijan. A state of emergency was declared in three southern republics, Armenia, Azerbaijan and Tajikistan. 'State power cannot abandon the use of force in extraordinary situations,' Gorbachev wrote in his memoirs, published in 1995. 'Such actions can only take place if absolutely necessary, and should be as limited as possible. The real solution to problems must always be found in political means.'

Of the 290 million people living in the Soviet Union, only half were Russians. When Gorbachev looked in the mirror, he could see a lot of faces he no longer recognised crowding around him. Each of the peoples of the Soviet Union had its own history, its own aspirations and its own string of grievances towards mother Russia.

At the Soviet barracks at Mátyásföld, Captain Krylov took me to a history class at the Soviet secondary school. The subject of the day was, appropriately enough, 'Russia during the capitalist period.' There were seventeen pupils in the class, all thirteen-years-old, well disciplined, but with strong views of their own. There were pictures in their schoolbooks of the leaders of the democratic movement in Russia between 1840 and 1900, and citations from Lenin. Lenin understood, the teacher explained, that ordinary people living in the last century could not go on living the way they had. The liberals understood that it was necessary to create capitalism out of feudalism. Communism was about equality—'but capitalism was better', piped up a girl in a green fluorescent blouse in the front row, and her girlfriend agreed.

They said they would be sorry to leave their Hungarian friends.

The headmaster of the school was mostly upset by the prospect of destroying school buildings and equipment. These had been offered to the Hungarians, but they didn't want them, he complained. They wanted a tabula rasa, with the Russians gone and no trace of their former presence.

That was going to be very difficult to achieve. As 260 military trains left Hungarian territory for the east, Moscow presented Budapest with a bill for nearly $3 billion for the buildings they had constructed on Hungarian territory over the past decades. Budapest hurriedly put together a hefty counter claim, citing the damage caused to Hungarian property during the years of occupation, especially the environmental damage they were leaving behind. As one barracks, training ground and airfield after another were handed over, the true scale of that damage only began to become apparent. Diesel oil poured for years straight into the soil and dumps full of rusting ammunition which threatened to explode at any time. Moscow wanted to sell the old ammunition to Hungary. Hungary said it had no use for it, and asked the Russians to simply take it away. Moscow proposed that Russia be allowed to store it on Hungarian territory while they searched for another buyer. Budapest was, to put it mildly, not keen.

Another Hungarian tactic was to point out, in a rather tongue in cheek way, that the Soviets had never had planning permission anyway.

Similar discussions were going on between Moscow and Prague and Moscow and Warsaw. 73,500 soldiers, 1,220 tanks, 173 helicopters and 103 fighter planes were due to be withdrawn from Czechoslovakia alone.

Increasingly stuck in the middle, Gorbachev offered compromises to the political leaders of the new democracies which his own generals were unable, or unwilling, to fulfil. The deadlines by which troops and equipment should leave appeared too tight to the Soviet top brass. Regarding the withdrawal from Poland, the Russians wanted to keep large garrisons there, until all troops were withdrawn from East Germany. In military terms, to cover their retreat.

Another important factor slowing the Soviet withdrawal was the simple fact that they had nowhere to go. The decision to withdraw the troops had come so suddenly that several hundred thousand Soviet soldiers had no alternative accommodation at home.

'Please understand our position . . .' said Captain Krylov. 'We are pulling officers and their families, their children, out of comfortable flats, and sending them to live in barracks and tents . . .' One of the main ideas behind claiming compensation from the east Europeans was to fund the construction of new flats—but the east Europeans were not in magnanimous mood.

'If there is any faltering in the Soviet willingness to keep to the signed agreement, the Hungarian authorities would make it public immediately, and seek international support,' Lieutenant General Antal Annus told me. He admitted to being concerned about the situation in the Soviet Union, but 'only in an extreme case' could he imagine that that might influence the withdrawal. What he meant was the danger of a coup against Gorbachev, which had been much on the mind of all the democratic forces in eastern Europe the previous year.

Even as the Soviet soldiers left, the new governments in eastern Europe braced themselves for a new Russian invasion, this time of economic migrants. As the Soviet Parliament prepared to liberalise laws on freedom of movement, an Austrian study suggested that eight million Soviet citizens might try to make a new life in the West. The east European countries grew increasingly alarmed that they might become buffer zones, flooded with Russians as the west Europeans closed down their borders along the line of the so-recently-dismantled Iron Curtain. Ever with an eye to the great ironies of history, the Czech and Hungarian authorities began making plans to turn former Soviet barracks into refugee camps.

'Any Soviet citizen will be eligible for a passport guaranteeing free travel abroad,' said Alexander Lebedev, the head of the consular section of the Soviet embassy in Prague. Over two hundred thousand people had left the USSR in 1988, he said, and he expected that to double in 1990— 'mostly young, unskilled workers, seeking El Dorado.'

Nevertheless, he felt fears of an invasion in central Europe were exaggerated. 'There is talk here of the re-introduction of a visa regime. We Russians have been justly criticised for years for depriving people of the right to travel . . . it would hardly conform to the spirit of a 'common European home' if they now try their hardest to keep Russians out.'

Anyway, they needn't worry, he concluded. 'We cannot print so many passports so quickly, and there are only a limited number of seats on Aeroflot planes . . .'

While the Soviet Union fell apart, Germany was re-uniting—under the careful gaze of the Russians, the Americans and the European powers.

* * *

Nie wieder Deutschland, nie wieder Deutschland—Germany, never again!—I had heard a crowd of at least ten thousand East Germans chanting in Berlin in December 1989. There was considerable resistance to the idea of a new Germany of 79 million people among those in the East schooled in shame over the Nazi regime in the Second World War. But they were far outnumbered by those in favour of re-unification. Germans leaders were keen to prove that this would be an opportunity, not a threat, to the European continent.

'We want a European Germany, not a German Europe,' said the West German Foreign Minister, Hans Dietrich Genscher, quoting the writer, Thomas Mann. Poland insisted that before the two Germanys re-unite, they guarantee the 1945 German-Polish border. Poland had disappeared once before between an expansive Russia and Germany, and wanted to make sure Polish borders were now inviolable.

In March 1990, the Christian Democrats won the East German elections with forty-eight per cent of the vote, with Social Democrats trailing on twenty-two per cent and the Democratic Socialists—the successor party to the communists—in third place with sixteen per cent. An astonishing ninety-three per cent of the electorate voted.

'All the political forces of Europe are taking part in the re-unification of Germany,' the Christian Democrat leader, Lothar de Maizière, said in April. 'In this great historical process of our liberation, we give thanks in particular to one politician, Mikhail Gorbachev ...'

In July, Mikhail Gorbachev was re-elected Soviet Communist Party leader, but the critical voices against him in his own party were growing—over a thousand voted against his candidacy, compared to less than a hundred the previous year.

In September, Transdniestria declared independence from the Soviet Republic of Moldova, which had already declared its intention of leaving the Soviet Union. Russians and Ukrainians together made up equal numbers to Moldovans in Transdniestria, and they were determined to prevent Moldovan re-unification with Romania, to the west. Ethnic conflict broke out and, again, Soviet troops were involved.

On 3 October, Germany was re-united after forty-four years divided between East and West. Mikhail Gorbachev was one of many world leaders to send his congratulations. In December, in the first all German elections since 1932, Chancellor Helmut Kohl and his Christian Democrats won a major victory, and the Social Democrats scored their lowest support for thirty years.

In January 1991, Soviet troops occupied the radio and television buildings, and several ministries, in the Lithuanian capital, Vilnius. Local people formed a human wall to successfully prevent them entering the Parliament. Fifteen civilians were killed in the struggle, and at least 160 injured. A few days later in the Latvian capital of Riga, clashes between troops of the nascent Latvian army and those of the Soviet Interior Ministry took ten more lives. Gorbachev was roundly condemned in many countries for the first time since he took office. When he distanced himself from the order to send the troops in, he succeeded only in showing how weak he had become—the leader of a country in collapse.

As Gorbachev stumbled, the former head of the Moscow Party, Boris Yeltsin, manoeuvred himself carefully forward. Yeltsin travelled to Lithuania as a Russian, not a Soviet, leader, and immediately reached agreement with the leaders of Estonia, Latvia and Lithuania for the mutual recognition of the Baltic States and Russia.

'Russian separatists ... used the events in Vilnius and Riga to strengthen their own positions by supporting the separatist endeavours of the Baltic states ...' Gorbachev wrote in his memoirs.

'Our forces made mistakes in the Baltic region,' Captain Krylov told me, a month later. His uncle was a Russian, living in Vilnius, so he had some personal information about the events. 'For example, when they stormed the television offices. Though there were some provocations from the side of local people, I am a military man, and I believe arms must not be used against civilians. With stability, we can solve all our problems.'

On the early morning of 19 August 1991, the nightmare which had haunted east Europeans for several years, since the moment each realised that Gorbachev was serious, finally came true. Tanks appeared on the streets of Moscow and several other Soviet cities, and a committee of army generals and ministers declared a state of emergency, as Gorbachev's 'illness was preventing him fulfilling his functions as head of state.' I went out onto the balcony of my Budapest flat, struggling for air.

*   *   *

Was everything I had lived through for the past five years going to unravel? Surely the changes in eastern Europe had gone too far? But what might a military dictatorship in Moscow mean for the region? Nothing good.

Opinion polls suggested forty per cent of the Soviet population supported the attempted putsch. With Gorbachev under arrest on the shore of the Black Sea, Boris Yeltsin took control of the situation, condemning the coup and calling for a general strike. On 21 August, military forces belonging to the Soviet secret police, the KGB, tried to seize the Russian Parliament, but outside the building army tanks and demonstrators loyal to Yeltsin prevented this. Two days later, Gorbachev resigned as leader of the Communist Party. Ten republics took advantage of the turmoil in the centre to declare their independence from the Soviet Union—Estonia, Latvia, Ukraine, Tajikistan, Belarus, Moldova, Azerbaijan, Kazakhstan, Kirgizia and Uzbekistan. The Soviet Union was, to all extents and purposes, over. On 21 December, the man who had opened the way for the collapse of his country, and the re-unification of Europe, Mikhail Gorbachev, stepped down as Soviet leader.

'Today, I am still convinced of the correctness of the democratic reforms we started in 1985,' he told the nation in a televised address on 25 December, 'but we have still not learnt how to live with freedom.'

The sudden withdrawal of that Soviet influence left a vacuum of power that no in-rush of western capital, western journalists or even western secret agents could fill.

155

'From Stettin in the Baltic, to Trieste in the Adriatic, an iron curtain has descended across the continent,' said Winston Churchill in Fulton, Missouri on 5 March 1946. 'Behind that line lie all the capitals of the ancient states of central and eastern Europe. [. . .] And all are subject, in one form or another, not only to Soviet influence, but to a very high and, in some cases, increasing measure of control from Moscow.'

Western Europe seemed even less prepared for the new situation than eastern Europe. It was as though a twin had woken from a coma.

9. The Man with the Knife

Even if we don't know how to work, or do business, we know how to fight!

Slobodan Milošević, speech to local mayors,
Serbia, March 1991

Something odd was happening beside the lamp-post. I walked a little faster, afraid to discover some dreadful crime. It was nearly midnight, close to a bridge over the River Vardar in Skopje, capital of the Yugoslav Republic of Macedonia, in November 1990. A young man with a black beard and a dark beret, sucking absent-mindedly on a pipe, was carefully gouging out the eyes of Petar Gusev, the leader of the Macedonian Communist Party, on every campaign poster he could find. As I was in his town to cover the same Federal Yugoslav elections, it seemed only fair to strike up a conversation. 'I hate communists,' the man explained, helpfully. So he was doing his democratic duty. Gouging all their eyes out on the eve of election day.

The collapse of communism in eastern Europe and the disintegration of the Soviet Union left Yugoslavia exposed politically, and ideologically.

After the Second World War, the single party system was organised on different lines in Yugoslavia than in eastern Europe, more closely mirroring the Soviet Union.

Under the 1946 constitution, the country was divided into six republics and two autonomous regions, both in Serbia, Kosovo in the south and Vojvodina in the north.

Power was held by the Party both centrally and locally by its loyal lieutenants in each republic. For the next forty-five years, the tension between the nations remained more or less under control, with occasional eruptions.

From a nationalist perspective, Yugoslavia held its many peoples together against their will. From an internationalist and communist

157

perspective, Yugoslavia was the answer to a problem created by the nationalists; how to live together in the name of progress and prosperity, putting aside national grievances.

Josip Broz Tito, the communist partisan leader who became the unchallenged master of Yugoslavia until his death in 1980, played the nations off against one another in order to keep his state firmly together. Initially, there were the 'main' nations: Serbs, Croats, Montenegrins, Slovenes and Macedonians. The Macedonians were especially pleased with this development, as their own identity had not been recognised when the country was first constituted in 1918 as the Kingdom of Serbs, Croats and Slovenes. Then there were the others—Bosnian Muslims (now also known as Bosniaks,) Albanians, Hungarians and Roma, guaranteed equality under the constitution, but without the comfort of their own national status. In 1948, just as most east European countries were being politically coerced into the Soviet Empire, Tito's Yugoslavia was expelled from it. Communism remained the dominant ideology, but in his foreign affairs Tito shunned the bi-polar world and went on to establish the so-called Non-Aligned Movement with India and Egypt.

In 1951, a young Cambodian student, Saloth Sar, came to Yugoslavia during the summer holidays from his studies in Paris, with other volunteers, to help 'build socialism'. He spent the summer digging ditches in Zagreb, and would later say that this, alongside his readings of the Chinese leader, Mao Tse-Tung, were the most formative experiences of his life. He was later known as Pol Pot, and oversaw the killing of some one million of his seven million fellow Cambodians.

In 1953, a constitutional law was passed, suppressing national, in favour of 'Yugoslav' identity. Socialist consciousness was to replace 'national consciousness'. But from 1956, the same year as the Hungarian Revolution, the smaller peoples of the federation were referred to as 'nationalities' rather than 'national minorities'.

In 1961, the 'Muslims' of Yugoslavia, concentrated especially in Bosnia but also scattered throughout the country, were granted the status of a nation.

The history of Yugoslavia was dotted with 'uprisings', of both a national and social character. In 1968, Kosovar Albanian students took to the streets, demanding recognition as a separate republic. Tito's skill lay in giving, as well as taking. A year after the riots, an Albanian language university was set up in Priština. In 1974, a new Yugoslav Constitution was passed, which devolved far more power to the republics than had been the case until then. The provinces of Kosovo and Vojvodina were granted a similar status to the republics, but without the right to secede, which the others theoretically enjoyed. Yugoslavia was defined as 'a federal state with the form of a state community of voluntarily united nations and their Socialist Republics.' Each had their own police, central banks, courts and schools.

In 1971, however, the Croatian Spring—a combination of Croatian national and liberal ideas—was crushed by Tito, just as the Soviet Union had crushed the Prague Spring three years earlier.

In 1981, less than a year after the death of Tito, student demonstrations in Kosovo which had been sparked by frustrations over two-hour queues at Priština's university canteen turned into nationalist protests and demands for better food and dormitories rapidly spread through the province. Tanks were deployed on the street and the police opened fire, killing dozens. The 1980s were marked by the growth of nationalist sentiment in all corners of the country, most noisily in Serbia, Croatia and Kosovo.

In Serbia, Slobodan Milošević rode the nationalist wave, abandoning the internationalism of Tito to proclaim to Serbs in Kosovo that 'no one'—meaning the Kosovar Albanians—'should dare to beat you.' The treatment of Serbs in Kosovo became a litmus test of Serbian nationalism, and also of how far the communists in Belgrade were prepared to bend to listen to, or even to steal the thunder of, the nationalists.

Instead of Tito's careful balancing of nations, each began to provoke the other. In the spring of 1989, Belgrade declared martial law in Kosovo, suppressed strikes and protests and amended the constitution again, stripping Kosovo and Vojvodina of their status.

Milošević's promises to make Serbia once more the top dog in Yugoslavia, after their 'subservient role' under Tito, were seen as both a threat, and an opportunity, by the other nations. Croatian demands for an independent state, dormant but not extinguished after the 1971 events, grew rapidly.

In January 1990, the Fourteenth Special Congress of the League of Communists of Yugoslavia (LCY) ended abruptly with the Croatian and Slovene delegations walking out. The elections in November and December 1990 were overshadowed by the question of what form Yugoslavia should take in future, and if indeed it should even continue to exist. With the teacher—Tito—strangely absent, the pupils began overturning benches and fighting among themselves.

In the narrow, cobbled streets of old Skopje, close to the River Vardar, the sun came out and men played chess or backgammon beneath the mulberry trees, and talked about the state of their country. Relative to most of eastern Europe in the communist years, the Yugoslavs were rather well off. There was incomparably more food in the shops. There was a far free-er press—the first reports of the unrest in Romania in 1987 were made public by the respected Yugoslav state news agency, Tanjug. But storm clouds were gathering, and as far as most non-Serbs in Yugoslavia in the Balkans were concerned, most of those clouds had Slobodan Milošević's name on them.

The initials of the Yugoslav army, the JNA, were mentioned almost as often as Milošević. Whatever the politicians did, the army was always regarded as a key player, as in the Soviet Union and Turkey.

'I personally don't think the army will allow Yugoslavia to disintegrate,' Milan Djurĉinov of the Party of Yugoslavs in Macedonia, told me.

'Some regard the use of military force with fear . . . Others see it as the last means to secure peace of any kind . . . because this agony has been lasting too long.'

I went to see Petar Gusev next, the Macedonian communist leader whom my bearded revolutionary had taken such exception to. His eyes—no longer visible on his defaced posters—were a deep brown and he sported a blue tie, flecked with red, and an elegant grey waist-coat. In an election fought between parties with long names, his had one of the longest: League of Communists—Party for Democratic Transformation.

He stressed the achievements of the years of communist rule, with a clear nod in the direction of Macedonian identity. Tito had established a Yugoslav Republic of Macedonia, he pointed out. The Communist Party in each of the republics had contributed most to good relations between the different Yugoslav nations. Of course there had been mistakes, he admitted. Communism as an ideology 'was not productive.' But they had decided to keep the name for the time being, as a link to the working class and to the poor. And they had a new, progres-sive programme, social-democracy, based on greater social justice. The survival of Yugoslavia would depend on the strength or weakness of the policies coming from Belgrade. He supported more independence for the republics, but linked together in a common, Yugoslav state. He had little time for the nationalists, in Macedonia or elsewhere. 'Little

Neros' he called them—'they want to burn down Yugoslavia with their national struggles.'

He was talking, among others, about Ljubčo Georgievski. His black beard set off nicely by his white suit, Georgievski was the leader of IMRO, the Inner Macedonian Revolutionary Organisation, usually known by its Macedonian acronym VMRO, the main conservative party in this election. Founded in 1893, the organisation had a long and sometimes violent history of fighting for a Macedonian identity.

He began our conversation, predictably, with a history lesson.

'The king had to die . . .' he said, referring to King Alexander of Yugoslavia, gunned down by a VMRO member while on a state visit to Marseilles in 1934. This was one of the first assassinations caught on film. He had to die because he opposed Macedonian national aspirations.

Georgievski came across as thoughtful, but fanatical. Macedonia needed its own army and its own foreign policy, he said. 'We want the world to realise that there is a country called Macedonia somewhere.' There was a need for a new Macedonian state, he said, within a united Balkans, within a united Europe. 'We're not getting ready for war, but for a new Europe, in which democracy is a fact.'

I was travelling with an artist, Charlie Foster-Hall, instead of a photographer on this long road trip. The next day Charlie and I were on stage with Georgievski, at his final election rally.

We stood on the stage among the floodlights and the election banners in the pouring rain. A sea of scarlet flags adorned with banners and golden Macedonian lions thundered below us. Georgievski, immaculately dressed as always, bellowed his nationalist, anti-communist message. In a crowded puddle of television cameras and photographers on the edge of the stage, I held an umbrella, as Charlie frantically sketched and painted the scene beside me. Besides the cameras and the sound system, it could have been any moment in the last few hundred years, of national hopes aroused, whipped up, crushed, but never quite extinguished.

My last call in Skopje was to the Alliance of Reformed Forces of Macedonia. The reformists had set up sister parties in each republic, and were rather proud of their image as the main, non-nationalist alternative to the communist parties throughout Yugoslavia. 'Our colour is white,' Georgi Hadži-Vaskov, the party's Vice-President, explained. 'Because we have no relations with the past.' It seemed an odd, even an outrageous claim in a country where the past tasted as strong as the plum brandy which the Serbs, in particular, excelled at making—and democracy was pale beer in comparison.

'But all this will pass,' Petar Gusev had concluded, confidently. 'Our passions are growing at the moment. These peoples quarrel loudly, but we make love passionately too.'

Compared to Romania under Ceaușescu, and to much of eastern Europe under communism, Yugoslavia was a consumers' paradise. Most families in the cities at least had washing machines, fridges, freezers and video players. The shelves were packed with food from north and south, and the Balkan peninsula, ever a trade route and sometimes a battlefield, boasted some of the best markets in eastern Europe. There were denims and sheep's cheese from Novi Pazar, red wines from Macedonia and Montenegro, white wines from Vojvodina and fresh fish from the Dalmatian coast in Croatia and Montenegro. The borders of Yugoslavia were open, and Yugoslavs travelled widely in Europe and beyond in large numbers, in search of work. The borders were also somewhat easier to cross for other peoples. A Hungarian friend of mine tried to cross the Yugoslav border into Greece in the 1970s, but was turned back by Yugoslav border-guards because his red passport was valid only for socialist countries. He found a quieter crossing, and the guards took pity on him and let him across after dark.

In the mid-1980s, National Geographic magazine ran a special edition praising both the colourful diversity of the country, and its tolerance and unity. I wonder what the writer felt later.

Across the border in Kosovo, we tried to book into the almost empty Grand Hotel in the centre of Priština, a vast communist-era edifice, but were told, rather rudely, that there were no vacancies. It didn't look a particularly friendly place anyway. There were policemen with machine guns in the lobby, as there were on the approach roads into the town. So we took a room at a smaller hotel just up the road. This one seemed empty, but three men in dark anoraks who refused to meet our eyes, and ignored our attempts to greet them, moved into the neighbouring room immediately.

The nationalists in Serbia, on whom Slobodan Milošević had based his rapid ascent through the Communist Party, were delighted by his moves to confront the Kosovar Albanians. Who would have thought a communist could prove such a good patriot? The restive Albanians who formed the majority of the population in Kosovo, and the restive minority of Hungarians in Vojvodina would be taught a lesson now, they hoped.

After the replacement of Kosovo's own curriculum by Serbia's, Albanian pupils boycotted classes, and their teachers set up a system of parallel, underground schools to teach as they wished. The Albanian language daily, Rilindja, was banned the previous July.

In the Albanian cafés, pictures of the Albanian writer, Ismail Kadare, torn from newspapers, gave people a sense of belonging to a bigger, prouder people—the Albanians of Albania, of Macedonia and of the diaspora. Kadare had left communist Albania, and now lived in Paris, where he spoke often of the plight of Kosovar Albanians.

In conversation, the Albanians competed with the Serbs about who suffered most at the hands of the other.

'Rape, particularly of little girls, is a serious crime located at the very apex of the pyramid of discrimination,' said a glossy pamphlet, distributed to foreign journalists by the Federal Ministry of Information in Belgrade. Serb tabloid newspapers were full of gory details. A Serbian farmer, allegedly abused with a broken bottle, was one of the most celebrated.

The Albanians countered with statistics of their own. One hundred murdered Albanians in the past decade was their usual figure. Various illegal papers circulated, full of gruesome pictures of the bodies of ethnic Albanian conscripts, tortured or killed by their fellow Serb soldiers while on national service in the Yugoslav army. In September 1987, one Albanian conscript, Aziz Kelmendi, went berserk and opened fire in his barracks, killing four soldiers, before killing himself. Eight fellow Albanian conscripts were later convicted as his 'accomplices'. After that, few Kosovar Albanian youths obeyed the call-up.

What was certain was that the Serbs were leaving Kosovo, 400,000 in the past fifty years, according to Serb figures, driven out by 'intimidation, violence and fear'.

The Albanians were portrayed as a nation of drug runners and terrorists. 'One kilo of heroin,' continued the same pamphlet from Belgrade, 'generated enough profit to buy the entire property of a Serbian family in Kosovo, or forty automatic rifles.'

Slobodan Milošević was seen by Serbs as the strongman who could stem the tide. Tito, until recently a revered national statesman, was portrayed as the leader of a conspiracy to keep Serbia 'small and weak'.

At Radio Priština, I talked to the editor, Rade Tomić. 'The communists gave Kosovo as a gift to the Albanian minority,' he said.

As Serbia struggled to re-assert its control, the Albanians had called a general strike. 'And after five days' absence,' said Tomić, 'they lost their jobs.' Tens of thousands of Albanians were dismissed from their work places in this way.

'Dignity is the question here,' said Neriman Kamberi, a student who was working as my interpreter, 'and we Albanians are very proud.'

She could have been speaking of any of the Balkan, or east European peoples. While the Serbian authorities were exploring just how much pressure the other nations could bear from them, their opponents were looking not so much for a united front against Belgrade, as for a multitude of fronts on which to oppose the central power.

'We need more peoples to be against the Serbs,' she said, 'like the Croats, and the Slovenes. And more division among the Serbs themselves.'

'We are revolting. . . . they are revolting.' She used the word in the sense of 'making revolution', like Shakespeare in Richard II.

> We'll make foul weather with despised tears;
> Our sighs and they shall lodge the summer corn,
> And make a dearth in this revolting land.

'We need a dialogue,' Neriman continued, 'but they do not want one.'

At the time of my visit, there were no prominent Albanians in prison, for a change. It was too dangerous to organise demonstrations, she said. 'We are just biding our time, waiting until we have something in our hands.'

She took me to meet Zenun Çelaj, a journalist and member of the Council for the Defence of Human Rights and Freedoms. He had just been released from one of his frequent prison spells, under article 136 of the Yugoslav penal code, for 'forming hostile groups endangering the territorial integrity of Yugoslavia.' He estimated that some two to three thousand people were in a similar position, often released on bail, awaiting trial, as a way to increase the pressure on them to desist from political activity.

'We're only a small nation,' he said, 'and we rely greatly on the democratic processes that have swept eastern Europe, and will hopefully become a reality in Yugoslavia and Kosovo too.' He bemoaned the sacking of Albanians in Kosovo—40,000 had lost their jobs since June. Ten thousand people sentenced over the past decade for opposing the regime, 100,000 families without an income.

'The Serbs definitely want us to become violent, so they can clamp down on us further,' he said. But peaceful resistance was now the philosophy of all Albanians in Kosovo, he added.

How would he feel if his son or daughter married a Serb? I asked before we left. He paused for a moment. 'I would not forbid it,' he said, 'but I would not be pleased.'

We were talking at an outside table at the Café Tropical, beneath the Hotel Grand, on an unseasonably warm November day. The man at the next table sported a handle-bar moustache, a brown jacket and arranged what looked like a fat pen, but was in fact a microphone, on the table top in front of him, pointing over the ashtray in our direction.

To travel through Yugoslavia in the autumn of 1990 was to see a country held together in places, it seemed, only by denim. The jeans and jean jackets, the denim skirts, mostly manufactured in Novi Pazar in southern Serbia, were like a uniform to rival the dress of the omnipresent army—an army which was still popular with the people, but only just. In photography shops there were little square, passport-sized pictures of boys, invariably in uniform, taken on their first day in the army. These were the pictures, of their brothers or their sweethearts, which girls carried in their purses.

'Many clever people think Yugoslavia is breaking up,' Georgi Marjanović of the League for Democracy in Skopje had told me. 'But it's not true! The communists didn't make Yugoslavia, and they won't break it apart either.'

Much was to depend on just how hard Serbia pushed its dominance, and how cleverly or toughly the various peoples resisted.

From Kosovo, we drove to Belgrade. Four years earlier, the Serbian Academy of Sciences and Arts had carefully defined in a leaked draft entitled "Memorandum" the nationalism which was to define public discourse for the next decade. Using strong and emotional language, it portrayed the Serbs as the main victims of first fascism and then communism, in Kosovo and in Croatia.

> In less than fifty years, for two successive generations, the Serbs were twice subjected to physical annihilation, forced assimilation, conversion to a different religion, cultural genocide, ideological indoctrination, denigration and compulsion to renounce their own traditions because of an imposed guilt complex.

Slobodan Milošević rode to power on the wave of such appeals, and from the summer of 1988 to the spring of 1989 had organised 'rallies for truth' to unite the Serb nation around its 'struggle for survival'. Estimates of how many people in total took part in these rallies vary from three to five million. At each, representatives of the Kosovo Serbs would arrive and give details of the 'genocide' against them. Serbian state television, RTS, run by Milošević's friend Dušan Mitević, made sure the message dominated airwaves which until recently had been among the most respected in eastern Europe for the standards of their journalism. Unlike in most socialist countries, Yugoslavs had grown used to believing their media.

In 1988 and 1989, the bones of Tsar Lazar, defeated by the Turks, according to Serbian legend, at the Battle of the Field of Blackbirds in 1389, were taken on a tour of Serbia and parts of Bosnia, moving from church to church and drawing enormous crowds. The tale of Lazar had been immortalised in the nineteenth century in a poem which every Serbian schoolchild knew. Until it was written down by Vuk Karadžić, the great Serbian writer, the story had survived as epic poetry, sung around the fireside and so handed down from generation to generation. It had helped keep Serb national consciousness alive during the centuries of Ottoman Turkish domination. Now the legend, as it were, shifted onto the offensive.

Milošević visited Kosovo on the six hundredth anniversary of the battle, 28 June 1389, and addressed a crowd of half a million Serbs.

> The battle of Kosovo contains within itself one great symbol. That is the symbol of heroism. [. . .] Six centuries later, we are again involved in battles, and facing battles. These are not battles with arms, but they cannot be excluded . . .

Slobodan Milošević was notoriously difficult to win an interview with, so I settled for one of his many right-hand men, Vladimir Štambuk.

'Serbia was never dominant, and doesn't want to dominate now either,' said Štambuk, over glasses of fresh orange juice.

'Serbia became important, because it is the biggest nation, with forty-five per cent of the total population. We are for a modern, federal Yugoslavia of equal citizens, with equal rights.' Russians were only in a slightly better demographic position in their even more composite country, I remembered.

I challenged him on recent comments by Milošević. If a federal Yugoslavia ceased to exist, he had said, the question of Serbia's borders would be opened. This had been taken as a less-than-veiled threat to include all territories where there were Serbs—in Croatia and Bosnia, in Montenegro, and also perhaps in Macedonia—in a future 'Greater Serbia'. This was the logical conclusion of the views propounded by Serb nationalists in the Academy's 1986 'Memorandum'.

'What Milošević said is: if someone wants to change Yugoslavia, we should talk about how to do it,'—in other words, an invitation, not a threat. But a barbed invitation, nonetheless.

'We're not making any preparations for an independent Serbia,' Štambuk continued, 'but we can't impose the federal Yugoslavia we want on anyone.'

'Was his party nationalist?' I asked.

'There's no Serb nationalism here,' he replied. 'We're a Socialist Party, which acknowledges national characteristics.'

Rilindja—the daily paper of Albanian communists—had been banned in Kosovo because it was promoting secession, he said. 'Albanians in Kosovo have all rights, except the right to secede.'

They would be won over by the economic development of their part of Serbia, he concluded, confidently, as would all other poor and backward parts of the country.

'Nationalism provides a simple answer to complex problems, which everyone can understand,' said Sonja Licht, a Serb human rights activist. 'We're better than everyone. But we are endangered by them.'

'The West should understand that the East is exhausted. That its people can no longer be the victims of experiments.'

*   *   *

In Sarajevo I stood in the crude, over-large footprints of Gavrilo Princip, which were imprinted in the pavement outside the museum dedicated to his memory, and looked towards the River Miljacka, just as he did on 28 June 1914, when he shot dead the Austrian Archduke Franz Ferdinand and his pregnant wife, Sophia. Inside the museum were pictures of the sickly, dark eyed, eighteen-year-old youth, and the secret correspondence between him and fellow revolutionaries in Belgrade, who supplied him with a Browning semi-automatic pistol; there was even his mother's distaff, the stick she used for carding sheep's wool into strands for weaving. Before the First World War, young Bosnia was a group of Serbs and some Croats and Bosnian Muslims, intent on the unification of the South Slavs in one state, if necessary by violent means. Austrian rule was the main obstacle.

I went to see Radovan Karadžić, leader of the Serbian Democratic Party at his down-town office.

'We have to persuade people that nothing bad will happen if we take power,' he told me. The man who would soon lead his people to war came across as a rather weak, pleading character, eager to impress. He was not for a Greater Serbia, he insisted. Most of all he wanted to talk about the sufferings of the Serbs throughout their history, culminating in the atrocities committed against them by the fascist Ustasha movement in 1941. No matter how hard I tried, on this and subsequent occasions, it was always hard to get Karadžić off the subject of 1941, and the Jasenovac concentration camp in Croatia. Without any disrespect for his people or their suffering, I had a job to do, and anxiously watched the hands of the clock move as I looked for a chance to ask him about more contemporary political questions.

* * *

The éminence grise of his party, a Sarajevo Serb historian, Milorad Ekmečić, was a better conversation partner. He had written the glowing eulogy to Gavrilo Princip I read in the museum.

Ekmečić spoke about the Croat leader, Franjo Tudjman, first. He was not a bad historian, he said, but he didn't like his brand of Croatian nationalism, which he called 'a revival of the old-fashioned nationalist movement of Croatia, founded on the political ideology of the Catholic church.' Most of all, he disliked Tudjman's 'identification of Croatian civilisation as something different from Serbian civilisation,' he said, 'something greater.' So I was treated to another history lesson, on the first Serbian constitution of 1844, and nineteenth century efforts to make the Serbs 'the centre of the southern Slavs—a European state, not a Russian satellite in the Balkans.'

Ekmečić was optimistic about Yugoslavia surviving its current trials and tribulations. 'In my opinion Yugoslavia will not disappear. Geographically, it will exist. No one should place bets on their destiny.'

What was happening now in many places in Yugoslavia, he said, was a 'Serbian uprising' comparable to the Serbian uprisings against Ottoman rule in the early nineteenth century. What he didn't mention was that those had been accompanied by the burning of mosques, and the forced expulsion of the Muslim population.

'When I was a child, before the Second World War, Serbs and Croats in Bosnia, with Muslim neighbours, would not raise pigs in order not to offend the Muslims,' said Ekmečić. But that traditional tolerance of one another had been badly damaged during the war by massacres of Muslims, Serbs and Jews, he said.

'We are all just a handful of misery,' concluded Ekmečić.

'Bismillah, irrahman irrahim, Ente ul Haadi, Ente ul Haqq . . .' 'In the name of Allah the merciful, the beneficent, you are the guide to the right path, you are the truth,' chanted some forty men, kneeling on sheepskin rugs in the old tekija, the dervish prayer hall, up the steep hill above the Baščaršija, the old Ottoman district of Sarajevo.

I had been tempted into the tekija by a half-open door into a courtyard, and the beautiful calligraphy, half-obscured by a pile of logs, stacked against it.

The men rocked gently from side to side, chanting the ninety-nine names of God. We were motioned to sit at the back, and invited to drink tea with them afterwards.

A black kitten played on the woodpile outside, among vines and rose bushes. 'All this country needs is understanding and love,' smiled a man in a light brown fez.

It was hard not to fall in love with Bosnia at first sight.

'We are not a religious party,' said Alija Izetbegović, of the Party of Democratic Action or SDA. He wore an open necked-shirt and thin blue cardigan, and was flanked by his son Bakir on one side, and another party official on the other. Almost alone of the leading candidates in this election, Izetbegović was not a former communist, and had spent many years in the notorious prison in Foča for his Islamic faith. During the election campaign he caused a stir at a rally in Kladuša, by suggesting that the Muslims might take up arms in Bosnia 'as a last resort, in self defence.'

He brushed aside the reference at our interview. 'We want people to be able to express their religion in a peaceful way.'

There was nothing to fear from his party winning the elections, as the polls were starting to predict, he explained. The Muslims would never be able to govern Bosnia alone, with their forty-two per cent of the population, compared to thirty-two per cent for the Serbs and eighteen per cent for the Croats. He imagined a grand coalition of national parties—his SDA, Karadžić's SDS and the Bosnian Croat HDZ, he said, as the real alternative to communist rule. He had even attended the founding meeting of Karadžić's SDS.

Across the street at the headquarters of the Yugoslav Reformist Forces, well-heeled young men in sharp suits, smoking Marlboro cigarettes, were equally confident about victory in the elections. They warned that the national parties would break up the country, and counted on the support of all those who felt themselves to be Yugoslavs, first and foremost. If the Reformists, led by Yugoslav Prime Minister Ante Marković did well in all the republics, they argued, that would make them strong enough to hold the country together.

'Everything depends on whether the enthusiasm of the people for their long-suppressed identities, or their fear of the consequences of that, carry the day,' I wrote in the Observer.

The enthusiasm won. Milošević's Socialists, decked out in their most nationalist colours, won forty-six per cent of the vote, and 194 of the 250 seats in the Serbian Assembly. Milošević himself defeated thirty-one other candidates for the post of Serbian President, with sixty-five per cent support.

In Croatia, Tudjman's HDZ had won some forty per cent of the vote in elections held in two rounds in April and May. Thanks to the system, this gave the HDZ almost two thirds of the seats in Parliament, which duly elected Tudjman as President soon afterwards. In December 1990, Croatia passed a new constitution, in which, crucially, the republic's Serbs were demoted to the status of a national minority, as opposed to the constitutional equals of the Croats. Serbs made up twelve per cent of the Croatian population.

The same month, Slovenes voted ninety-five per cent in favour of independence. In Bosnia, just as he had predicted when we met, Alija Izetbegović formed an uneasy 'nationalist' alliance between his SDA, Karadžić's SDS and the Bosnian branch of the Croatian HDZ.

The disintegration of Yugoslavia was speeding up and was about to claim its first victims.

On 25 June 1991, Slovenia and Croatia declared independence from Yugoslavia. The Federal Parliament in Belgrade condemned the move, and the army took control of the border crossings and surrounded the Slovene capital, Ljubljana. In the ten days that followed, forty-four JNA soldiers and eighteen Slovenes died.

Fearing civil war on their doorstep, European leaders scrambled to find a solution, or at least create a space for one. But they were each backing different horses. In Germany, Chancellor Helmut Kohl warned that Yugoslavia could not be held together by force. On 7 July on the Adriatic island of Brioni, Croatian and Slovene leaders reluctantly agreed to a three month moratorium on independence, under European Community pressure. The conditions included a return of JNA troops to barracks, and that a Croatian politician, Stipe Mesić, assume the Yugoslav rotating federal presidency—which Serbia had so far blocked.

After talks with US President George W. Bush, Mikhail Gorbachev spoke in favour of Yugoslav unity. The alternative, he said, 'was a chain reaction of national and ethnic minorities around the world. This is not just about Yugoslavia . . .'

Both Serb and Croat communities in Croatia had been arming and clashes had begun in earnest in spring. At the beginning, Croatia had no forces to resist the federal army, in which its own people were supposed to be an intrinsic part. The JNA was rapidly becoming a Serbian army in all but name. Croatian Serbs who lived in the Krajina region had already declared autonomy in the so-called "log revolution". A National Guard was quickly set up, and the Croats secured 20,000 Kalashnikovs from Hungary. This was a transaction made by the Croatian Defence Minister, who was then tricked into making inflammatory statements by Yugoslav military intelligence, who duly filmed the affair and had it broadcast on television. The Hungarians, especially, were greatly embarrassed.

The Serb position was clear—if nations wanted to break away they could, but there was no way they were taking those parts of their republics where there was a sizeable number of Serbs. Those regions should have the right to break away, too, and attach themselves to mother Serbia, Belgrade argued.

As Yugoslavia fell apart, my own life came together. In June, I was married in Budapest, and as we set out on our honeymoon, I tried for once not to follow the news.

The three months respite which Croatia and Slovenia had won soon expired. By mid-September, when I returned to Zagreb, 449 people had been killed in atrocities between Serbs and Croats in villages in Croatia. The Croatian Serbs pondered whether to defend their rights peacefully. Then they chose force. Armed by Serbia, backed by it politically and now also by the JNA, they seized that third of the country they felt belonged, also, to them.

That did not mean that Tudjman and Milošević could not do business together. In March they had already discussed in great detail the partition of Bosnia between them. Milošević always seemed to get the better of their encounters, a fox beside the owlish Tudjman. Tudjman was a genuine nationalist; Milošević, I felt, was only one by convenience, for as long as it would serve his much simpler goal of staying in power.

Gangs of youths sang old fascist songs from the Second World War in the streets and bars of Zagreb. Serbs were offended when the checkerboard symbol of Croatia was put back in the centre of its flag, charging that this was the Ustasha Croatian flag, with only cosmetic changes. There was talk of introducing a new currency called the kuna, as it was also known under the Ustashas. In Belgrade the state television dug out wartime films of Croat leaders meeting Hitler, and played them ad nauseam. The first bodies started to appear in the rivers—victims of ethnic hatred upstream. Fear rose like a dark tide.

* * *

The trains, amazingly, kept running, and my journey from Budapest was rather unusual. All the lights on the train were turned off at the border. The country was under night-time curfew, and we passed through town after town like a ghost train, each railway station adorned with huge checkerboard Croatian flags. That night in the Hotel Esplanade in Zagreb, I watched Tudjman speak on television.

'The army has been shaken by the blows we have given it in recent days,' he told the nation. 'Perhaps that is why they want to negotiate' Following a deal between Milošević and the Slovenes, the army had withdrawn from Slovenia soon after its first, hapless intervention in June, but JNA bases dotted across Croatia were bristling with weapons and extremely nervous soldiers. Croatian police forces, and its nascent army, surrounded them, and a tense stand-off developed.

There were air-raid sirens that night in the Croatian capital, and several loud explosions. I slept on the floor beside my bed, feeling rather foolish to be so wasteful of the five-star sheets. Flares dropped by military jets lit the sky, and there were reports that the television tower and the airport had been hit. Meanwhile, JNA soldiers besieged in their barracks opened fire on the homes of Croatian policemen in the city.

Snipers took up position in many streets. As I left the hotel each morning, staff at the reception desk advised which streets to avoid.

One evening, I went to visit Slobodan Lang, a prominent public health worker and human rights activist, at his home. Because of the fear of snipers, I had to decide whether to walk as quietly as possible, to avoid detection, or as loudly as possible, so no-one mistook me for the enemy. I chose the latter, then realised I was still wearing my soft-soled wedding shoes. No matter how much I stamped, they hardly made any sound on the pavement.

Croatian television put together a propaganda film of its new soldiers, running in slow motion through the undergrowth in combat fatigues, effortlessly defeating the Serbs. Serbian television ran another version about its own, heroic warriors. Folk music and national anthems underlay both. In the predominantly Serb village of Borovo Selo in Croatia, twelve Croatian policemen died in May, when they walked into an ambush.

As the conflict intensified in the coming months, I was in Zagreb one night, Belgrade the next. At the end of the news on both days, the state broadcasters showed exactly the same footage of a school of whales which had been washed up on an Australian beach. It seemed a peculiarly apt symbol for the death of Yugoslavia.

I joined a policeman training his rifle over the sandbags which surrounded the Borongaj army barracks in Zagreb. He had a little blue radio, and a pair of binoculars through which he watched for any movement behind the lace curtains in the windows of the long green squat building. There were 600 soldiers inside, he said. A Croatian militia car drew up behind us.

'What's going on?'

'We're waiting to see if there will be peace. The army don't want to give up so easily.'

A young Croatian woman wore a pink t-shirt beneath the camouflage jacket of the Croatian National Guard, her brown curls resting on the sight of her rifle, her grey eyes looking hard beyond her years. I stood at an upstairs window of the Esplanade, waiting for a BBC colleague to finish her report. At one point, someone slammed the boot of a Renault 4 loudly in the street outside. 'There goes another one,' I heard her say into the microphone. This was going to be a strange war. There were an estimated 57,000 Serbs living in Zagreb. Who could now trust whom?

I went to see one of the flats which had been targeted by the military, number 51 Jordanovac Street. There were three big holes in the side of the building, and about half the windows in the whole block were broken. The bedroom was a mess of smashed furniture and bits of a telegraph pole, blown in from the street outside. The occupants—a policeman's family—survived the attack in the cellar.

There was constant fighting around Osijek, in the east of the country, and in the wine-growing villages around Ilok. The siege of the exposed town of Vukovar on the River Danube had begun in August. By the time it fell on 18 November, it looked like post-war pictures of Hiroshima. But this was a far slower death, the buildings chewed away by constant shelling.

In October, the Yugoslav navy began shelling the medieval walled city of Dubrovnik on the Adriatic coast. As an act of state-sponsored vandalism, it did the Serb war cause enormous damage. Four naval commanders were eventually put on trial for the shelling, in which more than forty people died. Miodrag Jokić was commander of the 9th naval sector. Twelve years later he pleaded guilty at the UN's Yugoslav war crimes tribunal.

'The fact that these lives were lost in the area for which I was responsible will remain etched in my consciousness for the rest of my life. I am ready to bow before all the victims of this conflict, regardless of the side they were on, with the dignity of a soldier.'

Atrocities by one side were quickly mirrored by atrocities by the other. By September 1991, Croatia looked like a hiker who had been savaged by a bear in the Balkan forests, but still managed to limp home to the campsite. One third of the body had been chewed off by the Serbs. There were anti-aircraft batteries beside the main road intersections in Zagreb, the presidential palace was rocketed by Yugoslav jets and President Tudjman narrowly escaped with his life.

'Tudjman has done some useful things, but he thinks exclusively of power,' Slobodan Lang told me. 'He doesn't have the strength to develop a positive Croatian programme. He sees Croatia as a one-party system— his party, the HDZ.'

Meanwhile, Bosnia began to look as though it, too, would be dragged into the Serb-Croat war.

In September 1991, I boarded a Yugoslav Airlines DC9 from Belgrade to Sarajevo, only 200km south-west. On the row of seats in front of me, two men clutched large, 1/22 scale 'Invincible Thunder' toy helicopters. As the Balkans re-armed, how was the toy arms-race doing? I wondered. In the past months I had toured Czech, Slovak and Hungarian weapons' factories, all searching with one eye for a way to unload their unwanted goods on some likely South American or Central African republic and, with the other, for ways to switch production to something more peaceful, like radiators. Some of it no doubt made its way to the Yugoslav arsenals as well.

A small boy continuously kicked the back of my seat, all the way to Sarajevo. Belgrade had disappointed me, with its pop music and pornography. The flight to Sarajevo took thirty-five minutes, at 9,000 metres.

Mustafa Cerić—the most important Muslim religious figure in Bosnia, and perhaps all Yugoslavia—looked stern in his white and red turban. He was just back from burying another Muslim victim of the war in Croatia. Many young Bosnian Muslims died in the Yugoslav army, fighting the Croats. At the same time, more and more of them sympathised with the Croatian desire for independence from the increasingly pushy Serbs.

Many Bosnian towns were already affected by the fighting, just over the border, said Cerić. The psychological result was to drive people to gather in their majority areas, where they felt safer.

'If the fighting spreads, all Muslims in Yugoslavia will feel in danger. But we still believe common sense will prevail. '

'But if our biological existence is threatened,' he continued, fingering his prayer beads, 'we will fight to defend our lives.' It was a repeat of Alija Izetbegović's words in Kladuša.

In 1991, a population census had been carried out across Yugoslavia— an established practice every ten years. The resulting map of Bosnia was a colourful one—green for the Bosnian Muslims, red for the Serbs, blue for the Croats and yellow for those who declared themselves to be Yugoslavs. The map was to have a fatal effect in speeding up the spiral of war in Bosnia. I sometimes felt some way should have been found to cancel, or at least postpone, the census. Predictions by the CIA and others that war in Bosnia was now 'inevitable' were almost as damaging to peace. If someone had 200 Deutschmarks to spare, and was hesitating between buying a new cow or a Kalashnikov, and they read in the newspaper that war was certain, there was more chance that they would buy the gun. And each weapon made war more likely.

From Sarajevo I travelled to Banja Luka in the north of Bosnia, where the Serbs were in the majority. Here the Serbs had already declared a SAO, a Serbian Autonomous Region, no longer answerable to the central government in Sarajevo. From there I journeyed on to Bosanska Kostajnica, on the border with Croatia.

Sporadic machine-gun fire interrupted the drizzle and the birdsong along the Sava River—the boundary between Bosnia and Croatia. A few days earlier, the Croats had surrendered the sister town of Kostajnica on the other side of the river. Four hundred Croat soldiers had been captured, we were told. Now the triumphant Serbs were mopping up the last resistance. Three hundred and twenty captured Croats, many of them wounded, had been taken to prison camps near Banja Luka. We tried and failed to find them.

There was a victorious mood in Banja Luka town-hall. While the rest of Europe worried whether Bosnia would be drawn into the Serb-Croat conflict, here it was clear that it already had been. Yugoslav air force planes flew sorties against Croatian targets from Banja Luka airport; Serb soldiers trained in the hills around the city; and Croatian prisoners were held here. Most ominous for the future of Bosnia, the city already had an ethnic Serb leadership, and the Muslims and Croats trembled in their homes. In the lobby of the Hotel Bosna, when I came down to breakfast one morning, I heard Roberta Flack singing 'Killing me Softly.'

'The borders of Bosnia are artificial, imposed on us by Tito,' said Anđelko Grahovac, president of the self-proclaimed region of Bosnian Krajina. This was the standard argument of Karadžić's party, backed up by Milorad Ekmečić's historical ideology that Bosnia was something artificial, a bone in the throat of 'genuine' peoples like the Serbs and Croats. The Muslims themselves were regarded as 'renegade Serbs', or 'renegade Croats', who had treacherously chosen the Islamic faith during the Turkish occupation, and abandoned the 'true faiths' of Orthodoxy and Catholicism.

Bosniaks argued rather that their borders were among the oldest in the Balkans, hardly changed for the past thousand years, unlike those of the Serbian kingdoms and principalities which had often fluctuated. They pointed out that Bosnia was first mentioned in a written document under a tenth century Byzantine emperor. And they insisted that Bosnia was not the problem, but the solution to the restive Balkans, because it prevented both the Serbs and the Croats from getting too big for their boots.

On the 1991 ethnic map of Bosnia-Hercegovina, there was much to worry those on both the Serb and Croat sides who looked down on Bosnian Muslims.

The Muslim proportion seemed to be growing inexorably. In 1971 they made up nearly forty per cent of the population, in 1991, nearly forty-four per cent. Over the same period, Serbs fell from thirty-seven to thirty-one per cent, and Croats from twenty-one to seventeen per cent. Those calling themselves 'Yugoslavs' had shrunk from a high of ten per cent in 1981 to under eight per cent in 1991. Serbs in Banja Luka, their northern bastion, made up fifty-five per cent of the population, with Bosniaks and Croats on fifteen each.

'Every day we fear they will come and arrest us. I do not believe I will be alive in a month's time,' said Muharem Krzić, deputy leader of Alija Izetbegović's Party of Democratic Action in Banja Luka. A veterinary surgeon by profession, he slept with a small pistol under his pillow. At first his wife had been alarmed by it. Now she checked every night to see if it was still there.

'If the massacres start, by then it will be too late. Do not come back. Then we will defend ourselves,' were his parting words.

'Yes, there will be migrations,' said Anđelko Grahovac, the local Serb leader. 'We expect Muslims to move to where they are in the majority.' The Serbian Democratic Party had already armed its members and supporters, and was intent on using the ethnic map of Bosnia to rid 'Serb' areas of Bosnia of Muslims for ever. It would turn out the following spring that those who refused to leave, or who failed to leave in time, would be killed.

This was to be the 'final solution' imposed on the majority Muslim population, first by the Serbs, then by the Croats.

Although the Serbs and Croats were arming, most Bosniaks followed Alija Izetbegović's argument that to arm would only increase the likelihood of conflict.

I spent much of the next few months in Bosnia. In the Hotel Europa in Sarajevo, my wife complained when I got back one night from a string of interviews that people in the hotel had been slamming their doors all evening. It was actually the sound of shooting from the hills around. Bosnia was being sucked deeper and deeper into war. When a ceasefire finally held in Croatia in January 1992, the international community allowed the UN to deploy and the Serbs were told to withdraw the JNA and their heavy arms. The result was that they just moved over the border into Bosnia, ready for the next war. It was one of many, fatal diplomatic mistakes.

On the ethnic map, the red, Serb majority areas made up only the top left hand corner of the wedge-shaped Bosnia, minus its green tip, and a long swathe down its eastern side, interrupted by the green of many Bosniak majority areas. The green was darkest in Srebrenica, with a seventy-three per cent Bosniak majority. The Serb war aim would be to link all the Serb majority areas, and to do that they had to get rid of all the Bosniaks of eastern and northern Bosnia.

The fear of war began the work. People fled to where they were in majority. But that presented a problem to the Serbs, who needed the majority Bosniak areas as well. After the Second World War, and Tito's split with the Soviet Union in 1948, the Yugoslav Army continued to be trained in the partisan tradition which had proved so useful against the occupying German army. Each republic had its own territorial defence force, with its own arms depot and training schedule separate from the army. All Yugoslav boys were trained in guerrilla warfare. Not only was the country full of weapon stockpiles, the arms industry of Yugoslavia was concentrated in Bosnia. In 1991, the now Serb-controlled Yugoslav army confiscated the weapons from all Bosniak areas. They had tried, and failed, to do the same in Slovenia the previous year. Apart from one small armed unit, the Green Berets, Izetbegović continued to veto the arming of his own people.

'There won't be war in Bosnia,' he told me, 'because it takes two sides to make a war, and we are not going to fight.'

At the end of February 1992, the Bosnian government—minus its Serb component which had already walked out—organised a referendum on independence. My usual interpreter was not available, but she recommended a young Croat, Frano, in her place. He proved to be the most nationalist figure I had met so far in the Balkans. Serbs and Croats were chosen races, as far as he was concerned. There was no problem if a Serb or Croat man raped a Muslim woman, he said, because their offspring would be Serb or Croat, whose numbers would thus increase. Muslims, as far as he was concerned, were the scum of the earth. To cap it all, he said he was a Catholic, recited long passages from the philosopher Schopenhauer and was a music student.

As we travelled through central Bosnia, Frano got angrier and angrier. Every Croat we asked said they intended to vote for an independent Bosnia. Frano could hardly bring himself to translate their words. Finally he took us to his own village. His mother was his last hope. She was going to vote for independence too, she said bravely. Frano nearly tore out her hair, as well as his own. 'Stupid, stupid peasants . . .' he muttered, all day. His vision was of a Bosnia divided equally between Serbs and

Croats. The Muslims, as far as he was concerned, could go 'home' to Turkey.

Sixty-three percent of the population turned out for the referendum—pretty much all the Muslims and Croats, and even some Serbs who defied Karadžić's call for a boycott. There was a massive vote in favour of Bosnian independence.

* * *

The drive from Budapest to Sarajevo should take eight or nine hours. You had a choice of three roads—one through Serbia, entering the country near Zvornik, the others across Croatia. In April 1992, all seemed equally problematic. The war began in earnest in its first week.

European Community countries recognised Bosnia on the sixth of April, the US on the seventh, and I arrived for my latest visit on the eighth. The Serbs had already put their plan to seize up to seventy-five per cent of the country into motion.

I drove slowly in a rented car, via Banja Luka and Travnik, picking up hitch-hikers all along the way—people fleeing to the homes of their relatives in places they judged 'safer'—mostly women and children. On the edge of each major village, or sometimes in the middle of nowhere, barricades had been hastily erected. Men with Kalashnikovs, sometimes in uniform but more often not, barred my way. I had a black-eye—the result of too hastily opening the door of my flat before I left. This became my passport.

'I'm a journalist, going from Budapest to Sarajevo. I have no gun. Please let me pass,' was my formula at each road block. Having searched the boot of the car and checked my papers to make sure my story tallied, conversation invariably moved on to my purple eye. The joke in each case was that my wife must have beaten me up for some indiscretion, and I was happy to go along with this version of events. What could be more harmless than a hapless foreign journalist, tangled up in their foolish and unnecessary war, nursing his own, domestic injury?

Eventually I reached Sarajevo. It was after dark, and pouring with rain. I tried to go into the Holiday Inn, close to the centre of town, but the hotel was blacked out, and men with guns in the doorway blocked my way. I asked if the Hotel Europa was still open.

'It is, but you can't get there—there's a curfew, you might be shot,' I was told.

Rather than spend the night in an exposed car park, I drove on in the rain. I waited a while at a red light, as gunfire and the occasional dull thud of a mortar echoed across the valley. In my exhaustion, I just waited for the light to change, but it never did. So after a while, I drove on, through it, to safety.

I had to decide whether to drive fast to the centre of the city and risk being mistaken as a combatant, or to drive very slowly, thus making myself an easy target. I chose the latter. My car was United Nations white, carefully chosen in Budapest in preference to the green one I had been offered. Just to be sure they would not balk at renting it to me, I said I was driving to Slovakia.

At last I reached the Hotel Europa. As I got out of the car, bullets ricocheted off the walls all around me. Two policemen started yelling at me to get down. So I lay in a puddle in the pouring rain, my cases beside me in the street, until the shooting died down. Then I crawled into the hotel.

The local paper, Oslobodjenje, reported that more than twenty people had been injured by gunfire in the town the previous day, and that twenty-nine had been killed in the city so far. It was full of reports of massacres and waves of refugees, in other parts of the country. The presidency had taken the decision on Wednesday—the day I arrived—to form a Bosnian army, the paper wrote. Everyone who could was asked to volunteer. Bosnian television began showing classical music concerts and natural history programmes from its archive.

I went to find my interpreter, Alma Mušanović. She was away, but her parents related the dramas of the past days. Two girls had been killed on the bridge over the River Miljacka, when Serbian snipers in the Holiday Inn opened fire on the march for peace on 5 April. Several men had been caught by the police when they stormed the hotel—which was why it was closed—and accused of responsibility. One was Rajko Kusić, a former security guard at the casino, and now the bodyguard of Nikola Koljević, one of the SDS leaders. Radovan Karadžić, from his new base in the village of Pale, outside Sarajevo, had demanded the snipers be released, and had threatened to start bombing the city if they were not. They had been released, people believed, but the bombardment of the city began anyway.

'We were so mad at them, we didn't know where to hide,' said Alma's mother. 'We ran from room to room . . .' Her mood was not improved by the fact that the family's holiday home was also in Pale, now completely out of reach, and had possibly been taken over by soldiers.

The hills tower over Sarajevo on all sides. After the Serb besiegers took the high ground, it was an easy task to attack the valley. To add insult to injury, one of the Bosnian Serb leaders, Momčilo Krajišnik, appeared on television and described the Serbs as the victims.

That evening I went with Mirza, Alma's father, to see how his street was preparing to defend itself from the expected attack on the Baščaršija, the old city. Željko Živković was one of the defenders. 'My father is a Croat, my mother is a Serb and my wife is a Muslim!' he laughed. 'I am all mixed up—like wine and water!'

One teenager in the group proudly showed me a small handgun he had made himself for shooting rabbits. A few of them had bought guns in the past few weeks, as the situation deteriorated—'from soldiers . . . or on the black market.' Their pride and joy were two anti-tank missiles.

One of them had been down to the market and come back with a pile of green berets—his contribution to the defence of the street. 'Only a maniac would try to divide Bosnia,' said another man. 'We have all lived together for so long, why should we fight each other? There are three nationalities in this room. Those who are attacking Sarajevo are terrorists.'

I went to see Rusmir Mahmutćehajić, the Deputy Prime Minister. 'We're trying to re-establish the institutions of state,' he said, 'and to establish a territorial defence over the whole territory.' Civilians had been massacred in Bijeljina in the north-east. There were awful tales pouring in from many parts of the country. He gave me a long list of names.

'One of the most terrible things has been the slaughter of children. Serb paramilitaries have been crossing from Serbia, spreading terror . . .'

'We are continuing negotiations with the JNA, but there is no sign that they accept Bosnia. [. . .] And we are trying to open the door to negotiations with the SDS . . .'

The UN rapidly imposed an arms embargo on the whole of the former Yugoslavia. This was a gift to the Serbs. Yugoslavia had been the tenth biggest arms producer in the world before the start of the war, and the Serb authorities, as the main instigators of each conflict, had been careful to seize control of the arms factories before each war even began.

The hardest part of the war for the Bosniaks, and everyone who believed in a multi-ethnic Bosnia, was that they could not afford to either win, or lose. Bosnia could only exist, they argued, as a state of all its constituent nations—Serbs, Croats and Bosniaks. The Serbs, or rather, their main political party, the SDS, had now declared war on their own state. The Bosnian Croats, or rather, their main political party, the HDZ, would do the same the following year, in 1993. The Bosniaks were fighting for a draw. Military defeat would mean a small Muslim enclave and another log-jam of their bodies in the River Drina.

I found Milorad Ekmečić, Karadžić's adviser, still in his flat, still brooding about 'the Muslim threat'.

'The Muslims expect in ten years to have reached fifty-one per cent of the population,' he said, 'and then they will declare a Muslim Republic. The Serbs want to avoid such a process.'

He quoted von Clausewitz. 'When war starts, everything is possible, every end can be realised.' 'We expected a revolt, not a war,' he added. 'The spontaneous revolt of the (Serb) peasants of the east.' He didn't add that his party had been carefully arming them, and telling them that the Muslims were about to attack—and so goading them into attacking the Muslims first.

What did he think of the atrocities against Muslim civilians? I asked. In Bijeljina, in Zvornik ... I started reading him the list of names and the ages of the victims, which I had received from Rusmir Mahmutćehajić. 'Arkan (a notorious paramilitary leader) is not helping the Serbian national cause,' said Ekmečić. 'They decided to come, we did not invite them.'

'The Serbian revolution will take place in Bosnia-Hercegovina, with them, or without them.' It didn't look much like a revolution, I told him. It looked like a massacre.

Why couldn't Serbs just carry on living with their neighbours, in their villages, as he himself had told me they used to do so well? I asked.

'Serbs have to be exclusive, in order to survive.'

In spirit, it was the opposite of Thomas Mann's comment, about 'a European Germany, not a German Europe'.

The collapse of Yugoslavia had brought all the ghosts out of the closet, and there were plenty of west European, not just Balkan, ones among them.

The Germans and Austrians felt unable to intervene, perhaps because of their own role as 'aggressors' in the Second World War. The French always enjoyed a special relationship with the Serbs. The British, as traditional 'architects' of the Balkans, were also more in favour of a status quo which they had shaped. The British press was full of the rantings of retired generals who cited the bravery of Serb partisans against the Nazis as a reason for non-intervention now. And all the while Serb paramilitaries went from house to house, stealing fridges and televisions and raping any Muslim woman they could find. In the first four months of the war alone, an estimated 20,000 Muslim women were raped. They were seen as part of the 'spoils' of war, as the judges of the International Criminal Tribunal for the former Yugoslavia later recognised, when they defined rape as a war crime.

Driving to and fro across Bosnia in the spring of 1992 was to witness the sheer terror of an unarmed, civilian population before the Serb advance. The army, despite months of negotiations with the multi-ethnic Bosnian government, sided openly with Karadžić's Serbian Democratic Party. When it finally withdrew, after immense international pressure on Milošević and Serbia, it left much of its heavy weaponry, and all of its Bosnian Serb soldiers, behind. Then, from across the Serbian border, it continued to provide logistical support to this new Bosnian Serb army, which was largely paid from Belgrade.

While the Romanian army fought both against and then on the side of the people in the Romanian revolution, in the Yugoslav conflict the Yugoslav army allowed itself to be manipulated by two political parties, the Serbian Socialist Party, and then Karadžić's Serbian Democratic Party in Bosnia. That it allowed this to happen was in part a clumsy effort by the generals to defend their own privileges—the pensions, the holiday homes and, above all, its prestige as a defender of Yugoslavia. But as an institution of state, it was ill-prepared for an 'internal' threat. Like hundreds of thousands of people throughout eastern Europe who had faithfully served the regimes and had been amply rewarded, they were desperate to hang on to what they had. Elsewhere in eastern Europe, apparatchiks consolidated their wealth in the first, chaotic months and even years of privatisation.

In Yugoslavia, the officer class thought at first that they could use the military power of their army to defend the army itself, as one of the key pillars of the state. There are parallels with the Red Army's attitude to the collapse of the Soviet Union, and the staunchly secular Turkish army's distrust of both the Kurds and political Islam.

'I would gladly defend Yugoslavia if it was attacked,' nineteen-year-old Amer Čatković told me in Sarajevo, a few months before war broke out. 'But I refuse to kill or be killed by other Yugoslav peoples.' As we spoke, he was trying to avoid being sent to fight in Croatia. His mother,

Mensura, was active in a group called Mothers for Peace, which bravely tried in vain, in Sarajevo, Zagreb and Belgrade, to stop the spiral to war.

The basic failure of the European powers in Bosnia was to recognise that the multi-ethnic republic which existed at the start of the war, when Bosnia won international recognition, was worth defending. Instead, first under the Portuguese diplomat José Cutiliero, then under his many successors, it sought to appease an extreme nationalist group, the Serbian Democratic Party, which made nationalist parties like that of Jörg Haider in Austria or Jean Marie Le Pen in France, look positively moderate. And the failure of the Serbian people in Bosnia was that they blindly chose to follow their leaders. As they continue to do, to this day.

There were many reasons for this. Many actually agreed with the view that Serbia should win back the position of 'top dog' in Yugoslavia, which it had enjoyed before the Second World War, and which Milošević had promised them. The state media bear a huge responsibility for consistently under-reporting or ignoring atrocities carried out by Serbs.

Schools in Serbia, as in many countries, taught the glories and tragedies of Serbian history, without any attempt at a critical perspective.

'A Serbian man could never commit rape,' my friend Sasha, a receptionist at the Hotel Moskva in Belgrade, told me—the same hotel to which the Austrian ultimatum was sent on the eve of the First World War, after the assassinations in Sarajevo, as the Serbian government did not have a telegraph machine of its own. 'His sense of honour would prevent him making love to a woman who did not consent.'

Alternative media like B92 radio and the weekly Vreme waged a brave battle to provide a critical perspective of daily events, but they simply did not have the reach which the state media enjoyed. The economic crisis, and the flood of refugees into Serbia, added to the sense of dislocation people experienced.

Many Serbs simply fled the country, seeing no hope of change.

A strong part of the opposition to Milošević was actually more nationalist than he was—this was true of Vuk Drašković and his Serbian Renewal Movement, and of Vojislav Šešelj and his Serbian Radical Party.

'I respect you Albanians,' Vojislav Šešelj would later tell a Kosovo Albanian, Ramush Haradinaj, when they met in the television room of the Scheveningen detention centre in the Hague many years later, both facing war crimes charges. Haradinaj was surprised. 'I respect you because you are a real nation,' Šešelj continued, 'unlike these so-called Croats and Bosnians.'

The Serbs were also the victims of their own wars. Milan Popović, head of the Serbian Association of Psychiatrists, told me about the case of a young Serb soldier who had lost contact with his own forces during one of the battles in Croatia. Terrified by stories he had heard about what the 'fascist' Croats did to Serb prisoners, he lay in a crater in no-man's land for more than twenty-four hours, with his finger on the pin of a hand-grenade. He had resolved to blow himself up rather than fall into Croat hands. Eventually his own side found him, but by then something inside his mind had broken. More than a year later, the medical staff at the psychiatric institution in Belgrade to which he had been sent had still not succeeded in getting the grenade off him. He carried it everywhere and slept with it pressed to his chest each night, like a teddy-bear.

As a British newspaper journalist in the chaos of the opening months, there was no more protection than your own luck and common sense provided, and the speed you could get away from people who might harm you. There were no armoured vehicles, there was no support network, only the informal trust you established with your own colleagues, and the kindness and self-sacrifice of the local people. On a human level, there was as much generosity as viciousness. When you run out of petrol, you would accept a few litres from the devil himself.

Where did the hatred and the cruelty come from? Some of it, undoubtedly, from the previous war. The old Serb caretaker of an Orthodox Serb church in Foča told me that the town had changed hands forty-three times in the Second World War and the River Drina in the valley below had run red with blood. It would do so again, he predicted, as long as 'they', and he pointed with disgust at the beautiful sixteenth century mosque on the bank of the river, were still there. All these emotions had been frozen under the communist ice. And hatreds were passed down through families.

Long after the war, I interviewed a Bosniak woman from Skelani in eastern Bosnia, a village on the main road into Bosnia from Serbia. Her husband's best friend, and best man at their wedding, was a Serb. Yet in April 1992 the atmosphere in the village changed, she said, from one day to the next. The Muslims went to the Serbs and asked for protection, as had happened in the Second World War, when one side sometimes managed to prevent atrocities against the other in places like this. After all, you never knew when you might need to ask to return the favour. But this time, the Serbs refused. Her husband's best friend had then taken part, alongside Serb paramilitaries, in the massacre of Muslim men in the village, including her husband and her oldest son.

'Evil passed over us like a cloud,' she said. 'It hovered overhead.' While it lasted, those it filled became capable of almost any act of unspeakable brutality and murder, she said. But then it passed, as suddenly as it had come. Did she believe those who had committed such crimes would ever be brought to justice? I asked.

She pointed upwards. 'God alone will make sure that the murderers do not escape justice,' she said. She no longer believed in justice on this earth.

* * *

In late June 1992, the atmosphere was as heavy as lead in Bosanski Brod, a town just inside Bosnia, across a single bridge from its namesake, Slavonski Brod, on the northern bank of the River Sava in Croatia. The Serbs had already overrun the town once. The Bosniak and Croat defenders suffered from a permanent shortage of ammunition, but the Serbs always had bullets to spare. On their previous visit, they had even shot the little red and green figures in the traffic lights. Now the defenders estimated that the Serb infantry was only five kilometres away.

In the red-brick gym of the town secondary school, several hundred refugees cowered. There was the sound of machine gun fire from the suburbs, and sporadic shell fire on the town from Serb artillery on a nearby hill. The women and children in the gym were dazed. Many had already seen their men-folk murdered before their eyes. Now they seemed less afraid of death than of capture. The physical education and music teacher said they were just offering people somewhere to sleep, something to eat, and taking note of their identities, before they carried on northwards, on foot. Even if the Bosnian army were to win back territory in central Bosnia, he said, that would just make the refugee situation worse—'the whole population of central Bosnia would leave, if they could,' he said. What did they need here most? I asked.

'Do you really want the whole list?' he almost laughed, sadly. 'Food, blankets, medicines, soap, nappies, sanitary towels . . .'

In the misery and chaos of war, he still remained, first and foremost, a teacher, concerned for his classes.

'If Europe doesn't help us, I don't see how the children are going to go back to school on 1 September . . .'

Outside on the grass, exhausted soldiers slept among beer bottles. They had been fighting for days without rest.

'The Chetniks (a pejorative word for Serb soldiers) burnt my home, and slaughtered six members of my family,' a twenty-five-year-old soldier told me. His face was streaked with dirt, hardly old enough to grow a beard; his voice a monotone, drained of emotion.

'They cut the throats of men and women alike, and gouged out their eyes. Then they put their watches in the eye-sockets, as decorations. For me, this will only end when Bosnia is liberated.'

Down by the bridge, a pathetic line of about 2,000 people waited to cross. There were some men in battle fatigues among them. The only weapon they appeared to have left was a single anti-aircraft gun, but without ammunition. The Croats were refusing to allow them to cross the bridge. Many Croat soldiers felt embittered that the Bosnians had not come to their aid, in their fight with the Serbs a few months earlier, at a time when Alija Izetbegović was still desperately trying to keep Bosnia out of the war. Now they were paying them back. It was a grudge born by one people after another, as the domino of war knocked on through the peninsula. The Slovenes were upset that the Croats and Albanians didn't help them, the Croats that the Bosnians didn't come to their aid and the Kosovar Albanians that the Croats and Slovenes did not adopt their cause. The Bosnian Muslims were betrayed by the Croats, who first fought alongside them, then turned on them in 1993, when they were offered the chance—in the plan devised by Britain's Lord Owen and the American Cyrus Vance—to divide Bosnia to their advantage.

It didn't seem to matter to the Croatian soldiers guarding the bridge that many of those trying to seek refuge in their country were Bosnian Croats—from the Posavina corridor in northern Bosnia. 'Go back and fight,' they told the defeated army. The nervousness in the crowd increased with the sound of every shell from the nearby hills.

'We are not deserters, we are not refugees, we are the expelled,' the commander of an anti-aircraft battery, Esed Zolotić, told me.

'We're just local people, farmers, workers ... we weren't prepared for war. Now we have lost our homes, our factories, our farms. We have lost everything, there's nothing left to fight for.'

After several hours in the town, expecting to see the Serbs overrun it at any moment, we heard a massive explosion from the Croatian side of the river. People on the bridge begged us to go and find out what had happened. A Yugoslav air force plane had flown over the towns of Slavonski and Bosanski Brod that morning, on some kind of reconnaissance flight. It must have seen clearly that the football stadium in Slavonski Brod was full of people—refugees whom the Croats had allowed to cross.

When we reached the stadium, there were scenes of the most horrible carnage. Three or four howitzer 155mm shells had landed in the middle of a crowd of several thousand refugees. There was blood everywhere, and human body parts radiating out from craters in the grass, on what was still clearly a football pitch.

We went to the town's hospital. After the destruction of the hospital in Derventa, this was the last one trying to treat the injured from northern Bosnia—those who managed to make it here. Ninety-five per cent of the wounds they were treating were from shrapnel, and only five per cent from bullets, a doctor told us. It was a measure of the way the war was being fought—and the Serbs had all the shells, and the tanks, and the artillery with which to fire them. Eighteen children had been killed in one of the worst incidents, when a bomb dropped from a Yugoslav plane hit the cellar where they were sheltering.

The refugees who had reached the stadium must have thought they were safe at last. There were trails of blood leading down the corridors. Makeshift operating theatres had been set up in the hallways, and seven teams were operating. After a while, an anaesthetist, Dr Josip Jelić, came out to give a brief statement to the press. There were twelve confirmed dead so far, he said, and many more injured. Instinctively, he put out his hand to shake mine, then recoiled when he saw it was still covered in blood.

As I left the war in Bosnia, I met men returning there to fight. On the outskirts of Zagreb, a lone blue and white fleur de lys Bosnian flag fluttered above a warehouse, near a petrol station. Men of Bosnian origin, who had been working in Germany, had made the decision to come back and fight.

'We are just gathering here, the Croatian government doesn't allow us to train,' said a man from Zvornik. 'Then we will go to a mobilisation centre in Bosnia.'

The people of Bosnia had fled too easily at the start of the war, because they were unprepared, he said. 'Now we think we should all go back, because it is our homeland, and we have to defend it . . . Our morale is stronger now. The Chetniks don't fight like men, they just kill innocent women and children.'

'What would it take for the West to intervene?' they asked. 'How many more victims do you need? Tell us the number!'

They, like the refugees at several camps, were full of stories of atrocities carried out by Serb soldiers or paramilitaries, of torture, murder and rape. They also spoke of concentration camps.

A few days later, in Belgrade, I met the British Foreign Secretary, Douglas Hurd. He dismissed all talk of concentration camps with a wave of his hand as 'journalists' tales'.

'I have had a very full and detailed conversation with Slobodan Milošević,' he said, 'and he made it clear to me that he respects the integrity of the borders of Bosnia-Hercegovina.' He refused to be drawn on who was to blame for the war.

'Over the next few weeks it will become clear whether the different republics of the former Yugoslavia will find their way back to peace, or go further to disaster.'

British government policy, especially on maintaining an arms embargo which left Bosnian forces hopelessly out-gunned, had a decisive effect on that of the other European countries and, for a while, on the Americans, as the academic Brendan Simms has underlined in his book, *Unfinest Hour—Britain and the Destruction of Bosnia*.

'We have at each stage of the Yugoslav crisis agreed on what we should do—that is, we Europeans have avoided the disastrous rivalries of western powers in the Balkans which caused such harm in the first years of this century,' said Hurd.

He was right. The older democracies in western Europe, like the new democracies in the east, followed the British lead.

Bosanski Brod was my last trip to Bosnia during the war. My wife was expecting our first baby. I had seen too many orphans in my job. We decided together that I would not cover the war any more. Like the rest of the western world, I abandoned Bosnia.

10. Who is to Blame?

Some of these people would like those times to be totally forgotten, and in this way try to influence a model of behaviour in which the total disappearance of conscience goes together with a total disappearance of memory . . .

Jósef Życiński, Polish Bishop

To mark the fifth anniversary of the 1989 revolutions, I revisited old haunts in Prague, starting with Národni Street in the centre, where the students had been pursued and beaten so heavily by the police on the night of 17 November. Under the arcades, an austere sculpture of five, black iron hands had been set up, reaching to the sky, their fingers twisted into the 'V' for victory sign. On one of the sculptures the fingers simply splayed apart—a reminder of the hands I saw so many times above the crowds, searching for the right sign, symbol or gesture to scrawl on the grey, east European skies. In 1989 there was a poster for the Lithuanian 'Sajūdis' Reform Movement of just such a crowd. Some of the hands were formed into fists, in defiance of Soviet rule. Many in the two fingered victory salute. Many still open fingered, like this one, as though waving to one's parents on the railway stations of one's youth. Along the back of the monument in Národni Street, someone had thoughtfully arranged conkers, small dried horse-chestnuts, rather than flowers. Another reminder of the extraordinary glut of horse-chestnuts in the autumn of 1989. Of the crowds in Budapest and Prague, Leipzig and Berlin, marching ankle deep in conkers.

In a bar opposite the entrance of the huge ČKD Elektrotechnika works, in the Libeň district of Prague, men sat around drinking beer at the end of their shift. They were willing to talk, but not to give their names, they said. The old communist-era reflex of fearing the consequences of one's words died hard.

'We don't know what to do with democracy,' said one man, in his

190

mid-forties. 'We need a new generation, who are born into it, who know how to use it.'

The men were worried, above all, about their future. A foundry had just closed, with the loss of 800 jobs, and more were slated to go. The markets in the east, in the old Soviet Union, had disappeared with the revolution. The company had just lost a tender to build underground train carriages to a Swiss competitor.

This was the bar from which the workers had set out to join the students on Wenceslas Square, after the violence of 17 November. Some of those in the bar remembered the head of the Prague Communist Party, Miroslav Štěpán, coming to talk to the workers, to try to dissuade them from joining the revolution.

They whistled Štěpán down, but 'mainly the younger men went to support the students,' said one old-timer. 'We older guys, who had lived through 1968, were afraid. The students were young, they had nothing to lose,' he explained. 'But we felt we had a lot to lose.'

'And what had been lost, as a result of the revolution?' I asked. 'This pub has gone downhill, for a start,' they all agreed. In the old days, it served good cheap hot food. Now there were only drinks. The men used to play board games, darts and cards here. But that was over too, they said.

As we spoke, a fight began near the bar, apparently over a girl. 'Bring her here then, and she'll tell you,' shouted a youth in blue, oil-stained workers' overalls. The next minute his protagonist landed a fist on his jaw. The others separated them.

'The revolution was worthwhile,' said one man, thoughtfully. 'But they shouldn't sell the land, Czech land, to foreigners.'

'It was good to get rid of the police state,' chimed in another 'but now you can get mugged, and nobody cares.'

'There used to be a games room, but it was pulled down to make way for something else, which was never built. They're good at pulling things down, but they can only build if they sell it to a foreign owner . . .'

*   *   *

'After 1989, the stakes were too high,' said the Hungarian sociologist Elemér Hankiss. 'People realised suddenly that in the coming years it would be decided who would be rich, and who would be poor; who would have power and who would not; who would be marginalised, and who would be at the centre. And who would be able to found dynasties and whose children would suffer. The stakes were too high, and people panicked. They began to treat each other as enemies, even their friends . . .'

His words rang particularly true in Hungary, but were valid in all the former communist countries in the early 1990s. When the dust cleared, and people were able to survey where each had managed to claw his or her way during the dust-storm, there was a lot of dismay.

Efforts to conclude what Hankiss called 'a new social contract' between rulers and ruled failed in most countries. The rules of the democratic game were not clearly established. The rights and duties of the citizen were not debated and agreed. The systems of checks and balances, worked out over the centuries in older democracies, were not there.

Instead there was an uneasy hiatus. Oversight of the secret services, of state finances, of the finances of the new parties and of the mass media was concentrated in party hands. The media themselves were strongly influenced by political parties. Elected parliamentary deputies, and their political masters, treated election victory as an absolute, not a conditional victory. The chosen form of proportional representation meant that people voted for party lists, rather than individual candidates. So there was little sense of an elected parliamentary deputy being answerable to his or her constituents. The courts remained open to political pressures. The new rich felt hated and misunderstood by both government and the people, and carved out their own, new, high-fenced world. Suddenly, everyone was talking about money. The children on their way home from school on the tram argued over a coin they had found in the street; state employees argued about the size of their bonuses. These were cash economies, without cheque books or credit cards. If you bought a flat, it was paid for in cash, from a shoulder-bag. Money changers tried to trick tourists at railway stations with wads of notes from Yugoslavia, liberally sprinkled with zeroes. In the midst of all this, the Russians arrived—businessmen with a lot of money to spend, fast. Russian became a compulsory language for bank clerks. Little stickers appeared on the doors of Prague and Budapest banks—a pistol with a red line drawn through it.

On another level, there was a failure of 'the people' to defend themselves from the state. Civil society remained weak. There were individual victories, by environmental groups in particular, on single issue campaigns but, on the whole, people swung between meek subservience and sly rebellion.

Germany was a special case. As it re-united in October 1991 by the common will of most of its citizens, there was a strong sense in the east that, for all the 'sacrifices' west Germans were making to pay for re-unification, something was being imposed on them, rather than created together. It was not so much re-unification, some felt, as colonisation by the rich cousins. Many young east Germans had a strong belief in equality. A couple from Schwerin I met at a campsite in Hungary were appalled, even in 1987, by the gulf between rich and poor. It hurt their sense of fairness. In 1990, they could witness the growing abyss closer to home.

In Germany, as in many countries, there was also an acute awareness that western firms were buying factories just to get the market, then closing them down. Each state drew up lucrative tax regimes to attract investment, but tried to add clauses to protect jobs.

In Hungary, there was a growing trade in shop and business receipts. Taxes were too many, too high and too complicated, so people demanded a receipt for everything, to play it off against tax. Or the business went underground. No receipt, and twenty per cent off the price of the service. Something wrong with your car? Don't get it fixed, just pay extra for the road worthiness certificate. Doctor's salary low? Expect a fat envelope of cash from the patient, *in advance of the treatment* and treat them worse if you don't receive it, or if the envelope is thinner than you think you are entitled to. The system works, it limps along—but it is deeply corrupt, and corrupting.

While the state remained strong on one level, it was fatally weakened on another. In the euphoria of the early 1990s, people had the sense they had won back power. In communist times, Václav Havel had written of 'the power of the powerless'. So the powerless won power. But then they lost it.

As the state and, in particular, the political parties, re-occupied public space, the people withheld their consent. Just as under the old regime it was socially acceptable to travel on public transport without paying—to search for a million and one loopholes not to give 'the power' its due. Because they felt the power was not giving them their due. It was as though the Cold War between East and West had been replaced by a cold war between the citizens, and between the citizens and the state. Even the old solidarity *against* the communist system had gone.

In the new cut-throat capitalist world, you could only be against your fellow citizens.

Various efforts were made to map out the responsibilities of employers towards employees, in national labour laws or codes, and in work-place agreements between management and trade unions. On paper, these often looked rather reasonable. In practice, the new companies, especially foreign investors arriving in the region, ensured themselves the maximum possible room for manoeuvre, especially in terms of hiring and firing workers with little or no notice given. They had arrived in the jungle, they felt, so they had to keep their machetes to hand. And, in the rush to attract them, governments bent over backwards to address their every whim and fancy.

In communist times, trade unions had been little more than transmission belts for the Party. They relayed and explained Party decisions to the workers, and owned hotels or recreation areas beside lakes or on sea coasts to provide cheap holidays for members and their families. In those days, as the working-class allegedly 'owned' the means of production, they could hardly be expected to strike or even lobby against themselves.

Only in Poland did a trade union, Solidarity, play an active role in the fall of communism. Elsewhere, independent trade unions had to start from scratch in 1989 or 1990. They were, and mostly remain, shy of flexing muscles they do not know whether or not they have.

As the new rules were being written, some of the new leaders found the temptations of office too much. When politicians were caught out, they feigned surprise. In November 1995, as Alexander Kwaśniewski of the Democratic Left Alliance (ex-PUWP) prepared to win the presidential election in Poland, a scandal surfaced. It seemed a clear conflict of interest—he bought $15,000 worth of shares while he was a parliamentary deputy, in a non-transparent manner, in a company in which the state was heavily investing. He responded to the allegations with a simple 'I don't remember'.

'This is not a country in which you don't remember $15,000,' said the commentator, Konstanty Gebert. 'And public opinion is not sophisticated. It expects those at the top to grab what they can.'

Western companies entering this fray found themselves asking—how much is the bribe, and to whom should it be paid? If they were caught out, the phrase they could not utter, but one could see them mouthing, was 'but we were told this was the only way to do business here!'

* * *

The political process throughout the region in the 1990s was tumultuous, with so much wreckage from communist times still in the water and the shipyards of the new democracies turning out so many un-seaworthy vessels.

Throughout the region, it became the prerogative of the political right to emphasise the split between anti-communists (some of them albeit of very recent vintage) and former communists. This approach ignored the fact that many former communists had repainted themselves in national, sometimes extreme national, colours. It also placed the scales physically in the past—weighing the merits of individuals on their past activities, rather than their abilities or merits today. The political left put out a more inclusive message—they felt their skills were needed too. And they wanted to be loved again. 'Bring back the experts!' was the successful election slogan of the Socialist Party in Hungary in 1994.

In Poland, Lech Wałęsa lost the 1995 presidential election by dividing the country into 'us' and 'them'. He claimed the whole Solidarity tradition, which was not his to keep, for all the admiration and respect the people felt towards him. While in Romania and Hungary one spoke of 'red barons', Wałęsa described former members of the communist elite who were now doing well as 'the red spiders'. This left the way open to Kwaśniewski to present himself as the man of compromise, representing all Poles, including those who had suffered from the collapse of communism, or who had at least hoped for more—a rather wide category. Wałęsa, quipped Kwaśniewski in their television debate, was behaving like an old sportsman, harping on about an old medal.

Kwaśniewski's strongest support came from western Poland; from the more lightly-rooted population who arrived from the east fifty years earlier.

Wałęsa could count on stronger support from the south-east, the old Austro-Hungarian Empire, with a stronger democratic tradition and workers' movement. Wałęsa won support in the countryside, and in big cities like Warsaw, Kraków and Gdańsk. Kwaśniewski could count on the young urban vote in the provincial towns, which had had less chance to develop in the first years after the return of capitalism. Neither leader could be described as particularly democratically minded. The second and decisive round of the election became a battle between two authoritarian figures.

In 1990, the victory of centre-right parties in many countries allowed the former communists to focus on their business interests—their ill-gotten gains from the first weeks and months of the transition. Kwaśniewski's victory in Poland in 1995—like the victory of Gyula Horn and the socialists in Hungary in parliamentary elections in 1994—allowed ex-communists to win back political power as well. So now they had nearly everything—power, albeit more conditional than before, and wealth. Their raucous sons had close-shaven heads and drove the latest BMWs, their daughters dressed or undressed or under-dressed like Russian prostitutes.

In Hungary in 1994, the once stridently anti-communist Free Democrats were only too pleased to join a coalition with the ex-communists—the Hungarian Socialist Party. After five years in opposition, watching the power and influence and wealth of the country divided before their eyes, they felt it was time they tried their hand at steering the new ship. They also wanted to get their hands on the cake before it was all eaten up. Their supporters felt the time was right to go to bed with the socialists. Some of the more principled members of the party left. The increasingly conservative leader of the opposition, Viktor Orbán, muttered darkly that 'we let the socialists out of quarantine too soon.'

The polarisation in Hungary between the centre-left and the centre-right was particularly damaging. It divided families and friends, and soured all attempts at consensus. Gyula Horn, the Hungarian Prime Minister from 1994–98, had taken part in the mopping up operations after the crushing of the 1956 Revolution as a member of the workers' militia. His exact role was never clarified, but to all on the right of centre, he was anathema.

Horn himself stressed his own role in the 'change of system'. Especially as Foreign Minister in June 1989, when he symbolically cut a section of the Iron Curtain with his Austrian counterpart, Alois Mock.

Slovakia became independent from the Czech Republic in January 1993. It was a strange divorce, largely engineered by two men—the Slovak Prime Minister, Vladimir Mečiar, and the Czech Prime Minister, Václav Klaus. Klaus calculated that the Czechs would be better off without the less developed Slovakia. It was a logic similar to that employed by the Northern League in Italy—a ploy to allow the rich north—or in this case, the richer west—to keep more of the proceeds, and jettison the poor regions.

Václav Havel, as Czechoslovak President, disliked the idea of a split, but refused to call a nationwide referendum on the division, which would certainly have gone against the break up. Many Czechoslovaks felt their country would be bigger and more important as a central European state with fifteen million inhabitants, straddling the north and south of Europe, than of ten million, fixed in the north. Interestingly, a majority of Slovaks never backed independence either, according to opinion surveys. The Slovak National Party had campaigned vociferously for independence since 1990, but won less than eight per cent in the 1992 election. The large Hungarian minority in Slovakia were against independence, as they feared they would be left at the mercy of Slovak nationalists, without the more sober-minded Czechs to defend them. But Mečiar hypnotised his people.

'There is not a single Slovak,' Mečiar's biographer, Marián Leško told me, 'who has not felt at one time or another 'I like this man'.' In every speech, Leško noted, there was a key moment, at which Mečiar communicated to his listeners, 'We are listening to you. We will do what you, the people, say.' And the people felt all their frustrations in daily life dissolve.

Mečiar was larger than life, an amateur boxer turned lawyer turned politician. He won three elections in a row, and was eased out of power each time by moderate Slovaks who were appalled by a man who pursued power so single-mindedly, then so unashamedly divided the spoils of it among his cronies.

'Mečiar loves to beat, and be beaten ... that is his strength. His weakness is that he is enormously self-destructive,' said Leško.

'Mečiar can only be defeated by himself!' said one Slovak humourist.

His message to his people was that Slovakia should join the European Union, but only as a separate state. The ever-conciliatory Havel actually helped Mečiar. He sympathised with Slovak frustrations at always playing second fiddle to the more sophisticated, rather arrogant Czechs. And he certainly had no desire to be the man who shot down the balloon of Slovak identity, just as it was taking off. Instead, the two countries should become 'separate stars, close to one another' on the European flag.

In the first days of independence, in January 1993, I found out that the division of the Czechoslovak army was due to begin. The Czechs had more big Soviet-designed T-84 tanks than the Slovaks, so leaders of the two sides agreed that the Czechs would send some of theirs on the train. I rang the new Slovak Defence Ministry in Bratislava, to find out when and where the Czech tanks would arrive.

'That's a military secret!' an indignant spokesman told me. So I rang the Czech Defence Ministry.

'Thirty-two tanks, travelling from Plzeň, are due to reach Trenčín in Slovakia at 15.15,' a helpful woman told me. So I was there. The information was good, but the tanks were delayed for a couple of hours. I met a unit of Slovak soldiers at the station, waiting to take delivery.

'Does anyone speak German?' I asked. 'English maybe? French?' Nobody did. 'Or Hungarian?' I hazarded, aware of how much hostility there has been, traditionally, between the two peoples. A great burst of laughter followed. The whole unit were minority Hungarians from southern Slovakia! We settled down to chat in the station buffet to wait for the tanks.

'And I'll tell you one thing,' said one of the soldiers, after a few plum brandies. 'If there's ever a war with Hungary, I'm going to take this tank, drive it over the border, and join the Hungarian army!' I carefully avoided quoting him in the report I wrote. I didn't want to be the one to start that war.

In the corridors of the Slovak cultural organisation, Matica Slovenská, in Bratislava, I met a group of skinheads from central Slovakia, who assured me that they hated Hungarians. But also confessed that they had never met one. Slovaks from southern Slovakia, where the vast majority of Hungarians live, were much more relaxed about their neighbours.

I spent an evening with Hungarian skinheads in the 22nd district of Budapest, doodling Hungarian symbols on their arms with biros, listening to tirades against the Jews and the Gypsies by 'Uncle Potyka', a Hungarian who had returned after the fall of communism from Canada. Sporadically, through the 1990s, the western press ran stories about the danger of a 'new fascism' in eastern Europe. German and Austrian journalists in particular saw little Hitlers behind every tree, and their articles were much quoted by east European liberals who were themselves quoted in their scripts. I trailed the fringes of political meetings, election rallies and film showings to find out if such a threat really existed. And concluded, tentatively, that it didn't.

The problem was, as the writer György Konrád put it, that 'there is no map of the right' in Hungary. While there were many maps of the left. The communists had only won slightly less than seventeen per cent of the vote in the 1945 election, yet proceeded to terrorise the Social Democratic Party into a merger. It was as though an aggressive fish swallowed a more docile one, of a similar size. The red line between social democracy and communism was relatively well known. As the great rotten edifice of communism collapsed, there was also wide agreement among politicians in most of the new parties of the need for a 'social market economy'. That some way had to be found, in these relatively poor countries, to extend or reshape the old communist welfare system— of theoretically free health care, state pensions and all the rest—to cushion the inevitable fall from full employment to high unemployment. People day-dreamed about a 'Scandinavian model' for eastern Europe, with no idea where the money could be found to fund it. But what to do with all the 'right wing' baggage? Where could the line be drawn between a sensible patriotism and a rabid nationalism? On the one hand, there was a romantic inclination to rehabilitate wartime leaders, including Admiral Horthy in Hungary, Jozef Tiso in Slovakia and Ion Antonescu in Romania, without the critical assessment their careers and their sayings deserved. Because such men had been demonised by the communists, there was a tendency for some to hero-worship them now.

Politicians on the right, especially in Hungary and Poland, claimed a monopoly to represent the nation. Because of the communist experiment, they felt that the 'left' no longer had a right to speak for their countries. They wanted, even expected, 'the left' to die out.

On the other side of the political spectrum, the 'new left' proudly presented themselves as the champions of 'modernism', against what they saw as the narrow, provincial nationalism of the past. In Hungary, there was a debate in the early 1990s about the fate of the Crown of Saint Stephen, which had languished in the National Museum since its return from the United States, at the initiative of President Jimmy Carter, in 1978. Christian Democrats wanted the crown placed in the aula beneath the dome of Parliament, where they felt it belonged. And they wanted it back on the coat of arms. They won both arguments, but at the cost of more bitterness, more mutual incomprehension between the rival players in Hungarian public life. The liberal Free Democrats wanted the crown kept in the museum where they felt it belonged. It had as much relevance today, wrote the liberal philosopher János Kis, 'as a Swiss beret'. The liberal President of Hungary, Árpád Göncz, had a more conciliatory approach.

'The dismemberment of Hungary under the Treaty of Trianon, in 1920, is still an open wound for most Hungarians,' he said. Many Hungarians exposed that wound at every possible opportunity, but it was at least genuine. No-one seriously contemplated going to war to re-occupy Slovakia, Transylvania, Croatia or Vojvodina. Much later, as Serbia lost its access to the sea when Montenegro left, Kosovo with all its ancient Serbian churches and lands in Croatia and Bosnia which they felt belonged to them, Hungarians expressed understanding for their feelings. But the Serbs went to war to keep them. The Hungarians tried that in the Second World War, and it failed. They were not going to make the same mistake again.

The Democratic Forum (MDF) Prime Minister of Hungary, József Antall, said he was the Prime Minister of fifteen million Hungarians, and was attacked from many sides, although he emphasized that he meant this in a moral and a cultural sense, without any wish to redraw the borders.

Some ten million Hungarians live in Hungary, three million in the neighbouring countries, and a further two million scattered across the world. When his Foreign Minister, Géza Jeszenszky, suggested in Parliament that only the governing Hungarian Democratic Forum was truly patriotic, the entire opposition—Socialists, Free Democrats and Fidesz walked out. These were, and remain, extremely sensitive issues.

The absence of a map of the political right was also a problem for right-wing minded people. Within the MDF, István Csurka, the fiery playwright who had provoked the Writers' Union crisis in 1986, pressed hardest for former communists to be thoroughly investigated, for property they could be proved to have acquired illicitly to be taken from them and for them to be banned from public office.

József Antall challenged him: 'So you actually wanted a revolution?' The events of 1987–90 and the collapse of communism were referred to in Hungary as the rendszerváltás, 'the change of system'. Revolution implied great sacrifice and bloodshed, and was reserved for the national liberation struggles of 1848 and 1956. Csurka left the MDF, amid much acrimony, and set up his own Hungarian Justice and Life Party.

The MDF was routed by the revamped Socialists in the 1994 elections in Hungary, and lost its place as the main centre-right party to Fidesz. The young Fidesz leader, Viktor Orbán, under Antall's influence, steered Fidesz from its liberal origins carefully into the Christian Democratic harbour. And with an eye on Helmut Kohl's CDU in Germany, set out to absorb, sometimes ruthlessly, all right-wing parties under his own flag. As a result, Csurka's party struggled and only once managed to score over the five per cent threshold and enter Parliament.

'89: The Unfinished Revolution

Western visitors to eastern Europe are often struck by how people seem obsessed by their history.

'We're not interested in anniversary stories,' a foreign editor in London once told me. 'But you cannot cover eastern Europe without doing anniversaries!' I explained. 'They are already celebrating anniversaries of events which haven't happened yet!'

But the fascination with the historical past ran into trouble with the more recent, communist era, and died a sudden death with the 1970s and 1980s. The communist era became a public bone of contention within the new societies, a battle played out largely in the media and in the chambers of Parliament, rather than in the living rooms and kitchens of the region. Only in the former East Germany has any serious attempt been made by the public, with the help of the authorities, to confront their own recent past.

People had cut too many compromises. To get their daughter into university. To get their son or themselves a job. To get out of paying that speeding fine. To advance a little higher on their own nice ladder.

There was no record of those 'everyday' compromises, except in peoples' own consciences. But there were still a lot of fish rotting in the old secret police nets.

The old secret services had been rather efficient. In East Germany the Stasi, in Czechoslovakia the StB, in Romania the Securitate and in Hungary Department III/iii, the political police. The services had usually not kept just one copy of each file—as the politicians hoped as they quietly retrieved their own files from the shelves in the early 1990s and destroyed them; or quietly squirrelled away the files of their political opponents, ready to produce some damning detail to destroy them during the next election campaign. They had sometimes made as many as ten copies of each.

Throughout the 1990s, a battle was waged over the files. By human rights activists, to ensure unfettered access to them. By citizens, to find out who had spied on them, informed on them, betrayed them. And by politicians, to gather dirt on their opponents, or destroy the dirt on themselves.

The demonstrations in East German cities in the autumn of 1989 usually ended at the local Stasi headquarters. As symbols of the power of the communist regime, these invariably sinister buildings were rather useful landmarks. As the regime fell, the more diligent, more compromised Stasi officers tried to destroy the most incriminating evidence. But it was a thankless task. The files gathered on the citizens for the whole of the GDR, placed side by side, stretched for 180 km. There were eighty-eight million sides of paper. Some were shredded, but the shreds were recovered.

In August 1990, even before German re-unification, the first law dealing with the files was passed, followed by another in December 1991. The Gauck Institute was established in Berlin to house a large part of them—the last public institution in Germany with the name 'German Democratic Republic'—GDR—in its title.

While some had argued for the files to be locked away for thirty years because of the sheer human suffering they might unleash, the human rights activists won the day. The basis of the law is that any citizen has the right to read any file which affected them. Some names were blacked out in the copies they received, but it was usually possible, due to the circumstances, to work out who had informed on them. A period of soul-searching and bitterness began, but the ache of betrayal passed surprisingly quickly. By 1997, 1.3 million people had applied for and received their own files, and applications were still coming in at a rate of 15,000 a month.

None of this would have been possible without clear legal regulation, and a willingness on the side of the authorities to fund and facilitate the process—helped by the fact that the West Germans were involved, not just the old men and women of the East. Once again, some in the East felt the opening of the files was imposed on them according to a model over which they had no influence. But the sense of a boil being lanced was usually stronger.

The Gauck Institute has 3,100 employees. Uncovering the past has proven a time-consuming task. Especially reassembling the massive jigsaw puzzle of the shredded files.

'There is no sense, however, of victor's justice,' said Peter Busse, the director of the institute. 'It's just a case of "everyone must know what has been gathered on them."'

With no West Germans to hold their hand on the long walk through the files, other countries have had less stomach for the task. The most common argument against full public access has been that many former agents went to work for the new, democratic authorities. The first law had been passed in Hungary in 1993, but in January 1996, former dissidents felt the need to send this letter to parliamentary deputies, as they worked on an amendment.

We, the undersigned, have good reason to assume that prior to 1990 the Hungarian State Security Service was gathering information about our persons by illegal means. It was gathering information about those of us who, in emigration, ran the institutions of an "alternative Hungary"; who, in a minority status, represented the spiritual unity of the Hungarian nation; who, in the various dissident movements of Central Europe, propagated identical moral principles; who, in university lectures and through the press, expressed the opinion that Western democratic values did not lose their attraction in the East after 1948. The political police of the Hungarian People's Republic was gathering, storing and evaluating information about us, yet the government of the Hungarian Republic is now reluctant to grant us equality before the law as far as access to information about our own persons is concerned.

The burden of the dissidents' tale was that there were too many caveats, and that access to the files was far too limited compared to the Gauck model.

The former Hungarian secret services were divided into four main departments—III(i) Intelligence, III(ii) Counter-Espionage, III(iii) Internal Dissent (the political police), and III(iv) Military Counter-Espionage. The Hungarian law made the III(iii) files partially available to the public, but excluded files built up by the other departments. The reasoning was that while III(iii) had been abolished in February 1990, the other sections had continued their work, as part of the new NBH—Office of National Security.

Some of the staff—estimates varied between one third and two thirds—were the same. Disclosing the files, it was argued, could pose a threat to national security. Even the files of the political police were carefully vetted first, to find out whether they contained information which might incriminate still-active agents. As there was no public oversight of that activity, one was left with an impression that secretive people, obsessed with their treasure trove of secrets, were protecting their secretive predecessors or contemporaries from an inquisitive enemy—the public.

Eventually the Történeti Hivatal, the Historical Office, was established. On the day it opened, I was ninth in the queue on the pavement outside, to apply for my own file. I received thirty-five pages from my first three years in Hungary, half of which as the only western journalist permanently based there. With the folder came a key, explaining the meaning of the jottings in the margin and how the information had been gathered—by informer, telephone tap, active agent . . . To my relief there was nothing about my private life—those details languish, perhaps, in parts of the files not yet released. But there were details of conversations, opinions I had offered and, in particular, anything to do with the dissidents, the environmental movement and with neighbouring Romania.

'The so-called journalist makes no secret of his sympathy for the environmentalists,' was one of my favourites. Just how closely the different departments of the old secret services worked together was best revealed by the heading on each document of 'action to be taken'. More often than not, the conclusion was: 'inform Intelligence'. Or 'inform Counter-Espionage,' or even 'pass details to Military Counter-Espionage'.

As late as 2002, the Hungarian Socialist Prime Minister Péter Medgyessy was revealed as agent D-209. His defence was that he had been spying *for* his country, not against it, as a young official in the Finance Ministry in the early 1980s, winning Hungary a place in the World Bank and the IMF.

His critics countered that he had been clearly working *against* it, securing high-technology items from a list of goods the Americans were keen that the Soviets should not get their hands on—the so-called COCOM list. With Hungary in the West's good books, it would be easier to obtain such items. While the Soviets pretended to be angry with Hungary for its membership of international financial institutions, they were actually ordering and taking away these items through the back door.

Another tantalising question was the fate of the large funds controlled by the former secret services—especially the money made available to steal computer technology from the West, which was kept in legal businesses in the West. After the change of regime, it was never retrieved by the mother countries. In most cases, it was simply used to buy private firms and goods. In 1996, a scandal erupted in Vienna over the 'Gigastorage' project, in which Bulgarian and Hungarian secret service money had allegedly been invested alongside French and American funds.

'The former political police proved their loyalty to the new regimes,' said János Kenedi, a former dissident who has devoted years of his life to opening the files, 'and that's why the politicians of the new regimes don't fight against them.'

In those countries which allowed some access, the exact circumstances or background of revelations published against 'informers' were often not clear. In the Czech Republic, the former adviser and spokesman for Václav Havel, Michael Žantovský, was accused of tampering with a file which 'proved' he was an informer. His name had been crudely altered to the feminine form 'Michaela Žantovska' in another document, while the original document had been destroyed. He dismissed it as a crude attempt to smear him.

In Hungary, my friend and long-time source of wise comment and reflection, László Lukács, editor of the Catholic monthly Vigilia was also on the list. He laughed it off. He had been invited for a coffee, many years earlier, by a secret police colonel, he said, who asked him to collaborate in exchange for a bishopric. He didn't want to be a bishop, thank you very much, he told the colonel, and he had no wish to inform on his fellow-believers. He never heard from the man again, but there he was, twenty years later, turning up on someone's list. One explanation, he and others offered, was that some malevolent former agent was trying to poison either individuals, or social discourse, for reasons best known to her or himself.

Romania passed its first law dealing with the new Romanian Intelligence Service, and the former Securitate, in 1992, under President Iliescu.

'These papers should not be open to the whole Romanian population,' commented Oliviu German, a member of the old communist nomenclatura and, after the revolution, one of President Iliescu's men. 'This is wise law. What would I profit, from being able to read the information given by my colleagues about myself? Do you think this would improve the atmosphere in our country?'

Constantin Ticu Dumitrescu, a parliamentary deputy and head of the Association of Former Political Prisoners, disagreed strongly.

'Unfortunately in Romania, our former torturers are in high places, in the army, the police and in the leadership of the country.' He himself had been beaten up by thugs twice, suffered two mysterious car accidents and also received many death threats.

'I don't want revenge; I just want justice . . . to shed light on the past. The Nuremberg trials brought the crimes of the Nazis to light . . . Why doesn't the outside world help us?'

The outside world, however, often carried on as though eastern Europe had not been 're-attached'. If the East was like an arm, amputated in an accident of history long ago, western Europe had grown used to eating, feeding and growing prosperous without it. When the arm 'turned up', it expected to be treated as an equal, but this just didn't happen.

Virgil Măgureanu, a former Securitate officer who had taken part in the revolution and witnessed the trial of Nicolae Ceaușescu, ran the Romanian Intelligence Service, the RIS from 1990 to 1997. I arranged to see his deputy, and spokesman of the RIS, Nicolae Ulieriu.

'Take a bus to such and such a bank and stand outside. We will come out and fetch you,' were my instructions. The office proved to be in an unmarked building opposite Ceaușescu's monstrous palace, the House of the People. As we spoke, I cast my eyes over his bookshelves.

They included *Best Chinese idioms*, *A Dictionary of the French Revolution*, *The Watergate Files* and the poetry of Arthur Rimbaud.

He began, to my amazement, by defending the Securitate.

'From 1964 to 1989 the Securitate, with few exceptions, did not commit political murders,' Ulieriu assured me. 'Only a minority of its activities were repressive. On the whole it defended the fundamental interests of the state.'

The pastor who sparked the Romanian Revolution in Timișoara, László Tökés, Ulieriu tried to convince me, was a Hungarian spy. And Hungarian foreign policy 'had not changed one iota' since 1920—in other words, the real policy of successive Hungarian governments since 1990 was still to win back Transylvania. I knew this was not the case, but it was not my job, as a foreign journalist, to try to enlighten him. I could just express my incredulity.

Little wonder that the annual report of the RIS to the Romanian Parliament devoted several pages each year to the 'Hungarian threat', in language that mirrored that of the far-right Greater Romania Party led by Ceaușescu's former court poet, Vadim Corneliu Tudor.

'Today's RIS has two main tasks,' Ulieriu concluded. 'To counteract foreign espionage, and to counteract terrorist activity. The same as in any country of the world.'

At the end of 1996, the new Democratic Convention government vowed to reveal the truth about the revolution, and to open the Securitate files once and for all. Ulieriu's boss, Virgil Măgureanu, who had run the service for seven years, resigned immediately.

The government tried half-heartedly to carry out its campaign promise, but in 1998, the veteran reform communist, Silviu Brucan, could claim that Securitate agents and informers 'still control the media and are members of parliament and government as well'. His comments followed leaks which forced two ministers to resign, after sections of their files, proving that they had agreed to work as informers, were published to the intense embarrassment of the government.

In 1999, a law was passed, establishing the Committee to Study the Securitate Archives, the CNSAS. The RIS, despite its new, more liberal leadership, did everything it could to obstruct its work. Only 7,000 cases were initially handed over. Two million files were finally delivered at the end of 2007, and the CNSAS were eventually given their own building, that same year, to house the files which stretch along fifteen kilometres of shelves.

The numbers, as in the former East Germany, give a sense of the scale of the former Securitate's work.

Seven hundred thousand people were registered as informers—not the one in four alleged in communist times, but still bad enough, at one in thirty of the population.

One of the main tasks of the CNSAS was to vet candidates standing for public office, from the lowliest local councillor to the President of the Republic. Thousands were checked, starting with the local government elections in 2000. Those discovered to have links with the Securitate were contacted, confidentially, and shown the relevant documents. They were then given the chance to challenge their validity. After a fixed period, their names were made public, but there was no automatic disqualification, as in the Czech Republic or in Bulgaria. Many politicians just brushed aside the published details and carried on regardless.

In 2008, the 1999 law which established the CNSAS was declared unconstitutional by the Constitutional Court, throwing the results of years of work by the committee into a legal limbo.

*　*　*

The question of how to deal with the old intelligence agencies sat heavily on the desk of Ján Langos, the gentle Slovak I first met on the camping trip with Václav Havel in 1990. As Interior Minister of Czechoslovakia from 1990–1992, he was responsible for overhauling the Czech secret services and turning them, with a certain amount of US, British and German help, into partners for their western counterparts.

At the end of 1991, he visited Moscow with President Havel.

'We offered three conditions for future cooperation with the Russians,' he told me. 'A list of the names and ways to identify KGB agents in Czechoslovakia, which the Czechs would handle with the utmost confidentiality. The return of all information which the KGB had gathered over the years on the citizens of Czechoslovakia and information on all Czechoslovak citizens who had been taken to the Soviet Union.' Only on the basis of what they called 'a clean table' could new negotiations on cooperation start, the Czechs argued.

The Russians laughed in their faces. The Russian Minister for the Security Services made a joke: first the Czechs should withdraw all their agents from Russia!

To the second condition, he replied that information on foreigners was controlled by the foreign department of the KGB, the head of which was now Yevgeny Primakov, who was not in Moscow at the time. And, finally, any information collected was in the hands of the prosecution offices of the former Soviet Union. None of the conditions were accepted, and Czech-Russian cooperation on the emerging issues of the new world order, drugs and terrorism, got off to a bad start. For Langos, these were a 'veil' of issues which the Russians were trying to hide behind. The Russians did, however, return some files to other countries—notably Lithuania, where the first shipment alone included 2,400 boxes.

On the Havel-Langos visit to Moscow, various inter-state agreements were signed. Then the Russian President, Boris Yeltsin, stood up and ceremoniously handed several boxes to President Havel, which were presented as 'documents from the KGB archives on the Soviet invasion of 1968.'

'I went through them on the plane on the way back,' Langos said. 'There was not a single KGB file among them.' Instead, there were various communist documents, of little historical value, of meetings with Alexander Dubček, the reformist Czech leader at the time. And what he called 'a very obscure letter' from the Soviet Politburo, one day before the 1968 invasion. Havel could not say so publicly, Langos explained, but Yeltsin's gesture was an empty one.

Back at home, and after much bitter debate, a 'lustration' or screening law was passed in October 1991, following a similar law in August 1990 in what was still (just) East Germany. The word lustration came from the Latin, and meant 'to illuminate or purge by sacrifice'. This was the kind of law which István Csurka had been pushing for in Hungary, albeit a much milder version.

Communist Party officials, former members of the People's Militia, former secret service officers and various others, were banned from holding public office, initially for five years. This was later extended indefinitely. The list of jobs from which they were excluded was quite long. They could not be elected or appointed to government office, rise above the rank of colonel in the army, obtain management positions in state-owned companies nor reach the top jobs in public service media, universities or the justice system.

When the law was passed, there were howls of protest from all sides. Alexander Dubček, the leader of the Prague Spring and a significant figure beside Havel in the Velvet Revolution, found himself excluded from power, a situation he called 'ridiculous'. From Strasbourg, the Council of Europe condemned the measure as discriminatory. Human rights champions from across the continent expressed their dismay that the new democratic government appeared to be following down the same 'illiberal' path as the regime it had replaced. Tens of thousands of people were affected. In the first year alone, 210,000 people were screened.

At its worst, the law established the principle of collective guilt for the crimes of the communist years. At its best, it gave Czechs and Slovaks a sense of justice, or even revenge, that those who had ruled over them so long had been chastised. And that was a feeling which was sorely missing from most of the other former communist countries. There was little demand for a full-blooded witch-hunt against the communists. But there was a very public distaste with those, politicians and journalists in particular, who simply changed horses in midstream, and carried on with the same self confidence as before.

Efforts to open the files in most countries proved an ugly, unfair struggle, because they focused on the informers, not on those who had recruited them; the secret police officers whose job it was to blackmail citizens. The procedure was also unfair because it focused on just one uncomfortable aspect of collaboration with the old regime, that of the informers. And ignored the everyday collaboration of the majority, who now felt somehow exonerated.

Perhaps it would have been better to encourage more honesty from everyone, for them to judge themselves rather than judging, or failing to judge, others. Bishop Józef Życiński in Poland put it rather well in a letter to the Catholic faithful published on the eve of the 1995 presidential elections.

'We shouldn't forget that during those times when some people were imprisoned, others were busy with careers, which did not depend on honesty and hard-work alone. . . . some of these people would like those times to be totally forgotten, and in this way try to influence a model of behaviour in which the total disappearance of conscience goes together with a total disappearance of memory . . . If you cannot morally judge your own past, you should not be given an important function in the country, because you can once again form decisions based only on lies and tactics . . .'

11. Having a Baby

Women in Hungary . . . would rather forget the birth of their children. Their experience of giving birth in hospital is often of a barbarian place, akin to a slaughterhouse, in which they are the victims.

Mária Neményi, Hungarian social-psychologist

Home birth works best for women who want to *cope* with pain, rather than hand pain over to be reduced or eradicated by professionals. [. . .] The *meaning* of birth pain is different from the pain of, say, tooth or earache, broken bones or colic. It is the pain of creative activity. In a labour that is going well each contraction starts gently, builds up in a grand crescendo to a peak, and then fades away. It is pain with a purpose—*positive* pain.

Sheila Kitzinger, 'Birth Your Way'

In 1990, Mária Neményi researched Hungarian women's attitudes to motherhood before and after birth. The experience was so negative, she found, that many women cited this as a reason for deciding not to have any more children. Hungary's birth rate, like that of almost all the new democracies in eastern Europe, was falling disastrously, despite the immediate euphoria of the 1989 revolutions.

During the twenty years which have passed since the change of political system, my wife and I have had five children, all born at home, in Hungary. That experience, for both of us, has been central to the story of this book—of people taking back control of their lives from the state and its many institutions. Of people feeling empowered over their own bodies; over their own fate.

'I think we should take down the Christmas tree now,' Andrea said. It was dawn on 8 January 1993, and her contractions had started at midnight. Then stopped, and we had slept for a bit. Then started again. We had decided to have our baby at home, and we had somehow imagined it would be nice to give birth under the tree. But she now felt

211

that a bed of falling pine needles was not such a good idea. Everything needed to be very clean, and very tidy. This was her nest.

So down came the coloured lights, the damp-eyed angels and the silver baubles, and I wrestled the poor dry bare tree out onto the landing of our first floor flat in a rain of needles, then down into the yard below.

The flat was as prepared for the birth as we could imagine. A pile of clean cotton sheets on the edge of the sofa, folded plastic sheets to put underneath them, great wads of cotton wool and music if we needed it. An enamelled saucepan of water boiling on the stove, and clean, ironed cloths next to it, to apply hot compresses. Candles and low lights. A bottle of dark red wine, to celebrate her or his arrival. And the car parked immediately outside the house in the street, facing downhill, in case I needed to take her to hospital.

When the floor was all swept and hoovered, I set out across the city to fetch our midwife. There was snow on the ground, and the city seemed raw and dangerous in the early morning light. I felt as though I was back in Sarajevo. Life and death seemed very close, as though I was driving down a narrow causeway between them. Last night's drunks, still looking for the way home, teetered along kerbs and out onto the street, close to my front wheels. The tyres skidded for a moment on the ice, and then regained control, accelerating out of danger. It was an ordinary day for the rest of the city, but we were already under the spell of the baby, inside our own dream.

Ágnes Geréb was waiting at the door with a small bag already packed.

This was to be the twenty-fifth time she would break the law, and we were her accomplices. As Hungary's first and only independent midwife, she was risking a heavy fine, even prison, to help us satisfy our desire to have our baby at home. Under a 1951 government decree, never repealed, all medical staff in Hungary are legally obliged to call an ambulance when they ascertain that a birth is imminent, and get a birthing mother to the nearest hospital, immediately. That made home-birth impractical in Hungary, and more or less illegal. Most doctors could not, and still do not, understand what we are trying to achieve.

There were undoubtedly some positive motives behind the original regulation. A wish to lower infant and maternal mortality, and to guarantee free health care for all, as the communists had promised. But in practice it was the second devastating blow to maternity care in Hungary and many other eastern European countries in less than ten years.

'Now don't any of you go having babies till I get back!' one midwife called to her fellow Hungarian villagers, as she and her family were herded away, towards the train to Auschwitz. The story survives because she, incredibly, was one of the few who survived the death camps. Most didn't, and there was a big shortage of midwives to cope with the baby boom produced by the returning soldiers. Midwives were traditionally Jewish, like Ágnes.

And then came the communists, with their sweeping rules and regulations. By insisting on the primary role of the doctor and the hospital, the role of the midwife and the wisdom of centuries of women attending to birthing mothers in their hours of need was pushed into the background.

Birth was institutionalised. It became a medical event, not a natural process. Women were told they didn't know how to give birth. Instead of being attended to in birth by women who knew the meaning of each sigh and cry and bead of sweat, doctors, usually male, became the central figures on each occasion.

They were there to extract the child, like an infected tooth, at a time usually decided by the doctor's or the hospital's timetable. And there to pick up the big envelope of cash, long before they administered the drug to start the birth. Doctors were badly paid in Hungary, but those with direct access to their patients, especially obstetricians, were able to compensate by inviting 'gratitude money', originally given after the event, but increasingly given before it, to make sure that the care one received was good, or at least no worse than other families had paid for. In the mid-1990s there were 1,200 obstetricians in Hungary, and of these only eighty were women. Women were discouraged from the profession. It was and remains a male club.

During her research, Mária Neményi found cases where Roma families gave bigger bribes—so concerned were they to avoid the 'double stigma' of being a woman at the mercy of male doctors, and a gypsy at the mercy of a white-skinned man in a white coat.

Our midwife, Dr Ágnes Geréb, worked for seventeen years at the University Clinic in Szeged, the main city in south-east Hungary. She described a catalogue of mistreatment in the hospital, which bore out Mária Neményi's study. Of abortions carried out on healthy women who it later turned out had had perfectly healthy babies in their wombs— when specialists misread the ultrasound pictures or other tests. (The women, were, naturally, never told.) Of being forced by the hospital to alternate abortions and births. Of women told to lie on their backs and shut up. Of partners not allowed to attend births. And of sexual harassment of female staff by male colleagues.

A short spell at a British hospital in Leeds, convinced her that birth did not have to be as unfeeling and often unpleasant as the everyday Hungarian practice. Meetings with independent midwives in Britain and the United States convinced her that she should give up her doctor's glory, and become a simple midwife, and an independent one—a concept which did not exist in Hungary.

So she quit the hospital, to her colleagues' dismay, astonishment and, in due course, hostility. She began to attend home-births, at first of friends, but as word spread that this was now possible in Hungary, of strangers.

The first thing she did was to lay aside her scalpel. Episiotomy, a cut in the vagina made to enlarge the birth opening, was compulsory in Hungarian hospitals for all first births, according to hospital rules, and standard practice for later births as well. This is a medical intervention to prevent tearing as the baby's head emerges. From British and American midwives, Ágnes learned how to massage rather than cut the skin to prepare it for birth, how to hold her hands to deliver the baby and not to give drugs to induce labour. The use of oxytocin often meant that the baby was expelled too fast—increasing the danger of tearing.

She discovered to her satisfaction that by doing away with one intervention one usually did away with the necessity for other interventions. But because the medical profession treated each birth as the same, and saw birth as an 'illness' which only a doctor could cure, they were tempted to intervene from the moment the woman entered the hospital. The doctors, who were obliged by hospital rules to be present at every birth, wanted to justify their presence. So they meddled. And each meddling increased the danger of more meddling and, in some cases, endangered the life and health of mother and baby.

'It is true that doctors are inclined to intervene. That is why we stress to them in our teaching practices that they should only intervene when necessary. But I don't see this as a major problem,' Dr Zoltán Papp, Hungary's leading obstetrician, told me. I beg to differ.

The day when we were sure our first child was going to be born came and went. Andrea's contractions stopped and started. The mouth of the womb opened gradually, but still the baby wouldn't come. We disconnected the phone, and tried baths, hot compresses and hours of massage. We measured the baby's heartbeat often, with a small hand-held foetal heart monitor which had a loudspeaker. The sound of the heart was like the waves beating on the shingle beach near my parents' home on the south coast of England. But the baby wouldn't come. Its head couldn't quite get over the lip of the womb.

At just after midnight on the second night of labour, Ágnes asked quietly if we would like to go to hospital. There were no medical reasons for it, she said, but she could see how exhausted Andrea was. We looked at one another, the three of us. Andrea was indignant. Anything but that! Was there not something else we could try, that we hadn't tried so far?

'Have you got any wine in the house?' Ágnes asked. There was the bottle of red, waiting to celebrate the birth. I opened it and Andrea sipped from her glass. Then we brought a jar of honey from the kitchen, and she ate a large spoonful. Feeling much stronger again, she sat back on the edge of the sofa, seized my hands as I stood behind her, and began pushing. She shouted with pain, and ecstasy. The baby's head was in the channel! We wept with joy. The birth would be any moment now.

But it wasn't. The baby was there, on the way out, but something kept pulling it back. According to Hungarian hospital rules, this stage is only allowed to last a maximum of twenty minutes, and then there is massive medical intervention. With a vacuum or forceps or, most crudely, by male staff jumping on the mother's belly to push the baby out. This is the time when many 'birth injuries', which can mark people for life, occur.

As the foetal heart monitor kept lapping rapidly away, showing that the baby was not in distress, Ágnes allowed nature to take her course. Three hours later, with one final, gargantuan effort, he came out in Ágnes arms. A boy. Wet and red and screaming and perfect. This stage had lasted so long, we discovered, simply because his umbilical cord was very short.

For weeks, we lay either side of him, day and night, listening to his every breath. He was like the most ancient being, arriving, completely formed, from another world. The experience sealed our friendship with Ágnes, who became like a second mother to Samuel, and to each of the four boys who followed him, at almost regular two-yearly intervals. Three in the living room, one in the bathroom, one in our bedroom. In hospital, Sam's birth would almost certainly have been by caesarean, or emergency caesarean. And after two or three caesareans, it is unlikely that we would have had any more children. It is no exaggeration to say that today in Hungary many babies—since then she has delivered more than three thousand in the same, semi-illegal circumstances—owe their lives to Ágnes Geréb.

The legacy of poor maternity care was common to all countries in eastern Europe and the Soviet Union, but after the political changes it was an issue which began to engage human rights campaigners, in Poland first of all. With half a million births a year, no-one could dispute its importance in a young democracy.

Piotr Pacewicz was a journalist at Gazeta Wyborcza, the underground newspaper of the Solidarity movement, which transformed itself after the revolution into the main daily newspaper in Poland. Deeply disappointed by the birth of his own first child in a Warsaw hospital, he persuaded his editors to back what was then a small movement of parents, and turn it into a nationwide movement for more active, natural birth in Poland. Rodzić po ludzku, 'to give birth in a human way', was born.

'We had to fight for space in the paper with colleagues who really didn't understand why this was a human rights issue. But we won the argument,' said Piotr.

Journalists and their assistants, often medical students, toured hospitals asking obstetricians and midwives, but first and foremost women, to talk about their experience of birth. It was a massive effort.

'Our aim was to wake women up, as consumers of medical services, to what they can demand from hospitals,' explained Anna Otffinowska, another of the founders of the campaign. 'And to encourage them to use their power to implement changes in medical care.'

A typical communist-era approach to the issue would have been to ask only 'experts'—the doctors and specialists themselves. A democratic approach was to first ask birthing women about their experiences, and demote doctors down the line. And when doctors gave a different version of events, the woman's version was given priority.

As in Hungary, maternity care in Poland had been turned under the communist system into another industry, softened by individual acts of kindness by medical staff, but still an industry.

The Polish campaign developed a system of hearts and stars—hearts for the kindness of staff, stars for the objective facilities and possibilities allowed to birthing women. There were stars, for example, for the right to choose the position in which to give birth and the right to keep their baby with them afterwards, as well as the cleanliness and other facilities in the ward. The final aim was to produce a guide book to all

460 hospitals in Poland, and to campaign for better treatment and conditions in each. The guide even published information on the bribes doctors demanded at different hospitals, though this was sometimes concealed in the form of a 'contribution' for the welfare of future mothers, which often ended up in the pocket of the lead obstetrician.

Apart from their own visits to hospitals, the researchers encouraged women to write letters and fill out detailed questionnaires on every aspect of the treatment they received.

Some doctors reacted angrily at first. The doctors' letters were duly published, and responded to by women who felt they had been mistreated by exactly that doctor. The pages of Gazeta Wyborcza, in regional supplements and in the main paper, buzzed with debate. Some doctors wrote that the campaign was missing the point; that the real issue was underfunding of hospitals, and poor pay for the medical staff, and if only those issues were solved, everything would be fine.

'This has nothing to do with money, we are talking about your attitude to our bodies,' thundered the mothers in response. 'The question is, are you going to grant us our rights or not?'

There were also doctors who expressed support, and who acknowledged the need for change. And through the years, that support grew, from both mothers and medical staff.

In the first year, 7,000 letters and completed questionnaires arrived, an average of almost twenty a day. Maps were published in the paper, showing the areas where the most letters came from, and those where few were sent—to encourage more people to write, and to make the research as representative as possible.

'Even those who hated us, also feared us,' said Anna. 'So they implemented changes, in order to win more hearts and stars for their hospitals, and so for themselves.'

The question of visits to mother and newborn child was one of many issues. The official argument was always that visits should be severely restricted, for fear of bringing outside diseases into the 'sterile' environment of the hospitals. The campaigners argued that this was rather a totalitarian leftover exercised by hospital authorities, who enjoyed wielding their own absolute power over the patients.

Close examination of maternity wards showed that sales representatives from drug companies, plumbers, electricians and, above all, medical students trudged through the wards by the dozen—but the fathers, husbands, mothers and the siblings of the newborn were kept out. They waited in distant, draughty halls, smoking nervously by drinks machines which swallowed your money but rarely delivered a drink.

Some women complained that they had to bribe the 'guards' to receive a visit, or a gift, from their own loved ones. In one notorious case, in Świnoujście on the Baltic coast in north-west Poland, the chief doctor punished a whole ward of women for some minor infringement of the rules by taking all their babies away for a whole day.

In 1995 in Poland, after the publication of the first guide to maternity wards, the campaign became more focused. The criteria according to which the stars and hearts were allotted were explained in detail to give the hospitals a clear idea of how to improve their own score. The fourth star out of a maximum of six available, for example, was awarded if women were allowed to keep their newborn babies with them for twenty-four hours a day. If the baby was taken away during the night, only half a star was allotted, or if fewer than half the rooms were equipped to allow women to keep their babies.

Polish television also got involved, following the twists and turns of the campaign. In the first edition of the guide, there was enough data to assess 274 hospitals. In the second edition, 439. Each year, there were more innovations. Hearts crossed out or torn apart for hospitals who consistently mistreated women; black hearts to show indifference of the medical staff.

Inspired by the Polish example, we decided to try something similar in Hungary. After much debate, the Hungarian Ministry of Health paid for a single page each week for one year in the former trade union daily, Népszava, for the campaign.

We began to gather stories from women and to publish their accounts. This was to be a campaign of the consumers, not of the experts, we emphasised. We wanted to give space to the doctors to comment both on the readers' letters and on the services they provided, or said they provided. But the microphone was first and foremost with the mothers.

Using the Polish campaign as our model, we invited letters from mothers and fathers whose children were born at each hospital in the country. Then we invited the doctors in charge of the maternity departments at each hospital to describe their facilities, and their plans for the future. As well as our weekly page in Népszava we wrote articles in the main womens' and family magazines in Hungary, and gave countless interviews to other media, to drum up interest in the campaign.

The letters began coming in, not quite in the floods our Polish friends had experienced, but in sufficient numbers to begin to evaluate the hospitals through new mothers' eyes.

I was expecting my first child in 1989, when I was twenty-four years old. I was so happy, and enjoyed my pregnancy very much—it never occurred to me that anything could go wrong. My little son was in the breech position (feet, rather than head down) but my doctor told me that won't be a problem, just that I should go into hospital one day early. I packed my bags and went in innocently, as I had been told. When I arrived I was told that the practice at this hospital was to examine all women before birth with an amnioscope. I was surprised . . . this hadn't been mentioned at any of the four birth classes I had been to at the hospital.

The examination was extremely painful, and completely destroyed my self-confidence, and my sense of happiness. I began to bleed heavily, and my waters broke. I was told I should stay in the birthing ward, where the examination had taken place. I had no contractions, of course. During the next twenty-four hours no less than six different doctors came to examine me.

My contractions started, gradually. I felt a bit relieved—just pleased that no one should touch me any more. Among the other women I had spoken to at the maternity ward, the chief doctor was famous for his 'gentle' and polite examinations. He told me he would like to examine me between contractions. So I was placed up on the examining chair, my legs wide apart, while the whole team of doctors and specialists and medical students made their routine morning tour. The examination hurt so much, I could hardly breathe.

'So, what's the matter then?' was all he said to me. 'No contractions?'

The contractions which had been coming regularly till then, every five minutes, stopped, of course. I had to stay in that position for five to ten minutes, and no contraction came. Then the doctor said to his staff, without even looking at me, 'prepare the operating theatre'. Operating theatre? What operation?

Only half an hour earlier, my doctor had told me that the contractions were regular and that the mouth of the womb was already three fingers open. By the time they had shaved my pubic hair, and a catheter had been placed inside, my contractions had started again and were coming every two minutes, but no-one was interested in that.

I was given a spinal epidural and they carried out the caesarean. And that's how my first son was born. I wasn't allowed to be with him, as women who had had caesareans were not allowed into the mother and baby room. I cried the whole day, I was missing my baby so much. The next day they brought him for me to breastfeed for the first time (they refused to bring him even once during the first twenty-four hours, no matter how often I pleaded with them). And the very first time I held him, he threw up on my pillow some of the baby-formula they had been feeding him, with the best will in the world, so my tiny, caesarean baby wouldn't scream so much, or starve.

During the ten days I spent in that hospital, only the midwives showed any kindness to me—I'm still hugely grateful to them for that [...]

When I got home, I wept so much, every day, I don't know why. Because the child was healthy, my wound healed, the breast-feeding went well. My doctor reassured me that the same thing would not happen again.'

But it did, twice. Two more caesareans followed, at the same hospital, with the same staff. Unlike the practice in western Europe, in almost all east European hospitals, after one caesarean, women are usually not allowed to attempt a natural, vaginal birth.

Reading letters like this, we were astonished that women returned to the same doctors, in the same hospitals, to give birth. The explanation was simple. My doctor is bad enough, they thought, surely the others will be worse?

As the years passed after the change of system, some things improved. Pictures went up on the walls of the maternity wards, reproductions of Matisse, or Monet or Van Gogh. In many hospitals, husbands or partners were allowed into the birthing room, though doctors complained that they often fainted as they stood in the corner of the room in their green, hospital aprons, watching other men fishing around inside their wives. Some hospitals reluctantly introduced more active birthing practices, under pressure from younger doctors with experience abroad, and women who came to give birth.

The facilities for mothers to keep their babies with them improved too—usually for a cash payment, straight into the doctor's pocket. Some doctors distributed the money among the nurses and midwives; others did not.

We received and published positive letters as well. Especially from women whose babies came quickly, giving the medical profession no excuse to intervene—in the best cases, before the doctor even arrived, and with just the midwife present. Invariably, the midwives were kind, but inexperienced.

In Hungary, basic midwifery training was extended from nine months under the communist system to three years after the political changes. Midwives, however, had little chance to practise their profession. The doctor had to be called, and took over immediately. In the worst cases, the midwife was then relegated to a sort of secretarial role in the next room, typing out the birthing mother's details. More often, she was at least allowed to sit on the mother's bed, holding her hand during painful examinations.

Each week in Népszava we published letters like the one above, and dredged the postbag for more positive ones as well, so that the profession would not feel that they were under attack. But in vain.

The Hungarian Board of Obstetricians, the 'politburo' of the profession, saw the campaign from the start as an attack, and devised a strategy to neutralise our work. After pressure on the ministry to withdraw our funding failed, obstetricians were advised to have nothing to do with us, and not to fill out the questionnaires we sent them. Interviews which we managed to get with leading doctors reflected a wall of suspicion and hostility towards us.

'Our maternal mortality figures are as good as, or better than, some countries in western Europe, and we want to keep them that way,' said Dr Jenő Egyed, the head of the National Institute of Obstetrics and Gynaecology. He was very proud of the fact that in his hospital, eighty per cent of women were given epidurals, an injection into the spine designed to reduce or do away completely with pain. 'In our hospitals we have a very good doctor-patient relationship.'

His only complaint was a shortage of funds to buy new equipment—electronic foetal monitors, for example, which would be permanently strapped to the woman. 'But wouldn't that prevent her walking about?' I asked innocently, aware of how much walking, crouching, shouting and dancing helped my wife cope with pain during the birth of my own children.

He laughed when I mentioned Ágnes Geréb's attempts to encourage home-births. Her ideas were 'not modern', he explained, and in any case, Hungary was not developed enough to support home-births. The telephones and roads were not good enough, the ambulances not properly equipped, and there was a shortage of ambulance staff with gynaecological experience to help if complications arose. He, like other doctors we interviewed, was under the misapprehension that in countries like the Netherlands, where home-births top thirty per cent of all deliveries, ambulances are on stand-by outside every home.

At a press conference, Dr Egyed was asked by a female journalist whether he had ever witnessed a normal birth. He didn't answer the question but retorted, 'I've certainly seen many where emergency care was needed immediately.'

This was exactly the point of our campaign. By treating every birth as a potential emergency, the hospitals were denying that the psychological state of the birthing woman strongly affected the ease or difficulty of the delivery. The doctors were not only denying women the right to give birth in their own way, they were actually causing the complications they set out to avoid.

In the Szent Imre Hospital in the 11th district of Budapest Dr Sándor Bálint was one of the few doctors who said publically that he sympathised with Dr Geréb's methods. It would take 'a whole generation, ten or twenty years', however, for them to be introduced in Hungary, he believed. Opposition to active birth was so entrenched among his own generation of doctors, he said, they would simply have to die out before the system could be changed. Even he insisted on giving his strongest opinions off-record, for fear of his own job.

There were some achievements. His was one of the first hospitals in the country to allow partners to be present during birth. The practices of automatically shaving each woman's pubic hair, and giving each an enema, were no longer compulsory. There were less episiotomies than in many hospitals. The caesarean rate stayed below twenty per cent at his hospital, even as it soared towards thirty and forty per cent in others. At one provincial hospital, the caesarean rate reached forty per cent, simply because this was the favourite method of delivery of the two main obstetricians.

Some things also stayed the same. On one visit to the Szent Imre Hospital, I found five newborn babies, in identical purple jumpsuits, on top of what looked like a lunch trolley, about to be wheeled in to their mothers for feeding time. 'The babies keep the mothers awake, and stop them resting after the birth,' a nurse explained, as she fed them sweet tea from a bottle—sweetened with white sugar—making it even less likely that they would want to breast-feed.

As we toured the country, a common experience was this—younger, more progressive doctors, afraid to speak openly for fear they would be sacked. There might have been a political change in Hungary, with one-party rule swept aside, but in the maternity wards, the Board of Obstetricians still held absolute power with the old Leninist doctrine of 'the leading role of the Party'.

Other hospitals proudly told us that they had won international awards as 'baby-friendly' hospitals—largely, as far as we could see, by repainting the walls and cleaning the toilets more often. 'Creating the comfort of home, in a hospital environment,' became the new slogan, but the old rules remained in place. As new technology arrived, it was used to strengthen the doctor's control and to create a culture of surveillance of every movement of the baby inside the woman, always in the name of safety. New, and hugely expensive, birth-chairs were introduced, in which the woman could at last squat or crouch to give birth. Anything to avoid the 'indignity' for the doctor of having to get down on his own hands and knees.

Everywhere, we found evidence of the corrupting influence of money. All eastern European medical staff are underpaid compared to their counterparts in western Europe, but obstetricians had risen to an almost unchallenged position as the best paid doctors in Hungary, through the illegal system of gratitude money. The going rate was between one and two months salary. The women discussed among themselves how much each doctor expected, then often slipped in a few extra notes, just to make sure.

Ágnes Geréb continued her one-woman fight for active birth—not just for home-birth. She knew that only a minority of women would ever want to give birth at home, but she wanted to have the same effect on the hospitals that home-birthers have had in countries like Britain and the Netherlands—to create the opposite pole to the highly mechanised routines that hospitals gravitate towards, and remind them that birth is natural.

In 1993, the Hungarian Parliament voted to give her foundation more than £200,000 from the 1994 health budget, to set up Hungary's first 'Birth House'—a place where couples could come to take classes to prepare themselves for birth, with facilities to give birth there as well, if conditions at home were unsuitable.

Proposed by a Liberal deputy, it won cross-party, almost unanimous support. A Christian Democrat deputy described it as 'the best law enacted by the first parliamentary cycle'—but the money was never paid.

Throughout 1994, the Health Ministry stalled. The foundation had 'not handed in sufficient paperwork', according to one official. Behind the scenes, the Board of Obstetricians lobbied hard to make sure the money was never paid. The health budget was paid to other items on the list, and finally ran out. The doctors had won, and Ágnes and the foundation had to sell the house they had bought with a bank loan, on the basis of the parliamentary vote.

Nick Thorpe

The first edition of our *Birth Guide to Hungary* came out in 1999. Each hospital was evaluated on the Polish model, stars for objective conditions were offered, and hearts for the kindness and helpfulness of medical staff. The county hospital in Kecskemét, central Hungary, was a typical provincial institution, and received the following evaluation:

> The hospital arranges classes, and there is even a club for expectant mothers. Three quarters of those who wrote to us said they did not attend. Partners are theoretically allowed to be present, but were not present at eighty per cent of births, mainly because of lack of space. At the moment only one birth can take place at a time with the partner present, though the hospital plans to expand these facilities in future. Shaving and enemas are compulsory. There is one birthing room, divided by partitions. One of the toilets was dirty, the other clean at the time of our visit. Two thirds of births are induced, or accelerated by artificial means. Painkillers such as epidural injections, or in gas or tablet form, are given at the request of the patient. During labour one quarter of women were not allowed to move freely. Women have to give birth in a lying position. Episiotomies are compulsory. After the birth, the baby is given to the mother for a couple of minutes, then is taken away in every case, and the mother only sees her child again in the mother and baby ward. Forty-six per cent of mothers in our survey said the staff performed their tasks in an impersonal way, and that some were unfriendly. After the birth, two thirds of women were allowed to keep their babies with them in mother-and-baby wards.
>
> The vast majority of visitors were only allowed to see the mother and baby through a glass window. On average, women spend five days in hospital. 2,300 to 2,400 babies were born in this hospital in 1997.

The handling of birth and, above all, of the woman giving birth, was symptomatic of the way the citizen was handled by the state, and all its institutions, in Hungary and throughout the former communist countries of eastern Europe. As a dumb animal, to be manipulated, experimented on, harmed, healed and handled. The citizen was there for the state, rather than the state being there for the citizen.

In 1997, a mother turned to the parliamentary ombudsman in charge of human rights, Peter Polt, with a request to clarify the legal situation: did she have the right to give birth at home? Could she in such a case request professional medical help? And if so, could this please be regulated by law.

In March 1998, Polt ruled that home-birth is constitutionally possible. Two laws affected his decision, he said. The right of the woman over her own body, and the right of the unborn child. He concluded that a woman does have the constitutional right to give birth where she wishes, but this can only take place in cases where what he called 'the very large medical risks' of home-birth can be excluded.

We had taken one step forward, but two steps back. The profession would always argue that the risks could never be 'excluded'. We had failed to persuade him that in many cases, the risk of infection from the hospital environment, and the risks of psychological or physical harm to mother and child in hospital, could be greater than the risks posed at home.

Our second son was born safely and peacefully at home in 1995. Daniel, the third, was due in early December 1997. During the later stages of what had been, until then, a beautiful and complication-free delivery, the sound of his heart on the foetal heart monitor suddenly faded away. Ágnes remained completely calm, produced a small oxygen cyclinder from somewhere and gave Andrea a gulp.

'Now you need to push . . .' she said firmly.

Daniel was born with the next contraction. He was given oxygen too, but mother and baby were fine. I had turned on my BBC tape-recorder, earlier in the birth, to record the sounds of my wife singing in order to control the pain. I had forgotten the machine long since, assuming the tape had run out. We found out that the whole drama of Daniel's birth— including the sound of his heart ebbing away on the loudspeaker on the monitor, Ágnes's instructions and Daniel's first cries—was all safely recorded.

In February 2002, the ethical committee of the Board of Obstetricians published its view on home-birth.

> The committee does not dispute the right of Ágnes Geréb or other doctors to develop an approach which differs from those published in the textbooks. But it cannot be allowed that she conducts a medical practice which puts her clients in danger. The ethical committee is not in a position to judge whether conditions exist for home-birth today in Hungary, [. . .] but has come to the conclusion that as a result of Ágnes Geréb's continuous activity in this field, one part of her clients receive less safe care than would be possible. [. . .]
>
> Because alternative birth techniques are spreading increasingly quickly, the professional forums concerned should evaluate whether there is a genuine demand for home delivery. If they do, after being fully informed, then conditions should be created as soon as possible which ensure the safety of mothers and babies.

One step backwards we thought, but two steps forward. What has happened since has been a continuous struggle between Ágnes and the independent midwives and doulas—non-professional birth assistants—she has trained, on the one hand, and the obstetric profession on the other.

Ágnes and those who support her argue that midwifery needs to be recognised as a separate profession from that of the obstetrician-gynaecologist, as it is in many countries. This would allow for a separate protocol or list of duties and responsibilities to be drawn up for midwives attending births, to replace the current situation where they are, as nurses, mere assistants to doctors. Obstetricians have long opposed this, as it would undermine their own monopoly on birth, and their control over the gratitude money paid by mothers.

There has been some progress. Midwifery training has improved, and has been extended. But qualified midwives can still rarely move out of the shadow of the attending doctor who 'leads' the birth, in Hungarian parlance. Ágnes, and others who practise active birth, use a different terminology. Midwives attend birth. If anyone 'leads' it, it is the birthing woman and her baby. From September 2009, home-birth has appeared for the first time on the syllabus of new students of midwifery. But who will be able to teach it in Hungary, if the efforts to criminalise Ágnes and her circle continue?

The Ministry of Health has presided over several rounds of negotiations to establish rules and regulations governing home-birth in Hungary. But as health ministers come and go—almost every year—the subject is constantly moved down the list of priorities. Ágnes sees her work as a-legal, rather than illegal. She is simply helping women who have decided to have their babies at home. Both her Hippocratic Oath, and her duty as a member of the public, compel her to do so.

What is missing is a calm, sensible cooperation between independent midwives, the ambulance service and the hospitals. In Hungary, as in other countries where planned home-births take place, about one in ten end up in hospital. This is usually a decision taken by the mother—that she would, after all, feel safer in hospital—or by the midwife, who sees indications that hospital facilities might be needed. Only in rare cases does the woman need to be taken to hospital in emergency circumstances.

In the meantime, several court cases have been launched against Ágnes for the death of two babies, soon after birth in the mother's arms in one instance, and during birth in the other. She argues that a hospital birth would not have been able to save either child. Approximately forty babies die during birth in Hungarian hospitals each year. In some cases the hospitals but, under Hungarian law, never the doctors, are prosecuted. Ágnes cannot practise legally, because her right to do so was taken away by a professional body which dogmatically opposes home-birth. The same body gives professional advice to the court—the court has nowhere else to turn. It is one struck-off doctor's word against that of the profession. It appears impossible for her to get justice in her own country.

Some parts of the Hungarian media, initially quite sympathetic to her as a 'one woman show', turned against her after the death of the baby in September 2007. Journalists from tabloid papers started running front page pictures with her eyes pixelled out, to give the impression of a common criminal. They took photographs of the whole house in which she rents just the ground floor, with scurrilous articles implying that she has grown rich from the proceeds of her 'dangerous' activities. Plain clothes police turn up regularly outside the flat, at all hours of day and night. Tabloid journalists pose as students at birth classes.

She continues to attend births, in the midst of the storm. Banned from practising as a gynaecologist, she takes part as a birth-attendant. Her enemies in the profession feel they can rid themselves of this 'troublesome priest' once and for all.

* * *

One other case is worth quoting as an example of malpractice in even the best hospitals. In September 2003, János Szántai and his wife Ildikó travelled from Cluj in Romania, to the MÁV Hospital in Budapest, for the birth of their child. They felt they could be sure of better care in a Hungarian rather than a Romanian hospital.

They had been recommended a certain doctor by a friend, and cheerfully arranged for him to attend the birth. Ildikó had given birth to her previous child fourteen years earlier, and they didn't want to take any chances. The MÁV Hospital, formerly the Railway Workers' Hospital next to the West Station, had the reputation, confirmed in our surveys, as the best maternity ward in Hungary—though admittedly the best of a bad bunch. What János and Ildikó did not know was that this particular doctor took on several hundred deliveries a year. They were unlikely to get his full attention.

At eight o'clock in the evening the doctor examined her. No-one else was present in the room. János waited outside. The doctor then disappeared to examine his other patients, and they never saw him again. Ildikó's contractions began suddenly at nine-fifteen, and she was placed in the care of completely different doctors, who appeared to know nothing about her. At quarter past one in the morning, a baby boy was born, perfectly healthy, but János was told that 'a major tragedy' had happened. Ildikó's uterus ruptured during the birth, and she died almost immediately as air entered her arteries.

The doctor was temporarily suspended from the hospital, and a police investigation launched against him, on suspicion that he had administered prostaglandin to Ildikó and to other patients. This causes spasms in the muscles, including those of the uterus. It is legally used in Hungary and other countries to treat problems of the intestine, but not to induce birth because of the dangers it could cause, including rupture of the uterus. What made the case more suspicious were both the high number of deliveries this specific doctor took on, and the high number of complications during those births.

'This drug is not registered for use during birth, and such use would be totally against the medical profession,' a senior doctor at the same hospital told me, in an off-record conversation. 'But I cannot exclude that a doctor might use it, without the knowledge of the hospital and the patient.'

The doctor at the centre of the case denied the accusation, and the case was eventually dropped for lack of evidence. He continues to practise.

The cases against Ágnes persist.

12. Barbers of the Balkans

'The fight has started, our hearts are beating,' thundered the loudspeakers on the rickety opposition stage, *'we are here, facing our oppressors . . .'*

Nineteenth-century ballad, Bulgaria

The words of a nineteenth century song, composed as Bulgaria was breaking free from the Ottoman Empire. This time round, the people had had enough of the Socialist Party.

'I used to think the last hairs of Stalin's moustache would be shaved off in Podgorica. But now I think it will happen in Belgrade . . .'

Jevren Brković, Montenegrin novelist

The generals, for some reason, rode in a white Dacia, a sort of small Romanian Renault. But the car was squeaky clean, and sailed over the pot-holed streets of Bucharest like a swan. It was accompanied, ahead and behind, by two long, sleek, black Opels, full of security men. The Dacia parked at the back of the Democratic Convention headquarters and the generals, in their finest uniforms, got out. The black cars parked at the front. It was November 1996.

'I'm terribly sorry,' said Radu, President-elect Emil Constantinescu's son, 'you'll have to wait a little longer for the interview. These generals have requested an urgent audience.'

The generals left stony-faced, an hour later. Constantinescu brushed aside our request for details of their conversation.

They belonged to the Serviciul de Protecţie şi Pază (SPP), that much we knew; the Presidential Guard which formed one of the five separate secret services in Romania. During his presidential campaign, which had ended with his surprise victory the previous Sunday, Constantinescu had frequently criticised the secret services, both for their sheer number, and their apparent loyalty to the incumbent, Ion Iliescu. Although as a presidential candidate he was also expected to make use of the services of the SPP, he had chosen instead to surround himself with unarmed former fighters from the 1989 revolution. The SPP, he alleged, had 3,200 members, and he intended, if elected, to cut it back or abolish it altogether.

On the last day of the election campaign, the SPP hit back.

'We regret that Professor Emil Constantinescu wishes to accede to the highest function of state with lies and calumnies,' they said in a statement, released to the Romanian media. Their staff, they claimed, was half the size he had mentioned and they attacked him, in turn, for 'running a private, paramilitary bodyguard of his own, in contravention of the Romanian Constitution.'

Romania's first non-socialist government after the revolution was off to a rocky start.

The celebrations on the streets of Bucharest on the night of his victory were ecstatic. Young people, liberals, conservatives, small businessmen, intellectuals, workers—anyone who felt that their revolution had been stolen from them six years earlier, danced until dawn. Constantinescu himself came to the studios of the BBC Romanian Service at about two o'clock in the morning. Tall and professorial, he told us we could only have five minutes, then talked for more than half an hour. Then asked to listen back to what he said. Then asked us to increase the bass on his voice. My respect for him began to ebb rather fast.

His task would not be easy. Romania, like the other former communist countries, would have done better with an anti-communist, conservative or liberal-minded government for the first years after the revolution, I thought. It might have rooted out some of the most flagrant abuses of power, and given people a sense of change, not continuity.

Instead, Romania had had Ion Iliescu. And it was run by an incompetent elite, much of which had established its power in the communist era, and was riddled with corruption and cronyism.

Onto the battlefield strode the professor, fresh from seven years painstakingly rebuilding the opposition, but with no experience whatsoever of high office.

'The only true reconciliation must be initiated by those who suffered. On my side are the former political detainees of the communist regime, those who fought in the December Revolution, and those who suffered under communism,' Constantinescu told me.

'What did he plan to do with all those within the state apparatus who owed their jobs to their loyalty to Iliescu?' I asked.

'We will not exclude anyone who is honest, competent and willing to work,' he replied.

He was counting on western support to guide Romania towards membership of the European Union, and it had not been slow in coming. President Chirac of France had rung him from Tokyo at four o'clock in the morning, soon after his visit to our studios.

'We know that a united Europe is not a charity,' said the President-elect, '. . . and we can only be admitted to the EU if our economy is healthy and our society meets certain standards . . .'

It was to prove an uphill struggle, both for him and his Socialist and Democratic Party successors, over the following decade.

A few months earlier, I had waited at Sofia airport to see another great hope of the Balkan peoples, Tsar Simeon II, arrive back from fifty years in exile.

They were serving bread and salt on silver trays in the fourth century church of St Sophia in honour of the King's visit. An elderly woman with the platter in her hand looked at me suspiciously—are you Orthodox? Only a Protestant, I replied, but pointed upwards at the beautiful frescoes on the arched ceilings, and mimed, as well as I could, that there is only one God. She shook her head and pressed on among the true believers. A little later she relented, and pressed a salty dry crust into my hand.

The return of the King, the Tsar, cast a spell, an enchantment over many Bulgarians. As in Romania, the first six years after the fall of communism had been dominated by the Socialists, the successor party to the communists. In a smaller country, blessed by a better climate and the abundant fruit and vegetables, fish and meat of their southern position, the people had fared somewhat better. But there was still a sense of incomplete change, of corrupt leaders, of the new-old mafia running the show. Simeon was untainted, and many people invested great hope in his return.

'This is the last chance for our country,' a man in the crowd at the airport had told me, waiting to cheer his arrival. 'The communists won't let him come back to power. But a king is like gold in the bank. It is an investment. It provides security for a better future.'

By 1996, inflation in Bulgaria was rampant. A loaf of bread cost the equivalent of a dollar, and the average wage was worth only sixty dollars a month, down from a hundred and ten the previous year. After years of reluctance to start privatisation, the Socialists had just announced the closure of sixty-four loss-making state firms, and the loss of 25,000 jobs.

Their restructuring plans for industry, they admitted, would cost close to a quarter of a million jobs. This was not a popular government.

The television news focused on four subjects that evening—the shortage of bread, the shortage of petrol, the prevalence of crime and the return of the king. The previous year, Bulgaria had enjoyed a bumper wheat crop, but it had mostly been exported, the people were told. So where is the money? they asked. A plan by the Rover car company to set up a factory in Bulgaria was cancelled at the last moment—another blow to the Socialist government.

Simeon of Saxe-Coburg-Gotha left Bulgaria with his mother at the age of nine, in 1946, after a referendum officially abolished the monarchy. While other former monarchs now seemed too old to play an active role in their countries—King Michael of Romania was seventy-six—Simeon was a sprightly fifty-nine. People were also aware that he made a living as a financial consultant in Madrid—a Bulgarian who understands capitalism, at last! many thought. He had applied for and received a Bulgarian passport from his Spanish exile in 1991, but had put off his return 'until Bulgaria is stable'. It still wasn't, but he had decided the time was ripe anyway.

'Did he intend to reclaim his throne?' I asked him, in his suite on the eighteenth floor of the Intercontinental Hotel.

'My dear sir, that is a pretty odd question! I have considered myself the rightful monarch of Bulgaria since the day I was born!'

Simeon kept the authorities guessing about his true intentions. Not only the former communists, but many other Bulgarians felt monarchy was an anachronism—but as the King had suddenly appeared, like a new card in the pack, they were wondering how they could play him. Mr Saxe-Coburg-Gotha didn't especially want to be played. He had not decided yet how long he would stay, he said. President Zhelev invited Simeon and a group of private guests to a lunch of stuffed peppers and baked lamb at his residence.

'We had a very pleasant lunch among mutual friends,' Zhelev told reporters. 'We discussed the political issues of the world, of Europe and, of course, of Bulgaria, but we did not go into great detail. Such issues need a more serious discussion than is possible over a meal.'

Simeon toured the country, avoiding meeting politicians at all, where he could. His popularity lay in his ability to stand above politics. He was upset, he said, by the roughness of the security guards assigned to protect him. A ninety-year-old film maker presented him with a copy of a film he had made about the funeral of his father, Boris III, in 1943. Boris died in strange circumstances, soon after a meeting with Hitler, at which he refused to deport Bulgaria's Jews to the Nazi death camps.

As he toured the country with his wife, Margarita, Simeon stopped briefly in front of the crumbling pale green palace which once belonged to his father. It now serves as the National Ethnographic Museum.

*   *   *

To the west of Bulgaria, in another former kingdom, Slobodan Milošević was in trouble. Having come to power nearly ten years earlier, pledging to make Serbia great again, his country and his record were by now in rags. As President of Yugoslavia, he had presided over the loss of Slovenia, Croatia, Bosnia, and Macedonia. Montenegro was still loyal for the time being, but Kosovo was straining at the bit, and was only kept under control by a massive police presence and a catalogue of repression.

On the surface Serbia didn't look like a country heading for a crisis. In Belgrade, the markets were full of food, and the nightclubs and cafés were doing a good trade. Since sanctions had been lifted in December 1995 cheap petrol was once again available and the roads were packed with cars. But people were gloomy. The government had promised the lifting of sanctions would bring about an economic recovery but there were no signs of it.

Painful too for many Serbs, was the fact that mother Serbia was swollen by 700,000 Serb refugees from the breakaway republics. Belgrade, towering over the confluence of the Sava and Danube rivers, had once been one of the jewels in the crown of European cities. Now it was trampled daily under foot by wave after wave of protesters and refugees. Vojvodina, the province in the north which, like Kosovo, had enjoyed its own autonomy until Milošević stripped it away in 1989, was restless. It was also swollen with disgruntled, dispossessed Serbs from the Krajina region in Croatia, or Kosovo or Bosnia, upsetting a delicate ethnic balance, established over centuries between its many peoples.

The domestic opposition to Milošević was diverse, divided, but it was becoming more radical. The next flashpoint would be the local elections in November 1996. The opposition to Milošević was traditionally crippled by internal bickering, fuelled as much by personal differences between its leaders as policy differences over the degree of nationalism they should profess. But for now it was enjoying one of its more united periods, grouped loosely in the Zajedno or 'Together' coalition.

In two rounds of local elections, on 3 and 17 November, Zajedno won in fourteen major towns and cities across Serbia, including the capital Belgrade, Niš in the south, Novi Sad in the north as well as Čačak and Užice in the west.

For a moment it looked as though their success at local level might cement their unity at national level, and Milošević would face a formidable opponent at last. He moved fast to make sure it did not. As a former lawyer, he was a stickler for legality, in its outward form at least. Democratic elections and courts of law, provided the people voted, and the judges ruled in his favour. When they didn't, however, he lost patience quickly with the content of democracy.

The Central Electoral Commission, at his bidding, refused to recognise the election results, citing numerous irregularities.

'In these elections in Niš, the citizens of this town and the dreams of half a century have been victorious. I beg you to defend with all means our Niš and our and your victory in it,' thundered Vuk Drašković, a firebrand nationalist who had organised his own paramilitary militia to fight for Serbia in the wars in Croatia and Bosnia, and who was by now also a firebrand democrat.

The opposition organised daily demonstrations in each of the affected cities, to protest against the theft of the elections.

The Electoral Commission awarded Nis to Milošević's Socialist Party and ordered a rerun of the election in those Belgrade districts where Milošević had lost.

The rerun went ahead, but turnout was very low, with much of the population either too weary to vote again, or heeding an opposition call to boycott the elections. Protesters bombarded the offices of Radio-Television Serbia, the daily Politika, and Radio Belgrade—all mouthpieces of the regime—with eggs and stones.

The demonstrators were an odd and colourful mix. There was a strong 'patriotic' element, with old and new Serbian banners, carried by some of those who until recently had cheered Milošević for taking the country to war. There were trade unionists more concerned with job losses and labour rights, and students fed up with the tough visa regimes of western countries, who carried the flags of places they wanted to visit—Britain, Germany, France, Italy and Spain. Each day, the demonstrators followed the same route on their 'walk' through Belgrade, blowing whistles and chanting. The possibility of police reprisals was always present, but rarely materialised. In Belgrade, only a student who had the temerity to wield a giant puppet of Milošević was badly beaten by the police for his insolence.

Most worrying for the regime was the fact that the demonstrations became daily events; colourful, non-violent pageants of protest. Most worrying for the protesters was the weather.

Winter was bitterly cold in Serbia. Basic state-produced, cheap foods were in short supply. Sanctions might have ended after the signing of the Dayton Agreement in November 1995, but the people had few reserves left when imported goods returned to the shops. Belgrade's well stocked shops and busy cafés concealed a crumbling economy. Going home from the demonstrations, people huddled on broken pavements in the sleet, waiting for groaning, overcrowded buses to lurch round the corner, to take them home to the suburbs. Belgrade was beginning to look like Bucharest under Ceauşescu.

The authorities were caught off balance by the scale and the persistence of the protests. After initially trying to ignore them, they then set their pet commentators on them, labelling them 'fascists' and 'manipulated children'. The students retorted that the authorities had had no qualms about sending their contemporaries to their deaths on the battlefields of Croatia and Bosnia.

In Belgrade, the popular opposition radio station, B92, was taken off air for two days, as were its sister broadcasters in other towns. State television, RTS, turned its dislike and irony on the protesters, just as it had on the Croats in 1991. Milošević's wife, Mira Marković, suggested that the students wanted civil war—when in fact it was the state which was contemplating how much violence it could get away with—to get the non-violent protesters off the streets. Serbia was used to demonstrations in the early 1990s, but these were bigger, better humoured and potentially more revolutionary.

* * *

Back in Bulgaria, the growing opposition movement to the governing Socialists watched the Serbian protests closely, like students of revolutionary practice. In November 1996, the opposition candidate, Petar Stoyanov, won the presidential election. In December, Zhan Videnov resigned as Prime Minister, in the face of a deepening economic crisis, as inflation for the year topped three hundred per cent. The Bulgarian Socialist Party (BSP) still enjoyed a comfortable majority, and had the constitutional right to choose a new prime minister from their own ranks. Most expected the tough Interior Minister, Nikolai Dobrev, to be appointed. The opposition formed what they called the Union of Democratic Forces (UDF) on the model of Serbia's Zajedno coalition, and began daily protests in early January 1997. In Sofia and Plovdiv, Ruse on the Danube and other cities, a daily march past Socialist Party headquarters was held. In imitation of their Serbian counterparts, eggs were thrown at the buildings and, taking advantage of the wintry weather, snowballs. The UDF had several advantages over Zajedno. One was the support they received from the main trade union movement, Podkrepa. The other was the fact that the new President, Petar Stoyanov, came from their own ranks.

On 10 January, deputies assembled for the first session of Parliament after the winter break. They were supposed to debate a motion proposed by the UDF, a 'Declaration for Bulgaria's Salvation', which called for the immediate dissolution of Parliament and new elections. The declaration also demanded a new governing board of the Bulgarian National Bank, and talks with the IMF for the formation of a 'currency board' to stabilise the currency and tie it to the Deutschmark.

The Socialists found ways to prevent the debate, and angry protesters broke through the police cordon around the Assembly, smashing their way inside the building in an attempt to vent their fury on Socialist Party deputies. They destroyed furniture, and set fire to what they could. Smoke billowed from the second floor windows, and the television pictures showed the building apparently on fire. Police reinforcements forced them out, and a tense stand-off followed. By two in the morning, the police had regrouped, and the crowd outside was dwindling in the cold. Police formed a cordon, and shepherded more than a hundred frightened Socialists from the building, while riot police laid into any protesters they could still get their hands on. It was less an exercise in public order than revenge for the protesters' 'success' earlier on. More than a hundred people were hospitalised, and many more injured. As far as the Bulgarian opposition were concerned, as in Prague in November 1989, it was a 'massacre'.

The plane from Budapest to Sofia the following day was packed with journalists. 'Who do you work for?' I asked the woman sitting just across the aisle. 'The BBC—and you?' she replied. No-one in London had told either Orla Guerin, the Rome correspondent, or me, that we were being sent on the same story.

The old Lada taxi bounced over the potholes past the tower blocks onto the wide crumbling highway into town from the airport. There was something wrong with its suspension, and a piece of cardboard had been cellotaped to the right side of the taxi-meter with three extra noughts, to keep up with inflation. The average wage was now worth only $20 a month.

We found a city in ferment. Barricades had been set up by protesters at key road intersections, with braziers to keep the people warm and free food distributed to all comers. Miners, transport workers and dock-workers joined the students, as the shock-troops of the protest. Everywhere local radio stations crackled from small receivers—the protesters' very own supply of anti-regime news. Like B92 radio in Serbia, Darik radio in Sofia broke the protesters' sense of isolation from one another. Unlike in Belgrade, there were no attempts by the authorities in Bulgaria to close them down, or jam their frequencies.

Everywhere I went, the protesters spoke about what was happening in Belgrade. The Serb street was their model, they said. They blew their whistles, beat on their drums and waved their colourful flags. This was 'internationalism' such as the propagandists of the communist movement once dreamt of, but there was also a strong, patriotic streak.

'*The fight has started, our hearts are beating,*' thundered the loud-speakers on the rickety opposition stages, '*we are here, facing our oppressors . . .*'

The words of a nineteenth century song, composed as Bulgaria was breaking free from the Ottoman Empire.

One Sunday evening in Sofia, I sat down to watch *Kanaleto,* a satirical weekly television show. One sketch showed the triumph of the lev, the Bulgarian currency, 'the most stable in the world, after the Russian rouble', while the dollar collapsed on all fronts. Another sketch was silent, just a man holding up a 'no left turn' road sign. The programme was so popular that similar signs appeared on the barricades all over Sofia the next day.

At the front of the demonstrations in Sofia, Ivan Kostov, the leader of the Union of Democratic Forces, marched in scarf and woolly hat. To interview him, one had to walk alongside him, microphone in hand. There seemed no time to sit down anywhere. The opposition had drawn sharp criticism from foreign capitals after the storming of the Parliament, and Kostov was out to prove the non-violent means and goals of his movement.

'Our purpose is not to destroy but to provoke elections,' he told the crowd. 'Izboli!' they chanted, 'Elections!', or 'Pobeta!'—'Victory!' Each day, as they passed Socialist Party headquarters, they added another slogan to their repertoire: 'Mafia!'

The Socialists wobbled in late January, and offered early elections, but not until the end of the year. Too late, thundered the crowds, and protest leaders like Kostov, feeling the wind in their sails, insisted on new elections in the spring.

From an upstairs window of the National Bank, a chunky stone fortress of a building where the daily news of plunges in the value of the lev echoed like news of defeat in battle, I watched the demonstrators pass on one occasion. 'Those kids are crazy,' I could hear the bankers whispering in my ear. Let there be a government, any government, but let there be an end to this disorder. Only money is wise, only money creates order in the universe . . .

Bulgaria's debt had been rescheduled in 1989. The next instalment of interest, of $137 million, was due to be paid at the end of January. The government insisted that, despite the crisis, it would still be able to pay.

The man from the International Monetary Fund woke me from my reverie. He joined me at the window to watch the marchers pass.

'There are times in history,' he said, not without sympathy for the people on the street, 'when economic policy has to take a back seat.'

It was a relief to return to the heady, romantic atmosphere below. On a stage in front of the former mausoleum of Bulgaria's first post-war communist leader, Georgi Dimitrov, students were performing a play imaginatively entitled '10 January 1997'. Students dressed as riot police chased students dressed as students across the stage. The crowd roared with laughter. As in 1989, humour was one of the most useful cards in the protesters' hands. Riot police stood by, watching themselves through the upper corner of their transparent riot shields.

On every street and street corner in Sofia, on the barricades and in the bars, there was music. Gypsy violins, impossibly blonde and buxom singers, church bells chimed, folk music, jazz and rock ballads rang out. There was even a military brass band. Poor Socialists, I thought. It must sometimes seem to them that while they have a monopoly on grey power, the opposition have a monopoly on music.

I took a number 19 tram to the Graf bakery, one of very few private bakeries in Sofia. The boss was away, in Serbia, trying to buy flour, and his staff were reluctant to speak in his absence. Anelia was the bravest, having only worked there a month. I asked how much bread cost, and was puzzled when she couldn't reply. It's because it's not for sale any more, my interpreter explained. 'For the past few months, they have only been making bread here for the staff, not for customers.'

But there were cakes, like croissants but heavier, and stuffed with jam or chocolate. 'So let them eat cake . . .' I thought.

I asked a customer how the crisis was affecting her family. 'Well, we're not badly off compared to most,' she explained. 'Both my husband and I have work. But there are some foods we can no longer afford to buy, which the children would need. For example milk, and honey . . . and some kinds of sausage . . .'

On 21 January, Petar Stoyanov, who had won the presidential election the previous November, took the oath of office. As the protests had delayed a replacement prime minister for Zhan Videnov, Bulgaria had had no effective government for four weeks, and the currency was sliding further every day. A shortage of large denomination leva notes meant only small notes were available, which people began carting round in bags and suitcases. Pensioners saw a lifetime's savings evaporate in a few weeks. 'Zivoli!' chanted the crowds each day, 'Elections!'. Under Bulgaria's constitution, however, President Stoyanov was obliged to ask the Socialists, who still enjoyed a majority in Parliament, to form a government. Reluctantly he turned to Dobrev, but not before drawing up a plan for the Socialists to step down with dignity. Dobrev should immediately return the mandate he offered him, the new President suggested, a caretaker government should be formed to start talks immediately with the IMF, and new elections could take place in April.

Dobrev, under pressure from hardliners in his own party, thought otherwise, and tried to form a government. The situation on the streets escalated. The independent trade union bloc, Podkrepa, called a general strike. The main border crossings into Greece were blocked by protesters.

Dobrev struggled on for a week, then surrendered. Elections were called for April. The protests turned into a vast street celebration. But some in Dobrev's party were bitter.

'Will every government in Bulgaria now become a hostage of the street?' asked a leader column in a pro-government newspaper. Other commentators muttered darkly about the danger of 'blue revanchism'—

the threat of the new authorities putting on trial the 'reds' responsible for running the country since the 1989 Revolution.

This sense that 'the winner takes all' was common throughout eastern Europe in the 1990s and beyond. There was little sense of the idea that one could lose power with dignity.

The popular mayor and caretaker Prime Minister of Sofia, Stefan Sofiyanski, established a non-party government, and the lev was dragged back, with IMF and European Union help, from the brink of the abyss. Urgent negotiations began on the creation of a 'currency board' which would peg the rate of the lev to the Deutschmark. The popular uprising in Bulgaria had triumphed in barely five weeks. In the April elections, the UDF won 137 seats in the Assembly, with the Socialists reduced to fifty-seven. Ivan Kostov became Prime Minister of the tenth Bulgarian government in seven years.

* * *

It was to prove much harder to dislodge the ruling Socialists in Serbia. The 'power' stood firm as a cliff onto which the protesters broke, in wave after wave.

The Serb street lacked both the tools and the good fortune which brought down the government in Sofia—there was no presidential figure to sympathise with them; no wavering in the ranks of Milošević's men. All they had was their victory in the local elections, and eventually a deal was done with Milošević.

Zoran Djindjić, a former student protester and leader of the Democratic Party, became the first non-communist mayor of Belgrade since the Second World War. Only four months later, another opposition leader, Vuk Drašković, withdrew his support and Djindjić fell. Compared to Bulgaria, these were pretty meagre pickings, for months of popular pressure. The only consolation for the opposition was that they now had a foothold in power, on a local level. That would prove valuable the next time the street gathered the strength to challenge Milošević again.

* * *

Much neglected Albania was about to implode and make a dramatic contribution to the history of the Balkans. A series of pyramid or 'Ponzi' schemes, pseudo-banks offering huge rates of interest to investors, collapsed in the last weeks of 1996 and first weeks of 1997. There had been similar schemes in Serbia, Romania and Russia in the early 1990s—with tens of thousands making money, hand over fist, but hundreds of thousands losing their life savings when the bubble finally burst. In Albania, however, the sheer scale of investment in the schemes, the millions brought or sent back from Albanians working abroad, led to the phenomenal growth of the pyramids, and their equally spectacular collapse. In a country of just three million, over a billion dollars was lost. Two thirds of Albanians had invested in the schemes. The banking system was in its infancy. The police and army had little experience of crowd control, and angry investors flooded the streets. The governing Democratic Party of President Sali Berisha was also deeply involved in several of the pyramids, which it tried to protect as similar schemes fell all around them. The intrigue of foreign governments—British, American, Greek and others, each backing rival parties—added to the maelstrom. A general uprising against the government began in the south of the country, centred on the port city of Vlora. Berisha's response was to open fire on the demonstrators. Protesters broke open army barracks, and seized the arms stockpiled during the communist era to protect the country, partisan-style, from 'foreign invasion'. Two thousand died on the streets of Albanian towns, as Berisha lost control.

In Albania, as in Bulgaria, elections provided a way out of the crisis. At the end of June, the Socialist Party decisively defeated the Democratic Party, and Berisha resigned as President. The arms seized from the barracks would prove invaluable to Albanian insurgents in neighbouring Kosovo, as they abandoned non-violent resistance to Serbia and formed the Kosovo Liberation Army (KLA). Hundreds of thousands of guns at $10 a piece fell into their hands. And as parts of Albania slipped from central government control, KLA training bases and supply routes sprang up. In each country, the failure of the new political elite to feed its people, or to provide the basic conditions for a normal life, was rebounding in their faces. Another Balkan war drew closer.

* * *

'Milošević is a pig' read the grafitti on a prominent wall near the Danube in Budapest. 'No, people are the problem' read the riposte. The graffiti stayed there through the mid-1990s. The two sides in the debate were presumably young people fleeing the implosion of mother Serbia, escaping the draft into her armies, or simply hoping for a Hungarian girlfriend. What the exchange did illustrate was a deeper debate within the Serbian opposition—to what extent they were themselves to blame for the fall of their country into war, civil strife and poverty. Milošević had, after all, been democratically chosen at election after election. This was no Ceauşescu.

The opposition to Milošević came in waves through the 1990s. One hundred thousand people marched through Belgrade in the early summer of 1992, to oppose the siege by Serb forces of one of their favourite weekend destinations, Sarajevo. But to no avail. Opposition leaders and parties came and went, but mostly came and quarrelled, then arranged marriages of convenience with Milošević. Vuk Drašković, the bearded patriarch of the opposition, and Zoran Djindjić, his elfin counterpart, outdid each other with their support for Radovan Karadžić and the Bosnian Serb war against Bosnia. Vojislav Koštunica, a prominent nationalist lawyer with a gloomy expression which made his occasional wry smiles the more endearing, did the same. But the deal with Milošević in February 1997 to partially recognise the November 1996 local election results crippled the opposition for a long time. A new generation stepped into the breach. Otpor —the word means 'resistance'.

It began with graffiti. From August 1998, black fists clenched in protest, or their negative image of white fists stenciled on a black background, began appearing on walls and underpasses, bridges and hoardings, initially in Belgrade, but then they spread like a virus, all over Serbia.

'We knew it was an aggressive, even a Nazi image,' said Milja Jovanović, a plump, serene twenty-five-year-old, one of a dozen or so founders of Otpor in October 1998.

'The communist workers movement used it, and the students used it. And especially in Serbia, where the extreme left and the extreme right are very strong, it made an instant impact. Everyone started to wonder what these fists were.' The red star had been removed from buildings across Yugoslavia and eastern Europe. Otpor proved that the time of symbols was far from over.

The youth of Serbia were angry. Angry with the failure of the opposition protests of 1996–97, angry with opposition leaders who seemed to spend more time attacking each other than attacking the regime, but angry first and foremost with the regime itself. A tape-recording of Slobodan Milošević using the word 'resistance' was cheekily cut and looped to give the impression that the President supported the movement against himself!

'Otpor came naturally as an individual answer to this overwhelming bad thing that was happening to us. You couldn't deal with that rationally, you just had to go out and express your anger in whatever way you could, and this spraying was a good beginning,' said Milja.

The first reprisal by the authorities was to beat up and then imprison four Otpor activists for ten days.

'After that we tried to build our organisation, but it was not a real organisation, just a group of friends at first. And we spread the word among people we trusted. Because the fear of the police is very great here. Maybe the strongest fear in Serbia is fear of the police.'

Another big difference between Otpor and their predecessors was that they didn't get bogged down in history.

'It's not important to make a new interpretation of the history of Serbia, or make a new interpretation of who did what to whom during the Second World War. What is important is that we have to face the problems that are happening right now.'

Patriotism had been one of the strongest driving forces of the protests in 1989 in eastern Europe. Patriotism in the early 1990s led many Serbs to support Milošević's wars. But by the end of the decade, Serbs were overdosing on patriotism. Anti-patriotism, resistance in itself to everything the regime stood for, attracted young people. And with all the narcissism of youth, they were less willing to put up with shortages which their grandparents, their life savings swept away, by now considered almost normal.

Before Otpor could gather steam, one more war had to be lost—the war for Kosovo.

Through the autumn of 1998, another fist hung in the air over Belgrade—not the slim, bare, bony fist of the boys and girls in Otpor, but the vast military tonnage of the North Atlantic Treaty Organisation.

For much of the 1990s, since my first visit to Kosovo, the Albanian opposition to Serbian rule in Kosovo was led by Ibrahim Rugova, a chain-smoking, scarf-wearing intellectual who was deeply committed to non-violence. As leader of the Democratic League of Kosovo, he was elected president of the province in a virtually underground ballot in May 1992. The Serbs didn't recognise Kosovar Albanian elections, and the Albanians boycotted the Serb votes. The two communities, never close, separated out entirely into two separate and parallel systems. The Serbs held the whip, but the Albanians were in the majority.

Rugova argued that any confrontation with the Serb security forces would leave thousands of casualties. There was already ample evidence of that on the battlefields of Croatia and Bosnia, and for a long time his people accepted his argument. It was also clear that Serbia would never relinquish Kosovo, but more radically minded Albanians grew tired of non-violence, and were hankering for a fight. The 1995 Dayton Accords, signed with American mediation in Dayton, Ohio in November 1995, ended the war in Bosnia and were limited only to a Bosnian settlement. In 1996, Rugova reached agreement with the Serbian authorities that the Kosovar Albanian schools could continue independently of the Serbian educational system. It was a move that would lose him his reputation as a leader, and allow radicals to take control. After Dayton, the great powers stated unequivocally that since Kosovo had been a province and not a republic it had to remain part of Yugoslavia. The EU recognised the rump Yugoslavia—Montenegro and Serbia—and Kosovo as part of it. Rugova's passive resistance had got his people nowhere.

A series of drive-by shootings and bomb attacks in 1996 and 1997 on the Serbian police, prominent Albanians who collaborated with the Serb authorities and public figures from the Serb community, like the dean of Priština University, suggested the existence of increasingly determined and well-equipped underground cells. Bank-rolled by the Albanian diaspora in Switzerland, and largely armed by the insurgents in Albania, the Kosovo Liberation Army took shape.

The Serb authorities responded with mass-repression. In early 1998, the KLA finally emerged from the shadows as a guerrilla army, and began claiming territory. The army surrounded and shelled their villages. In the most famous case, in the Drenica valley in March 1998, commander Adem Jashari and fifty-three members of his extended family were killed. With martyrs like these, hundreds of thousands of Kosovar Albanians rallied to the cause. Eighteen thousand were recruited into the ranks of the guerrillas. Serbian police and military controlled the main roads, but the guerrillas the hinterland. Police and army units wrought a terrible revenge on villages which harboured or even fed the rebels.

In Vojvodina, Serbia's northernmost province, nineteen-year-old Tibor Szeles came back in a coffin from Kosovo in July 1998: the first ethnic Hungarian casualty of the latest war. His family were told he had committed suicide. But no-one I spoke to believed that. There were rumours of bullets in the back of the head. When I visited his grave, in Subotica, there were cigarettes, planted by old school friends, filter down, for him to smoke in the after-life. And there was a bottle of red wine, corked, half-drunk, leaning against his gravestone, for him or his friends to swig from when they came to visit him there.

The Hungarians in Vojvodina felt that they were being called up in disproportionate numbers, as proxies for Serbia's war against another Yugoslav minority, the Albanians, while their Serb schoolmates fled north, to Hungary, to avoid the call-up. Not only raw conscripts were taken, but reservists who had already done their military service, and were now expected to serve their country with live ammunition.

As in Bosnia and Croatia, parents gathered to protest against their sons being taken away. József Kasza, the Hungarian mayor of Subotica and the Hungarians' most prominent politician, sat down to talks with Milošević and other Socialist Party leaders. The Socialists promised to compromise, then didn't. The police patrolled the streets of sprawling Vojvodinian villages, the homes and work places of the missing boys, trying to hunt them down.

In Subotica, under a canopy of trees on one of the main streets, a fountain had been built with the names of young men from the town who had died in the Yugoslav wars. There were already forty or fifty Hungarian names, mostly from the conflict in Croatia. And room left further down the weather-darkened bronze for plenty more. 'For their loyalty,' ran the inscription at the top. 'To a country', one might have added, 'which no longer exists.'

In the largely ethnic Hungarian village of Bački Vinogradi, with a population of 2,300 people, ten Hungarian boys were sent to Kosovo in April 1998. In September, eight more were called up, but six went into hiding. I helped Pál Bajtai, the father of one of them, pick peaches in his orchard. Even here, he spoke in hushed tones, as though even the fruit might be listening. 'The night my son came back from Kosovo, I met him in the corridor of our house. He put his head on my shoulder and wept. "Dad," he said, "I did my duty, but I'm never going back there."'

On a small rowing boat, nervously hiding among the reeds on a nearby lake, I found their son. He was in even worse trouble than the others. He hadn't just dodged the call-up, he had been caught, sent to Kosovo, served for a few weeks, and then deserted.

'When we arrived in Kosovo we were taken straight to the front,' he said. Not to shoot, he was told, 'just to get used to being shot at.' That lasted a week, then they returned to barracks. At that point they asked for volunteers to go back to the front. Everyone was taken, whether they volunteered or not.

It was after dark. They surrounded a village. He was given a heavy machine-gun and 2,000 bullets. 'You've got ten minutes to shoot them all,' he was told.

'If I didn't shoot, I knew I would be shot in the brain, by my own comrades.' So he carried out the order. He didn't know if he had hit anyone. It was dark. When his bullets were used up, he fainted.

'I only remembered who I was, and where I was, about a week later,' he said. 'And I knew I had to get out of there, to get home.'

There were no accurate figures for how many men had left Serbia, how many were hiding, and how many were actually serving in Kosovo.

'The unity of the country is endangered,' Pavel Domonji, the government official responsible for minority issues in Vojvodina, told me.

'We are fighting an armed uprising, and the call-up is valid for everyone, without exception.'

As their grandfathers and great-grandfathers had done before them, the men tried to dodge other men's wars.

One night at the Hotel Hyatt, among the ugly housing blocks of new Belgrade where Radovan Karadžić would eventually seek refuge, my phone rang at two in the morning. An apologetic BBC editor in London informed me that the police had raided Dnevni telegraf, the opposition-minded newspaper of Slavko Ćuruvija. Could I find out any more? I rang Ćuruvija. He was sitting with his friends from what was left of the independent media, drinking whisky at his flat. I was welcome to come and join them.

'They took one hundred tables and chairs, and thirty-one telephones,' Ćuruvija told me. He had already memorised the inventory he received from the police; all the office equipment and computers they had taken away. Thirty or forty policemen had come to his flat, he said, after raiding his offices. Everything on which a newspaper could be produced had been taken.

'I have been accused of calling for the destruction of the constitutional order.' He poured me a large tumbler of whisky. There was water in a jug on the table. The room was sparse, and crowded with the cigarette-smoking, hard-drinking, hard-core reporters and editors of the independent media.

A new law had just been passed by the youthful Serbian Information Minister, Alexander Vucić, from the Serbian Radical Party. Ćuruvija was to be its first victim.

What appeared to have annoyed the authorities most was a personal letter partly written by Ćuruvija, addressed to Milošević, accusing him of responsibility for 'everything which has happened to Serbs for the past ten years'. There were also thirteen proposals, which included new elections, independent courts, making peace with the increasingly independent-minded President Djukanović of Montenegro, Serbia's co-state in the rump Yugoslavia, and a 'turn to the West' and the European Union.

'This is not just an attack on the independent media,' said Miloš Vasić of the weekly Vreme, 'it's an attempt at a coup. Mr Vucić has effectively suspended two constitutions, the Serbian and the Yugoslav. ... This is the first step to a fascist dictatorship, and I say that with full responsibility.'

'We shall fight, of course, we don't have any other choice,' said Ćuruvija, as I downed the last of his whisky and prepared to return to the hotel and write my story, hoping the night air would sober me up.

'We are going very soon to establish a committee for the defence of media freedom ...'

In the autumn of 1998, Richard Holbrooke, the architect of the Dayton Agreement in Bosnia, began making regular visits to Belgrade, as President Bill Clinton's special envoy to the Balkans. Guilt over doing so little to stop the war in Bosnia, as the media carried daily, hourly reports of the atrocities there, had lowered the tolerance of western public opinion for more ethnic cleansing in the Balkans. Despite the KLA role in provoking the conflict, most sympathy in the West lay with the Albanians. And in Kosovo, as elsewhere, the Serbs made themselves few friends.

John Major's Conservative government in London, with its pro-Serb sympathies, had been replaced by Tony Blair's Labour administration.

Blair, the 'Vicar of St Albion' as the British satirical weekly Private Eye portrayed him, brought a new moral passion to the Prime Minister's job. Blair believed, as did most of us who had covered the wars in Croatia and in Bosnia, that more resolute action in 1991 and 1992 to confront the instigators of conflict would have saved many lives. This had earned us the then British Foreign Secretary Douglas Hurd's scorn, for the 'selective spotlight' we shone on world events. In Hurd's world, Bosnia had nothing to do with Britain. Might European statesmen finally be waking from their post-Berlin Wall siesta, to see the Balkans, and Kosovo in particular, as a European problem? In tandem with the US President Bill Clinton, Blair set about persuading his reluctant European counterparts that it was.

Richard Holbrooke insisted that the Serbian government withdraw some 25,000 troops and special police who had been drafted into the province in recent months. Milošević ordered some token troop movements, and said he had complied. Holbrooke visited Kosovo in the morning, and was back in Belgrade for more talks in the evening. 'We have done everything you asked . . .' the poker-faced Milošević began. 'You have not . . .' countered the American. 'I have been there, and have seen the situation with my own eyes. And you have not.'

For a few days at the start of October, NATO airstrikes against Serbia—Richard Holbrooke's last card—began to look almost inevitable. The government introduced a special war tax, to improve the readiness of the armed forces, and began testing air-raid sirens and cleaning up air-raid shelters. Shortages of basic goods—diesel, wheat, sugar and oil began to bite deeper.

'The graveyards of the Balkans are filled with Milošević's broken promises,' President Clinton told Congress. Watching the conflict worsen from the Hotel Moskva in Belgrade, I jotted down his words in my journal, and added—'. . . and the living rooms of western statesmen are filled with their ghosts.'

The Americans proposed a peace deal: considerable autonomy for the province, with its own parliament, police and courts, with Yugoslav troops still on the international boundaries, and a final decision on status postponed for three years.

The US and Europeans also wanted to put international peacekeepers, led by NATO, into Kosovo. The Serbian government refused such a loss of sovereignty, but offered to limit the number of its own troops and police on the ground, and to accept unarmed observers, under the auspices of the Organisation for Security and Cooperation in Europe (OSCE). The Russians backed the Serb position. At the last moment, both Milošević and the Albanians agreed to face-to-face peace talks at Rambouillet Château, south-east of Paris, a short drive from the Grand Trianon Palace at Versailles where the Austro-Hungarian Empire was carved up after the First World War. What was it about chateaus and palaces on the outskirts of Paris which wielded such an influence over the fate of peoples on the other side of Europe? Yugoslavia had been created in 1918 partly as a result of the Trianon treaty. Were its death-bells to sound from just across the same park?

It was not to be—or not quite yet.

The Kosovar Albanians agreed to the terms of a draft agreement, but refused any further negotiations. The Serbs refused to sign—largely because of the inclusion of an annex on the deployment of NATO-led peacekeepers in the province. The sweeteners offered by the West—an easing of the ban on foreign investment in Serbia, the disarming, by NATO, of the KLA, a guarantee of the borders of Yugoslavia, including Kosovo, and the saving of money and lives which a last minute decision not to bomb might still avert—proved not sweet enough.

When another Hungarian was killed in the uniform of the Yugoslav Army in Kosovo, I went to his funeral. Twenty-one-year-old Zoltán Nemes was buried in the village of Mohol, Mol in Hungarian, on 20 March. Four days, though none of us knew that then, before the NATO bombing of Serbia began.

All morning the bells tolled, a single monotonous chime. All 3,000 inhabitants of the village were there. Two horses drew the cart carrying his coffin, loaded to heaven with flowers, slowly through the flat streets. At the graveside there were speeches. First from his commanding officer, about how much he was liked, his bravery in action and his sacrifice for his country. Then from the local Hungarian deputy in the Yugoslav Parliament, Attila Széchy, about what a waste of a life, in a stupid, unnecessary war. But there was no tension, no animosity between such diametrically opposed views. The state media would report one speech; the independent media, if it was still broadcasting, the other. At the graveside, the boy's father moved his head slowly, interminably, from side to side, as I did as I rocked my own boys to sleep in my arms. Zoltán was his only son.

Milošević tried to exploit the differences between the members of the so-called Contact Group—the US, UK, France, Germany and Russia—apparently believing that their divisions would stop an attack. In the meantime, he sacked his top general, Momcilo Perišić, apparently for saying Serbia should not go to war 'with the whole world'. His replacement, Ojdanović, was a yes-man for the President.

Another top general, Nebojsa Pavković, in charge of the 3rd Yugoslav Army, promised a 'settling of accounts' with internal traitors. Zoran Djindjić, the leader of the Democratic Party, disappeared after finding he was next on the hit-list after Slavko Ćuruvija. He took refuge in neighbouring Montenegro.

Beneath the gathering clouds of war, the regular bus route between Belgrade and Zagreb, suspended since 1991, resumed up and down an empty motorway increasingly overgrown by weeds.

I tried to find out the latest developments over supper with a British diplomat at the BBC flat in Belgrade.

'So, are you going to bomb?' I asked.

'Well, the way we're going to explain it is this . . .' he grimaced. 'To get Milošević back to the negotiating table, and to prevent a humanitarian catastrophe.'

'What about the Russians?' I asked.

'The Russians are really pissed off with Milošević, he said. 'We think they're on board . . .'

The diplomats left, and Richard Holbrooke held his last press conference at the Hyatt.

'I've just had my forty-second meeting with Slobodan Milošević,' he announced, 'and I'm sorry to say there was no progress. It's been good knowing you all. You're a great press corps.' With these words, he left for Washington, via Brussels.

On 24 March, a Thursday, I canvassed opinions on the streets of Belgrade. Will NATO bomb you?

'No way, they're too smart,' said a young businessman.

'No, they're just fooling around,' said a bunch of schoolboys, fooling around themselves with a football.

'No, they're too dumb to bomb us,' said the bricklayers from southern Serbia.

We retreated to the glitzy interior of the executive seventh floor of the Hyatt, and waited.

At seven forty-five that evening, the phone rang. For once it was an editor in the newsroom not asking us something, but telling it. 'The planes have just taken off from RAF Lakenheath . . .' Probably the same ones I had blockaded in my peace-loving youth, I thought. And here I was, an enemy journalist, in the enemy capital, about to be bombed by the Royal Air Force.

We didn't have enough satellite dishes, so my colleague Jonathan Paterson asked me to get the main BBC news switchboard to ring us or, if that failed, I should get through to them myself on the hotel phone. They tried for a while, but failed. Then I got through straight away. We kept the line up for twelve hours, until eight the following morning. 'By the way . . .' he asked at breakfast, '. . . was that our call or theirs?' When I told him the bad news, he took it in his stride, and didn't complain. I had, after all, just been sentenced to death.

The first missiles struck at about eight-fifteen in the evening. We watched the flashes in the night sky from our hotel windows, about fifteen kilometres away at the military airfield at Batajnica. We reported from the roof of the hotel, and from the rooms below, hour after hour until two in the morning, phoning friends and contacts between times in Novi Sad and Niš and other cities in Serbia, speaking to spokesmen and women for the different ministries and to colleagues from the BBC Serbian section.

Everyone was amazed by the extent of the bombing. We had expected, perhaps, a shot across Milošević's bows, a few token missiles. But this was a show of force. B52 bombers high overhead; cruise missiles fired from destroyers and submarines in the Adriatic, raining down on bridges and power-transmission lines as well as military targets. Excluding a few very limited attacks during the Bosnian conflict, it was the first time that NATO had gone to war.

Soon after two in the morning the boyfriend of one of our interpreters rang. Palma Plus TV, available throughout Serbia and owned by a senior figure in the Serbian Radical Party, had just shown photographs of Christiane Amanpour of CNN, and of myself, on the screen. Anyone who saw either of us should kill us, viewers were told. We were enemy journalists, the bearded presenter explained. Nothing that either of us had actually reported was held up as evidence for the prosecution. Simply the fact that, on the night, our faces more than any others were on the BBC and CNN screens.

A few days earlier, the head of the Radical Party, Vojislav Šešelj, had said that if it came to war, journalists from NATO countries should be rounded up in stadiums and shot.

BBC editors in London decided that I should be taken off air immediately. For safety's sake, all BBC staff in Belgrade were concentrated at the Hyatt Hotel. Now we were sitting ducks for anyone who took a dislike to us.

As the bombing began, I remembered an anecdote recorded by Richard Holbrooke in his book, *To End a War*, about the Dayton Accords. The day dawned at the talks, Holbrooke wrote, when the future of the Bosnian capital, Sarajevo, was finally put on the table. US and Bosniak negotiators approached the day with foreboding, expecting Milošević to strike a hard deal, and for the city to be divided, like Berlin after the Second World War.

As they sat down, Milošević looked Alija Izetbegović, the Bosniak leader, in the eye.

'You can have it,' he said, referring to Sarajevo. 'At least you fought for it, unlike those cowards from Pale!'

Pale was the wartime base of Karadžić and his team—the very men Milošević was supposed to be standing up for at Dayton. The story said a lot about Milošević's character. 'Those cowards from NATO' bombing from 30,000 feet could expect pretty short shrift from him now. While the NATO top brass assumed that the Serbian government would bow to the inevitable after only a few days, I guessed Milošević's determination would strengthen. And that the country, once again, would rally behind him. It actually took seventy-eight days of bombing, death and suffering to bring Milošević back to the table.

On the morning of 25 March, reporters were out on the streets as soon as the all-clear sounded, but I was confined to the hotel. The Serbian Information Minister, Alexander Vucić, who was also responsible for closing newspapers like those of Slavko Ćuruvija, repeated his demand that all 'NATO journalists' should consider themselves expelled, and leave the country immediately. But Goran Matić, the Yugoslav Information Minister, said we were welcome to stay.

We packed our bags, but sat tight. That evening, the bombing began again after dark. As I walked down the corridor on the seventh floor of the Hyatt, I met Julius Strauss, the correspondent of the *Daily Telegraph*, running towards me.

'Arkan's coming up the stairs!' he said. 'They're taking journalists from their rooms at gunpoint!' Željko Ražnatović, better known as Arkan, was a much feared paramilitary leader from Serbia's earlier wars. He was shot dead in the lobby of the Intercontinental Hotel, just across the block from the Hyatt, in January 2000. He knew too much about Milošević.

*   *   *

We had a quick vote among the nine BBC staff. Seven to two in favour of leaving. We grabbed our bags, and fled down to reception in the lift.

252

As we drove north across the Serbian plain, there were flashes from Batajnica again. The road to Hungary went close to the military airfield, and as a curfew was in force, it seemed foolhardy to go that way. So we branched west, on the empty motorway towards Croatia, instead. As I drove, I gave a long interview to Radio New Zealand on my mobile phone. Milan, a friend from the BBC Russian Service, sat beside me in my old GB-plated Saab. When I had driven into the country in the same car a fortnight earlier, the Serbian customs officer had teased me about it. 'Greater Britain, eh? So why not Greater Serbia?'.

There were to be no jokes at the border that night. Serbian plain-clothes police were waiting for us, and they were in a foul mood. We were ordered to line up our bags on the tarmac, and then turn out the contents one by one. All video and audio tapes were taken away. A money belt containing 5,000 Deutschmarks, belonging to one of the cameramen, was confiscated as well. When they got to BBC World Affairs Correspondent John Simpson's bag, no-one claimed it. He had decided at the last minute to stay in the hotel. The plain-clothes man ordered Jeremy Cooke to cut the bag open. It was John's entire CD collection.

They were looking in particular for electronic items, of which we were not in short supply. 'Locator' one of the security men kept shouting— an electronic device for guiding bombers to deliver their bombs. At one point, he found an electric toothbrush, still in its case, and started brandishing it about in triumph, 'locator, locator'.

It was as much as we could do not to laugh.

I spoke my few stock phrases of Serbian, to try to break the ice. 'So you speak Serbian—you must be a spy!' he shouted. 'You stay here!'

If his view spread, a lot of language schools around the world would be out of business.

Eventually they let us go, after stealing any items they liked the look of. In the excitement, they didn't notice that Milan had no Serbian visa in his British passport.

He had come into the country on his Serbian passport, and if he had tried to leave with that, he would have been arrested and then press-ganged into the armed forces. So we had reason to celebrate, as we drove wearily towards the Croatian capital, Zagreb.

13. To Make A Revolution

It only takes three thousand people to make a revolution.
Miklós Vásárhelyi, former press chief to Imre Nagy

The fist . . . is as strong as a thousand words . . .
Milja Jovanović, Otpor activist

At five-thirty on the afternoon of 11 April 1999, day nineteen of the NATO bombing, Slavko Ćuruvija was approaching his flat with Branka Prpa, his partner, when two men in black leather jackets approached him. They shot him at close range, and while one pistol-whipped Prpa, his companion, the other stood over his body, pumping more bullets into him. The editor of Dnevni telegraf had long used his contacts with highly-placed figures in Milošević's regime to stay ahead of the game. Now the regime had identified him as the enemy.

'He was a brave man, braver than those who shot him in the back like cowards and braver than those who bombed him from the skies,' Ljiljana Smajlović, an editor at Evropljanin, a magazine he had founded, said at his funeral. Copies of his newspapers were thrown with the flowers into his open grave, as air-raid sirens split the Belgrade sky.

The bombing went on and on. My BBC colleague, Mike Williams, who had left the country with us on the second night, managed to get a visa to return. As he was passing Batajnica, the military airbase near Belgrade which had already been hit many times, soldiers stopped his car. They beat him and kicked him into the ditch, then tore all the money they found on him, several hundred Deutschmarks, into shreds in front of him. This was not theft. This was sheer fury, the bitterness of men who had witnessed their comrades blown to smithereens by an enemy they could only hear, but would never see. It was enough for them that Mike was born on the same island as some of the bombers.

From the start, NATO targeted Defence and Interior Ministry buildings, barracks and training grounds, then moving on to bridges, electricity transformer stations and factories and anything which might serve the war effort, however indirectly. The Serbs built decoy planes, decoy tanks, and performed any manner of tricks to avoid the missiles and the bombs.

The situation in Kosovo went from bad to worse. Paramilitaries and all kinds of other thugs joined the army and special police in Kosovo, massacring Albanian civilians and looting and burning wherever they went. Prominent Albanians were targeted and murdered. There was a clear design in the actions of the Serb forces—to drive up to two million Albanians out of the province, and restore a Serb majority which had not existed for hundreds of years. As they crossed the border, their identity papers and car or tractor number plates were taken away. It was a cold-blooded act of revenge by the Milošević regime. You bomb our country, we expel your 'friends'.

NATO bombed Yugoslavia for seventy-eight days. Around 500 civilians died, according to Human Rights Watch. They included fourteen people (some Yugoslav sources said fifty-five) on a passenger train crossing the bridge across the Grdelica gorge in southern Serbia, on 12 April. The train appeared 'suddenly', when the pilot was closing in to destroy the bridge, said the NATO commander, General Wesley Clark, 'it was really unfortunate.'

With John Simpson and Mike Williams in Belgrade, other BBC reporters tried to find different ways into the country. Word spread that Montenegro, which had distanced itself from Milošević's war, was allowing western journalists in without a visa, even though the mountainous coastal republic was still part of Yugoslavia. But as the Yugoslav army still patrolled the main roads, we had to work out an alternative strategy.

I flew into the Croatian port of Dubrovnik, was met by a car and driven down the sparkling Adriatic coast to the Montenegrin border. The sight of the beaches, the ancient olive groves on hillsides sloping down to the sea and the smell of the pines reminded me of passing Lake Balaton in Hungary on my way to cover the Croatian war seven years earlier. On the way out, it always scandalised me—how could girls wear bikinis and tan their skin in the sun while young men were dying fifty miles away? How could people enjoy themselves so close to a war? But on the way back, I would always feel relieved to see exactly the same people.

Normality at last! People were right to enjoy their short time on earth to the full. The soldiers were breaking the laws, not the sunbathers. What is the point of killing one's neighbour? Or dying for one's country?

In Bosnia, the sheer brutality of the aggression made me change my mind again. Seeing the people of Sarajevo trying to defend their homes in April 1992, the boy with the rabbit gun on the edge of Baščaršija, the old Ottoman heart of the city, talking to the refugees whose menfolk had been slaughtered like cattle the day before, I understood finally the need to defend one's home, and even one's homeland.

Watching the bombing of Yugoslavia, I felt that western leaders were trying to assuage their guilt over Bosnia. Bosnia was a multi-cultural society which would have been worth defending. Far braver journalists than I spent the war documenting each twist and turn of the fighting, and the sheer uselessness of the United Nation's effort. People were kept alive by humanitarian supplies, so that they could be target practice for the snipers for another day, or month, or year longer. But no effort was made, by the European powers at least, to address the core of the problem. Even-handedness did not mean, and should never mean, equalisation of the blame for what happens.

In Kosovo, the Kosovo Liberation Army knew they could never liberate their country on their own. Their only chance lay in provoking the Serbs into massive retaliation, in the hope that the West would come to their aid. The strategy worked perfectly, but at huge human cost, as Ibrahim Rugova, their President who had espoused non-violence, had always said it would. But without the sacrifice, they would never have won independence. It was a carefully calculated risk. It was also hugely unfair on the Serbs who had lived in Kosovo for at least as long, if not several centuries longer, than the Albanians had. In Kosovo, I could understand both sides. I could only respect those, however, who didn't rape or pillage or murder, and who treated prisoners with a modicum of decency. And those who didn't order their soldiers to shoot randomly into villages and homes and rooms where they knew non-combatants were sheltering.

Sasha, my old friend from the reception desk of the Hotel Moskva in Belgrade, finally got his way. At last the Serbs had their chance to die at war with the Americans.

The car dropped me on the Montenegrin side of the border, and I walked up to the Yugoslav customs post. They studied my passport. 'No visa,' they pointed out. 'Not a problem,' I replied, 'it's ok to go through, yes?' They shrugged and waved me on with a warning. 'Be careful—Serbian soldiers up ahead.'

Momo, our Montenegrin interpreter, was waiting for me just round the next corner on the mountain road. This was our strategy for skirting the roadblocks. Other media hired fishing boats, to loop round the coast. This was easier.

Momo drove me to the next town, where we stopped briefly at the police station. A courtesy bottle of whisky changed hands. Then I was bundled gently into a minibus full of enormous Montenegrin policemen, each at least two metres tall, all sporting flak jackets and armed to the teeth. Then we were snaking down the road, between the concrete blocks of a Yugoslav army checkpoint. The army and the Montenegrin police were both keen to avoid a clash with one another. I doubt the Serbs even saw the diminutive British journalist, squeezed among the policemen.

Back in Belgrade, the war ended with a climb down by Milošević on 3 June. Six days later, Yugoslav army commanders signed an agreement with NATO at Kumanovo in Macedonia specifying that all Serbian police and military forces had to leave Kosovo within eleven days. Under the Rambouillet accord, rejected three months earlier by Milošević, only Serb military reinforcements would have had to leave the province.

Under UN Security Council Resolution 1244 passed on 10 June, which endorsed the entry of NATO-led forces into Kosovo and instituted a UN administration there, Kosovo remained technically part of Yugoslavia, pending a final agreement. In practice, with all Serb police and military expelled, this was the end of eighty-seven years of almost unbroken Serbian rule over Kosovo. Milošević had lost another chunk of Yugoslavia. Montenegro would soon go as well.

The Serbian opposition were as demoralised and traumatised as the rest of the Serb population by the NATO bombing. Weak and divided, they had little in common besides a desire to overthrow Milošević. Their unity was further undermined by the fact that it was lead by vain and self-important politicians.

In Belgrade, after the war, there were no demonstrations. Columns of tanks and armoured cars drove along the motorway through Belgrade again, and though the government presented their retreat from Kosovo as a military victory, no-one was fooled. Government propaganda now focused on the rebuilding effort—the many bridges and transformer stations destroyed by NATO. No-one could criticise the government for that without appearing unpatriotic—except Otpor, the student based protest movement whose name meant "resistance".

The presumed state sponsored murder of Slavko Ćuruvija was followed by the assassination of the paramilitary leader Arkan, in January 2000, and then by the kidnapping and murder of Ivan Stambolić in August. Stambolić had been leader of the Serbian Communist Party and became President of Serbia in 1986. He was also the kum, both best man, and something like blood-brother to Milošević, and as such had helped Milošević, who was four years younger, at every stage of his career. But Stambolić was on the liberal wing of the Party, while Milošević was a hardliner. Their biggest differences were over Kosovo, with Stambolić advising a gentler approach than many in his party, and Milošević cynically using Serbian nationalism over Kosovo as a stepping stone to power. In 1987, Milošević leap-frogged his best friend, and then stabbed him in the back. Wounded, Stambolić went into banking, another career he had in common with Milošević.

Stambolić remained fiercely critical of Milošević over the war in Bosnia. He visited Sarajevo during the conflict and spoke publicly in favour of Otpor.

In the days before he was abducted friends had been trying to persuade him to re-enter the political fray and to challenge Milošević for the presidency.

On 25 August 2000, a van pulled up beside him in a Belgrade park, and he was pulled inside. His body was eventually found in woodland near Belgrade in March 2003. In July 2005, a judge found eight police officers from the Special Operations Unit guilty of his murder, and sentenced them to between fifteen and forty years in prison. The order for the murder, the judge said in his summing up, came from Slobodan Milošević.

The killings of Ćuruvija and Stambolić represented the lowest point of the Milošević years. The regime had gone from waging unnecessary wars, to cheating in elections, and finally to murdering its opponents. There was an ugly mood in Belgrade. Life, so precious when the country was at war, had become cheap.

The NATO bombing caused a wave of introspection in Serbia. Ordinary people were inordinately proud of having been on the Allied side in the Second World War, of having stood up to Nazi Germany, and now to be bombed by former allies like the US and Britain, not to mention old enemies like Germany and Italy, was particularly painful.

People found some consolation in the opening scenes of Emir Kusturica's film *Underground*—the Luftwaffe bombing of Belgrade in April 1941. The film was praised by pacifists the world over as an anti-war film. It was easy, I thought, to ridicule all warriors, but Kusturica, who was born a Bosnian Muslim, with a controversial relationship with Milošević which made him a loathed man in his home town of Sarajevo, should have known better than to equalise the guilt in his own homeland.

The old protesters had run out of steam, but Otpor, like a crop sown before the winter freeze, started to come up strong and early in the spring. And what made the movement so radical was that they dared to point the finger at what they called the 'Nazification' of Serbia under Milošević.

'The problem is not only in politics, it's deeper than that. It's not just the political system. It's the whole system of living and deciding and thinking in Serbia . . .' Milja explained, as we sat in the tumbledown headquarters which her organisation was squatting in, on what was once one of Belgrade's most elegant streets, Knez Mihailova. 'Because we represent not just resistance to Milošević's regime, but resistance to this whole chaos that's been on our shoulders for the last ten years.'

Unlike the mainstream opposition parties, they focused on individual pain.

'We do not want people to forget or cover up for a single moment their feeling of being misused and robbed. So our strategy is to promote the fist, because the fist itself is as strong as a thousand words.' She was referring to Otpor's clenched fist symbol which was being busily spray painted across the country. 'And once we have got Serbia covered with fists—when it is constant and not just there for a specific reason, for a date or something that's important in our history, but when it is constant and without any obvious reason, then I think people will start to react.'

'After the war ended the situation was even worse than before . . . It became clear to us what we had to do. We must become the moralistic, pure, anti-regime organisation which promotes a symbol to which a lot of people can feel connected. And we must be outside the party political system.'

A central core of Otpor activists began touring the country and recruiting. It reminded me of what we had done, as CND activists, touring Britain in the spring of 1985, organising small groups for action. But while we just wanted to close an airbase for a week, the goals of Otpor were much more far-reaching—to bring down a government.

259

During the 1956 revolution in Hungary, youth of a similar age, the *'Pesti srácok'*, the lads of Pest, gave the uprising its vitality. 'It only takes 3,000 people to make a revolution,' Miklós Vásárhelyi, Imre Nagy's press chief in 1956, once told me. In the right place, at the right time.

Thanks to Otpor, Serbia soon had twice that number of active 'recruits', 6,000 to 7,000, in 100 towns and cities across the country. The number of supporters of the movement soon swelled to many times that, as young people already active in other parts of the democratic opposition found a new home in Otpor. There were four basic centres, Belgrade, Novi Sad, Kragujevac and Niš—all university towns. The Otpor organisation in each place was autonomous, but had to be true to the basic principles of 'resistance'.

'The thing is, you do things yourself and show the ways you have to resist on a personal level. You are prepared to go out on the street and do something that will probably provoke the police, that will probably get you arrested, taken into a police station, interrogated, and then maybe prosecuted —or not,' said Milja.

As Otpor spread, the authorities tried different tactics to destroy or neutralise it. Many activists were arrested and beaten. In many cases this backfired. The parents and uncles and aunts of Otpor activists might have voted for Milošević in one or more previous elections, but they took a dim view of the police violence. Repression made martyrs for Otpor. Some were thrown out of work, schools and universities. Nikola Šainović from Milošević's Socialist Party of Serbia described Otpor activists as 'vermin', 'hooligans' and even 'terrorists'.

Otpor responded with an 'I love Serbia' campaign.

'We carried out several actions to make people remember the civilians and soldiers who died during the NATO bombing,' said Milja. 'We did that in front of 30,000 people, when they came onto the square to celebrate the New Year. We said: Serbia doesn't have a reason to celebrate. Go home and think about why we were bombed.' Otpor were looking right into the heart of the Serbian darkness, and inviting the rest of the population to do the same.

They were treading a knife edge between treachery, and patriotism. The knowledge that it was a well-worn knife edge in Serbian history did not make it any less jagged. It was rather as if all the feet that had walked it before had sharpened the blade.

It was one thing to blindly resist and build up an impressive list of detentions and beatings, but Otpor also needed a strategy for the future, and they struck on the simplest, most democratic one of all—elections. Activists like Milja knew they could never replace the Milošević regime themselves, that that was the task, for better or worse, of opposition parties. So, they set out to persuade young people to vote in the next election—no matter when that would be.

Milošević had originally been a lawyer, and he remained to the bitter end a stickler for 'legality'. He had remained in power for so long, not only by using foul tactics, but by paying lip-service, at least, to fair and democratic elections. The Socialists had always been good at mobilising their own voters. The Socialist fraud in 1996 only involved 'topping up' the vote they had actually received. Otpor knew their recent history, and set out to prepare first time voters for the next election, and to shame the divided opposition into working together. The polls were to prove Milošević's Achilles' heel.

Milošević's enemies abroad, led by the United States, began to support Otpor and the rest of the Serbian opposition financially. The US allegedly poured in some $77 million, but there were also sizeable contributions from Britain, the European Union and Norway. Money was sent into Serbia for computers, badges, t-shirts, paints for the ubiquitous graffiti and printing equipment. A conference was organised for opposition activists, including Otpor, in the southern Hungarian city of Szeged.

The movement's bank account in Szeged was ironically in the same bank where allies of Milošević were beginning to squirrel their money out of Serbia, just in case the great leader fell—or they fell foul of one of his sourer moods. In the space of a few months, Szeged became the second biggest banking centre in Hungary after Budapest, largely thanks to money flowing into or out of Serbia.

Milošević's reluctant acceptance of the results of the November 1996 local election results meant that the opposition ran thirty-two municipalities across Serbia.

In the winter of 1999, the extremely able EU representative in Belgrade, Michael Graham, began to funnel support, especially oil for heating, to the opposition towns, as an alternative power-base to Milošević. During and after the war, oil shortages had become acute in Serbia, both for heating and fuel, as a result of international sanctions. This had been largely resolved over the years by smuggling oil into the country from Romania and Bulgaria, but now the EU and the Norwegians devised a more subversive approach. Convoys of oil tankers were organised to opposition-run cities like Niš, as a sort of 'democratic dividend'. Many of the convoys were prevented by Serbian police and customs from entering the country. Some got through. But the whole exercise undoubtedly increased the pressure on Milošević and his government. The public could clearly see that opposing him carried material rewards, and that when he stopped the convoys, he was depriving his citizens of warmth. It was a battle which, despite his control of the police, the army and the state media, he could never win.

The atmosphere in Belgrade grew darker. The usual fear of the police doubled. The killing of Ćuruvija, the abduction of Stambolić and the beating of Otpor activists helped create a growing sense of deliberate or arbitrary violence.

'We are trying not to let Milošević use his only remaining power, the police,' said Milja. 'And we try not to provoke things to such a level that people feel that we are asking them to fight.'

I went to an opposition gathering in a district council hall in Belgrade, and left my tape-recorder running by mistake after the meeting ended. Listening back later, the sound of hundreds of wooden chairs being scraped together and stacked up sounded just like the rattle of machine-guns. Was there to be a 'Romanian scenario' now in Serbia? And might Milošević, like Nicolae Ceauşescu, end up in front of a firing squad?

Most people in opposition circles in Belgrade seemed to find a second Tiananmen Square massacre more likely, and the re-imposition of single party rule by a strengthened Milošević, who, within months or years, would find a way once again to cajole the support of the West.

The demonstrations began again, first in provincial cities like Novi Sad and Čačak and then in the capital. Through the spring of 2000, the government stepped up its attacks on what was left of the independent media. Heavy fines were imposed on newspapers and magazines like Vreme, for allegedly falling foul of media laws drafted with just that purpose.

'Of course we are more careful than before,' Dragoljub Žarković, the editor of Vreme said at a gathering of the independent media in nearby Hungary. 'Because we don't have enough money to pay all the fines.'

'Serbia is a prison, Serbia is a closed society,' lamented Stevan Nikšić, editor of the NIN weekly, at the same meeting. His country was like a door, he continued, locked from both sides. The regime locked it from the inside, and the international community, with sanctions, bombing and its visa regime, locked it from the other side. A generation of Serbs were growing up without experience of the wider world. If Milošević was unmovable, perhaps the door could at least be unlocked from the outside?

Next, the state moved against Studio B, the only television channel which dared breathe a critical word. Overnight, the editorial team were thrown out, and replaced by a new, pro-regime team. Demonstrators gathered in Republic Square. In the crowd, I met another Otpor activist, Branko Ilić.

'This is all about power, and they've decided to hang on, whatever the price,' he said. 'And I think the price may be very high.' The Otpor offices in Knez Mihailova had also been closed down. 'We're all terrorists now,' grinned Ilić. Talk of the introduction of a state of emergency, and the banning of opposition groups and parties intensified.

'Do not be afraid!' the head of the Democratic Party, Zoran Djindjić, told the crowd from the stage. 'No regime ever won a war against its own people!'

As I was walking back to the hotel after the rally, the riot police attacked without warning from the side-streets, wielding batons and spraying tear gas. It was as though they wanted to provoke an incident which could be used by the authorities to impose martial law. I fled with a section of the crowd into the city hall, squeezing in just before the students managed to close and bar the doors to the riot police. Inside there was mayhem. Someone tried to nurse a woman with a bad head-wound; people lay on the velvet chairs, choking from the tear-gas they had inhaled. In an upstairs room, I talked to Zoran Djindjić.

'We are trying once again to remove Milošević with peaceful methods,' he said. After ten years on the streets, even a simple interview, under police siege, sounded like a speech from a balcony.

'We have only people, only protests, only rallies, as a tool. We do not have armed forces, we don't have police forces, and really, we don't have parties . . . in a dictatorship parties are a very relative force. Ten years ago Milošević was the leader of this nation with the support of the majority . . . and now he's a kind of occupier in this country.'

On the telephone from the city hall, I started sending live reports to the BBC on the situation. For several hours, it looked as though the police, who had surrounded the building, were preparing to storm it. Eventually someone negotiated our safe exit. And so we trooped, several hundred people, out of the building, under the batons of the police, who kept their side of the deal not to beat us.

'Is Serbia close to civil war?' Nikola Šainović, a deputy minister in the government, was asked at a press briefing the next day.

'We have a duty to protect citizens,' he replied. What were his views on Otpor?

'A group of hooligans who break windows.'

In June 2000 Slobodan Milošević made his biggest mistake. He stepped suddenly into the trap which Otpor had prepared for him. Assuming the opposition were too weak and divided to come up with a common candidate, and assuming he could 'massage' the figures in case of any unpleasant electoral surprises, he called an early presidential election.

'Milošević had real support in 1989, and it was a support without boundaries—it was endless. This cannot and must not ever happen again,' said Milja.

After some hesitation, eighteen opposition parties—a measure in itself of just how bitter the personal and policy disputes of the past decade had been—produced a single champion to challenge Milošević: Vojislav Koštunica.

'Unlike Milošević, Koštunica is a real nationalist,' said Aleksandar Tijanić, a columnist who had also briefly served as Information Minister in a Milošević government, '. . . and also unlike Milošević, he is a real democrat.' It was a crucial combination. There were even photographs in circulation of Koštunica brandishing a Kalashnikov on a visit to northern Kosovo during the war. By contrast, Zoran Djindjić was seen as too close to NATO states which had bombed Serbia only a year earlier, and could not be so easily forgiven. Vuk Drašković, the old battle horse of the Serbian opposition, had joined a Socialist Party government just before the bombing, and was seen as a turncoat by another part of the opposition electorate. I spoke to him on the fringes of a march. He was extremely emotional.

'Don't talk to me, talk to the young people, the beautiful people . . . they are very afraid for the future . . . I'm an old man, and I have no right to talk in the name of the young, beautiful people. I have no future. My future is in the past . . .' And he waxed lyrical about taking part in the student protests in Belgrade, in 1968.

Only Koštunica collected enough support to stand a chance against Milošević.

Besides Otpor, another valuable weapon in the opposition arsenal was the pollsters. As election day approached, both Strategic Marketing, an independent company run by Srdjan Bogosavljević in Belgrade, and

SCAN, another independent agency, suggested Koštunica was well ahead in the polls. This was the case even in the old communist heartlands in the south and west of the country, and wherever the opposition had a foothold, and any access to the media.

In Niš, in Serbia's south, one poll suggested Koštunica would receive more than sixty per cent of the votes. The pollsters also studied the level of fear among voters on the eve of the election.

'People are afraid of losing their jobs, of getting poorer still, and most importantly they are afraid of getting ill and having nowhere to turn for treatment,' said Milka Puzigaća, of the SCAN agency in Novi Sad. 'And that is the biggest fear of all.' A decade of neglected investment in health care, of doctors and nurses leaving for other countries, of wave after wave of refugees coming in, especially to the province of Vojvodina in the north, had overloaded the hospitals and local clinics. Socialism in Yugoslavia, as elsewhere in the region, had promised a job for life, free health care and a good pension. The jobs were gone, inflation had reduced pensions to a tenth of what people had expected and, for many, health seemed the last straw. In a competition of fears, fear of the regime was overshadowed by fear of the regime staying in place.

Milka's research also showed that the vast majority of those under thirty had had enough of Serbia, and wanted to leave. But before they left, it seemed, they would make one last determined effort to push the Milošević bandwagon off the road. Such strong indications that the opposition were in a winning position allowed opposition activists to focus less on winning votes, and more on making sure that they were not stolen. That was not to prove an easy task.

The twenty-fourth of September 2000 was a Sunday, and the weather was fine. Unable this time to get a visa to enter Serbia, I sat in a makeshift press centre in faraway Budapest, five hours drive north of Belgrade. Courtesy of the global conspiracy against Milošević, there were good phone lines to Belgrade and other cities, and good contacts to CeSID, the independent agency trying to monitor the elections.

Turnout was heavy in most districts. If any one candidate won over fifty per cent in the first round, he would win outright. If no-one scored over fifty, it would go to a second round in two weeks time. There was mounting excitement on the night. Exit polls gave fifty-six per cent to Koštunica, suggesting an outright victory.

A stage erected by the Socialists in Republic Square remained empty. The Socialist press conference scheduled for ten o'clock in the evening was moved to eleven, then to midnight, and then finally cancelled, while the opposition celebrated.

The Federal Electoral Commission then announced the 'official' results. Koštunica was narrowly ahead, with almost forty-nine per cent to Milošević on almost thirty-nine per cent. Most of the remaining votes went to the candidate of Vojislav Šešelj's Serbian Radical Party, which had been in a coalition government with the Socialists. A run-off would be held on 8 October.

The opposition spat fire, and turned to the Constitutional Court. Thanks to CeSID and to Otpor, and the efforts of thousands of activists with good contacts to local election commissions, even to those where they had been refused entry, they had amassed piles of evidence of fraud. Milošević's trick, they argued, had been to reduce turnout by several per cent, and to stuff ballot boxes at strategic locations, most notably in Kosovo, which was now under UN administration. UN observers had only witnessed a trickle of voters there, but 100,000 extra votes miraculously appeared for Milošević, either from Serbs still living in Kosovo, or from those living in refugee accommodation. As most refugees and displaced Serbs from Kosovo felt betrayed by Milošević, such blanket support for him seemed, at best, unlikely.

The Constitutional Court, itself appointed by Milošević supporters over the years, dithered. On 2 October, Milošević addressed the nation on state television.

'The events unfolding around our elections are part of the organised persecution of our country and our people because we constitute a barrier to the full domination of the Balkan Peninsula. [...] These Imperial powers do not want peace or prosperity in the Balkans. They want this to be a zone of permanent conflicts and wars which would provide them with an alibi for maintaining a lasting presence.'

The opposition announced they would boycott any second round as their candidate had already won. Even Šešelj, Milošević's old playmate, called on Milošević to admit defeat.

On 5 October, massive demonstrations were planned and coordinated by the opposition with Djindjić in overall charge. Columns of protestors were also organised to converge on Belgrade from five cities outside of the capital. The focal point of the protests was in front of the Federal Parliament. Suddenly they turned violent. Ljubiša Djokić, an unemployed bulldozer driver, drove his vehicle through a police cordon as bullets ricocheted off it. In the chaos, crowds poured through the breach and broke into the building, setting one wing of it on fire. The police ignored orders to retaliate, and began fraternising with the protesters. According to Marko Nicović, a former top Belgrade policeman, of the 47,000 uniformed police officers in Serbia at that time, 45,000 refused the order to crush the protest.

Opposition leaders contacted the police, the secret police and the army, and pleaded with them to change sides, or at the very least, not to oppose change with force. After several hours of waiting, and frantic phone calls to the Ministry of Information in Belgrade, several hundred journalists, including myself, queuing on the Hungarian-Serbian border, were finally allowed into the country on emergency visas. The surly border-guards who stamped them into our passports still sat beneath portraits of Milošević, his fringe brushed upwards in a porcupine-like quiff.

At Novi Sad, I branched off the motorway to report on the progress of the revolution in the provinces, while my colleagues pressed on to the capital. Jeremy Cooke, a friend since our sojourn together in Belgrade at the start of the bombing, handed me a black computer bag, and a hard grey plastic case.

'What's this?' I asked.

'A satellite phone.'

'How does it work?'

'I dunno,' he laughed—and handed me a mobile number in Moscow. A colleague there might know.

In Novi Sad, Mile Isakov, a local opposition leader, had heard from secret police sources weeks earlier that Milošević had 'lost contact' with them, and that the organisation was in disarray, and without instructions. Communications between the centre and the services had apparently never recovered from the sacking of Milošević's right hand man, Jovica Stanišić, in October 1998, apparently for trying to persuade Milošević to take a softer line over Kosovo.

The revolution, nevertheless, hung in the balance, Isakov said. On the morning of the sixth, at four or five in the morning, there were signs that forces loyal to Milošević were going to hit back. Then there were rumours of a plane, packed with gold, waiting to take Milošević away to safety.

Isakov was now cautiously optimistic that the progress made could be consolidated.

That evening, Koštunica met Milošević. The Constitutional Court had declared that the latter had lost the first round of the election after all, and so there was no need now for a second. Koštunica began to make clear that his predecessor could stay in the country and that he would not be extradited to the International Criminal Tribunal for the Former Yugoslavia in The Hague.

'If he stays here . . .' said Isakov, '. . . he will end up in prison. For many things he has done, from stealing votes, to stealing public money, to torturing the people, individually and collectively. There are many reasons to put on trial every one of his team. And behind each of them, we will find Milošević.'

'If you want to cook a frog,' Isakov concluded, citing an old Serbian proverb, 'you don't drop it into boiling water. You put it in cold water, then turn up the heat.'

The Socialists still had a majority in the Serbian Parliament for which elections had not been held. The opposition had only knocked off their head. The body was still running around—and the head could re-attach itself at any moment.

Eventually, Milošević agreed to stay at his hilly home in the Dedinje district, protected by an army detachment and his own chief bodyguard, Nenad Batočanin. The bodyguards of all of Serbia's leaders were to play a crucial role throughout this period, keeping lines of communication open during the chaotic events from the opposition electoral victory to the fall of the President.

Batočanin knew Djindjić's bodyguard, Zoran Vasiljević, who knew Vuk Drašković's bodyguard, Rajo Božović. They all attended the same gym.

On 12 October, the Federal Electoral Commission finally released the formal 'unadulterated' results. Turnout had miraculously increased to seventy-two per cent of the electorate. And Koštunica had narrowly scraped to victory in the first round, with just over fifty per cent. No-one cared about the margin anymore. Milošević had fallen from power after thirteen years at the top. Vojislav Koštunica was the new Yugoslav President.

In December, the eighteen-party opposition bloc behind Koštunica, known as DOS, the Democratic Opposition of Serbia, won the Serbian parliamentary elections handsomely, and Zoran Djindjić became the country's Prime Minister.

One of the most burning issues facing the new authorities was what to do with the man they had so laboriously, but so dramatically, dislodged from his throne. Milošević spent the winter nursing his wounds in Dedinje and, for all anyone knew, plotting revenge.

His fall had been loudly applauded in western capitals, but what was still preventing Serbia's return to the community of happier nations was his indictment by the UN court at The Hague which was demanding that he be arrested and handed over. Milošević had been indicted first of all for the ethnic cleansing of Albanians from Kosovo. Koštunica, as a nationalist, albeit a democratic one, tried to use his new position as darling of the United States, the European Union and the Kremlin, to dodge or, better still, deflate the question. But the same nationalist credentials which had served him so well in hoovering up votes on the right of the Serbian spectrum, now tripped him up on the international stage.

'History teaches us that you should never push the Serbs into a corner,' a British diplomat had warned Richard Holbrooke, when he embarked on his first mission to Sarajevo. 'The Serb view of history is their own problem,' he replied. 'Mine is to end the war.' And as far as most countries were concerned, the war was still going on, as long as the top war-crimes suspects, like Milošević, were out of prison.

Zoran Djindjić, with weaker nationalist credentials in the West, but strong democratic ones, came gradually to the conclusion that Milošević should be extradited. But he knew how unpopular such a move would be, both among Milošević's lingering band of supporters, and among many in the former opposition, the current government, who felt Milošević should face a Serbian court to answer for his 'crimes' against the Serbian people.

The US Congress named 31 March 2001 as the deadline for Milošević to be arrested; otherwise it would suspend aid. Zoran Djindjić, now Prime Minister, hesitated. I spoke to him at the airport on his return from Washington on 23 March. Silver-haired, thin-faced, the best-looking of the new men in power, he had spent most of his time in the United States answering, or trying to avoid answering, that question.

'To be totally frank, I don't know,' he admitted. 'Our priority is the maintenance of political stability.' Even to put the issue on the parliamentary agenda seemed too big a risk.

As the US deadline approached, I found myself, one midnight, warming my hands beside a fire with Duško, a Serbian police commando, in a wooded glade a few hundred metres from the Milošević residence. All the signs were that Djindjić had decided to go for gold, and that the commandos, clad in dark blue camouflage uniforms, were about to stage an operation to seize their former leader.

Only twelve months earlier, the same men might have beaten me to death on the steps of the city hall. Only two years earlier, British planes had bombed their barracks. Now I was sharing jokes with them around a camp-fire, as they prepared to arrest their former boss. Who would want to be a journalist anywhere else in the world?

A week earlier, on the second anniversary of the start of the NATO bombing, 50,000 diehard Milošević supporters had attended a rally organised by the Socialists in Republic Square in Belgrade.

'I'm the mother of a soldier who was killed by NATO,' a woman at the rally told me. 'He was nineteen-years-old, a conscript in the army. He didn't even have the chance to defend himself . . .'

The new authorities and their supporters kept their distance, but Otpor activists, armed with brooms, arrived just as the demonstrators were leaving.

'What are you doing here?' I asked one.

'Sweeping up all the rubbish the Socialists have left,' he replied.

The new slogan of Otpor after the fall of Milošević became 'Tko je kriv?'—Who is guilty?

There was a stampede among former supporters of the regime to forget their past, and side with the new power in the land. And DOS faced a dilemma. With little experience of anything but the politics of the street, they could hardly replace the whole civil service overnight, however compromised it was by the years of subservience to Milošević and his predecessors. In many ways they faced a similar task to the Poles and the Czechs and Hungarians in the spring of 1990—with the important distinction that the latter had not just had the infrastructure of their countries destroyed.

Outside the Dedinje villa, the commandos prepared for action. The previous evening, an anti-terrorist unit had secured entry by blowing up the back door of the compound, but had been thwarted in their efforts to arrest Milošević by bodyguards still loyal to him. The negotiations had ended in deadlock. Inside, on what was then the second night of the drama, Milošević was warning the negotiators that they would not take him alive.

* * *

President Koštunica had ordered an elite unit of the presidential guard, who were still in charge of Milošević's security, to leave the premises.

They appeared to have complied. So the stand-off developed between, on the one hand, Milošević, some members of his household and his bodyguards—twenty to twenty-five armed people—and the government team, led by Čeda Jovanović and backed by police commandos on the other. A former Milošević aide, Gorica Gajević, also arrived, and announced later to Serbian media that Milošević might be willing to give himself up, provided 'the correct legal procedure' is followed.

'We're trying our best to avoid casualties. . . . that is why this is taking so long,' said Vladan Batić, the Minister of Justice. 'No matter what he did in the past, all he has to do now is obey the law.'

A court order had been issued for his arrest, to face questioning on corruption charges. He was to be charged with 'enriching himself and his supporters, and breaking the law to ensure his party held onto power in Serbia.'

At around two in the morning, we heard a single pistol shot, followed by a round of automatic fire, and assumed that the police assault had started. At four-thirty, journalists at the main gate, further down the hill on the other side of the villa, rang to say that a convoy of police jeeps had just left, and were heading for the city prison. Milošević had agreed to go quietly. It turned out later that his daughter Marija had fired at Čeda Jovanović as her father was surrendering.

No-one was injured. My last report of the night was just after sunrise from the gate of Belgrade's central prison, a drab, four-storey building in a residential suburb of the city. The stand-off had lasted thirty hours.

On 28 June 2001, after more hesitations by the authorities over whether he should be put on trial in Serbia for crimes including the murder of Stambolić, Milošević was bundled aboard a helicopter and then, in Tuzla in Bosnia, onto a military plane to the Netherlands. His trial, on sixty-six counts of genocide, crimes against humanity and war crimes in Croatia, Bosnia and Kosovo began a year later at the International War Crimes Tribunal for the former Yugoslavia.

Poker-faced, he conducted his own defence. He only showed emotion once, when the name of Ivan Stambolić was mentioned.

In March 2006, he died in his cell at the Scheveningen detention centre after nearly five years on trial, and only months before the verdict.

As I interviewed people waiting to sign the book of condolences in Belgrade, I suddenly found myself at the front of the queue, with everyone looking at me expectantly. I took the pen which was offered me, and thought quickly.

Nick Thorpe

'There are so many questions I would have liked to ask you,' I wrote, 'Nick Thorpe, BBC.'

* * *

We had written so much about the victims of war in the Balkans, I felt it was time to go looking for the perpetrators. Ten years after the Dayton Peace Agreement ended the Bosnian war, and sixty years after the liberation of Auschwitz, I went for a drive with Lola, aka Milorad Batinić, a Bosnian Serb historian, used car-dealer and the best man for the job. Lola had fought briefly on the Bosnian Serb side in the war, and had then been recruited by the British military as an interpreter, on account of his excellent, if somewhat fiery English. He also had the rare skill of being able to laugh himself out of the most threatening situation.

For weeks in advance, we drew up lists of men who were still on the run, and of those who had already been tried and convicted by the war crimes tribunal and had served their sentences and been released. We rented a flat in Banja Luka, the Bosnian Serb capital, and began to explore the hinterland of war crimes, and punishment.

We arrived mid-morning at the Hotel Prijedor, in the town of the same name. A man at the bar in a bright blue sweatshirt and jeans climbed down off his stool to shake hands. Dragan Kolundžija looked younger than his forty-six years. If you saw him in the street, you might mistake him for a football coach, not a reserve policeman, and certainly not a former concentration camp guard.

He hadn't agreed to an interview yet—and had turned down the approaches of other journalists.

It took Lola ten minutes to persuade him to speak, while I watched the women cleaning the glass panels which dotted the lobby of the hotel. Then we went upstairs to a big empty room with a gas heater. The hotel staff seemed afraid of us, or of Kole, as Kolundžija was known. I couldn't decide which. Kole was a guard at Keraterm, one of several concentration camps in north-west Bosnia where nearly seventeen hundred Bosnian Muslims were tortured to death in three months in the summer of 1992. These were the camps that Douglas Hurd, the British Foreign Secretary, had told me in Belgrade that same summer did not exist.

He was indicted by the Hague Tribunal for crimes against humanity, and violations of the laws and customs of war. He pleaded guilty to one

272

count of persecution as a crime against humanity, and got three years in jail. He was also one of the first to be released. Five of his fellow guards were still serving sentences when I spoke to him. There were thirty guards in total.

Sitting with him, it was easy to remember that the Serbs were also victims of the Bosnian war—that the jailors, too, suffered.

His hands and his lips trembled. He tried to hold his hands still on the pure white tablecloth. We made small talk for a while, but I couldn't pretend I had come to talk about the river, which flowed lazily beneath the windows.

I tried to be gentle, a storyteller, not a prosecutor. So the first question was: what ways were open to you to show kindness to the prisoners? He broke down immediately. We sat in silence for a while, listening to children playing on the river bank.

After a while, he suddenly asked if he could invite a friend to sit with us, as that might make it easier to speak.

Ten minutes later, Suad, known as Duda, arrived. He hadn't had time to shave, and he too was shaking. Duda had been a prisoner in the camp, when Kole was a guard. They were friends before the war, and friends again after it. Duda even testified at the Tribunal in Kole's defence—one of the main reasons why he only got three years.

The Serb and the Muslim, the guard and his prisoner, sat side by side, broken faced, broken eyed, drinking stupid soft drinks as though there was no war, no cruelty, no injustice in this world. But there was none of the gaiety about them that they must have shared, in the back row benches of the primary school class where they first met and became friends.

'What the hell are you doing here?' Kole had asked, when he first saw his friend in the camp.

'How the hell should I know?' Duda had replied. He had been rounded up, like all other Bosniak men in this region where Bosniaks had slightly outnumbered Serbs at the outbreak of war.

In June 1992, two months after the start of the war, Serb police had surrounded Duda's house, and taken him, his brother and a neighbour to the police station for questioning 'about a Muslim uprising in another town'. Then they were taken across the road, to the Keraterm camp.

The two men explained to me, in fits and starts, what a concentration camp means. What the *concentration* of men means. It is where men are concentrated to death. Four rooms with 400 to 500 men in each,

120 metres square. In the summer heat. With no space to lie down. Civilians, fifty to ninety years old.

Every night Serb soldiers, back from the front, came to the camp. They wanted revenge for lost comrades. They asked the guards for the keys to the rooms, and committed acts of unspeakable barbarity, of sexual humiliation and horror.

'I really don't know how it came to this, because before the war we lived together. We'd go to the same cafés together . . .' said Kole. 'It still doesn't make sense, how overnight some people could become beasts.'

'Thinking about it now, I think we were much closer to robots than to human beings. We were all doing things which were not connected to ourselves, to our minds. It was as though someone else was doing them. No-one could feel guilty. Whatever a soldier did, he was not held responsible for murder, or robbery or anything. No-one was held to account for their actions.'

Of all the guards, only Kole refused to hand over the key to the soldiers, said Duda. That was the only shift when there were no beatings or killings. But one night, the barbarians got inside, on Kole's shift.

'It was dark, the soldiers somehow got into the room, and Kole was shouting, "stop shooting, stop shooting!"' Duda said.

'By morning there were two hundred dead bodies.' The ICTY indictment spoke of at least one hundred and twenty.

Kole was hunched up at the table, staring at the back of his hands, as though he didn't know what they were.

'That was a dark, black night,' he said, after a long silence. A silence in which he waited, in vain, for something to heal inside himself.

After the interview, I tried to find the toilet. But my brain was fogged up. I walked head-first into a plate glass door—the women had cleaned it too well. It quivered but did not break. After that, I walked with my hands in front of me, like a blind man.

On the way out of Prijedor, we passed Keraterm, the ex-camp—once a factory for bathroom tiles. It was a low, meaningless building beside another factory, which boasted a chimney, at least, for making bricks. Twenty-five thousand five hundred Muslims are back in the Prijedor region—out of the 45,000 who once lived here. I wondered how people could come home to a place where things like this happened.

Some of the returnees turned their backs on Kole in the street. Some shook his hand. The camp commander, Duško Sikirica, is still in prison. He got fifteen years.

14. Welcome to the Club

The giant wheel rested next to where the statue of Lenin used to stand, on his red granite plinth. Inside it was a huge egg-timer, filled, as you would expect, with sand.

The egg-timer had been János Herner's dream for many years. He had first told me about it in Szeged, in 1986, when he helped me find anti-regime students at the university. Now European Union entry was making its realisation possible. The idea was simple. Instead of taking one minute to run through the timer, the sand was to take exactly a year. To the split second, grain by grain. So he had to get his calculations right. At first he wanted to use a mixture of sand from all the deserts of the world. That would have been more romantic, but he found the wide ranges of temperature in Budapest, from cold winters to hot summers, played havoc with the speed of his sand, as the levels of moisture changed. So he found a synthetic mix instead. Each year, at the stroke of midnight, the wheel would turn, and the sand start to flow back into the empty container. This was what the people of eastern Europe had waited fourteen years for. The regular and predictable passing of time.

* * *

Eight former communist countries from eastern Europe joined the European Union on 1 May 2004, alongside Malta, and the Greek half of Cyprus. A long time had passed since the Iron Curtain came down. A long time had passed since the two Germanies had re-united. Some of the enthusiasm for Europe had dampened in the process, like moisture penetrating real sand, but the goal had still been achieved, and people were more or less pleased. There was, after all, no other club in town.

275

In June 1947, the US Secretary of State, George Marshall, announced the intention, but few concrete details of what came to be called the Marshall Plan—US help to rebuild Europe from the ruins of the Second World War.

'We are remote from the scene of these troubles,' said Marshall, from the steps of Memorial Church at Harvard University. 'It is virtually impossible at this distance merely by reading, or listening, or even seeing photographs and motion pictures, to grasp at all the real significance of the situation. And yet the whole world of the future hangs on a proper judgement. [. . .] What is needed? What can best be done? What must be done?'

His speech was broadcast in full on the BBC. Over the following five years, $13 billion was distributed in western Europe. The central and eastern Europeans, newly swallowed by the Soviet giant, were forbidden to apply by Stalin. The Russians were busy stripping the industries of East Germany, Hungary and Romania of goods and equipment and, in Hungary's case, even of people, to rebuild the Soviet Union. The economies of most of the states of eastern Europe were well behind the West, even before this, but Marshall Plan aid undoubtedly reinforced the gulf between East and West.

In 1989, many commentators compared eastern Europe emerging from communism to Europe emerging from the Second World War, but there was no serious discussion of a new plan on the same scale. The European Union provided the framework of what might be possible, once each country met increasingly tight economic and political criteria.

The accession process was financially rewarding and institutionally valuable, too. Money was pumped into the poorer half of Europe like never before. The sewage systems of towns from the Baltic Sea in Estonia, to the Adriatic in Slovenia were upgraded. No longer would raw sewage harm rivers where children swam, or would like to swim, in summer, and fishermen fished regardless of what their fish had eaten for breakfast. Potholed roads were ironed out; grain silos rebuilt.

The justice systems were sharply criticised and, in many places, repaired. It became harder for politicians or businessmen to interfere in court proceedings. Judges were picked for cases at random, to avoid the possibility of them being bribed. Human rights legislation was drafted and passed by obedient parliaments, although once inside the Union, there would be little will to check that the spirit, or the letter, of the laws was kept.

Animals, as well as people, were to benefit. Slaughterhouses were closed down in droves as unhygienic. Tougher rules were introduced to try to minimise the suffering of animals in factory farms, and on the road to the slaughterhouse. All eggs would have to be free-range by the year 2010.

Along the new borders of the European Union, infra-red night vision equipment was installed, to keep unwanted aliens out. Germany and Austria could breathe a sigh of relief. The buffer zone with the barbarians had moved east.

The terms of admission were fought over for many months, years if one takes as the starting point the invitation to Hungary, Poland and Czechoslovakia to start accession proceedings, issued at the Dublin summit of the EU in April 1990. The accession chapters were closed in Copenhagen in December 2002. The deal on offer was not as good as the candidates had hoped, but not as bad as they had feared. The addition of ten new members was set to cost the existing fifteen members a total of €40 billion over the next three years, up to 2007.

In many countries, referenda were held and passed in favour of membership. In Hungary in March 2003, a dispute between the ruling Socialists and the opposition Fidesz almost led to the vote being declared null and void because of the low turnout. The government plunged billions of forints into the 'Yes' campaign, while critics of membership were left to spray their message on walls and pavements, unfunded by the state. At a secret location on the outskirts of Budapest, a team of young people with headsets tried to answer all the questions people had.

Fidesz, in opposition, said, 'Yes, but . . .' to membership, and were criticised as traitors to the national interest for suggesting that some people would suffer, in the first years of membership at least. In the event, the referendum was just valid, but many opposition supporters stayed away. There was no resounding endorsement of 'Europe' as one might have expected had accession come earlier.

On accession day, Freedom Bridge across the Danube in Budapest was closed to traffic, and completely turfed. I walked barefoot on it with my laughing children in the early morning, and bumped into the mayor, Gábor Demszky, and his assistant, taking photographs. For once, the bridge was quiet enough to set up my satellite dish on the ramparts, and send reports about how the Hungarians were feeling. This was normally the favourite bridge in the city for suicides, on account of the gentle camber of the supports, allowing almost anyone to climb up onto the very top and leap to their doom if they dared. Most didn't, and the fire brigade would come to coax them down. But there were no desperate Hungarians on the top that day. Disillusion, for some, would come later.

Once inside the Union, the impact on agriculture was the most complex and, in many countries, the most disputed. Existing EU members quarrelled with one another about how to reform, or abandon, the Common Agricultural Policy. Farmers in France, who got most from it, were particularly worried about the addition of millions of poor Polish farmers, and made sure that the new peasants would not enter on the same terms that they themselves had enjoyed for years.

Used to heavy state subsidies, farmers in the East wanted to know how much money would come from Brussels to replace it, and how soon. They were intensely alarmed by the fact that they had only been allotted twenty-five per cent of the payments which went to the far richer farmers of western Europe. Last minute sweeteners were added to the package under the Danish Presidency of the EU, but east European farmers still had the strong impression that the ploughing field was sloping against them, and that they would be on the receiving end of an invasion of surplus foods from the west of the continent, against which they would have no protection.

Another central issue for the farmers was to what extent they could trust their own governments to act in good faith as intermediaries between themselves and Brussels when it came to paying out the money.

In the event, the Polish government got it more or less right, and the Hungarians didn't. The Polish Agricultural Ministry took on 10,000 staff to streamline payments to the country's large farming population. The money was paid on time, and Polish farmers, in the first years at least, often noticed they were receiving more money for their produce than before. The Hungarian Ministry found jobs for less than 2,000 people and, within a year, angry farmers invaded Budapest and set up a tractor city on Heroes' Square. They were not protesting against the EU, only against their own government's delays. They had planted crops and bought equipment, they said, on the basis of promises which had not been fulfilled. City and village dwellers stared at each other in mutual incomprehension. There is a marked tendency in Hungary for each to regard the other as idiots.

The farmers did not remain united for long. Large farms had nothing to do with the protest from the start. They were favoured by the governing Socialist-Liberal administration, while the owners of small and medium-sized farms felt discriminated against. It was the other way round when a centre-right government was in office. Under both, the Hungarian countryside was starved of capital. The first democratic government of József Antall was much criticised for breaking up the large farms which formed the backbone of the rather productive Hungarian agriculture, and for throwing away the large markets to the east in the former Soviet Union, which were crying out for cheap Hungarian goods like wine and apples. In its defence, Antall's government argued that it was trying to address a historical injustice—the confiscation of land by the state. In the end, everyone was disappointed, and this played an important role in the devastating defeat of the Hungarian Democratic Forum in the 1994 elections, and the return of the Socialists.

That was long ago, but the decisions about ownership of the early 90s, with all their benefits and faults, had prepared the way for the European Union. And now people were supposed to change their way of thinking too.

'Hungarians are used to considering the EU in terms of 'them' versus 'us' . . .' said Györgyi Kocsis of the HVG weekly. 'Now we will have to learn that we are all together. We're going to have to learn to behave as part of the family—how to be creative, how not to downplay, and how not to overplay our role.'

* * *

Even as the central Europeans and the Baltic democracies were trying to find their place in the EU, the Romanians and Bulgarians were bending over backwards to qualify for the next round of enlargement in, they hoped, 2006. Enlargement fervour in the bulky, twenty-five member EU was cooling fast, and some politicians in the older member states were looking for reasons not to let any more countries in. Deep-seated corruption in both Romania and Bulgaria seemed to provide the perfect excuse. The conduct of the parliamentary elections in Romania in November and December 2004 was an important test of whether the country could qualify for EU membership. Romanians traditionally trusted two institutions above all, the Orthodox Church and the Army. Parliamentary deputies were seen as the most corrupt group in society, closely followed by doctors, judges and policemen.

The Democratic Convention, a mixed bag of anti-communist groups led by the National Peasants' Party, won the elections in 1996. It survived four years, but proved rather ineffective in government, and was swept aside by the power of the resurgent Socialists, or as they were now known, the Party of Social Democracy (PSD), in 2000. That government, under Prime Minister Adrian Năstase, was sitting rather prettily in the saddle in 2004, and looked set to win another term in office. Năstase was self-confident, coming across as a rather effete, somewhat arrogant figure. As President of the Romanian Hunters' Association, one could imagine him as a Conservative in Britain, or a Christian Democrat in Germany, hob-nobbing with leading businessmen over the steaming carcasses of wild boar and bears from the Carpathian forests. According to his declared assets, he also owned a number of properties, which redoubled suspicions that he was corrupt.

Civic groups in Romania had always played second string to the political parties, but had also proved surprisingly resilient. Ahead of the local elections in June 2004, and the general elections in the winter, several groups set up what they called the Coalition for a Clean Parliament (CCP). Their starting point was what they considered the ruling Socialists' failure to tackle corruption in high places, and the threat that Romania might miss its chance to join the EU.

'Communism left many scars in east European societies,' wrote the CCP in a booklet, 'amongst them, the tradition of a fully unaccountable political elite ranks as perhaps the most important.'

The CCP set six criteria for a candidate running for office to be categorised as 'clean'. She or he should not have changed political parties repeatedly (this was proving something of a Romanian disease—fifteen per cent of parliamentary deputies had done so between 2000 and 2004); they should not have been accused of corruption 'on the basis of published and verifiable evidence'; they should not have been exposed as a former agent of the Securitate; they should not be the owner of a private firm with substantial debts to the state budget; and they should not have profited from conflicts of interest involving their public position. Thrown onto the defensive by the CCP's well researched, nationwide approach, and not wishing to be seen as 'pro-corruption', all parties except the far-right Greater Romania Party initially said that they would cooperate with the campaign.

The atmosphere turned nasty when the CCP presented its findings. No less than 143 PSD candidates and a smaller percentage from other parties were deemed 'unfit for office'. The list included no less than seven ministers in the government—those of Foreign Affairs, Defence, the

Economy, Finance, Transport, Education and Health. There was a deafening silence. Then the party dropped some thirty lower profile candidates and went on the offensive, attacking the CCP at every opportunity.

'We consider that this gesture . . . constitutes a flagrant violation of a fundamental political right guaranteed by the Constitution, namely the right of a citizen to be elected,' read a PSD press release, one month before election day. A number of candidates began libel suits against the CCP.

I spent an eventful election day following buses full of PSD supporters who appeared to be driving from polling station to polling station, voting at each.

Observers from the CCP suggested that the so-called 'domino' technique of election fraud was being used. Genuine ballot papers were 'procured' illegally from voting stations, then the box for the favoured party was filled in, and these were then handed out to members of the public who were recruited in advance. They would then put the already filled in paper into the box, and leave the polling station with their own ballot paper intact. These were then collected by trusted party activists, filled in, then passed on to more members of the public. Only in this way can a party be sure that the person who is paid to vote for a certain party actually does so.

Having gathered a certain amount of evidence of the practice in the capital, I drove to the Danubian port of Olteniţa, south of Bucharest, for a change of scene.

I began by asking random voters my stock opening question at election time, as they left a school.

'Please tell me why you went to the trouble of voting today?'

'Because I was paid to,' replied a middle-aged, rather scruffy individual.

I checked my interpreter's translation, then edged the microphone a little closer under his chin.

'And were you just paid to vote, or to vote for any particular party?' I asked.

'For the Socialists of course, they always pay us to vote for them, at every election.'

He cheerfully explained the procedure. At each election, he and his friends approached PSD activists putting up posters, offering their votes—at a price. There was always a brief negotiation—taking inflation into account, of course—and then a deal was struck. The poor man even gave his name—which I was careful to cut out of the broadcast version. I was afraid his paymasters would beat him up. Later that evening I had calls both from the US embassy in Bucharest and the CCP, asking for copies of the tape.

After the first round of the election, the PSD were marginally ahead. But, partly as a result of the scandal raised by the CCP, and aided perhaps by my own work on the day, maximum publicity was given to the question of vote-rigging. With Brussels breathing heavily down their necks in the second round, two weeks later there were markedly fewer incidents, and the result of the first round was reversed. The opposition Liberals and Democratic Party won a historic victory.

*   *   *

While the Socialists fell from power in Romania, in Hungary the Socialist Party won a second term in the April 2006 elections—the first party to do so since the return of democracy. Ferenc Gyurcsány, a tall, extremely hard-working businessman and former Young Communist, played a central role in their victory.

A month later, Gyurcsány gathered his 189 parliamentary deputies at a summer retreat on the southern shore of Lake Balaton. They had every reason to be content—but there was nothing to be complacent about, he told the party faithful. The Hungarian economy was in a terrible state, and the budget deficit was ballooning over ten per cent of the GDP. Worst of all, in order to win the elections 'we lied morning, noon and night'.

His speech was also peppered with expletives, the most common being 'ezt a kurva orzság' literally, 'this whore of a country', but more accurately translated as, 'this fucking country'. It was broadcast in full by Hungarian radio on 17 September. Most probably, the main conservative opposition party, Fidesz, had got a copy of it, and the Socialists knew they were planning to make it public just before the autumn local elections. So the Socialists leaked it themselves, early, in perfect broadcast quality, to spoil the timing of the opposition's plan, at least.

Hungary was scandalised. If a minister or any public official was caught lying in a normal country, he could be expected to resign immediately. But now the Prime Minister had not just been caught lying, he had admitted to it—three times a day, for eighteen months! But was Hungary 'normal' yet? Apparently not.

Gyurcsány hit back at his critics. He had been trying to wake his party up, he explained, and then warmed to his theme. He was determined to turn his back on sixteen years of dishonesty, from all political sides, he said. Even better, he was going to be the first leader to tell the people the truth. And he waited for the applause. He got it from Socialist camp-followers in the media, but the anti-Socialists lost no time. Demonstrators gathered outside Parliament on the Sunday evening, within minutes of the broadcast, calling on him to resign.

The next day, a Monday, thousands joined them, a motley bag of respectable middle class people, lawyers and dentists and teachers, and a rowdy fringe, former supporters of the far-right Hungarian Justice and Life Party. Rebels searching for a new cause.

At about six in the evening, a group of the more radical participants took the petition they had drawn up a few hundred metres to the building of the state television in Freedom Square, to demand that it be read out, on air. Among the demands was the immediate resignation of the Prime Minister. Guards blocked their way, and when the petitioners got violent, a police unit arrived on the main steps. They were provincial cops, drafted hurriedly into the city, with no experience of crowd control. They were brushed aside, in a hail of stones, and the crowd started smashing their way into the building, hurling metal bars and Molotov cocktails at police. When a water cannon was brought up, the police were overpowered and beat a humiliated retreat. A part of the crowd then set fire to several cars in the car-park, and broke the rest of the windows of the sturdy old television building, which had once served as a stock exchange.

It was a scandal of European proportions, but who was going to pay the price?

I had gone to bed early, and only got there around eleven, roused from my slumbers by a phone-call from London with the news that the television headquarters was on fire.

I set up my satellite dish on a low wall, and broadcast live from the square till four in the morning, interviewing protesters, gathering information on the numbers injured and trying to find out what was going on. Everyone spoke happily, and even gave their names, except for three lads with football scarves who I had just seen actually breaking windows. Unlike most of the crowd, they had no obvious political insignia. They seemed just to be there for the fun of attacking a building.

After the first retreat, the police kept their distance, on the far side of the building, and despite sporadic rumours that they were about to clear the square, they never moved.

One of the most peculiar aspects of the police action, or rather inaction, was that they had left a large square police bus unlocked, and completely abandoned, on the southern edge of the square from which I was sending my reports. I watched one of the demonstrators try the door in passing and, when it opened, he climbed inside and pretended to be a policeman. He was quickly joined by others, who proceeded to wreck the vehicle, inside and out. The police, who watched from a distance, made no attempt to prevent this happening. It was almost as though they deliberately let the crowd do as much damage as possible.

The following day, a taxi driver told me this story. He had picked up a young couple, perhaps fifteen or sixteen-years-old, from near the TV headquarters at about four that morning, and driven them home to the far suburbs of the city. All the way, they quarrelled on the back seat. The girl was in favour of violence against property. 'If we don't smash anything up, no-one will listen to what we're saying,' she argued. The boy disagreed.

'No one will listen to us if we do that . . .' he argued.

The siege of Hungarian public service TV was condemned in Brussels and other European capitals, and the government were quick to seize on it as proof that the Prime Minister was the calm point in the storm, and not the reckless seaman who had whistled it up.

The demonstrators set up camp on the grass in front of Parliament, and announced that they were going to stay until the government stepped down. Various organising committees were established with their own podiums and speeches. During the day, numbers dwindled to a few hundred, but each evening, as people finished work, the crowd swelled to a few thousand.

Police tactics, overly passive the day before, switched suddenly on 18 September. In imitation of 23 October 1956, a part of the crowd in front of Parliament started marching towards the Hungarian radio building in Sándor Bródy Street. Riot police blocked their path, then attacked what was then still a peaceful demonstration. The youth hit back with bottles and rubbish bins, and the city centre turned into a battleground.

At one police road block I asked politely what was happening, and was told, very rudely, to go to hell.

The stand-off lasted for weeks, with the Christian Democratic opposition, Fidesz, at almost as much of a loss as the Socialists about how to react.

Though they agreed with the sentiment of bringing down the government, as a democratic exercise this was much too direct for them. Pro-government media suggested that they were behind the protests anyway. They weren't, but they were trying to find ways of steering them.

'This is a middle-class uprising,' the philosopher, Gáspár Miklós Tamás, told me, underlining a point which many other commentators seemed determined to avoid. By portraying it as a bunch of hoodlums, in league with the parliamentary opposition, they were missing the point. And the point was that the Prime Minister had a moral duty, after such a speech, to step down. It was no good arguing, as he did, that other politicians had lied in the past and got away with it. He was responsible for his own actions, not for theirs.

Hungary had been divided for years, on an artificial, left-right divide. The protests of September and October polarised the country still further. In quiet country villages, the older people tended to take the side of the state, against the street. All they saw were hoodlums, setting fire to cars and attacking the police. What has this country come to, they thought, where people attack the police?

As a parent with three children at Hungarian schools and two at kindergarten, I could follow the dispute from the inside. My dentist was a dedicated participant in the daily demonstration outside Parliament, spending an hour or two there, 'performing his democratic duty' as he saw it, to peacefully call for the government to step down, on his way home after twelve hours in his dentist's surgery. Several architects, fellow parents at the school my children attended, also took part.

I knew the opponents well too. A man who organised skiing trips for my sons walked along the edge of the crowd, cursing them all. Liberal friends dismissed the movement as a neo-fascist revival against an elected government, especially on account of the red and white striped 'Arpád' flags.

The flag was one of the historic emblems used by Hungarians through the centuries, older than the tricolour of the national flag today, and was named after the first ruling dynasty in the eleventh century. There were even examples of it on the beautifully painted walls of the Prime Minister's office, standards carried into battle during the 1848 revolution. But, like the chequerboard Croatian flag, it had also been used by a fascist group in Hungary during the Second World War, the Arrow Cross. Jews and Gypsies had been persecuted by people brandishing this flag, and it seemed deeply insulting to their memory to revive it now.

The twenty-third of October 2006 was the fiftieth anniversary of the outbreak of the 1956 revolution, and notwithstanding the continuing street protests, preparations were well advanced to mark the anniversary with all the pomp and glory it deserved as the proudest moment in Hungarian history.

The high point of the official celebrations, the raising of the national flag in front of Parliament, was attended by heads of state or top officials from eighty-two countries around the world. A whole fleet of limousines was hired for the day from the German car manufacturer Opel, some of them armoured. Gyurcsány felt threatened enough to order one of the latter for his personal use. He was feeling particularly vulnerable. On his blog, he commented that the current debate was about power, lies and style. On the first, the government was in its place—in harmony with the constitution and the norms of parliamentary democracy, he wrote. He dismissed his own confession to deliberately misleading the public as 'a dramatic monologue, rich in emotions', in which he had 'occasionally got carried away'.

In terms of the style, the 'foul-mouthed expressions' he had used, the Prime Minister wrote that this had been a 'brutal stylistic reflection of the intense emotions in the language'.

In an interview for the American TV network, CNN, he did not manage to express himself quite so well.

The reporter stuck to his one, simple question. 'But why did you lie?' This was repeated, politely but firmly, time and again. The Prime Minister wriggled on the hook, and finally went limp.

A few days later, when I went to interview him, he refused for the first time to speak in English, though his English was rather good.

'What's the matter?' I asked.

'Didn't you hear about my CNN interview?' he asked, with a crestfallen expression. 'It was awful!'

'Who was awful, the reporter?' I asked, innocently.

'Not the reporter, me!'

In the five weeks of street protests leading up to the anniversary, police tactics swung wildly from violent and sometimes brutal intervention to total passivity.

Local elections were due, and the protest camp in front of Parliament argued that it was actually a political rally, related to the elections, which gave it the right to continue through the campaign period. The government decided that they were an embarrassment, and wanted them moved before the foreign dignitaries arrived.

Early on the morning of 23 October, riot police cleared the camp, dragging some of its dozy organisers from their sleeping bags, and erected a double metal shell around the gardens in front of the building. Through the morning, protesters marched in disorganised groups around the city. A gathering of the opposition Fidesz party had been arranged for early that afternoon, at the Astoria Road junction, to commemorate the 1956 revolution.

The city council had arranged revolutionary paraphernalia around the city—flags and photo exhibitions and other mementoes, including a T-34 Soviet tank, parked strategically at an intersection and draped with the symbol of the revolution, a Hungarian tricolour flag with the centre cut out of it.

A part of the people on the street was there to call for a new revolution. Another part was there to remember an old one. Some were bitterly opposed to one another, others blurred in the middle. The result was chaos.

I joined the crowd at about midday, on the main boulevard in front of the Corvin cinema, scene of the centre of resistance to the Red Army in 1956. The cinema had been carefully restored, in Habsburg yellow and white, and a bronze statue outside of a fifteen-year-old boy, carrying a gun which looked too big for him, was always garlanded with flowers.

From there, they marched to Astoria, to join the Fidesz protest. I interviewed some of them on the way. Pleasant, non-violent people. Several tens of thousands of Fidesz supporters took part in the rally.

'There are many parallels between 1956 and today,' the writer and artist, Gábor Karátson, told me. 'Revolution is something which has a value in itself. For those weeks, or for that time, it instils in people the feeling of their own energy, of their own health, and of their own friendliness. When you look around here, everyone is smiling, greeting each other . . .' As a student in October 1956, he had participated in the toppling of the Stalin statue, then began running towards the radio building, as word spread through the city that the secret police had started shooting there. On the way, somewhere near Blaha Lujza Square, he picked up a cobble-stone. The cobble-stones in Budapest are square, like big black dice, unlike their rounder relatives in Paris. Gábor meditated on the stone as he ran. Am I really going to throw this at someone and hurt, perhaps even kill them with it? he asked himself. He put the stone down, then carried on running towards the radio.

Those in the city not taking part in the protest bitterly challenged any parallels with the events of fifty years earlier.

'There could not be a bigger difference between the events of 1956 and those of today,' said the historian and head of the 1956 Institute, János Rainer. 'Then, there was national unity. Now there's division. Then we fought against a dictatorship. Those fighting today are a minority, fighting against a democracy.'

* * *

Viktor Orbán, the Fidesz leader, took the rostrum at Astoria. He has a peculiar speaking style—first practised, to great effect, at the reburial of Imre Nagy in June 1989—of pronouncing the main phrases slowly and repetitively, to make sure that everyone hears what is said. This has fuelled his opponents' accusation that he is a populist. For his supporters, it has become a factor of endearment, much imitated among his fans. 'They–shall–not–pass.'

After some hesitation, Orbán and the Fidesz leadership struck on a way to channel popular anger with the government to their own advantage. In his speech, he announced the start of a campaign to gather signatures for a referendum, opposing the five or six least popular policies of the government—the introduction of a per-visit-fee to the doctor, the break-up of the national insurance system into one based on competing insurers, fees for students in higher education, and so on. The proposal drew polite applause, but was hardly revolutionary, on this revolutionary anniversary. Orbán had clearly considered, then decided against, trying to place himself at the head of this popular movement. Given the choice between leading a parliamentary party or a street movement, he knew where he belonged.

Word spread through the crowd that the police were shooting rubber bullets at protesters just up the road, in Deák Square. I pushed my way through the throng.

The scene was as spectacular as any I had seen anywhere in eastern Europe in the past twenty years. A line of blue police water cannons were ranged across Bajcsy-Zsilinszky Street, where demonstrators had passed on 15 March 1988, chanting 'multi-party system'.

In front of the police vehicles, a line of police marksmen crouched, each with a fat, double-barrelled shotgun aimed at head height straight into the crowd. There were several thousand people in the square, protesters and tourists, children on their parents' shoulders, stragglers from the Fidesz rally and others just out for a walk on a national holiday, the day of the new republic. Though some of the protesters wore face masks to hide their identity, none of them were actually throwing anything at the police, as I arrived.

Then a loudhailer from the police lines began barking instructions. It was faint, and so distorted I couldn't make out a word. I asked others standing next to me in the front row of the crowd—but no-one could understand it.

I had just taken up a safer position, on the edge of the crowd close to a wall, with a good escape route planned, when the shooting started without warning. Volley after volley of rubber bullets, straight into the crowd. At the same time, a police jeep parked at one side fired tear gas grenades in the air, looping down towards the back of the square. The water cannon began moving forward, spraying what looked like blue paint into the crowd.

The wail of ambulance sirens mingled with the loud retorts of the shotguns. A man fell on the pavement close to me, blood pouring from his eye. As the Fidesz rally ended, half a kilometre away, a large part of the crowd began walking towards Deák Square, either on their way home or to find out what all the noise was about—just as people began fleeing the rubber bullets, the water cannon and the tear gas.

Squads of riot police then charged the crowd, hitting indiscriminately with batons.

Some people asked the police for advice as to how to leave the scene. They followed the instructions they were given, only to be beaten by other police, coming the other way. At some point in the confusion, a man got into the T-34 tank, managed to start it and, billowing black smoke from the exhaust, began driving it crazily towards police lines. The police scattered, and the surrealist atmosphere redoubled. One revolution now sat inside another, like Russian dolls.

The pursuit and the violence continued late into the evening. A Canadian-Hungarian businessman, who had taken no part in the protest, was beaten to the ground by police as he came out onto the street from a restaurant in the city centre.

Some people fought back. But most fled, some with more success than others. Unlike in a 'standard' riot, there was no looting of shops. This was very much a confrontation between the people and the state.

I decided it was too dangerous to set up my satellite equipment on the street, so found my way through the backstreets back to my office, near the West Railway Station, and sent reports from there. For several hours, the air was thick with sirens. I wondered what the foreign dignitaries, ensconced behind the walls of the Parliament, made of it all. Hungary's fiftieth anniversary revolution celebrations were transformed into an international scandal. The final tally for the night: 88 hospitalised, several with serious eye injuries, and 131 arrested.

The Minister of Justice and Public order, József Petretei, offered his resignation, but it was not accepted. The opposition called for the head of the Budapest police chief, who was responsible for the action, Péter Gergényi, but it was not offered. Gergényi held a press conference at police headquarters a few days later.

'How many riot police took part in the disturbances?' I asked.

'That's a service secret. In a war, you don't tell the other side the strength of your forces.'

'So this is a civil war?'

He laughed—'Of course not, it was just an example.'

'How many rounds of rubber bullets did you use?'

'We didn't count.'

'A lot of the injured were hit in the head. Is there no regulation to aim for the legs?'

'These are weapons which cannot be aimed accurately.'

On display was a selection of offensive items, mostly taken from the protest tents when they were pulled down at dawn on 23 October. They included an axe—for chopping wood, said the protesters. And socks stuffed with charcoal—'they pour lighter fuel on them, set them on fire, and throw them at the police,' said Mr Gergényi. 'Nonsense,' said former protest campers. 'The charcoal is to protect us from the tear-gas. You hold the socks in front of your nose and eyes.'

Human rights groups tentatively reached the same conclusion as the mainly right-wing protesters; that this had been a disaster largely of the police's own making.

On 4 November, the anniversary of the Soviet invasion in 1956, Fidesz organised another peaceful, almost silent march, carrying flowers and candles. The police kept a low profile, and there was no violence.

The government had won its battle to stay in power, at the cost of the country's damaged reputation.

It is a strange anomaly of the new laws passed by the 'godfathers' of Hungary's new democracy in the early 1990s, that the right to strike and to demonstrate is strong. But the ability for the street, or for the parliamentary opposition, to remove an elected government is almost non-existent. The only way a government can fall is by passing a 'constructive vote of no-confidence' in itself, using its parliamentary majority. As Ferenc Gyurcsány made clear, that was not his plan.

Eventually, both the Budapest and the nationwide police chiefs did resign. I felt sorry for the national chief, László Bene, a gentle soul who admitted that the police intervention had been unnecessarily heavy-handed. Rubber bullets were subsequently removed from the police arsenal—or at least not replaced, and the stocks were much depleted. The police also lost a string of legal cases by claimants who were able to prove police brutality, but few individual police were found guilty. They had worn black masks, and no numbers. It was almost impossible, even from the copious television footage and still photographs of the day, to establish their identities.

'The problem is that the police are an over-centralised, over-militarised institution, without any civilian oversight of their activities,' said István Szikinger, a constitutional lawyer.

In other words, their actions, on occasion too weak, on others too strong, were signs that they were out of control, not under someone's control, as the opposition alleged.

A nine-member commission appointed by the government—and therefore of dubious independence—drew up and published their investigation into the troubles. They were not granted full access to the minutes of meetings between minsters, the secret services and police chiefs, but only to the 'unclassified' parts of those discussions. The experts 'did not primarily strive to determine responsibility, but endeavoured to formulate recommendations . . .'

In the section on the historical and social background, the commission found that there was 'still an unhealed feeling of injured national consciousness' in Hungary.

It criticised the government for 'poor communication'—surely one of the biggest understatements in Hungarian history, but levelled the far more serious charge against the opposition—of intending to overthrow the government.

'Groups representing the . . . extreme right wing attached themselves to (the commemorative events) and exploited them to carry out acts of physical aggression,' the report continued. And it concluded that 'the desolation of certain groups (of the youth, and rural communities) poses a serious problem for the entire society.'

Perhaps the most controversial conclusion was that 'certain dangerous ideas are spreading regarding the notion of democracy . . . that the constitutional representative system of parliamentary democracy may be replaced by the uncontrollable democracy of the street.'

According to István Stumpf, the head of the Századvég Institute and a former minister in a Fidesz government, the problem lay less outside Parliament than inside it.

'Eighteen years after the change of system the political elite have lost their popularity. People believe that those in power . . . cannot deal with their problems—education, health care, pension reforms—any more.'

As a result, he said, new groups were emerging, in a similar way to the 1987–88 period, with a more or less political agenda, looking for ways to 'breathe life back into politics'. Parallel to that, there was, he said, 'a new radicalism' in the air.

'The challenge of the political elite is how they are going to hear what people say, and how they are going to merge or apply the new forms of activism to politics.'

The real hope, he believed, was in a 'new generation' born around 1989, preparing not for the 2010 elections, but for those in 2014. 'Of better educated people, better at communicating with each other, with experience of the world, and able to identify the room for manoeuvre which Hungary has.'

One can only hope that he is right.

* * *

Separately from the political drama of the anniversary, I had prepared my own investigation into the Soviet side of 1956—how and why the revolution was crushed. The voice of the defeated is sometimes missing from the historical narrative, but on 1956 the voice of the conquerors was strangely silent.

Twelve months earlier, I had asked Anastasia, a friend in Kiev, to search through military archives, to try to make contact with veterans in Ukraine. I suspected it would be easier there than in Vladimir Putin's Russia.

After much painstaking research, and rebuttals from the Ministry of Defence and Veterans Associations, she finally struck lucky in Bila Tserkva, a town with a large military base, sixty kilometres south of Kiev. A friendly source at an archive found no less than twenty-four names and addresses of Ukrainian soldiers who had fought in the Red Army in Hungary in 1956.

She rang each in turn, and came up with six names of men who were willing to talk about their experiences.

Volodymyr Taranenko was twenty-six-years-old, a senior lieutenant in an artillery regiment in the 39th Mechanical Division of the Red Army. He had served in Austria, but when Soviet troops withdrew from there in 1955, he was moved to Transcarpathian Ukraine, just across the border from Hungary. On the night of 23 October, just as the first victims of secret police fire at Hungarian radio fell, his regiment assembled near the border, with tanks and heavy weapons. Nothing was explained to the soldiers about the mission, only that there might be some 'provocations', and they were not to fire back. At dawn on 24 October, the armoured column crossed into Hungary.

'We passed through little villages and towns, where people were sleeping. Sometime after sunrise we made a brief halt. While we were smoking, a Hungarian on a bicycle stopped. He spoke some Russian he had learnt when he was a prisoner of war. He asked where we were going. We don't know, we said. 'Haven't you heard? he said There's a revolution in Budapest.' It was a total surprise for us.'

Near the town of Szolnok, they came to a barricade of old vehicles and telegraph poles across the road, with Hungarians brandishing their fists at them and some throwing stones. But there was no shooting there.

'We called up the tanks, and they cleared a path through. Then we carried on to Budapest, and from there to Tamási in the south.'

Wherever they went, they saw Soviet monuments torn down, and people threw stones and taunted them. Once they were installed in Tamási, workers from local factories sent a delegation to negotiate with them. They asked them to leave. The commander refused, because he was under orders.

'We reserve the right to disarm you,' the delegation told the Soviets, then left.

On the night of 3 November, the division commander summoned his officers, and read out a letter from Marshal Konev, commander in chief of Warsaw Pact Forces. Counter-revolutionary forces, profiting from the discontent of the Hungarian people and led by Imre Nagy, had taken power. All Soviet troops in Hungary were ordered to disarm the rebels.

They started with the Hungarian army base in Tamási. The first man the Russians sent forward to negotiate was shot. The tanks opened fire and destroyed the cabin with two shells. Then the Hungarian soldiers were assembled in the main square, at gun point, and all their weapons collected and disabled. Seventy-five local communists, imprisoned by the rebels, were released.

Then they were ordered to drive to the southern city of Pécs.

'Rebels—who were actually university students—had got hold of guns and had taken refuge in holiday cottages in the forest—with their weapons, medicines and typewriters. I went with my division into the forest, and reached some kind of metereology station. We caught two Hungarian students there—they must have been eighteen or twenty years old. We were ordered to kill them. I didn't, but my commander told another lieutenant and a private to take the two students a little further down the path, and shoot them in the back. I saw it with my own eyes. I felt so sorry for them.'

Then Volodymyr read out a poem for me, '*Talpra Magyar*'—'on your feet, Hungarian!' or in Russian '*Stavaj magyar!*'. It was a translation from Sándor Petőfi, the Hungarian student leader from 1848, who had inspired the 1956 revolutionaries as well. Volodymyr had felt so bad about his own role in crushing the revolution, that he had found out as much as he could about Hungary after his return. He had carefully written out Petőfi's words, by hand, in his red notebook.

Before leaving Bila Tserkva, we called on one of Vlodymyr's neighbours, Svetlana. Her husband Mykola had also fought in Budapest in 1956. She opened for us, for the first time since that fateful autumn, a small wickerwork basket, and took out a small bundle of letters, tied with a ribbon. Letters home from Mykola to Svetlana, his pregnant wife. They had married seven months before the revolution.

In a sanatorium where he was recovering from an operation, we returned the letters to Mykola. He read them aloud to us, by the lake.

He had been flown in to a military airfield at Tököl, near Budapest, on 28 October 1956.

'On the morning of 4 November, we entered Budapest at high speed. I was in command of the artillery in our division. As soon as we entered the city, we were fired at from the balconies and windows of houses. We took up positions, and opened fire with the artillery at the city centre, at the Corvin cinema . . .'

Who did he think he was fighting against? I asked. And how did he feel?

'What could the emotions of a young man be, who had left his pregnant wife at home? Who had never been shot at before? Who had just finished military school? Of course I was afraid. But then we all calmed down a bit and felt brave, and we even took our helmets off . . .'

In the battle to retake Budapest, several of his comrades were killed, and many injured in the fighting.

On 1 November, Svetlana received her last letter from him. It was triangular, with no return address. 'I'm fine, but I don't know when I'll be back.'

On the evening of 28 November, Svetlana received an official cable that her husband had been killed in battle.

'I couldn't bear it' said Svetlana. 'Everything fell apart.' They had met at a dancing club, and fallen in love immediately. Within two months of their wedding, she was expectant, with twins.

She was taken to hospital at midnight, bleeding, and gave birth to a boy and a girl, prematurely, the next morning. They died a week later.

'My father made a little coffin for them, and buried them while I was still in the hospital. And I saw all the other mothers, with all their living children, and my eyes were so tired from crying.'

Then another letter arrived from Mykola. She looked at the postmark, and didn't know what to believe anymore. Soon another letter arrived, then another.

In a colossal blunder of Soviet bureaucracy, Mykola had been confused with another soldier when the notices were sent out. Mykola and Svetlana had two more sons, and now have three grandchildren, and a great grandson.

15. Borderlands

'Attila (the Hun) is our ancestor . . .' said the short, dark-skinned man standing at the foot of a great cliff of smouldering, compressed garbage. It was March 2002 and I had come to visit the Roma settlement just outside the Transylvanian city of Cluj with the nationalist mayor of the city, Georghe Funar.

Romania was about to hold a census, and the mayor was trying to persuade the Roma to declare their identity as 'Roma' or 'Romanian'— anything but 'Hungarian'. This was important to him, because if he could prove that the city was less than twenty per cent Hungarian, he could deprive them of the right to use their own language in official business, and might even be able to close down some of their schools. But the Roma were having none of it. 'We're Hungarians, descendants of Attila,' the man repeated. Funar's puffy pink face darkened. His entourage shifted nervously beside their black limousines.

About a thousand Roma lived on the municipal rubbish dump near Cluj. When the wind blew from the west, the inhabitants of the city choked on the fumes.

From the air, flying into Cluj airport, pilots navigated using the plumes of smoke. On the ground, the Roma lived in little shacks made entirely from waste materials, and scraped a living salvaging paper, glass, metals and rubbish from the junk their fellow Romanian citizens threw away. This was the Third World, embedded in Europe. Romania was well on the way to joining the European Union, and this was a side of their continent I felt European leaders in Brussels knew too little about.

As we talked with the mayor, a line of garbage trucks arrived from their morning collection round. The Roma children ran whooping towards them, then leapt with amazing alacrity onto the tail-plates, even as the drivers accelerated down the uneven road. Hanging on with one arm, the kids began sorting through the rubbish, picking off choice items, even before the trucks reached their final destination, and the whole load, plus the children, was jettisoned onto the ramp.

'It is a little bit dangerous,' Gabi, a twelve-year-old girl, grinned impishly, pushing her long black hair away from her mouth with a hand covered in sores. 'But there's a certain technique . . . if you know how to jump on the truck, you can avoid getting cut by the wheels!'

'Have you ever been cut?'

'Never!' she shouted proudly.

'Do you go to school?'

'Sometimes . . .' she giggled, and ran off to play with her friends.

Mikel Alexandre gave his age as twenty-five, but he looked much older. He said he was born in Cluj, grew up in an orphanage, then came here. He said he would declare his identity as Roma in the census.

'My nation is the Roma, and I'm not ashamed of it.'

'Can the mayor help you?'

'It's good that he came here to visit us today. That's the first step. Maybe he will start to address some of our problems.'

'And what are your problems?'

'The main problem is that there's a threat to close the dump. That would deprive us of our homes, and our livelihood.'

Julia Eötvös—her name means 'metal smith' in Hungarian—said she was forty-five, and had fifteen children. 'That's right darling, fifteen—and our life is hard.'

And what would she write in the census?

'That we're Hungarians, and Catholics. We're also Gypsies, but we speak Hungarian. We're just passing through here. We'll stay a month or two, then go home, or find work somewhere else. It's hard to make a living, especially in the winter, with so many mouths to feed . . .'

In the early 1990s, the orphanages of Romania overflowed with Roma children. Television crews stumbled on them in January 1990, on their way home from covering the revolution, and the scenes of appalling squalor shocked the world. Charities and especially churches collected money, and food and clothes arrived by the lorry-load.

One of the more successful civic initiatives in 1989 was called 'Operation Romanian Villages.' Designed to organise international resistance against Ceaușescu's plan to raze thousands of villages, the campaign encouraged villages in Britain, France and Belgium to 'adopt' a Romanian village. In the aftermath of the revolution, the campaign meant that an infrastructure of sorts was already in place, and villages organised emergency relief to the grateful Romanians, most of who had not even heard of the twinning arrangement.

As aid flowed to the orphanages, however, they became even more attractive than before as dumping grounds for Roma children. By 1999, the number of inmates had doubled from one hundred thousand to two hundred thousand.

I visited one in Cluj, a few days before Christmas of that year. Two sounds remain imprinted on my mind. The creak of the iron cots, as babies abandoned at birth rocked to and fro in hungry unison. And the crackling of paper in another room, as older children tore open Christmas presents from the West.

Abandoned children in Romania were a largely, but not uniquely Roma problem. Many Roma still travelled the country with horse-drawn wagons. Their life was extremely hard in the winter, and they used to drop the children off at a convenient orphanage in the autumn, and pick them up again, or not, in the spring. They believed they would at least be properly fed, and kept warm.

Luminica, six-months-old and born prematurely, and her brother Gheorghe, twelve-months, were the sixth and seventh children of a Roma mother who explained when she dumped them that she had a large family, no flat, her mother was out of work and her grandmother and grandfather were both alcoholics. Half the children in that orphanage were Roma.

As I walked through the garden, small children ran all around me. I felt a little hand rummaging in my shoulder bag, and turned round to find a small boy tying a knot in the corner, to stop other children from stealing anything. He was concerned for my belongings.

A scandal developed in the 1990s about the orphanages and the international adoptions. For a time, it was comparatively easy to adopt a Romanian child. Then, stunned by newspaper reports of a 'trade' in Romanian children, with middlemen and middlewomen getting rich in the process, the government cracked down. A British member of the European Parliament, Baroness Emma Nicholson, did much to publicise and campaign against the trade.

To the shame of many Romanians, their country's European Union membership came to depend on an improvement in the lot of their children, as well as proof that the government was finally tackling corruption.

'The objective is to have more and more children protected within their natural families,' Gabriela Coman, the senior government official in charge of the issue told me in June 2004. 'If one effect of the new legislation is the stopping of international adoptions for a period, then so be it.'

Two new laws, on Adoption and Child Protection, were passed in rapid succession. Dozens of orphanages were closed, and the children were either returned to their own families, sent to foster families or installed in new family-style houses where no more than twelve children of different ages would live together in a family-like environment with adults caring for them.

I visited the first orphanage to close, in Bacău, eastern Romania. Ominously known as Orphanage Number One, it was home to three to four hundred children, from babies to eighteen-year-olds. Many were anaemic and suffered from rickets. A large centralised bureaucracy in Bucharest had kept the system in its fossilised state. The key to dismantling the system was to decentralise authority to local councils, and order them to move the children to families. Deadlines were also drawn up to close big orphanages like this one. In the old days, children were always accepted from parents who said they could not cope with them. So the orphanages actually served to divide families. Under the new system, women who arrived at the door were told to take their babies home, then began to receive regular visits from social workers. A new social category, 'endangered families', was introduced.

The decentralisation of the state, I felt, would solve many problems in east-central Europe, including those of the minorities. More local autonomy would give people a greater sense of control and influence over their own lives, and less sense of depending on distant capitals. If more of the money they were paying in taxes stayed in their communities, people would also have more sense of ownership over local institutions.

In social affairs, the idea that the local council might send someone to the homes of vulnerable people, to check they were alright rather than to belabour them for unpaid bills, was also radically new in Romania. It was a similar story in the prison system in several countries. Convicts used to be released from the high-security Csillag prison in Szeged, in south-east Hungary, at five in the morning, with a train ticket, some pocket money and not much else. Post-prison support for former convicts has gradually been introduced, to help them find accommodation and work again.

The wasteground between the state and the citizen is being planted with trees. They are still rather small, but they are signs that the oppressive state can turn into a more caring one.

* * *

Another problem in Romania in the 1990s was what became of children when they left the orphanages at sixteen. In communist times, a bus would arrive to take them to live in workers' hostels, with a guaranteed job in a factory or working on the fields. After the end of communism, there was no-one to send a bus, no workers' hostels and, with unemployment over ten per cent, probably no job either. As the system changed to a family-centred one, more and more foster families agreed to look after the child till eighteen. After that, they would also keep contact and support the teenager into adulthood.

In the predominantly Hungarian-speaking county of Hargita, high in the Carpathian Mountains, Robi waited patiently by the garden gate. He wore a little blue peaked cap with a red anchor on the front, his ears protruding from the sides, and his big brown eyes lit up when he spotted his foster-father cycling up the hill towards him. Then he was hoisted up onto the handle-bars, and the two of them wobbled the last few metres up to the house, laughing uproariously.

The couple had lost their own eldest child in a car accident when he was thirteen and had adopted Robi, they told me, as a kind of consolation. They took him from the orphanage, where he had been placed when his father went to prison for murder, and his alcoholic mother couldn't cope.

'He was so pale and ill when he arrived. Now we love him like our own,' said his foster-mother.

Not all babies in Romania were so lucky. Contraceptive pills and condoms, banned under Ceauşescu's fanatical efforts to raise the population, swamped the country in the 1990s. But there was no culture of using them and abortions, also banned under Ceauşescu, soared. By 1997, Romania had the highest abortion rate in the world, one hundred and ninety-seven for every one hundred live births. Between 1990 and 1997, 4.6 million abortions were carried out, according to a UN report, in a country with a population of 22 million.

'89: The Unfinished Revolution

* * *

At Lom on the Bulgarian shore of the vast Danube, the river stretched across to the far Romanian bank like an ancient, pungent, grey-green lion.

'Ten years ago, when we started our association, only five per cent of the Gypsy children finished high school. Now its seventy-five per cent,' said Nikolai Kirilov, a local activist. Until the year 2000 only five Gypsies from the town had ever finished university. That number multiplied to forty over the next seven years.

'Everything depends on education,' said Nikolai, 'If kids don't get good marks at school, they can't play in the football team.'

The population of Lom was 32,000 people, about half of them Roma; there were also many mixed marriages.

'It's important that we teach Romany culture and language,' he said, 'but even more important that we teach Bulgarian. That will be more useful to them.'

After an hour of conversation, I pointed out that he had not uttered the words discrimination, segregation or prejudice even once. The normal narrative of the Roma activist. He shrugged.

'Those words have been devalued by overuse.'

So we talked about politics. Was he not afraid of Bulgaria's new, ultra-nationalist party, Ataka, which blamed all Bulgaria's ills on Gypsies and Turks? 'My nightmare is that we create a crazy ethnic party of our own. Then the conflict would really start,' he said.

Pastor Iliya was pouring concrete when I arrived. From all around him came the sound of hammering. Humata, the suburb of Lom where he worked as a priest of the Pentecostalist church, resembled a shipyard. Everyone seemed to be working, making the most of the fading light, as a bloodshot sun painted their homes, their arms and their faces, and the willows by the distant river a deep orange.

In predominantly Orthodox Romania and Bulgaria, Protestant churches like the Baptists, the Pentecostalists and the Seventh Day Adventists have instilled in Roma communities what can only be described as a Protestant work ethic. We were back in the early days of capitalism, it seemed, and while Karl Marx argued that human relations were shaped by the economy, the sociologist Max Weber argued that the Protestant church, and the blessing it bestowed on physical work, had powered the rise of capitalism. In Lom, Weber was winning the argument.

'I stole, I drank, I was lazy,' said Iliya, with a twinkle in his eye, playing the caricature of a Gypsy villain, on a stage of his own carpentry. 'And then I got a life-threatening illness, and I started to pray.' With God's help, he said, his whole neighbourhood had turned to Christianity. Together they built a church, rebuilt their own homes and found an energy and purpose in their lives which bordered on the miraculous.

After sunset, he directed me to a prayer meeting in a private house. Sixteen people—as diverse in age as a young toothless babe and an old toothless crone, but most in their twenties and thirties—squeezed into a tidy room. All Gypsies.

'Does anyone have a problem they would like us to mention in our prayers?' asked the man in the denim jacket, leading the meeting. Many volunteered. A teenage girl asked us to pray for her mother, who was away from home, working in Italy, and had a heart problem. Another woman wanted us to pray for the safe delivery of her baby. A man said he was deep in debt. The prayers came thick and fast, like a chant, as the people swayed to and fro in the wind of faith.

'Now I'm going to tell you a story,' said the prayer leader.

'A man was driving a packed bus down a steep hill, when suddenly a child walked out into the road in front of him. There was a cliff on one side, a ravine on the other. He had to choose between killing the child, or all his passengers. It was his own child.' The room was sunk in silence, everyone was watching him.

'The driver agonised for a moment, then smashed into the child. There was blood all over the windscreen . . .' He paused, for dramatic effect, then continued.

'That driver was God, and that child was Jesus Christ.'

*   *   *

Marcel Lakatos was the Baptist priest in Batar, a village near the city of Oradea in north-west Romania. It was July 2009 and he was fretting about whether his new kindergarten would be ready for the children in September. The basic shell of the building was there. There were even tiles down on the floor in some of the rooms, but no handrail up the stairs, and not enough money, he feared, to finish it in time. We stood together at an upstairs window, looking out over fields of maize and sunflowers on both sides of the small Crişul River. The good thing about standing at windows with priests, I noticed, not for the first time, is that neither of you feels the need to speak.

Just across the road, Iosif Fechete showed me round his house, while his wife peeled potatoes in the yard. He was one of more than a hundred Roma from Batar who regularly went to work in Belfast, Northern Ireland. A local Roma entrepreneur lived there, and smoothed the way for his fellow villagers. They got cheap housing in a run-down, Protestant area of the city, and jobs at the car-wash, or working on the fields, or selling the Belfast Telegraph to drivers at the traffic-lights. Iosif was a study in what they could achieve if they were diligent. He had two houses now, he explained proudly—a smaller, older one with just two rooms, where he and his wife and their six children used to live, and the new one just across the yard which he had built from the money he saved in Belfast. But the work was unfinished. In June 2009, he and the other hundred or so Roma from Batar fled Belfast after their homes were firebombed by local youths.

The Roma took refuge for a while in a local church, but when the windows there were smashed as well, the Roma pleaded for repatriation.

The heavens opened in Batar when I arrived, and I sheltered under a mulberry tree. Some of the younger girls stayed out in the rain. They were soaked to the skin anyway, as they scrubbed carpets clean under the village tap. There was no running water in their houses. Ioan Fechete offered me shelter in his house—but he was only joking. There was no roof! The sudden end to their Irish adventure left the Roma stranded, at home, without work or prospects.

'People were kinder to us in Belfast than in other countries, until this happened,' people told me. They had tried France and Belgium, with little success, and ended up begging on the streets to get home.

'There are very few chances for the adults to learn a new profession . . .' said Marian Daragiu, chairman of the Ruhama (Empathy) Foundation in Oradea, 'but there are chances for the young people, so our first target is not to lose another generation.' Ruhama is one of the best non-governmental organisations I have come across in many years visiting Roma communities. It gives the people a sense of their own worth, lifting them out of the trap of sitting at home, complaining and waiting for the next welfare cheque to arrive.

Tina Daragiu, Marian's wife and the co-chairperson of Ruhama, told me a story. A Roma child she knew was always in trouble, skipping school and thieving. She asked him what he would most like in the world.

'A pair of Adidas trainers.' But where would you keep them? she asked.

He showed her a place near the door, and she helped him hammer nails into the wall to hang them on. The boy got his shoes, and began attending class.

* * *

Hungary made some of the furthest reaching efforts to tackle Roma segregation after the fall of communism. Minority councils were established at local elections, to give the Roma their own elected representatives. Radio C (for 'cigány', the Hungarian word for gypsy) was set up with private money but official support in Budapest. Roma were proud to have their own, unashamedly Roma station at last. There were stories in the Romany language, and World Music as well as Gypsy music. 'This is our radio' ran the jingle, and the listeners believed it. Non-Roma youth also listened to it, as it was one of very few stations playing good music in the capital.

In more than a hundred villages across the country, András Nyírő championed a 'WiFi Village' project, to try to bridge the growing gap between those who have the new technology, and those who don't.

In Királyegyháza in southern Hungary, near the Croatian border, I went into a classroom and saw ten-year-olds with small laptop computers on each desk. The children were studying the period of King Matthias Corvinus, Hungary's most successful medieval king, and had looked up the heraldic emblems of his mercenaries, known as the Black Army, on the internet. Then they had drawn and coloured in the emblems on paper, and cut them out for a montage. In the centre of their drawings was a black crow, holding a ring in its beak on a blue background—like a window on the red and black lions and stripes of the rest of the flag.

But even as progress was made in some areas, there were setbacks in others.

Many Roma in eastern Europe have traditionally been dumped in schools for the mentally or physically handicapped. Integration has to start at school or, better still, before school, to make serious progress. Different ways have been tried to end a system which deepened segregation. In Hungary, the state tried paying primary schools extra money to accept Roma pupils, but abandoned it after the scheme back-fired. School directors began taking in more and more Roma pupils, to get the money on offer, and non-Roma parents, fearing for educational standards, began taking their children to other schools. Aid was recalibrated to encourage schools to take Roma pupils, but with no more than twenty-five per cent in one class.

It was a difficult balance to achieve. In eastern Hungary, where the majority of the Roma live, some village schools have a third, two thirds, or even three-quarters, Roma pupils—for demographic reasons. Only the Roma keep having children. Should such schools be classified as 'segregated'? Viktoria Mohácsi, a liberal member of the European Parliament of Roma background, said they were, and should be closed down and their children bussed off to the nearest town, to integrate in majority white schools. After 2002, this became the policy of the Socialist-Liberal government to which she belonged. Others disagreed, and argued that better teaching in the villages was the answer. That only there, would the parents have a chance to get involved in their children's education, and keep in contact with the teachers. I found more in common with this approach. Many villages had already lost their post offices, their shops and their police stations. Should they now also lose their schools?

Behind this debate lay another, about Roma identity, and what should actually be taught at school. Liberals who had fought heroically for equal rights for the Roma for so long were often rather luke-warm to the idea of teaching Roma history and Roma culture in mainstream schools.

If the Roma are finally accepted as the same, don't encourage them to be different, ran the argument. More traditionally-minded observers said that Roma pride was as important as equal opportunities in lifting them out of their ghettos. It was an old argument I had first heard as a student in Senegal, in West Africa. 'The word 'negro' is a stone, thrown at us,' the Algerian writer Frantz Fanon argued. 'We should pick it up, and smash the windows of our oppressors with it.' Léopold Senghor, the Paris-educated first President of an independent Senegal argued instead that the 'stone' should be picked up and polished, and presented to the world. 'Black is beautiful' was one of the slogans of the movement Senghor participated in, and which became known as 'Negritude'.

* * *

In the Czech Republic, eight Roma pupils won a historic judgement at the European Court of Human Rights in Strasbourg, stating that by placing them in a so-called 'special school' their right to education had been severely curtailed. The same court, however, ruled against a group of Croatian Roma who argued that by putting them in special 'Roma' classes within a normal school, their interests had been harmed.

Events in Hungary since 2006 suggest that all the money, time and effort poured into helping the Roma integrate, have done little more than scratch the surface of the problem.

In October 2006, in the sprawling village of Olaszliszka in eastern Hungary, Lajos Szögi, a geography teacher from a nearby town, was driving slowly home with his two daughters, when a Roma girl ran out suddenly in front of him. He caught her a glancing blow, and stopped his car to check she wasn't badly hurt. She picked herself up, and ran off. A crowd of local Roma then surrounded him and beat him to death in front of his own, terrified daughters. The father of the girl who had been hit was heard to say 'if necessary, I will kill a hundred Hungarians'.

The words were repeated at his trial. He and seven accomplices were sentenced to long prison terms, in a trial which ended in May 2009.

The incident has had a disastrous effect on race-relations in Hungary. 'Gypsy-crime' was a term which had been used during communist times, when the racial origin of offenders was noted on their police records, but was then banned under human rights and data protection legislation in the early 1990s. But from 2006 onwards, the phrase was resurrected by a section of the far-right, who blamed the Roma for the deteriorating public order in the countryside. Politicians and parts of the media began using the term, too.

A re-organisation of the police under the liberal Interior Minister, Gábor Kuncze, had made the situation worse. In order to save money, many local police stations were closed, and the already demoralised, under-paid police concentrated in the main towns. Villages which had already lost their village shop, post office and school now lost any personal, everyday contact with the police. One could drive fifty or even a hundred kilometres through the Hungarian countryside without seeing a policeman. There were parallels to France, where police reforms under Nicholas Sarkozy as Interior Minister, before he became President, also took the police out of communities where they used to be accepted. This was one of the causes of the Paris riots in the autumn of 2005.

In Hungary, the segregation of the Roma from the non-Roma population grew rapidly after 1989, instead of decreasing. High rents and unpaid bills squeezed them out of the towns to which they had gravitated since the 1960s. They either went back to villages they had left long before, or anywhere they could find. Roma ghettos spread out on the lower ground near the stream in many villages. Without land of their own, and with little prospect of anything other than seasonal agricultural work, they festered. Petty theft, politely known as 'crimes of survival', grew.

At a press conference held by an animal welfare group, devoted to the problem of battery chickens, a journalist innocently asked just how many hens there were in Hungary. Pál Földi, chairman of the Poultry Board, gave a number, then added that 'for reasons we all know, very few people keep hens in eastern Hungary anymore.' I asked him afterwards to forgive my ignorance, and to tell me why. 'Because the Roma steal them—but I'm not allowed to say that, because I will be accused of racism,' he said.

The only factor keeping the Roma from starvation was a well-developed system of state welfare payments, especially child support—which was more or less equal to the minimum wage. Second and third generation Roma grew up without ever having seen their parents work, let alone having held down a job themselves.

'The welfare cheques arrive on the fifth of the month,' Robi, a father of eight children told me in the village of Magyargéc in northern Hungary, 'but by the time our debts to the local shop are paid, the rest of the money only lasts till the middle of the month.'

Under communism, Robi had a job in the glass factory, 30km away. That job had gone in the early 1990s. Then there was occasional labouring work, as local builders drove through the ghettos, looking for able-bodied men, and paid them a day rate. By the late 2000s, with the recession beginning to bite, that work has dried up too.

The Roma also did each other few favours. One of the better-off Roma families in Rakacaszend, in north-east Hungary, proudly showed me the pigs in their yard, and the good marks their children had received at school. In the gloom of the single room in which eight of them lived, the childrens' eyes and teeth gleamed white with pride as their parents spoke of their achievements. But their father said that it was not worth repeating last year's experiment, when he had negotiated with the mayor to work a plot of common land in the village, and to plant several rows of maize—tengeri as it is known in Hungarian slang—meaning 'the sea', because of its distant origins. Just as it was getting ripe, poorer Gypsies stole their whole crop. This year he wouldn't bother to plant any, he said sadly.

Rakacaszend had a primary school, at least. András Tóth, the local Greek Catholic priest, and his wife, Anna, had restored the derelict building, raised the funds and re-launched the school and kindergarten in the late 1990s. It was the only new primary school to open in the whole country. They even offered lunch to the pupils, some of whom never received a hot meal at home. Officious inspectors from the ÁNTSZ, the state hygiene authority, finally put an end to the meals. There were not enough taps in the kitchen, they said, and withdrew their permit to prepare food. Under the more radical definition of segregation, that school too would have been forced to close, because in the lower classes, the majority of pupils were Roma.

The practice of usury, the lending of money at an exorbitant rate of interest, was also a serious problem within the Roma community. It was hard enough for non-Roma farmers, with land and a home and even a steady job, to borrow money from the banks. How much harder for the Roma, who could only turn to unscrupulous businessmen within their own community. When Roma mayors were elected in majority Roma communities, the mayor sometimes ran the racket himself. But the system worked in a way, however unfairly. It brought money into villages where there might otherwise have been none.

In the capital, sociologists and, occasionally, politicians wrung their hands about the Roma issue. Scholarships were announced and awarded, integration projects were financed and did have a limited impact, but the situation for the majority got worse.

There was also little dialogue in society about the growing problem of rural poverty and, within that, of Roma poverty.

In a normal country, neighbourhood watch groups might have helped bring order to the countryside. In Hungary, however, to join the organisation you had first to prove that you had an unblemished past. Most Roma have a criminal record, often for as small an offence as repeatedly not sending a child to school, or cycling at night without a lamp. In their unlit, frequently muddy streets, the Roma got on with their increasingly segregated lives, and sometimes fell back on theft—of firewood from privatised woods, corn from privatised fields, or worse.

'Our fellow nationals from the minority are not interested in co-existence,' commented Albert Pásztor, police chief of the eastern Hungarian city of Miskolc in January 2009. Then he went further. 'We can state clearly that robberies committed in public places are carried out by Gypsies. Apart from bank-robberies and petrol-station holdups, all other robberies in Miskolc are carried out by them.'

As news of his comments reached Budapest, he was fired by the Interior Minister, and then reinstated within forty-eight hours. A large demonstration was held, supported by all the main parties, and even by some Roma organisations. There was a growing comprehension gap between the capital and the provinces.

A far-right youth group, Jobbik, was founded in 2003, and began to grow rapidly during the street protests against the Gyurcsány government in the autumn of 2006.

While István Csurka's Hungarian Justice and Life Party had blamed Hungary's problems on the Jews, and an alleged conspiracy of international capital rooted in Tel Aviv, Jobbik identified the Roma as a scapegoat for Hungary's ills. They called for action against 'Gypsy crime', and decided it was time to root it out.

In August 2007 they set up a paramilitary organisation, the Hungarian Guard Association for the Protection of Traditions and Culture, to 'restore law and order' in the Hungarian countryside. They held marches, shows of force, in towns and villages which were home to a large Roma community. By the time they were banned by a Budapest court in December 2008, they had three thousand members. The ruling was upheld in July 2009 and, from then on, Hungarian police have attempted to break up any attempt by the Guard to hold public rallies in uniform.

In the elections to the European Parliament in June 2009, Jobbik won fifteen per cent of the vote, largely on an anti-Roma platform.

The leader of Jobbik, Gábor Vona, strenuously denies that they are racist.

'What we're saying is that there is a problem in Hungary which has been swept under the carpet for quite a while now. And Jobbik is basically just trying to open a discussion about it.'

'Please define the problem.'

'As we see it, petty crime is associated with the Roma in the countryside. It is, unfortunately, widespread, and the statistics which are of course not official, but also press statements and leaked information show that the criminality rate amongst the Roma population is much higher than among the Hungarians.'

András Biró, a longstanding champion of Roma rights and integration, surprisingly agreed.

'It's terrible that in Hungary only the far-right, including the neo-Nazis, dare to speak without inhibitions, and that is how we have reached a situation in which today the only people offering a clear, strategic 'solution' to the problems of the Roma are the Hungarian Guard with their 'Gypsy crime' slogan.'

A time-bomb was ticking in Hungarian society, Biró said, in relations between the minority and majority.

Unlike Vona, he called on the majority to confront their own racism, and speak honestly about all the other problems the country faced as well.

Parallel to the rise of Jobbik, armed attacks began on outlying Roma settlements in July 2008, and carried on into 2009. In the early morning of 23 February 2009, Robert Csorba and his five-year-old son were woken by a Molotov cocktail thrown through their window. As Robert ran from the burning room, his son in his arms, they were hit at close range by the blast of a shotgun. Both died. They were the third and fourth victims.

Jenő Koka was the fifth. As he came out of his house in Forget-Me-Not Street in the Roma settlement near Tiszalök at nine-thirty in the evening two months later, he was killed with a single shot to the heart, probably from a car parked across the street. He was on his way to work on the night-shift in the local chemical factory where he had been employed for most of his life.

On the morning of his funeral, boys cycled with wreaths, instead of their brothers and sisters, on their handlebars, through the sleepy streets of Tiszalök. More than a thousand people gathered for the funeral. The wind blew the candles of white flowers in the horse-chestnut trees, and a band playing clarinet, violins and double-bass followed the coffin to the graveside.

'Am I my brother's keeper?' Beside the coffin, Pastor Gábor Iványi quoted Cain, addressing God after killing his brother Abel, in the Biblical story. After the funeral, I drove north, towards the vine-clad hills of Tokaj, and waited beside the wide, blonde Tisza for the river ferry to take me across.

'We just feel sorry for them, really sorry,' said the ferryman. 'There is no ethnic hatred here.'

Forty-five-year-old Mária Balogh was the sixth victim, and the first to be killed as she lay sleeping in her house in the village of Kisléta, 50km east of Tiszalök, at the beginning of August. Her thirteen-year-old daughter, Ketrin, suffered multiple gunshot wounds. They had planned to spend the day together, picking tobacco in the fields.

The police offered a half million dollar reward to trace the killers, and set up a fifty member task force to hunt them down. The task force was gradually increased to one hundred and twenty.

Common features of each of the attacks—the weapons used, the fact that only homes right on the edge of Roma settlements were hit and the proximity of a motorway each time—led the police to believe the same group was responsible.

There were atrocities, too, against the 'white majority', which Jobbik and the Hungarian Guard emphasised on their web-sites. While much of the media carried maps of the attacks on Roma settlements, Jobbik questioned whether some of the Roma victims were Roma in the first place, and put another map on the same page, listing alleged 'Gypsy crimes'. As of July 2009, their map had thirty dots, ranging from 'Roma mob' to murder. There was no separate category for 'white mob', or for attacks by people with grey, blue or brown eyes.

In early February 2009, Marion Cozma, a Romanian star in the handball team in Veszprém in western Hungary, was enjoying a night out with other team-members in a night club, when a group of Roma, known locally as the Enying Mafia after the small town they lived in, started smashing the place up. Subsequent newspaper reports suggested the club had not paid its protection money. When the handball team tried to confront the vandals, Cozma was stabbed in the heart, and died almost immediately. Two other team members were badly injured. The culprits were caught within hours, but the damage was done. Media reports and locals who came to lay flowers or light candles at the scene blamed the Roma collectively for the killing. The handball team, very successful in international competitions, was the pride of the town and a force to be reckoned with in international handball. It was as if David Beckham had been killed in England. A documentary film *A Country Stabbed in the Heart* was made, and shown in cinemas across Hungary.

'The Gypsies have been the losers of every political system . . .' János Kozák, President of the Roma Local Council in Veszprém told the weekly HVG, '. . . and we are now drinking the juice (suffering the consequences) of the present crisis, because crimes like the one in Veszprém have turned public opinion against us.'

'Unfortunately the possibilities available to the police are limited, and their outlook is not what it used to be,' added his father, a Roma politician on the national level.

'A part of the Hungarians believe the police cannot protect them any more, and the Gypsies have never seen the cops as partners ... For as long as the Gypsies don't find new work-places, and as their level of education does not rise, it will be hard to reduce criminality in their ranks.' If a white politician had said it, he would have been ostracised as a racist.

Mária Balogh was the last to die at the hands of the serial killers who targeted the Roma. Until midnight on 20 August 2009, shots had been fired at sixteen houses, endangering the lives of fifty-five people, according to the police squad investigating the incidents. Eleven Molotov cocktails had been thrown. From the police side, the details of one and a half million cars, and data from several million telephone calls, were processed. At two o'clock in the morning of 21 August, a Friday, police commandos raided Perényi-1, a nightclub in the eastern city of Debrecen, and arrested four men—a former drummer, a pastry chef and two security guards—who worked there. DNA samples taken from them corresponded to traces found at the scene of the crimes, the police claimed. Weapons found at their homes furnished further proof, they added. The biggest manhunt in Hungarian police history was over.

* * *

The crimes committed against Roma, like the crimes allegedly committed by them, concealed a bigger picture of grinding rural poverty. In 2006, the Hungarian Academy of Sciences drew up a National Programme to Combat Child Poverty, to run until 2032. It is a bold and complex vision, to protect even the interests of those not yet born.

In Szécsény, in the Ipoly River valley in north-west Hungary, up on the Slovak border, I saw some of its first fruits. As the children at the village kindergarten, about half of them Roma, chanted the songs and poems they had learnt at the end of term concert, I slipped next door with Judit Berki, the local manager of the programme, to see the Childrens' House she had established. Above all, it served the Gypsies of Petőfi Street, the poorest of the poor, who had no running water, no indoor toilets, and whose homes were infested with rats. Walking home after the kindergarten concert, hand in hand down the squalour of their street, pretty and bright in their freshly-ironed shirts as two poppies at the roadside, the two Rácz sisters reminded me of girls I had seen on the outskirts of Indian cities, brushing their hair neatly, pulling on their school satchels, almost floating above the slums around them.

In the Childrens' House, there were washing and cleaning facilities for the families, hot food once a day, and a place for mothers and children to play. Poverty reproduces itself endlessly in Hungarian villages like this one. Roma children arrive at kindergarten, if they attend one at all, years behind the development of non-Roma children, who have books in their homes, and at least one working parent. Part of the aim of the programme is to restore a sense of dignity to the poor, and to the Roma in particular.

In countries with large and growing Roma communities, the problems of the minorities are becoming those of the majorities. The future of social peace and prosperity depends on each country finding answers, with support from the rest of Europe.

Afterword

> But when society was given freedom it could not recognize itself, for
> it had lived too long, as it were, 'beyond the looking glass' . . .
> Mikhail Gorbachev

In the autumn of 2008, the world that the brave countries of central
and eastern Europe had endured such pains to join, began to fall
apart. They were back in Gorbachev's mirror at last, but the mirror
developed a crack. Respected American lenders crashed, Iceland went
into financial meltdown, and even the sturdy Germans admitted they
were in trouble. For eighteen years, east European economies had
grown steadily. In terms of foreign investment, Hungary led the way
at first, then fell behind as the Czech Republic and Poland, then the
Baltic Republics, and finally Romania and Bulgaria boomed. Medieval
Transylvanian cities like Braşov and Cluj, wounded but not killed by
Ceauşescu's architectural nightmares, disappeared behind shopping
malls, multiplex cinemas and brash car showrooms. It was fast, it was
tasteless, it brought a lot of work in the construction industry, and
the public relations officers insisted it was just what the people wanted.
Then the bubble burst.

At one point around the turn of the millennium, the mayor of
Budapest, Gábor Demszky, told me there were twenty-five big shopping
malls under construction in his city at that very moment. Can't you stop
them? I asked, naively. 'The market decides . . .' he shrugged. As we flew
over the city in a small private aircraft, he even seemed quite proud of
them. Only the 14th district of Budapest resisted, as the district mayor,
Tamás Derce, tried to defend local shop-owners. He was sued by one of
the mall operators. Deprived of the thrills of the consumer society for
so long, east and central Europeans spent their weekends in the corridors
of Tesco or Praktiker or Auchan or Ikea—or stuck in the traffic on the
stretches of motorway which connected them to their homes.

The global economic meltdown would prove the biggest test so far of the new institutions—political, social and economic—which have been built in each country since the collapse of communism. That test has only just begun, but there are some early indications.

Eastern Europeans, unlike their western European cousins, have always found it hard to get credit. Interest rates were high and many people found it hard to prove their regular income, as so much of it came from moonlighting, and the poorest of the poor—the Roma—often had no title deed to their homes, or at least not to the land they were built on. The fact that somewhere in America, banks had cheerfully lent vast sums to tens of thousands of people who had no hope of paying it back, and that this had triggered the domino effect which brought the global financial system to its knees, added insult to injury.

EU membership has made it somewhat easier for the population to borrow money. Low interest loans, offered by the banks in Euros or Swiss Francs, proved especially attractive. The public sank or, in their own eyes, grew rapidly into debt.

One Sunday afternoon in early October 2008, the Hungarian Prime Minister, Ferenc Gyurcsány, picked up his phone and dialled the British Prime Minister, Gordon Brown. Gyurcsány had enjoyed a particularly warm relationship with Brown's predecessor, Tony Blair, and hoped he could count on British help now, too.

Most observers assumed, initially at least, that eastern Europe would not be hit by the crisis. Most banks in the region were in foreign hands, daughter branches of large Austrian, German, Italian, Dutch and Belgium mother institutions. Central and eastern Europeans felt well tied-in to the EU economy. Slovenia was already using the Euro, and Slovakia was about to adopt it. Several countries, led by Slovakia, had attracted car manufacturing plants, to the chagrin of west European workers, who lost their jobs as a result. A new Nokia city was under construction in Cluj in Romania.

Unlike some of those from the richer world, central European banks had not made 'poisonous loans'—reckless transactions—to people or institutions which were unlikely to pay them back. Austerity policies, pursued at high speed in Hungary, and more reluctantly in Poland and the Czech Republic, but from a less awful starting position, were having a tangible effect. Hungary's budget deficit had been cut back from a record eleven to five per cent, and was still falling. In its most recent reports to the Foreign and Commonwealth Office in London, the British embassy in Budapest had recorded progress, not panic.

Then Gordon Brown picked up the receiver. 'Hello Gordon, it's Ferenc.'

The British Prime Minister listened patiently as his Hungarian counterpart outlined the problem. Hungary was in big trouble after all. Its whole financial system ran on credit, especially the selling of state bonds to finance its burgeoning debt. If the life blood of the global markets was reduced, the Hungarian patient would rapidly become anaemic. In Gyurcsány's view, it was going to faint. He wanted British support to obtain a stop-gap loan from the International Monetary Fund.

Three days later, Brown mentioned Hungary in the same breath as Iceland and Ukraine, as a country whose example the United Kingdom should not imitate. It was a horrible blow to Budapest.

The cat was out of the bag, and the kittens were in shock. A colleague from a BBC Radio business programme rang Márk Kotsis, chief political correspondent at Hungarian radio, to interview him about the 'collapse' of the Hungarian economy. He did the best he could to deny knowledge of any impending disaster, and then rang me.

'Why on earth do the British think we are in such trouble?' he asked.

I promised to try to find out.

The extent of the crisis only leaked out in dribs and drabs. The mother banks abroad starved their local branches in Hungary of cash. Household borrowing proved another huge problem. The Hungarian currency, the forint, plunged like the Polish zloty. The big loans that Hungarians had taken out on their homes and cars became more painful. The little college car-park behind my flat, which used to have a couple of broken down Trabants and Wartburgs, plus a few contraptions which engineering students built and rebuilt themselves from scrap, was now full of little Suzukis, Opel Astras and other shiny models which students' parents bought for them on the never-never. The number of cars on the Hungarian roads had leaped from 1.73 million to 3.06 million in twenty years. Of these, the number of legendary Trabants fell from a proud 376,000 to 66,000.

But in the wake of the economic crash, the Hungarian currency lost value, and the cost of the monthly repayments soared.

Thousands of people lost their homes as the bailiffs moved in. Tens of thousands lost their cars. On the lamp-posts of the city, desperate pieces of paper appeared—'100 square metre flat, 13th district, urgent sale.' Even on smart pedestrian streets, second-hand clothes shops multiplied. Most had a British flag in the shop-window. 'Genuine used British clothes—complete stock replacement every Thursday!'

Late one Saturday night in November, I was trying to drive the foxes from my garden—unsure whether their tameness was due to the neighbours who fed them or from rabies—when the phone rang. The news had just been announced in Washington. Hungary was to be provided with a \$25 billion, IMF-led loan.

There is a certain procedure among us BBC correspondents at such times. We carefully close the doors of our partner's and our children's bedroom, if they haven't thrown us out long ago, on account of the strange hours we keep. We rig up a satellite dish in an upstairs window, or on a table in the yard, trained on an invisible satellite locked into orbit above the Indian Ocean. We set a computer to downloading the latest wire agency reports, and relevant interviews translated by the indefatigable staff at the BBC Monitoring Service, in their white, Victorian-era stately home in Caversham, Berkshire. Known as 'the ears of Britain' it was set up on the eve of the Second World War to monitor broadcasts. Imre Nagy's last desperate plea for international help was recorded there at dawn on 4 November 1956, as Soviet tanks swept into Budapest.

We then read back through any research and reports we have done recently and, if it is not too late, we ring a few people whose opinions we respect, and whose take on the situation ideally differs from one another. We then tap out short, forty-five to seventy-five second summaries of the information we have gleaned, and what it might mean. In the meantime, we answer questions through ancient-looking brown microphones, one bar of which rests on our top lips, where moustaches used to grow. Once I did all this at gunpoint, in Turkey, while a young soldier waited politely for me to finish before he questioned me. I had inadvertently set up my equipment next to an army base. But that is another story.

A few days before Christmas 2008, Zsolt Magulya arrived as usual at the glass factory in Salgótarján in northern Hungary where he had worked for nine years. As he left home that morning, his wife Nikoletta reminded him to ask if there was going to be any Christmas bonus. Instead he was told not to bother to come in from the following Tuesday. His job, along with several hundred others, had been axed.

In the first three months of 2009, sixteen per cent of Hungarians asked in one poll had recently lost their jobs. Some found new ones, others did not. Unemployment reached ten per cent.

A deeper, longer term problem in Hungary is how few people actually work in the legal economy, and pay tax on their earnings. Early retirement, disability and a host of other factors have conspired to keep the employment figure among the lowest in Europe—around fifty-four per cent of the working age population. The European Union average is sixty-four per cent, and some countries, like the Czech Republic, stand at over seventy per cent. As a result, in Hungary the working population are tortured by ever more, and ever more complicated, taxes, to carry the rest of the population on their back. This also further fuels the hostility towards the Roma.

A more common problem through the region is the aging of the population. In 1990, women married, on average, at twenty-two. By the twentieth anniversary of the revolutions of 1989, that figure had risen to twenty-nine—for those who bothered to get married at all. Under communism, adults usually became grandparents in their late forties. If they then retired at fifty-five, they could play a central role in caring for their grandchildren. More often than not, they also helped out by providing accommodation or money for their children. Nowadays, the children are more financially stable, and often live further away. Millions of grandparents have become redundant, but they have little money to enjoy their new leisure. Living on small pensions, they watch with astonishment, from the park-benches of Prague and Warsaw, Kraków and Budapest, as their comparatively wealthy counterparts from America or western Europe wander past in fashionable clothes, and wile away their retirement at expensive riverside cafés and restaurants.

* * *

As the global financial fortress crumbled, the sound of fireworks split the air above the muddy streets of Zizin in central Romania. I stood in a crowd, talking to the priest and the owners of the many horses and carts which plied the lanes. Then realised suddenly that these were not fireworks at all. On the top of a hummock overlooking the village, lads cracked long horsewhips in the wintry air. They sounded good, and they were in any case, all the kids here had.

The recession had hit this mainly Gypsy village hard. 'We used to be paid half a dollar a kilo for this stuff,' said Ion Otelas, gesticulating at a pile of metal stacked up in the corner of his stable. It included a car door, a coil of barbed wire and a contraption radiating metal spokes which might have been a giantess's hairbrush. 'Now we only get five cents a kilo.' The Chinese building industry had frozen, thanks to the recession. It was a shock to find out that the scrap metal trade of Gypsies in the long shadows of the Carpathian Mountains was so closely tied to the production of reinforced concrete, three or four oceans away. Tramp steamers en route to China and India on the high seas received radio messages to turn back. And Ion Otelas's metal rusted in his stable. There was no longer any point in loading it up onto his cart.

There was another problem nagging at the Romanian Gypsies' minds. On the day their country and Bulgaria joined the European Union, 1 January 2007, the Romanian government decreed that horses and carts were henceforth banned from all main roads. It was true that there were many accidents. A speeding car on an unlit road might turn a corner to discover a long wooden cart, loaded with timber or the worldly possessions of a family, travelling at only 5km an hour, three seconds away from impact. But the problem could have been solved with better lights on the carts, more reflective clothing and a better driving culture among the new rich. Instead, the horses and carts were driven off the roads, and repeat offenders faced stiff fines. I felt that the real reason for the ban was that the ruling bureaucrats in Bucharest were ashamed that the horse and cart remained, in twenty-first century Romania, the main means of transport in many rural communities. They tried to solve the 'problem' with one cruel stroke of their pens.

It was the same story when it came to the production of sheep's cheese in Romania, in the hills above Sibiu. Shepherds still practised transhumance—taking their herds down onto the distant plains to overwinter, each autumn. They walked vast distances up to their home villages in the mountains in time for Easter; keeping the sheep in pens to protect them from marauding wolves and bears, as far away as six hours' walk from the nearest road. They churned their milk in wooden barrels to make brindza, a delicious sheep's cheese which fetched a decent sum in the twenty remaining open markets of Bucharest. Then the hygiene officials arrived, with their new regulations. Only stainless steel drums should be used from then on. Cheese must be produced in new factories beside the main roads. Identical packages must be manufactured, for mass distribution to the supermarkets and hypermarkets which scar the landscape. The bureaucrats who thrived under Ceauşescu, whose main pleasure in life seemed to lie in persecuting others, had won a new lease of life with European Union membership.

'Do you actually like brindza?' I asked the head of the Food Safety Inspectorate, Marian Avram, in his Bucharest office.

'Of course I do, provided I'm sure its not going to poison me. I am not against traditional producers. What I am against is extremist traditionalism.'

He made it sound like a new front in the war on terror.

As the recession bit, the Dacia car works at Piteşti, producer of the rugged Logan, extremely popular on the pot-holed roads of Romania and Columbia, announced compulsory extended holidays, as orders plummeted. Other car-makers, in Slovakia, the Czech Republic and Hungary, followed.

In his prison cell a kilometre away from the Dacia factory where he used to work, Ion Galant groaned. He was serving a twelve year sentence for trafficking women to Italy. He also had gangrene in his feet.

'I will never get out of this prison alive,' he told me, in despair. 'Instead, I'm leaving here bit by bit,' and he gesticulated at one of his rotting limbs. When he felt well enough, he worked, suitably bandaged, in the prison bakery. Before I left, he gave me three fresh baked loaves, still hot from the oven, round as cannonballs, or cobble stones from the French Revolution.

*   *   *

From his new vantage point at the entrance to the Budapest Statue Park, Vladimir Ilyich Ulyanov, better known as Lenin, appears to be having second thoughts. The bronze sculpture, cast by Pál Pátzay in 1965, used to stand next to where János Herner's egg-timer now safeguards the free-flow of history.

For a society which used to lionise Lenin, this one was small. At only two metres, the statue was only a bit bigger than the man himself. In his original position, Lenin was designed to seem accessible, a real man of the people. To distinguish him from them, however, and to emphasise the power of his message, a fifteen metre high concrete column, dressed in Swedish red granite, stood behind him. In his left hand is some kind of scroll—presumably his speech. His right hand is thrust deep in his coat pocket. At the Statue Park, he has lost his granite, and now stands much smaller and more humble, in a cavity in the tall brick wall to the left of the entrance. Unlike other Lenins—the one that used to stand at the entrance to the Iron Works in Csepel, for example—this one looks as though he is about to return to the stage, because there was one more thing that he forgot to mention. 'Always remember,' I would have added in his place, 'that this is only an experiment. Don't take yourselves too seriously.'

On the right side of the entrance, Marx and Engels, chiselled from grey Mauthausen granite in the Cubist style, grace a similar cavity, gazing impassively beneath sharp eyebrows towards the family homes, electricity pylons and an image of a palm tree, advertising a garden centre.

The Statue Park on a late September day is full of the customary tourists. 'Some of the art is much better than I expected,' a Swedish man with a sketch pad tells me, as we rest at the feet of a limestone monument to the Soviet liberation. At the centre of the park is a reproduction of the flower-bed which used to be maintained in the middle of Adam Clark Square, between the bridge and the tunnel; the centre point of the star was taken to be the geographic centre of Budapest.

To walk between the forty or so exhibits is to be reminded of the vast scale of the communist dream. The dark bronze 'liberating Soviet soldier' is six metres high, and used to stand guard at the foot of the 'Genius of Liberty' statue on Gellért Hill. We could see it from our old bedroom window. The Soviet soldier was modelled on Vasili Ivanovich Golovcov, according to the Statue Park brochure. The 'spirit of liberty' has survived the outbreak of liberty, and still holds her palm branch over the city. There was some debate in 1990 over whether that statue too should be removed, with its connotations of Soviet domination. But the daughter of the actress after whom it was modelled argued successfully that her mother had nothing to do with the ideology imposed on Hungary for four decades, but was chosen on account of her physical beauty.

Exhibit twenty-four in the park used to be one of my favourites. It was erected on the edge of Budapest's Vérmező Park in 1986, the year I moved to the city. It shows Béla Kun, a Hungarian revolutionary who witnessed the Russian Revolution, standing beneath a street light above a crowd of protesters. His outstretched left arm, holding his hat, directs them forwards though he leans back, away from them. As they march, they are transformed from civilians into Red Army soldiers. Kun believed in revolutionary violence, and that the end justifies the means. He also believed, as did Lenin, that the Russian Revolution had to be exported in order to succeed. He tried first of all in Hungary, where communist rule lasted four months in the chaos at the end of the First World War. In Austria, Kun directed the communist attempt to seize power, but was thwarted by a police raid in June 1918. In Germany in 1921, the workers were only luke-warm to the comrades' exhortations to violent revolution, and the police nipped the protests there too in the bud. Kun died, a broken man, in one of Stalin's many prisons at the height of the purges in 1937. The beauty of Imre Varga's statue is that it manages to incorporate all of this.

Looking through the small shop as I left the park, I spotted a poster from the Young Democrats (Fidesz) 1990 election campaign. At the top, Brezhnev and Honecker, the greying former Soviet and East German leaders, are passionately kissing one another on the lips. Beneath, a young couple on a park bench are caught in the same posture. 'Please Choose' reads the slogan—'Association of Young Democrats.'

'I loved that one,' a girl who must have been born around 1990, laughs to her friend as they leave the park. The taxi driver who picks me up confides that he has not been to the Statue Park at all, but has been out for a romantic walk with his lover in the woods beyond.

* * *

For the twentieth anniversary of 1989, I made a radio programme about the role of environmentalists in bringing down the communist system in Hungary. The big demonstrations against the Gabčikovo-Nagymaros hydro-electric project on the Danube were one of the first fruits on the tree of popular protest. First of all, they succeeded in dragging people out of their apathy, and onto the streets. Then they succeeded in stopping the Hungarian side of the project, though the Slovak's completed their side, as related in Chapter Seven.

'I sincerely believe Hungarians made two big contributions to the history of the twentieth century,' Gábor Karátson told me, as we sat on the terrace of my flat in the late September sunshine. 'The 1956 Revolution, and the prevention of the dam at Nagymaros.' He had played a role in both, and was sent to prison for his troubles in 1956.

The next day I drove along the dykes of Szigetköz, the land of a thousand islands, which the Slovak diversion of the river left high and dry in October 1992. In lower Szigetköz, dry weeds stand shoulder high among the poplars and the willows in the old flood plain of the river.

There is water in the side-branch, but the levels are three or four metres lower than they should be at this time of year, I was told by an angler on the bank. He had been there six hours so far, without a single catch. The tasty bream used to be especially large and plentiful, he said. Now they were rare. The main river is so low that the fish cannot make it up into the side arms to spawn.

In the upper Szigetköz, József Kertész from the Northern Danube Environmental Authority took me to see the work he and other civil engineers had done in a desperate attempt to save the region. Slovakia only provides a fifth of the water which used to run in the old river bed. Four-fifths goes to drive the turbines at Gabčikovo, in the canal they built as a kind of water motorway. Since 1992, the Hungarians have diverted water from the old bed into the side arms, and then let it flow through a complicated system of channels to wherever it is needed. It has had a huge impact, keeping the surface and ground water levels up and saving, they dare to hope, the huge underground reservoir of drinking water stored in several hundred metres of gravel, beneath the area.

'We have this great river, like an artery flowing through the country,' said Karátson. 'And it is not only the physical greatness of this river, but its energy. Not the energy which engineers think about, that we can use for electricity, but the vitalizing energy which goes through the whole region.'

'What we need now is an ecological change of system, not a political one. The political system under which we suffered for forty years was, after all, just a side branch of a global capitalistic system, which is destroying the earth.'

* * *

When and how do revolutions end? Some historians place the end of the French Revolution in December 1799, when Napoleon's Constitution of the Year VIII came into force, giving Napoleon dictatorial powers. Others might say that the simple repetition of the mantra 'liberty, equality, fraternity' is like breathing on the old, still glowing embers.

As I have argued in this book, I see the revolutions in east-central Europe as a work in progress—and far from complete. In their current form, they began in 1989, though their roots lie much earlier—in 1980 in Gdańsk, in 1968 in Czechoslovakia, in 1956 in Hungary, in 1953 in

East Berlin. As outbursts of patriotic spirit, and the desire for national sovereignty, they date back to 1848.

What they have in common is the simple desire of ordinary people for the freedom to influence their own lives. The totalitarian state established in Stalin's shadow mellowed to an authoritarian state long before 1989 in most countries. The 'infrastructure of oppression' was dismantled in 1990, and a new architecture set up in its place. The padded doors of ministries, which once muffled so efficiently the sounds within, were replaced with glass—albeit frosted glass. The people can now at least see the moving shapes of their elected representatives, even if they cannot, or do not, hold them to account.

The problem is that the authoritarian reflexes, in both rulers and ruled, run very deep.

'For about five years after 1990,' according to the Hungarian sociologist Elemér Hankiss, 'people genuinely felt that 'this is my government.' For as long as the euphoria of 1989 lasted, the sense of empowerment lasted with it. But the people proved, in most cases, unable to consolidate their power, or the power they imagined they now had. As the political parties grasped this, they moved to re-occupy the space in society, and above all in peoples' minds, which the single party used to occupy. Life became over-politicised, over-party-politicised, and to a large extent, still is. The media have played a significant role in this, by turning to party politicians for their opinions on subjects which economists, trade unionists, scientists or lorry-drivers would be more competent to answer. And once one has the opinion of one politician, the need for balance requires one to seek the opinion of her or his rival, and the downward spiral continues.

In many countries, there has also been a fundamental misunderstanding of the art of politics by its new practitioners. It is not just the art of eloquence, but also of compromise. There is too little recognition that it is a game. There is still too much fear, and loathing.

The Programme for International Student Assessment (PISA) of the Organisation for Economic Co-operation and Development compares the abilities of students in many countries, to 'analyse, reason and communicate effectively'. The east Europeans in general, and the Hungarians in particular, had long prided themselves on their educational achievements. Historical and geographical dates and names were drilled into the pupils heads, mathematics was well taught, literature, it was assumed, was cherished—especially national literature.

The PISA project results in 2000 came as a great shock in Hungary. The pupils were very weak when it came to comprehending a text, as opposed to simply learning it. It was as though their teachers had forgotten to encourage their critical faculties. For me, that is symptomatic of one of the main problems for the new democracies—the citizens feel weak, and as reluctant to challenge their elected rulers as they once were to challenge their unelected ones. The institutions of state get away with too much.

Maternity care, as I tried to show in Chapter Eleven, is a useful gauge of the empowerment of women, in the most powerful, but also the most vulnerable moments of their lives. I could equally have chosen the handling of death in institutions, or for that matter, the handling of disease.

Too little has been said in this narrative about workers' rights. As western investment poured into the region after 1990, big companies created literally millions of jobs to absorb some of those who found themselves unemployed when the old 'socialist' industries went to the wall.

New codes of conduct were drawn up in labour relations, often without the involvement of trade unions. Some of the new companies do not even allow trade union activity at the workplace. Others offer generous sick pay, but maintain clauses which make it very easy to dump surplus labour from one day to the next. Trade union web pages from eastern Europe read like the blog of Napoleon's officers during the retreat from Moscow.

On the other hand, the power of lobbies is very strong. Industrial lobbies, professional lobbies, even citizens' lobbies. It is a picture full of contradictions. As I showed in the chapter on birth, a small clique of obstetricians has so far prevented the normalisation of home-birth in Hungary, against the best efforts of the public. Midwives, who ought to have strong lobbying powers themselves, have failed to organise and to fight for their rights as a separate profession. That would be an important part of the solution to the artificial wall of hostility which Ágnes Geréb now faces. Another important step would be an independent audit of maternity services, as frequently carried out in more advanced democracies, and indeed, of all hospital care. The patients have a right to know what is on offer. Especially as, one way or another, they are paying for it.

At the other end of the scale, local lobbies have so far prevented the broadening of Route 10 from the Pilis Hills into Budapest.

As a result, tens of thousands of people lose valuable hours of their lives each day in endless traffic jams. The Hungarians have proved, in public life, singularly incapable of striking compromises with one another.

* * *

I would not like to paint too grim a picture. The achievements of 1989 are tangible everywhere. There is, on the whole, freedom of movement. There is freedom of thought and expression. There is freedom of assembly. The courts work better than they used too, though are still far from perfect.

The revolutions of 1989, 1997 and 2000 were also successfully exported to Ukraine, Georgia and Lebanon, to be reborn as Orange, Rose and Cedar revolutions. These in turn have inspired the people of Belarus, and of Moldova. Will we see, one day, another Russian revolution?

European Union membership was most valuable as a set of standards to which to aspire. But monitoring ended the moment the countries got through the door. How much further Romania might be in integrating its huge Roma population, for example, if this had been set as a precondition of EU membership. Even the idea might have caused nightmares in Brussels.

The countries of the western Balkans are still beating on the big iron gate of the European Union fort. The drawbridge is down, but the gate is still closed. No timetable has been set for Albanian, Bosnian, Kosovan, Macedonian, Montenegrin or Serbian entry, though the Thessaloniki EU summit of June 2003 at least established the principle that all will one day be allowed in. Croatia already has its foot in the window. In 1989, the west chose not to make more sacrifices to let the eastern neighbours in sooner. In 2009 history is in danger of repeating itself.

The standards of democratic and economic behaviour are useful. But one has the distinct impression that they are sometimes applied to fend countries off, for political reasons, because the old members have not reached consensus about the need for further enlargement. If that is the case, it should be stated openly and honestly. Bureaucratic excesses should also be exposed at every turn. It is important that the recent members, and the future members, learn to shape the Union from within, to their own needs. The shipyard workers of Gdańsk, like the sheep farmers of the Carpathian Mountains, and the raki distillers of the Bulgarian plains, must have a voice.

Just as the new technology can be used to oppress, it is being used to liberate. In September 2009, tens of thousands of cyclists in Budapest organised themselves to campaign for better cycling lanes in the city. The decision of the mayor's office, led by former dissident Gábor Demszky, to quietly strike out a planned bicycle route from the reconstruction of Margit bridge was widely publicised, thanks to the cyclists and their 'Critical Mass' event.

In Bulgaria, an anti-government protest drawn up on Facebook in January 2009 drew 30,000 signatures in a matter of hours, and several thousand onto the street the next day—a colourful alliance of students, farmers, the disabled and Green activists. No party or trade union movement was involved. The protest probably also contributed to the defeat of the governing Socialists—again—in the summer elections.

The street still has an important role to play in the forging of democracy in east and central Europe. The people are on the march.

Select Bibliography

Quotations at the top of some chapters were taken from:
Collected Poems of Vasko Popa, Anvil Press Poetry, 1999
The Collected Poems of Kenneth Patchen, New Directions, 1968
Interview with Milovan Djilas, from: Stalinism—Its Impact on Russia and the World, Ed. G.R. Urban, Maurice Temple Smith 1982
'Kelet Europa' by Géza Bereményi and Tamás Cseh from www.cseh-tamas.hu
Leipziger Volkszeiting, 30/31 December 1989
Vladimír Merta, 'Konec Experimentu' 1986

The following select bibliography have proved valuable reference works:
The Patriot's Revolution, by Mark Frankland. I.R.Dee, Chicago 1992
Tearing Down The Curtain, by a team from the Observer, Hodder and Stoughton 1990s
With God, For the People, by László Tökés, with David Porter, Hodder and Stoughton 1990
Danton's Tod, by Georg Büchner, ed. Margaret Jacobs, Manchester University Press, 1954
The Wasted Generation, by Silviu Brucan, Westview Press, 1993
Hungary's Negotiated Revolution, by Rudolf L. Tökés, Cambridge University Press, 1996
The Lawful Revolution, by István Déak, Columbia University Press, 1979
The Polish Revolution, by Timothy Garton Ash, Jonathan Cape 1983
We The People, by Timothy Garton Ash, Granta Books 1990
The French Revolution, by Christopher Hibbert, Allen Lane 1980
Living in Truth, by Václav Havel, Faber and Faber 1987
To the Castle and Back, by Václav Havel, Vintage Books 2008
The Serbs—History, Myth and the Destruction of Yugoslavia, by Tim Judah, Yale University Press, 2000
Serbia under Milosevic, by Robert Thomas, C. Hurst and Co., 1999
Unfinest Hour—Britain and the Destruction of Bosnia, by Brendan Simms, Allen Lane, 2001
In the Shadow of Stalin's Boots—a Visitor's Guide to the Statue Park, by Ákos Réthly, Private Planet Books, 2008
A nemzetkozi élet kronikája 1945–1997, by Attila Pók, Historia—MTA Történettudományi Intezete, 1998
Egy Döntés Története, by András Oplatka, Helikon, 2008
A Quest for Political Integrity, Romanian Coalition for a Clean Parliament, Polirom, 2005
The Albanian Question, by James Pettifer and Miranda Vickers, I.B. Tauris, 2007

DONATION

Part of the profits from '89: *The Unfinished Revolution* will go to the Alternatal Foundation, which promotes natural birth in Hungary and east-central Europe.

The right of a woman to choose who will attend her in child-birth, where she will give birth, and how she will give birth are basic human rights. As I explain in this book, this is a central, not a peripheral issue in the new democracies. To improve the situation would need the combined efforts of mothers, their partners, midwives, doctors, and the health authorities in each country. Sadly, this is still far from the case.

Most of Alternatal's work lies in patiently explaining to parents, the medical profession, state officials and the general public through the media, why this issue is so important. And why midwifery needs to be recognised as a profession in its own right, with its own rules of conduct.

It is a peaceful, deeply democratic, and in eastern Europe at least, still a revolutionary message.

Alternatal Foundation
H-1015 Budapest, Batthyány u. 31
Hungary
www.szules.hu

REPORTAGE PRESS

REPORTAGE PRESS is a new publishing house specialising in books on foreign affairs or set in foreign countries; nonfiction, fiction, essays, travel books and memoir. Good books like this are now hard to come by—largely because British publishers have become frightened of publishing books that will not guarantee massive sales.

At REPORTAGE PRESS we are not averse to taking risks in order to bring to our readers the books they want to read. Visit our website at www.reportagepress.com. A percentage of the profits from each of our books go to a relevant charity chosen by the author.

You can buy further copies of *'89: The Unfinished Revolution* directly from the website, where you can find out more about our authors and upcoming titles.

REPORTAGE PRESS